Designing a Microsoft Windows 2000 Directory Services Infrastructure

Designing a Microsoft Windows 2000 Directory Services Infrastructure

iUniverse.com, Inc.
San Jose New York Lincoln Shanghai

Designing a Microsoft Windows 2000
Directory Services Infrastructure

Published by iUniverse.com, Inc.

For information address:
iUniverse.com, Inc.
5220 S 16th, Ste. 200
Lincoln, NE 68512
www.iuniverse.com

Cover Creation by Shay Jones

Graphic Production by Matt Bromley, Associate Consultant
Domhnall CGN Adams, Corporation Sole—http://www.dcgna.com
5721-10405 Jasper Avenue
Edmonton, Alberta, Canada T5J 3S2
(780) 416-2967—dcgna@yahoo.com

CD-ROM Duplication by Paragon Media, Seattle, Washington

ISBN: 0-595-14811-5

Printed in the United States of America

Acknowledgments

We are pleased to acknowledge the following professionals for their important contributions in the creation of this study guide.

Technical Writer—Dr. Joyce Wood, Associate Consultant

Technical Writer—Barbara Kowalik, Associate Consultant

Technical Writer—Joseph H. Rawlings III, Associate Consultant

Layout—Dr. Joyce Wood and Barbara Kowalik

Technical Review—Dr. Joyce Wood and Joseph H. Rawlings III

Editor—Nina Gettler

Indexer—Loral Pritchett

Cover Creation, Text Conversion and Proofing—Shay Jones, AA, MCSE, MCP

Graphic Designer—Matt Bromley

V.P., Publishing and Courseware Development— Candace Sinclair

Course Prerequisites

The Designing a Microsoft Windows 2000 Directory Services Infrastructure study guide targets individuals who have the following skills:

- Proficiency in updating Microsoft Windows NT 4.0 to Microsoft Windows 2000
- General knowledge of implementing and administering Microsoft Windows 2000 Directory Services or equivalent knowledge and skills

The Designing a Microsoft Windows 2000 Directory Services Infrastructure exam tests an individual's knowledge and skills to design a Microsoft Windows 2000 Directory Services infrastructure in an enterprise network. Strategies are also presented to assist the student in identifying the information technology needs of an organization, and then designing an Active Directory structure that meets those business needs.

In addition, we recommend that you have a working knowledge of the English language, so that you are able to understand the technical words and concepts this study guide presents.

To feel confident about using this study guide, you should have the following knowledge or ability:

- The desire and drive to become a certified MCSE professional through our instructions, terminology, activities, quizzes, and study guide content
- Basic computer skills, which include using a mouse, keyboard, and viewing a monitor
- Basic networking knowledge including the fundamentals of working with Internet browsers, e-mail functionality, and search engines
- IP, remote connectivity and security

Hardware and Software Requirements

To apply the knowledge presented in this study guide, you will need the following minimum hardware:

- For Windows 2000 Professional, we recommend 64 megabytes of RAM (32 megabytes as a minimum) and a 1-gigabyte (GB) hard disk space.
- For Windows 2000 Server, we recommend a Pentium II or better processor, 128 megabytes of RAM (64 megabytes minimum), and a 2-GB hard drive. If you want to install Remote Installation Server with Windows 2000 Server, you should have at least two additional gigabytes of hard disk space available.
- CD-ROM drive
- Mouse
- VGA monitor and graphics card
- Internet connectivity

To apply the knowledge presented in this study guide, you will need the following minimum software installed on your computer:

- Microsoft Windows 2000
- Microsoft Internet Explorer or Netscape Communicator

Symbols Used in This Study Guide

To call your attention to various facts within our study guide content, we've included the following three symbols to help you prepare for the Designing a Microsoft Windows 2000 Directory Services Infrastructure exam.

Tip: The Tip identifies important information that you might see referenced in the certification exam.

Note: The Note enhances your understanding of the topic content.

Warning: The Warning describes circumstances that could be harmful to you and your computer system or network.

How to Use This Study Guide

Although you will develop and implement your own personal style of studying and preparing for the MCSE exam, we've taken the strategy of presenting the exam information in an easy-to-follow, ten-lesson format. Each lesson conforms to Microsoft's model for exam content preparation.

At the beginning of each lesson, we summarize the information that will be covered. At the end of each lesson we round out your studying experience by providing the following four ways to test and challenge what you've learned.

Vocabulary—Helps you review all the important terms discussed in the lesson.

In Brief—Reinforces your knowledge by presenting you with a problem and a possible solution.

Activities—Further tests what you have learned in the lesson by presenting ten activities that often require you to do more reading or research to understand the activity. In addition, we have provided the answers to each activity.

Lesson Quiz—To round out the knowledge you will gain after completing each lesson in this study guide, we have included ten sample exam questions and answers. This allows you to test your knowledge, and it gives you the reasons why the "answers" were either correct or incorrect. This, in itself, enhances your power to pass the exam.

You can also refer to the Glossary at the back of the book to review terminology. Furthermore, you can view the Index to find more content for individual terms and concepts.

Introduction to MCSE Certification

The Microsoft Certified Systems Engineer (MCSE) credential is the highest-ranked certification for professionals who analyze business requirements for system architecture, design solutions, deployment, installation, and configuration of architecture components, as well as troubleshooting system problems.

When you receive your MCSE certification, it proves your competence by having earned a nationally-recognized credential as an information technology professional who works in a typically complex computing environment of medium to large organizations. It is recommended that a Windows 2000 MCSE candidate should have at least one year of experience implementing and administering a network operating system environment.

To help you bridge the gap between needing the knowledge and knowing the facts, this study guide presents Designing a Microsoft Windows 2000 Directory Services Infrastructure knowledge that will help you pass this exam.

The MCSE exams cover a vast range of vendor-independent hardware and software technologies, as well as basic Internet and Windows 2000 design knowledge, technical skills and best practice scenarios.

Note: This study guide presents technical content that should enable you to pass the Designing a Microsoft Windows 2000 Directory Services Infrastructure certification exam on the first try.

Designing a Microsoft Windows 2000 Directory Services Infrastructure Study Guide Objectives

Successful completion of this study guide is realized when you can competently design a Microsoft Windows 2000 Directory Services infrastructure in an enterprise network. Furthermore, the objectives require skills and knowledge for identifying the information technology needs of an organization, and then designing an Active Directory structure that meets those needs.

You must fully comprehend each of the following objectives and their related tasks to prepare for this certification exam:

- Describe how to gather business and administrative information from an organization, and explain how to utilize that information when designing an Active Directory structure for an enterprise
- Design an Active Directory naming strategy that supports a business organizational structure
- Strategize how to secure and assign administrative authority over Active Directory objects based on an organization's administrative model
- Identify business needs and real-life scenarios that require Active Directory schema modification, and also create a schema modification policy
- Design an Active Directory based on administrative Group Policy requirements defined by business needs
- Set up an Active Directory domain and its organizational unit hierarchy within the domain
- Identify business scenarios where a multiple-domain Active Directory structure meets the administrative and security needs of an organization, and then design a structure that reflects those needs
- Design a site topology to manage Active Directory replication, and optimize the available bandwidth for the physical network
- Design an Active Directory structure that combines administrative, replication, and naming requirements of an organization

Figures

Figure 1.1 Active Directory Service 5
Figure 1.2 Logical Structure Components 7
Figure 1.3 An Organizational Unit 11
Figure 1.4 A Domain Tree 12
Figure 1.5 DNS 13
Figure 1.6 A forest of trees 14
Figure 1.7 Global Catalog 15
Figure 1.8 Flow of Information through the Logical Structure 16
Figure 1.9 A Trust Relationship 21
Figure 1.10 Security Subsystem 23
Figure 1.11 Local Security Authority 25
Figure 1.12 Directory Service Module 27
Figure 2.1 A Domain Hierarchy 50
Figure 2.2 An Implemented Plan 60
Figure 2.3 Domain Model Echoes the Business Model 71
Figure 3.1 Location of Active Directory within Windows 2000 105
Figure 3.2 Inheritance of Permissions 109
Figure 3.3 Sample Active Directory Structure 124
Figure 3.4 OU Creation 126
Figure 3.5 New Object User Window 127
Figure 3.6 Management Properties Window 129
Figure 3.7 MMC Snap-in After Sector OU is Added 131
Figure 3.8 ID Permission Selection Verification 132
Figure 3.9 Security Properties 134
Figure 3.10 Inherited Permissions 135
Figure 3.11 New Object—User 136
Figure 3.12 New User Properties 137
Figure 3.13 View and Edit Permission Entry 139
Figure 4.1 A Model for OU Structure 160
Figure 4.2 Opening Screen for Active Directory Installation 173
Figure 4.3 Specifying a Domain Controller Type 174

Figure 4.4 Create Tree or Child Domain Decision Screen 176
Figure 4.5 Choosing a New Forest or Joining an Existing Forest 177
Figure 4.6 Default Built-in Container 179
Figure 4.7. Right-Clicking an Object 186
Figure 4.8 The First FIND Dialog Box 186
Figure 4.9 Object Attributes 187
Figure 4.10 Advanced FIND Features 188
Figure 5.1 Multiple-Domain Tree 209
Figure 5.2 Domain Trusts 211
Figure 5.3—Cross-link Trusts 213
Figure 5.4—The Multiple-Tree Forest 215
Figure 6.1 Opening Screen for Active Directory Connector 259
Figure 6.2 Component Selection Screen 260
Figure 6.3 Installation Location Screen 261
Figure 6.4 Bridgehead Server Configuration Screen 266
Figure 6.5 From Windows Screen 268
Figure 6.6 From Exchange Screen 269
Figure 6.7 Schedule Screen 271
Figure 6.8 Object Deletions 273
Figure 6.9 Advanced Tab Screen 274
Figure 6.10 Single-Site, Single-Domain Model 282
Figure 6.11 Single-Site, Multiple-Domain Model 285
Figure 6.12 Multiple-Site, Multiple-Domain Model 287
Figure 7.1 Domains 306
Figure 7.2 Directory Replication 308
Figure 7.3 Directory Synchronization 309
Figure 7.4 Intra-Site Replication 317
Figure 7.5 Inter-Site Replication 319
Figure 7.6 Replication Topology 325
Figure 7.7 Site Topology 334
Figure 7.8 Site Link Bridge 340
Figure 7.9 Site Link Bridge Two 341
Figure 7.10 Schedule Window 349

Figure 8.1 Active Directory Schema 368
Figure 8.2 Active Directory Components 371
Figure 8.4 Schema Snap-In 374
Figure 8.5 Active Directory Schema in MMC 375
Figure 8.6 Schema Management Dynamic Link Library Registration 376
Figure 8.7 Active Directory Services Interface Snap-In 377
Figure 8.8 Two Copies of the Schema 380
Figure 8.9 Administrative Schema Modifications 381
Figure 8.10 Schema Cache 381
Figure 8.11 Schema Modifications 382
Figure 8.12 Class Definitions 383
Figure 8.13 New Schema Class Creation 385
Figure 8.14 Class Properties Attribute Property Page 386
Figure 8.15 New Attribute Creation 389
Figure 8.16 Attribute Properties 390
Figure 8.17 Attribute Property Specifications 391
Figure 8.18 Global Catalog Replication 393
Figure 8.19 Schema Object Deactivation 395
Figure 8.20 Class Deactivation 396
Figure 8.21 X.500 OID Frame 398
Figure 8.22 Active Directory Users and Computers 400
Figure 8.23 Schema Modification on a Server 401
Figure 9.1 Active Directory Data Store Model 420
Figure 9.2 Data Store Process 422
Figure 9.3 Data Store Files 423
Figure 9.4 Transaction Log Files 428
Figure 9.5 Checkpoint Files 429
Figure 9.6 Reserved Logs 430
Figure 9.7 Patch Files 431
Figure 9.8 Disk Management Window 434
Figure 9.9 Disk Defragmenter 435
Figure 9.10 Backup and Recovery Tools 439
Figure 9.11 Restore Wizard What to Restore Page 441

Figure 9.12 Backup Options 446
Figure 10.1 Mixed-Mode Domain 470
Figure 10.2 PDC Emulator in a Windows 2000 Domain 471
Figure 10.4 FSMO Maintenance Prompt 475
Figure 10.5 Trust Relationship Comparison 479
Figure 10.6 Windows 2000 Group Policy Snap-In 481
Figure 10.7 Upgrade Paths for Different Operating Systems 485
Figure 10.8 Upgrading from a Single Microsoft Windows NT Domain 487
Figure 10.9 Upgrading a Master Domain Model 488
Figure 10.10 Upgrading a Multiple Master Domain Model 489
Figure 10.11 Upgrading a Complete Trust Domain Model 491
Figure 10.12 A Single Forest with Multiple Domains 492
Figure 10.13 The First Upgraded Domain Controller 493
Figure 10.14 Active Directory Users and Computers 497
Figure 10.15 Event Viewer Console 498
Figure 10.16 Hierarchical Forest with Root Domain 502
Figure 10.17 Account Domains 503
Figure 10.18 Retaining Access to Resources from a Separate Domain 504
Figure 10.19 Physical Sites in a Forest 505

List of Tables

Table 1.1 Comparison of Namespace and Sites 19
Table 1.2 LSA Components and Functions 26
Table 2.1 First Level Domain Names 52
Table 2.2 Second-Level Domains 52
Table 2.3 Implementation Checklist 59
Table 2.4 Exercise 3 Table 81
Table 3.1 Standard Permissions 108
Table 3.2 Groups and Properties 115
Table 3.3 Delegation of Control Wizard Options 120
Table 3.4 User Accounts 128
Table 4.1 Advantages and Disadvantages of OU Nesting 163
Table 4.2 Security Groups 165
Table 6.1 Installation Options 255
Table 6.2 Mapping between Objects 269
Table 6.3 Logging Categories 278
Table 6.4 Logging Levels 279
Table 6.5 Properties of the First Connection Agreement for a Single-Site, Single-Domain Scenario 283
Table 6.6 Properties of the Second Connection Agreement for a Single-Site, Single-Domain Scenario 284
Table 6.7 Properties of the First Connection Agreement for a Single-Site, Multiple-Domain Scenario 286
Table 6.8 Properties of the Second Connection Agreement for a Single-Site, Multiple-Domain Scenario 286
Table 6.9 Properties of the First Connection Agreement for a Multiple-Site, Multiple-Domain Scenario 288
Table 6.10 Properties of the Second Connection Agreement for a Multiple-Site, Multiple-Domain Scenario 289
Table 6.11 Properties of the Third Connection Agreement for a Multiple-Site, Multiple-Domain Scenario 289

Table 6.12 Properties of the Fourth Connection Agreement for a Multiple-Site, Multiple-Domain Scenario 290
Table 7.1 Replicating Partitions 310
Table 7.2 Update Request Types 320
Table 7.3 Performance Monitor Counters 331
Table 9.1 Log Files 424
Table 9.2 Log Files 427
Table 9.3 File Color Key 435
Table 9.4 Estimating Guidelines 448
Table 10.1 Mixed and Native Mode Management Features 484

Table of Contents

Acknowledgments vii
Course Prerequisites viii
Hardware and Software Requirements ix
Symbols Used in This Study Guide x
How to Use This Study Guide xi
Introduction to MCSE Certification xii
Designing a Microsoft Windows 2000 Directory Services Infrastructure Study Guide Objectives xiii

Lesson 1: An Overview of Microsoft Windows 2000 Active Directory Services 1

Basic Directory Service 3
- Extending the Active Directory 3
  - Conformance to Standards 3
  - Extensibility 4
  - Fault tolerance 4
  - Interoperability 4
  - Scalability 4
  - Security Controls 4
  - Single Access Point 5

Active Directory Logical Structure 5
- Unique Names for Active Directory Objects 6
- Logical Structure Component Objects 7
  - Object Classes 8
  - Object Class Attributes 8
  - Instances of Objects 8
- The Schema 9
  - Attributes 9
  - Classes 9
- Organization of Logical Structure Objects within Active Directory 10
  - Domain 10
  - OU (Organizational Unit) 10
  - Tree 11

Forest 13
Global Catalog 15
Replication 16
Queries 17
Active Directory Physical Structure 18
Understanding Sites 18
Domain Controllers 19
Active Directory Security 20
DACL 20
Delegation 21
Access Rights 21
Trust Relationships 21
Active Directory and the Windows 2000 Architecture 22
Security Subsystem 23
Local Security Authority 24
Directory Service Module 27
Directory System Agent 28
Database Layer 29
Extensible Storage Engine (ESE) 29
Data Store 30
NT File System (NTFS) 30

Lesson 2: Designing an Active Directory Naming Strategy 45
Active Directory Naming Conventions 46
Understanding Naming Convention Standards 46
Domain Name System (DNS) 46
Lightweight Directory Access Protocol (LDAP) 47
Understanding the LDAP Distinguished Name 48
Understanding the LDAP Relative Distinguished Name 49
Assigning a User Principal Name 49
Using a NetBIOS Name 49
Domain Name System (DNS) Components 50
Understanding Domain Namespace 50
Root-Level Domain 51
First-Level Domain 51
Second-Level Domain 52
Sub-domains 53
Host Names 53

Understanding Zones 54
Reasons for Dividing a Namespace into Zones 54
Zone Database Files 54
Understanding Name Servers 54
Primary Zone Database File 55
Secondary Zone Database File 55
Name Resolution Process 55
Resolving Services 56
Resolving Active Directory Objects 56
Locating Active Directory Objects 56
Locating IP Addresses 57
Understanding Lookup Queries 57
Forward Lookup Query 57
Reverse Lookup Query 58
DNS Naming Strategies 58
Defining Your Active Directory Scope 58
Choosing a DNS Root Name 61
Registering a DNS Root Name with InterNIC 61
Creating a Domain Name Hierarchy 62
Root Domain 62
Domains Derived from the Root Domain 62
Choosing a DNS Service 63
SRV Records 63
Dynamic Update Protocol 63
Incremental Zone Transfers 63
Storing DNS Zone Data 64
Text Files Storage 64
Active Directory DNS Zone Data Storage 64
Active Directory Domain Names 65
Selecting a Domain Name 65
Using a Registered DNS Domain Name 66
Using a Delegated DNS Sub-Domain Name 66
Using a Reserved Private DNS Domain Name 66
Using a Single DNS Domain Name for Public and Private Networks 67
Separate DNS Zones by Using a Firewall 67
Allow Internet Access to Internal Clients 67
Choosing Public and Private Network Domain Names 68
DNS Deployment Strategies for Active Directory 68
Planning for Active Directory 69

Creating A Forest Plan 69
Creating a Domain Plan 70
Assessing the Logical Environment 71
Assessing the Physical Environment 71
Accessing the Administrative Requirements 72
Domain Organizational Needs 72
Domain Requirements 72
Assigning DNS Names to Create a Domain Hierarchy 73
Creating an Organizational Unit Plan 74
Deciding Which OUs to Create 74
Creating a Site Topology 75
Site Topology Planning Process 76
Designing a Site Structure 76
Objective 77
Exercise 1—Configuring your Computer to be Part of a Domain 77
Exercise 2—Creating a Custom MMC Console 78
To save an MMC Console File 79
Renaming an Item on the Console Tree 80
Exercise 3—Evaluate a Naming Strategy 80
Business Requirements 81
Proposed Naming Strategy 81
Exercise 3—Answers 82
Exercise 4—Create a Naming Strategy 83
Scenario 83
Business Requirements 83
Proposed Naming Strategy 83

Lesson 3: Administrative Authority Delegation 103

Active Directory Security 105
Understanding Active Directory Security Principals 106
Granting Permissions 107
Standard and Special Permissions 107
Inheriting Permissions 109
Preventing Permission Inheritance 110
Understanding Security Descriptors and Identifiers 110
Security Descriptors 111
Owner SID 111
Group SID 111
Access Control Lists 111

Access Control Entries 112
Taking Ownership 113
Administrative Authority Delegation 113
Defining OU Administrator Access 114
Levels of Administration 114
Mapping Administrators and their Level of Authority 116
Delegation Methods 117
Delegating Administrative Control 117
Using Container Properties 118
Delegation Tools 119
Using Control Wizard 119
Using Security Properties 120
Using the DSACLS.EXE Tool 121
Administrative Control Implementation 121
Granting Access Permissions to Groups 121
Granting OU Level Control 121
Working with Group Policy Inheritance Flow 121
Assigning Domain Administrators 122
Lab A—Step by Step Guide to Using the Delegation Control Wizard 124
Populating Active Directory 125
Using the Delegation of Control Wizard 130
Verifying the Permissions Granted 131
Lab B—Examine Inheritance of Permissions on Directory Objects 133
The Inheritance of Permissions when Creating a Child Object 136
Lab C—Blocking Inheritance of Permissions 138

Lesson 4: Domain Structure Implementation 157
Organizational Units and Domains 158
Understanding Domains 158
Understanding OUs 158
Defining Physical Locations 159
Reducing Network Traffic 159
Considering Administrative Issues 159
Planning Organizational Units 160
Developing an OU Design Strategy 161
Identifying Administrative Tasks and Operations 161
Selecting Administrative Features 161
Establishing an Administrative Model 162

Defining the Number of OU Levels 162
First Level Organizational Units 162
Additional OU Levels 163
Organizational Unit Nesting and Performance 163
Deploying the OU Structure 164
Security Groups 164
Understanding Group Types 164
Security Groups 164
Distribution Groups 165
Understanding and Planning Group Security 166
Domain Local Groups 166
Global Groups 166
Universal Groups 166
Understanding Nesting Groups 166
Nesting Levels 167
Group Membership Permission Assignments 167
Universal Groups 167
Global Groups 168
Domain Local Groups 168
Developing an OU Delegation Plan 169
Planning for Delegation Using OUs 169
Levels of Delegation 169
Delegation at the Object and Attribute Level 170
OU Administration Model 170
Designing a Centralized Administration Model 171
Designing a Distributed Administration Model 171
Designing a Model that is a Combination of Centralized and Distributed Administration Models 171
Recommended Best Practices 171
Active Directory Domain Creation 172
Creating the First Domain 172
Using the Active Directory Installation Wizard 173
Using the Installation Wizard to Promote a Server 173
Promoting a Server to a Domain Controller 174
Active Directory Installation Wizard 175
Creating the First Active Directory Domain 177
Verifying Server Promotion 177
Database 178
Shared System Volume 178

Default First Site 178
Global Catalog Server 178
Root Domain 179
Default Containers 179
Default Domain Controllers OU 179
Adding Domain Controllers 180

Active Directory Installation Verification 180
Verifying Active Directory Installation 180
Verifying SRV Resource Records 181
Integrating a DNS Zone 182
Delivering Secure Dynamic Updates 183

Fault Tolerance Issues 183
Implementing Fault Tolerance 184

Native Mode 184
Switching to Native Mode 184

Object Management 185
Locating Objects 185
Find 187
In 187
User, Contacts and Groups Tab 187
Advanced tab 187
Search Criteria 188
Results 188
Moving and Deleting Objects 189
Moving Objects Between OUs Within a Domain 189
Deleting Objects from a Domains 189
Publishing Objects 190
Enabling Accessibility to Global Catalog Information 190
Relative Uniqueness 190
Easy Availability 191
Static in Nature 191
Reasonable Size 191

Lesson 5: Multiple-Domain Structures 207

Multiple-Domain Tree 208
Understanding the Multiple-Domain Tree Model 208
Sharing a Single Tree Root 209
Infrastructure Models Requiring Multiple Domains 210

Sharing Information with Automatic Trusts 210
Establishing Inter-Domain Trusts 211
LDAP Queries 211
Transitive Trusts 212
Cross-Link Trusts 212
Implementing Domains in a Tree 214
Plan Each New Domain Individually 214
Multiple-Tree Forest 214
Unifying Multiple Trees into a Single Forest 216
Distinct DNS Names 217
Controlled Access 217
Locating Resources between Trees 217
Accessing Resources between Trees 218
Implementing Trees in a Forest 218
DNS Domain Name of the New Tree 218
Domain Organization in the Tree 219
Multiple Forests 219
Creating a New Domain in an Existing Forest 220
Creating a Replica Domain Controller 220
How Replication Works 221
Querying the Global Catalog Server in a Forest 222
Resource Access between Domains 222
Creating One-Way Trusts between Domains 222
Creating Explicit Trusts 223
Defining Domain Boundaries 224
Accessing Resources in an Active Directory Forest 224
Exercise A. Creating a New Domain 224
Configuring a Child Domain 225
Exercise B. Creating a Replica Domain Controller 227
Exercise C. Searching the Global Catalog 228
Exercise D. Create an Explicit Domain Trust 229
Exercise E. Identify Trust Relationships between Domains 230

Lesson 6: Microsoft Active Directory Connector (MSADC) 253

Active Directory Connector Structure 254
Microsoft Windows 2000 Server 254
Active Directory Connector and LDAP 3.0 255
Exchange Server 255

Establishing and Maintaining Synchronization 256
Connection Agreements 256
Starting and Stopping the MSADC Service 256
Active Directory Connector Installation 257
Obtaining Information before the Installation 257
Installing the ADC 258
Active Directory Connector Wizard 259
Connection Agreement Configuration 262
Selecting Synchronization Direction and Service Location 263
Two-Way Synchronization 264
From Exchange to Windows Synchronization 264
From Windows to Exchange Synchronization 264
Service Location 264
Choosing a Synchronization Formula 265
Active Directory Synchronization Formula 265
Exchange Synchronization Formula 265
Configuring a Bridgehead Server 265
Polling Bridgehead Servers 266
Container Synchronization 267
Selecting Source and Destination Containers 268
Synchronizing a Schedule 270
Synchronizing Object Deletions 272
Selecting Optimization Settings 274
Paged Results 275
Primary Connection Agreement for Connected Exchange Organization 275
Primary Connection Agreement for Connected Windows Domain 276
Options for Replicating a Mailbox Whose Primary Windows Account Does Not Exist in the Domain 276
Managing Directory Object Synchronization 276
Managing Synchronization from Active Directory 277
Managing Synchronization from Exchange 277
ADC Troubleshooting 277
Using Diagnostics Logging for Monitoring Events 278
Using Performance Monitor Counters 279
Technical Requirements and Recommendations 280
Ensuring a Successful Deployment 280
Requirements 280
Recommendations 281

Examining Test and Production Scenarios 281
Single-Site, Single-Domain Model Scenario 282
Single-Site, Multiple-Domain Model Scenario 284
Multiple-Site, Multiple-Domain Model Scenario 287
Choosing a Scenario 290
Additional Considerations 291
Selecting Bridgehead Servers 292
Identifying Resource Usage 292
Identifying Initial Synchronization Strategy 292

Lesson 7: Active Directory Replication 305

Active Directory Replication Concepts 306
How Replication Works 306
Understanding Replication Terminology 307
Directory Replication 307
Directory Synchronization 309
Active Directory Replication Model 309
Replicating Partitions 309
Schema Partition 310
Configuration Partition 311
Domain Partition 311
Replicating Latency and Convergence 311
Replication Latency 312
Replication Convergence 312
Understanding Single Operations Masters 312
Forest-Wide Operations Master Roles 313
Schema Operations Master 313
Domain-naming Master 313
Domain Operations Master 313
Primary Domain Controller (PDC) Emulator 314
Relative Identifier (RID) Operations Master 314
Infrastructure Operations Master 315
Site Replication 315
Configure Inter-Site Replication 316
Understanding Intra-Site Replication 316
Understanding Inter-Site Replication 318
Updating Requests 320
Originating Updates 320
Replicating Updates 321

- Update Sequence Numbers (USN) 321
- Propagation Dampening 322
- Preventing Unnecessary Replication 322
- Understanding the Up-to-Date Vector 322
- Understanding the High Watermark Vector 323

Conflict Resolution 323

- Minimizing Collisions 323
- Resolving Collisions 324

Replication Topology 324

- Connecting Replication Partners 325
  - Connection Objects 326
  - Unidirectional Replication Pathway 326
  - Single Connection Object 326
- Automating Topology Generation 327
  - Knowledge Consistency Checker (KCC) 327
  - Default Bi-directional Ring 328
- Modifying Replication Topology 328
  - Active Directory Sites and Services 328
  - Modification Rules 329

Replication Traffic Measurements 329

- Using Network Monitor 329
- Using Performance Monitor 330
- Using Replication Monitor 332

Active Directory Site Roles 333

- Using Sites Control 335
- Establishing Site Parameters 335
- Understanding Site Server Objects 335
- Creating the First Site Automatically 336
- Using Site Links 336
  - Transport Site Link 338
  - Site Link Cost Factors 338
  - Site Link Replication Schedule 339
- Creating Site Link Bridges 339
- Placing Domain Controllers in Your Network 342
  - Connectivity and Bandwidth 343
- Controlling Workstation Logon Traffic 343
- Controlling Replication Traffic 344

New Site Creation and Configuration 345

Creating a New Site 345
Create Site Links 346
Adding a Site to a Site Link 346
Moving a Domain Controller between Sites 346
Exercise A—Transitive Sites 347
Exercise B—Changing Replication Schedule between Two Domain Controllers in a Site ..348

Lesson 8: Active Directory Schema Modifications 367

Active Directory Schema 368
Understanding Schema Components 370
Classes and Attributes 371
Attribute Syntax 373
Object and Attribute Naming 373
Schema Modifications 373
Modifying the Schema 373
Installing Active Directory Schema in an MMC Console 376
Processes for Modifying the Schema 376
Using Active Directory Schema in MMC 377
Using Scripting with ADSI 377
Installing software applications 378
Schema Modification Decisions 379
Replication Latency and Recovery 379
Write Conflict Prevention 380
Creating Class Definitions 382
Creating a New Class 384
Class Types 387
Modifying an Existing Class 387
Schema Attributes 388
Creating and Modifying Attributes 388
Creating a New Attribute 388
Modifying an Existing Attribute 390
Indexing and Replicating Attributes 391
Indexing Attributes in Active Directory 392
Replicating Attributes in the Global Catalog 392
Deactivating Classes and Attributes 394
Schema Object Identifiers 398
Understanding the Object Identifier Format 398
Obtaining and Extending Object Identifiers 399

Schema Admins Group 399
Adding Members to a Schema Admins Group 399
Enabling Write Access to the Schema 401
Schema Modification Policy 402
Developing a Schema Modification Policy 403
Schema Modification Policy Guidelines 403
Initiating Schema Modifications 404
Planning schema modifications 404
Modifying the schema 404
Best Practices 404

Lesson 9: Active Directory Data Recovery and Maintenance 419

Active Directory Data Store Model 420
Using the Data Store Process 421
Data Store Files 423
Working with Database Files 424
Object Table 425
Link Table 425
Schema Table 425
Understanding Log Files 425
Transaction Log Files 426
Current Transaction Logs 426
Previous Transaction Log Files 428
Checkpoint Files 429
Reserved Log Files 430
Patch Files 431
Active Directory Maintenance 432
Understanding Automatic Database Cleanup 432
Deleting Transaction Log Files 433
Deleting Obsolete Objects 433
Defragmenting Online Databases 433
Disk Defragmenter 434
Understanding Manual Database Cleanup 436
Offline Database Defragmentation Tool 436
LostAndFound Container 437
Active Directory Recovery 437
Backup and Recovery Tools 438
Activating a Non-Authoritative Restore 439

Activating an Authoritative Restore 442
Using a Transaction Logging Restore 443
Active Directory Backup Process 444
Configuring Hard Drives 444
Determining Hardware Needs 445
Creating a Backup Strategy 445
Database Planning 447
Estimating an Active Directory Database Size 447

Lesson 10: Windows 2000 Upgrade Strategies 469
The Mixed-Mode Domain 470
PDC Emulator Single Operations Master 472
PDC Emulator and Replication 473
PDC Emulator and Downlevel Client Authentication 473
PDC Emulator Failure and Recovery 473
The PDC Emulator in a Fully-UpgradedFully Upgraded Domain 475
Security Principles 476
Services in Mixed Mode 476
Logon Services 476
File Replication Service 477
Remote Access Service 478
Security in Mixed Mode 479
Trust Relationships 479
System Policy 480
Group Policy 480
Enabling Windows NT 4.0-style Microsoft Windows NT 4.0 style Group Policy 481
The SAM Database 482
Choosing Native Mode 483
Choosing Mixed Mode 484
Upgrading to Native Mode 485
Microsoft Windows NT Operating Systems 486
Microsoft Windows NT 3.51 Client Issues 486
Windows Client Operating Systems 486
Upgrading a Single-Domain Model 487
Upgrading a Master Domain Model 487
Upgrading a Multiple Master Domain Model 489
Building a Single-Domain Tree 490
Building a Domain Forest 490

Upgrading a Complete Trust Model 490
Upgrading to a Single Forest with Multiple Domains 491
Upgrading to Create Separate Forests. 492
How to Upgrade to Windows 2000 492
Upgrading the Primary Domain Controller 493
Upgrading the Backup Domain Controllers 494
Upgrading Workstations and Member Servers 495
Testing Your Upgrade 496
The Domain Upgrade 496
User and Group Accounts 497
System Policies 498
Active Directory Install 498
Hardware Configuration 499
Planning a Windows 2000 Upgrade 499
Existing Domain Structures 499
Domain Model 500
Existing Trust Relationships 500
Number and Locations of Domain Controllers within Each Domain. 500
Your Current DNS Structure 500
Recovery Plan Strategies 500
Designing the First Tree 501
Examine the existing domain structure 502
Examine Existing Explicit Trust Relationships 503
Identify Domains You Do Not Want to Include in the Forest 503
Determine the member Number of Domain Controllers and Their Locations within Each Domainn. 504
Identify Where in the DNS Naming Hierarchy You Will Place Your Active Directory Root Domain. 504
Designing a Site Topology 504
Ordering Domain Upgrades 505
Upgrading Domain Controllers 506

GLOSSARY 525
INDEX 543

Lesson 1

An Overview of Microsoft Windows 2000 Active Directory Services

Active Directory is a directory service that is completely integrated with Windows 2000 Server. It offers the hierarchical view, extensibility, scalability, and distributed security that all business customers need. Using Active Directory, network administrators, developers, and users gain access to a directory service that:

- Is seamlessly integrated with both Internet and intranet environments
- Provides simple, intuitive naming for the objects it contains
- Scales from a small business to the largest enterprise
- Provides simple, powerful, open Application Programming Interfaces (APIs)

Active Directory is a critical part of the distributed system. It allows administrators and users to use the directory service as a source of information, as well as an administrative service.

Active Directory provides a method for designing a directory structure that meets the needs of your organization. You use Active Directory to uniquely identify users and resources on a network. Active Directory provides a single point of network management. It allows you to manage resources easily and is a significant enhancement over the directory services provided in former versions of Windows.

Active Directory provides numerous benefits, which include:

- Information security
- Policy-based administration
- Extensibility

- Scalability
- Replication of information
- Integration with Domain Name System (DNS)
- Interoperability with other directory services
- Flexible querying

This lesson introduces the concepts of Active Directory and the function of each of its components.

After completing this lesson, you should have a better understanding of the following topics.

- Windows 2000 Active Directory
- Active Directory logical structure
- Flow of information through the logical structure
- Active Directory physical structure
- Active Directory security
- Active Directory and the Windows 2000 architecture

Basic Directory Service

One of the challenges of large, distributed computing environments has been to identify and locate resources such as users, groups, printers, and documents. With this directory service, when a name is given for a resource, it provides the information necessary to access that resource. Network administrators are not required to use specific binding information to access a network resource.

This directory service provides distributed applications such as Intranet applications with the features they need to lower the total cost of ownership. A directory service like Active Directory Service is part of a distributed computing environment, providing a way to locate and identify the users and resources available in the system.

Active Directory Service is a directory service within Windows 2000 that stores network information that can be queried efficiently and enables distributed security and distributed administration. Through a set of COM programming interfaces called Active Directory Service Interfaces (ADSI), Active Directory Service provides several standard interfaces for open synchronization and application integration. This enables interoperability of Windows environments with numerous devices, applications and other directory services, including Novell Directory Services (NDS).

Extending the Active Directory

Active Directory provides the following enhancements to what a basic directory service can offer:

Conformance to Standards

Active Directory follows and supports the following standards and protocols:

- International Standards Organization (ISO) X.500, which makes recommendations for implementation of directory services
- Lightweight Directory Access Protocol (LDAP), versions 2 and 3, which allows for integration between Active Directory and other directory services that support LDAP
- Request for Comments (RFC) 822, which is familiar to most users as an Internet e-mail address, for example: johndoe@somewhere.com
- HyperText Transfer Protocol (HTTP) Uniform Resource Locator (URL), which is familiar to users with Web browsers

- Universal Naming Convention (UNC), which is used in Windows 2000 Server-based networks to refer to shared volumes, printers, and files
- LDAP URL, which supports a draft to RFC 1779 and specifies the server on which the Active Directory services reside and the attributed name of the object
- Internet-standard naming, name resolution, and query protocols, which make integration with the Internet immediate and seamless

Extensibility

New object classes or class attributes can be added to the schema and you can add new attributes to existing classes of objects.

Fault tolerance

Data is mirrored in multiple locations, ensuring integrity and reducing the chances of data loss should hardware failure occur.

Interoperability

Active Directory integrates with other operating systems, platforms, services, and protocols.

Scalability

Active Directory can contain any number of objects. The administrator does not need to be concerned with the minimum or maximum number of objects in the directory.

Security Controls

Administrative control can be decentralized and delegated to multiple groups. This includes granting users access and usage rights.

Single Access Point

With the Distributed Directory organization, administrators can log on anywhere on the network to manage objects located all over the network. In addition, users can log on anywhere on the network and access resources, making it seem as though the resources are all located locally.

Figure 1.1 illustrates these concepts.

Figure 1.1 Active Directory Service

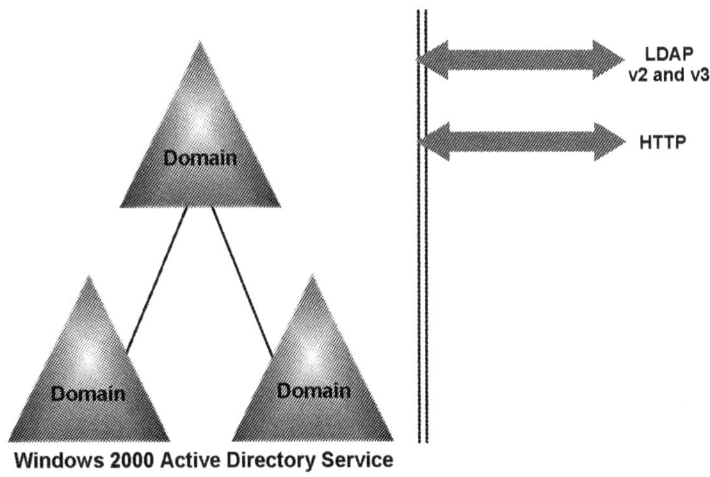

Active Directory Logical Structure

The structure of your business provides the first step in designing the logical structure of Active Directory. Starting with this concept will provide the basis for customizing your Active Directory to the unique needs of your business.

Tip: At this point, do not be concerned with hardware and connectivity issues. Connectivity will be covered later.

At this time you should consider three concepts:

- Unique names for Active Directory objects
- Logical structure component objects
- Organization of logical structure objects within Active Directory

Unique Names for Active Directory Objects

Developing naming conventions and structures at this time will save time, money, and confusion later. You must plan carefully at this point to be sure that all objects you are going to place in Active Directory have a unique name, because Active Directory will use the naming conventions you define to locate objects or resolve these unique names to objects.

Note: Some objects, known as containers, can contain other objects. For example, a domain is a container object that can contain users, computers and other objects.

For example, if you want to locate Garden City within an Active Directory structure, will you choose Garden City, New York, or Garden City, Kansas? If you have defined a Country object that contains a State object that contains City objects, you will have no trouble getting to the right city, nor will Active Directory. Think further about the possibility of two employee objects in the same organization named John Smith. How would you resolve this yourself? How would you structure an Active Directory object to resolve this name and locate the correct John Smith?

The process that Active Directory uses to translate a unique name into an object or information is called name resolution.

Logical Structure Component Objects

In Active Directory, you can organize resources in a logical structure that mirrors the logical structure in your organization. Grouping resources logically, allows you to find a resource by its name rather than its physical location. Since you group resources logically, Active Directory makes the network's physical structure transparent to the user.

Figure 1.2 shows the logical structure of component objects.

Figure 1.2 Logical Structure Components

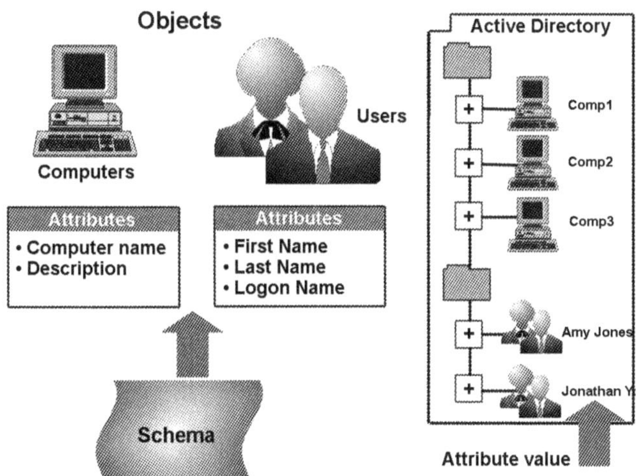

To define these objects in the logical structure, you should understand the following characteristics of objects:

- Object Classes
- Object Class Attributes
- Instances of Objects

Object Classes

Object classes define the types of objects that can be created in Active Directory. They do not contain data but are a format for creating data.

Object Class Attributes

Object class attributes define the characteristics of object classes. They have structure but not value in an object class. For example, an Employee class could consist of these attributes:

- Social Security Number
- First Name
- Middle Initial
- Last Name
- Street Address

Instances of Objects

Instances of objects take the template and put values into the attributes. For example, our employee of the day has the following values:

- 999999999 (Social Security Number)
- John (First Name)
- E. (Middle Initial)
- Smith (Last Name)
- 125 AnyStreet (Street Address)

The Schema

Now it is appropriate to consider the role of the schema, which contains definitions of object classes, but not the values. The definitions are stored as objects so that Active Directory can manage the schema objects in the same manner as the rest of the objects in Active Directory.

A schema consists of two types of definitions:

- Attributes
- Classes

These are also referred to as schema objects or metadata.

Attributes

Attributes are defined separately from classes. Each attribute is defined only once and can be used in multiple classes. This enforces consistency in naming standards, and aids resolution.

Classes

Classes are also known as object classes. They describe the possible Active Directory objects that can be created. Recall that each class is a collection of attributes.

The schema is extensible, which means that new object classes and their attributes can be added at any time. Applications then have immediate access to the new classes. A set of basic classes and attributes is shipped with Windows 2000 Server. For development and testing purposes, you can also view and modify the Active Directory schema with the Active Directory Schema snap-in, included with the Windows 2000 Administration Tools on the Windows 2000 Server compact disc.

Warning: Be sure to plan and prepare before extending the schema because it cannot be deleted, only deactivated. It is automatically replicated.

Organization of Logical Structure Objects within Active Directory

The basic objects that create the overall structural hierarchy in Active Directory are:

- Domain
- Organizational Unit (OU)
- Tree
- Forest

Domain

A domain is the basic building block of Active Directory. It is a container of objects that share a common directory database. A domain has a unique name and provides security requirements, replication processes, and administration. It defines a single security boundary of a Windows 2000 computer network.

Domains provide several benefits:

- Security policies and settings (such as administrative rights and access control lists) do not cross from one domain to another
- Delegating administrative authority to domains or organizational units eliminates the need for a number of administrators with sweeping administrative authority

Domains help structure your network to reflect the structure of your organization.

A domain stores only the information about its own objects. This way, Active Directory can scale to very large numbers of objects.

A single domain can span multiple physical locations or sites. Using a single domain greatly simplifies administrative overhead.

OU (Organizational Unit)

An OU is a container object that the administrator uses to organize objects within a domain into logical administrative groups. It can contain only objects from its parent domain. These groups should be based on the company's administrative model. An OU is the smallest scope to which you can apply a group policy or delegate administrative authority.

Using organizational units, you can create containers within a domain that represent the hierarchical, logical structures within your organization. This enables you to manage the configuration and use of accounts and resources based on your organizational model.

The OU can contain objects such as user accounts, groups, computers, printers, applications, and other OUs from the same domain. Each domain can implement its own OU hierarchy. An organizational unit cannot contain objects from other domains. Figure 1.3 illustrates an Organizational Unit.

Figure 1.3 An Organizational Unit

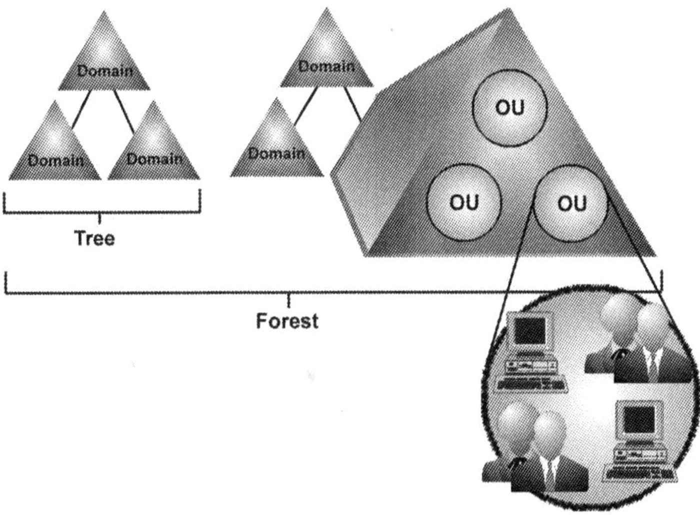

Tree

A tree is a hierarchy of one or more domains with a single root name. You create it by adding one or more child domains to an existing parent domain. These domains within a tree share a contiguous namespace and a hierarchical naming structure. Domains within a tree share information through automatic trust relationships, sharing a common schema, configuration, and the Global Catalog. Figure 1.4 illustrates a domain tree.

Figure 1.4 A Domain Tree

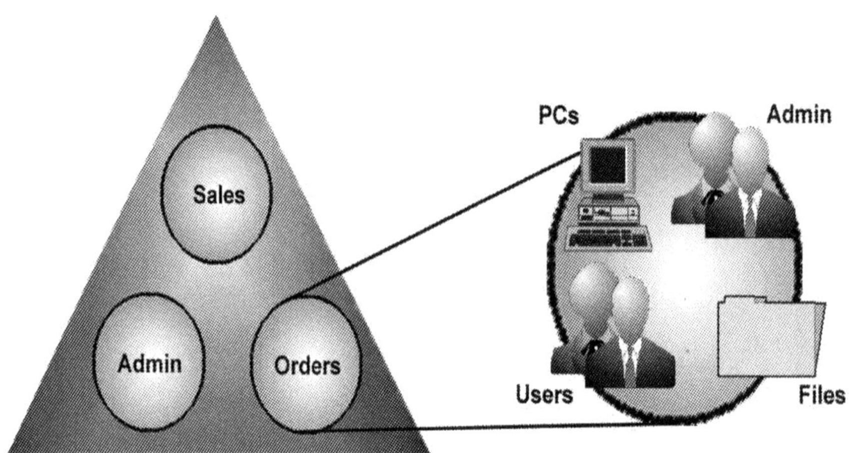

In addition, trees follow Domain Name System (DNS) standards by appending the name of the parent domain to the relative name of the child domain. For example, a child domain of mycompany.com might be oregon.mycompany.com

DNS is an Internet standard service that translates easily readable host names to numeric IP addresses. This enables identification and connection to processes running on computers on TCP/IP networks.

Domain names for DNS are based on the DNS hierarchical naming structure, which is an inverted tree structure: a single root domain. Underneath these can be branches and leaves, which are the parent and child domains.

Each computer in a DNS domain is uniquely identified by its DNS fully qualified domain name.

Active Directory is integrated with DNS in the following ways:

Hierarchical structure—Active Directory and DNS have the same hierarchical structure. Although separate and implemented differently for different purposes, an organization's namespace for DNS and Active Directory have an identical structure. DNS zones can be stored in Active Directory.

Domain controllers—Active Directory clients use DNS to locate domain controllers. To locate a domain controller for a specified domain, Active Directory clients query their configured DNS server for specific resource records. Figure 1.5 illustrates DNS.

Figure 1.5 DNS

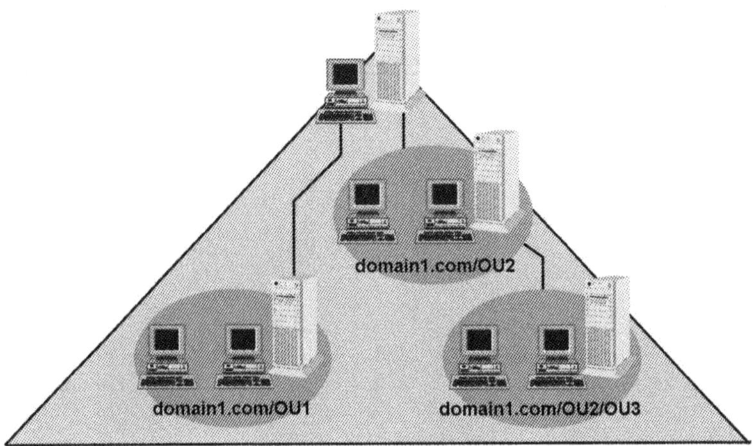

Forest

A forest is a collection of one or more trees. Multiple trees within a forest do not share a common root domain name, but share information through automatic trust relationships. Multiple forests can share information only through explicit trusts. Forests also share the following:

- Transitive trust relationships between the domains
- Transitive trust relationships between the domain trees
- A common schema

- Common configuration information
- A common Global Catalog

Tip: Using both domain trees and forests provides you with the flexibility of both contiguous and noncontiguous naming conventions. For example, this can be useful for companies with independent divisions that must each maintain their own DNS names.

Figure 1.6 illustrates a forest of trees.

Figure 1.6 A forest of trees

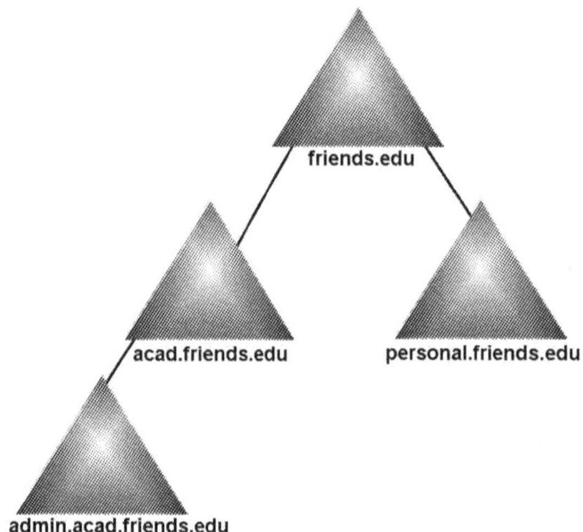

Global Catalog

All objects stored in the Active Directory have entries in the Global Catalog (GC). This service contains directory information from all of the source domains in a tree or forest. The GC allows users to easily find an object, regardless of where it is in the tree or forest, by searching selected attributes, which are contained in an abbreviated catalog. This technique, known as partial replication, allows many common queries to be resolved from the GC without requiring a lookup in the source domain. The Global Catalog may contain any type of object, for example, Users, Services, or Machines.

Figure 1.7 shows the structure of the Global Catalog.

Figure 1.7 Global Catalog

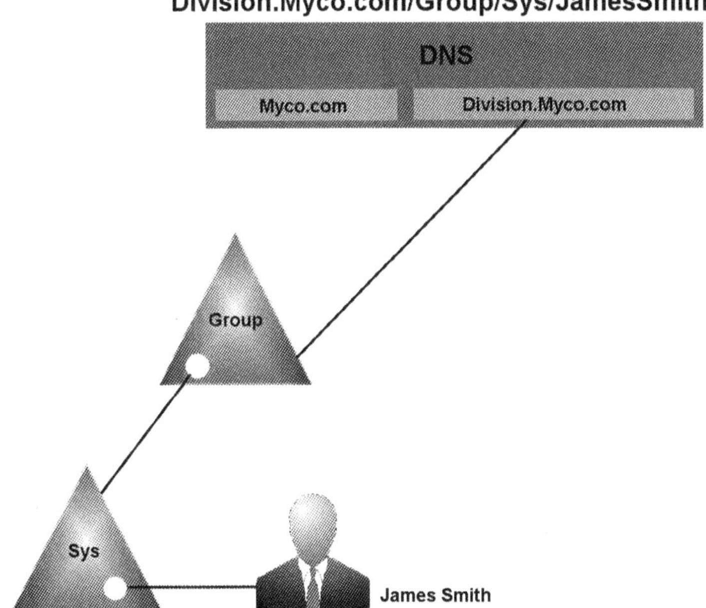

Figure 1.8 shows the information flow through the logical structure.

Figure 1.8 Flow of Information through the Logical Structure

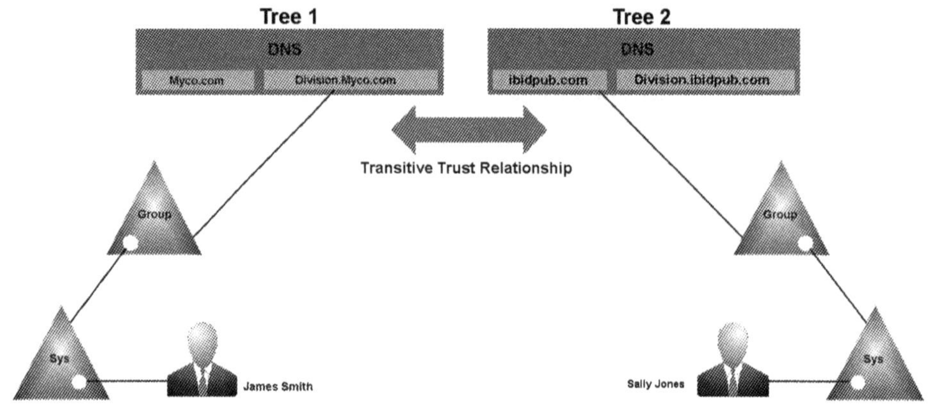

After comprehending the structure of Active Directory, the next step is to understand the way information flows through your Active Directory. This flow of information consists of two processes:

- Replication
- Queries

Replication

Active Directory uses *multimaster replication*, which means that each domain controller maintains a write-enabled copy, or replica, of the domain's partition of the directory. When an update is made to the directory, it is *replicated* to all domain controllers within the domain. This means that the same data resides in multiple locations. If one location becomes corrupted, several backup locations are always available.

As the administrator and planner of Active Directory, you can control the flow of replication traffic throughout Active Directory by using *sites*, which are collections of subnet addresses.

Two different categories of sites give you flexibility in controlling and directing replication. They are:

- Intra-sites
- Inter-sites

You should only place well-connected computers within intra-sites. Inter-sites communicate over more expensive and slower connections.

A site definition is stored as a site object in Active Directory. Collectively, all sites form a site topology. Because sites represent the physical structure of your network, they do not need to map to your Active Directory logical structure.

Queries

The *Global Catalog* stores information centrally to make information widely available to users. Domain controllers called *Global Catalog servers* can maintain a copy of the Global Catalog. Clients can query a Global Catalog server for information about any object in another tree in Active Directory without needing to know where the object is located.

Global Catalog servers contain a partial replica of the entire directory to conserve storage space. A *partial replica* means that each Global Catalog server contains a copy of all objects contained in the forest but only a subset of attributes for each object. For example, a user's logon name and password are frequently used attributes that are maintained in the partial replica of the Global Catalog.

Note: Members of the Domain Admins group are able to log on to the network even when the Global Catalog is not available.

Active Directory Physical Structure

In addition to the logical structure, you must also understand the physical components of Active Directory. You will use these tools to develop a directory structure that mirrors the physical structure of your organization. The physical components are:

- Sites
- Domain Controllers

Understanding Sites

A site is a combination of one or more Internet Protocol (IP) subnets connected by a link to localize network traffic. The typical site has the same boundaries as a local area network (LAN). You must plan your network carefully. When you group subnets on your network, you should combine only those subnets that have fast, cheap, and reliable network connections with one another. At this time, fast network connections are at least 512 kilobits per second (Kbps). Usually, a bandwidth of 128 Kbps and higher is sufficient.

Warning: Do not confuse sites with namespace. Sites are not part of the namespace!

Active Directory is primarily a namespace. A namespace is any bounded area in which a name can be resolved or translated into some object or information that the name represents. When you browse the logical namespace, you see computers and users grouped into domains and OUs, not sites. Table 1.1 shows you how to distinguish between a namespace and a site.

Table 1.1 Comparison of Namespace and Sites

Namespace	Sites
Computers	Computer objects
OUs	Connection objects used to configure replication between sites
Domains	
OUs	

Domain Controllers

A domain controller is a computer that runs Windows 2000 Server. It stores a replica of the domain directory—the local domain database. A domain can contain one or more domain controllers, and each domain controller in a domain has a complete replica of the domain's portion of the directory. This replication provides the robust fault tolerance that is characteristic of this environment.

Tip: A single domain can span multiple sites located in different geographical areas, and a single site can include user accounts and computers that belong to multiple domains.

Domain controllers perform the following services:

- Store a complete copy of all Active Directory information for the domain
- Manage changes to that information
- Replicate those changes to other domain controllers in the same domain
- Automatically replicate all changes to objects
- Immediately replicate certain important updates, such as the disabling of a user account
- Use multimaster replication, in which no one domain controller is the master domain controller

- Provide fault tolerance because if one domain controller is offline, another domain controller can provide all required functions
- Manage all aspects of users' domain interactions, such as locating Active Directory objects and validating user logon attempts

Active Directory Security

Understanding and using domains in your security administration will make your job much easier. This section provides basic information about security on the Active Directory. The following features are involved in maintaining security:

- Discretionary Access Control List (DACL)
- Delegation
- Access rights
- Trust relationships

DACL

DACLs determine:

- Who can see an object
- What actions a user can perform on the object

DACLs also apply to:

- Object attributes
- Object classes
- Individuals
- Groups of individuals

Delegation

As an administrator, you can delegate authority to other administrators to manage a specific container, domain, or subtree.

Access Rights

Access rights allow you to authorize users or groups to access objects in the network. You can grant or deny which user rights or actions individuals and groups can exercise or perform on a container, object, or class of objects.

Trust Relationships

A trust relationship is a link between two domains in which the trusting domain honors the logon authentication of the trusted domain (Figure 1.9). Stated another way, trust relationships allow users in one domain to hold access to resources and information throughout the forest.

Figure 1.9 A Trust Relationship

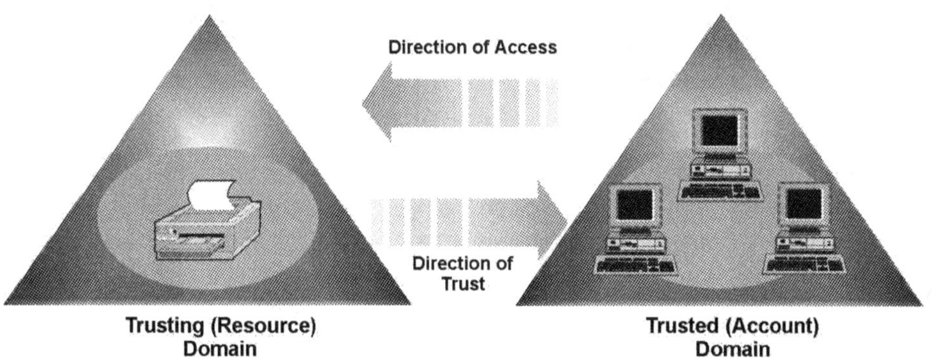

Activity Directory consists of two types of trusts:

Transitive trusts—Two-way trusts between domains. When domains are created within a forest, transitive trusts are automatically created. These are called implicit trusts because of this automatic creation.

Nontransitive trusts—Explicit trusts that are one-way relationships. They limit access to the member domain that is explicitly trusted. The administrator can manually create these trusts to improve authentication performance in a large tree or to create a trust with a domain that is not part of the forest.

Note: When a user is authenticated by a domain controller, this does not imply any access to resources in that domain. This access is determined by the rights and permissions granted to the user account by the domain administrator for the trusting domain.

Active Directory and the Windows 2000 Architecture

Understanding Active Directory architecture involves knowing where Active Directory fits into the overall Windows 200O architecture. Windows 2000 has separate and distinct components, each responsible for its own functions.

Windows 2000 uses modules and modes that combine to provide operating system services to applications. Two processor access modes, kernel and user, divide the low-level platform-specific processes from the upper level processes. This shields applications from platform differences and prevents direct access to system code and data by applications. Each application runs in a separate module in user mode, from which it accesses system services through an API that gains access to the system data.

An application begins in user mode and transfers to kernel mode to obtain the system services; the process is then transferred back to user mode. Active Directory runs in the security subsystem in user mode. The security reference monitor, which runs in kernel mode, is the primary authority for enforcing the security rules of the security subsystem. Active Directory is a component of the following:

- Security subsystem
- Local Security Authority
- Directory Service module

Security Subsystem

Active Directory is part of a component called the security subsystem (Figure 1.10). DACLs protect all objects in Active Directory. Access validation routines check the DACL whenever a user or a process attempts to gain access to an object or attribute in Active Directory.

Figure 1.10 Security Subsystem

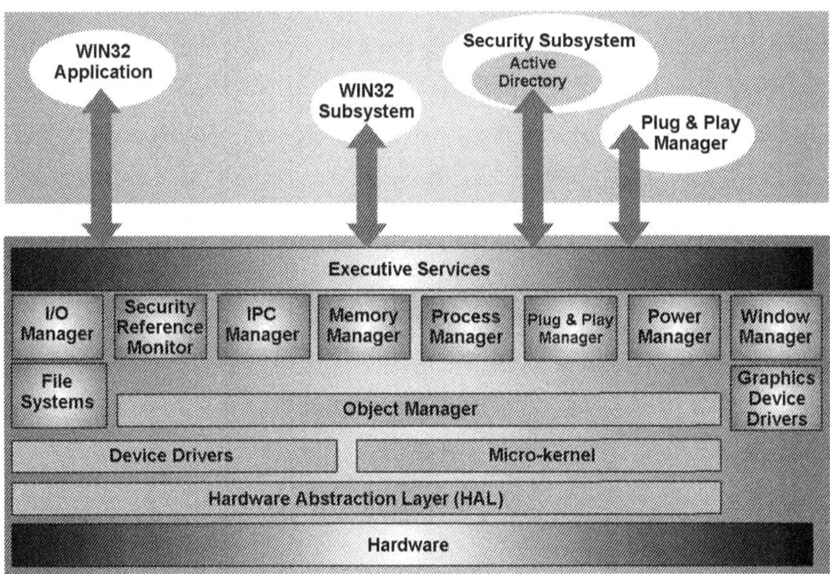

The Windows 2000 security infrastructure has four main functions:

- Directory service store for security policies and account information
- Implements security models for all objects
- Authenticates Active Directory access
- Stores trust information for Active Directory

Windows 2000 architecture includes:

- Addition of Plug-and-Play Manager and Power Manager to both user and kernel modes
- Quality of Service (QOS), Asynchronous Transfer Mode (ATM), and other drivers to the I/O Manager
- Changes in the operating system kernel (Ntoskrnl.exe) with the addition of Terminal Services

Local Security Authority

The Local Security Authority (LSA) is another component of the security subsystem (Figure 1.11). LSA is a protected subsystem that maintains the security for the local computer. LSA ensures that users have system access permissions by doing the following:

- Generates tokens, which contain user and group information and the security privileges for that user
- Manages local security policy
- Provides interactive user authentication services
- Manages the Audit policy and settings

Figure 1.11 Local Security Authority

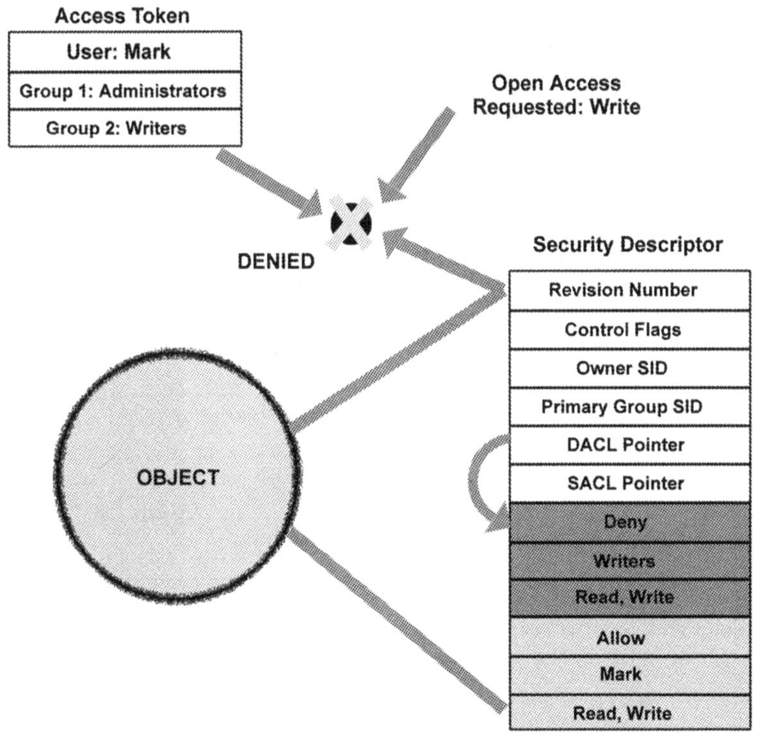

Note: When you configure a Windows 2000 system as a member of a domain, the system's LSA uses the domain's authentication services to authenticate users. These services are in addition to the system's own local account database. The system *trusts* the domain to provide accurate information about security principals on the network.

The following table describes the LSA components and functions.

Table 1.2 LSA Components and Functions

Component	Function
Netlogon.dll	A service that maintains the computer's secure channel to a domain controller
Msv1_O.ddl	The NTLM authentication protocol
Kdcsvc.dll	The Kerberos Key Distribution Center (KDC) service, which is responsible for granting tickets to clients
Schannel.dll	The Secure Sockets Layer (SSL) authentication protocol
Kerberos.dll	The Kerberos version 5 authentication protocol
Lsasrv.dll	The LSA server service enforces security policies
Samsrv.dll	The Security Accounts Manager (SAM) enforces stored policies and supports earlier Application Programming Interfaces (APIs)
Ntdsa.dll	The Directory Service module is the Windows 2000 replication protocol that supports LDAP and manages partitions of data
Secur32.dll	The multiple authentication provider that holds all of the components together

Directory Service Module

Active Directory is contained in the Directory Service module (Figure 1.12) within the LSA. The Directory Service module consists of three layers and several interface agents that work together to provide directory services, which are compatible with earlier systems. It is important to understand the function of each of the following four components of the Directory Service module.

- Directory System Agent (DSA)
- Database layer
- Extensible Storage Engine (ESE)
- Data Store

Figure 1.12 Directory Service Module

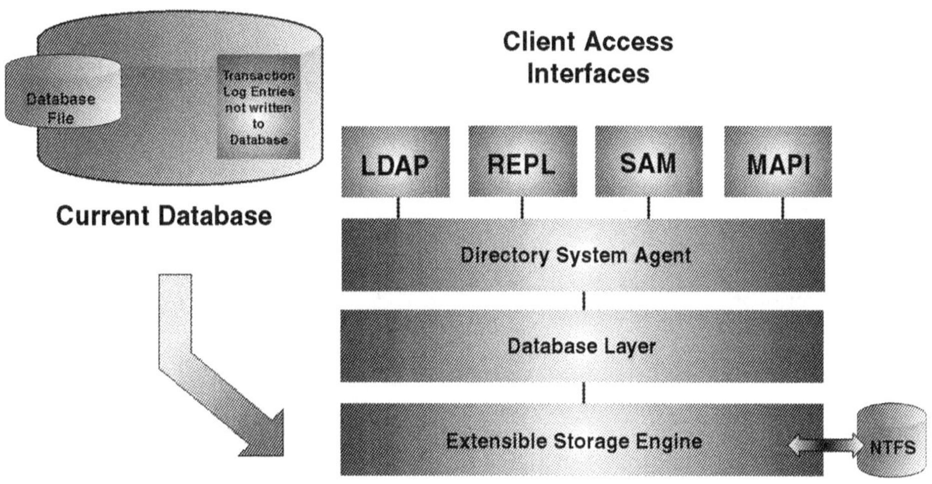

Note: The terms *directory* and *directory* service refer to the directories found in public and private networks. A *directory* provides a means of storing, managing, and retrieving information related to the network resources. A directory service identifies all of the resources in a network and makes them usable to users and applications. A directory service is different from a *directory* in that it is both the source of the information and the services making the information available to the user.

Directory System Agent

The DSA enables you to view users in a more logical, hierarchical manner. The DSA performs the following functions:

- Enforces all directory service semantics
- Processes transactions
- Enforces the schema
- Supports replication
- Provides Global Catalog server logic
- Propagates security descriptors
- Builds a hierarchy from the parent-child relationships stored in the directory
- Provides APIs for directory access calls

Client applications access Active Directory through DSA supported directory system interfaces such as:

LDAP/ADSI—Clients that support LDAP use it to connect to the DSA. ADSI is a means of abstracting LDAP API. Active Directory uses only LDAP. To make it easier to write directory-enabled applications that access the Active Directory and other LDAP-enabled directories, Microsoft developed Active Directory Service Interfaces (ADSI).

Messaging API (MAPI)—Legacy MAPI clients, such as Microsoft Outlook, connect to the DSA by using the MAPI Remote Procedure Call (RPC) address book provider interface. RPC is a call by one program to a second program on a remote system.

Security Accounts Manager (SAM)—Windows clients that use Windows NT 4.0 or earlier use this interface to connect to the DSA. In addition, replication from backup domain controllers in a mixed-mode domain goes through the SAM interface.

Replication (REPL)—Active Directory DSAs connect to each other by using a proprietary RPC interface when they are replicating directories.

Database Layer

The database layer provides the following:

- An abstraction layer between applications and the database
- Access to database storage and search functionality
- Routing for all database access

Extensible Storage Engine (ESE)

The ESE provides the following functions:

- Stores all Active Directory objects
- Enables you to create up to a 17-terabyte database that can theoretically hold up to ten million objects per domain
- Reserves storage only for space that is used and when more attributes are added, more storage is dynamically allocated, for example, if a user object has 50 attributes and you create a user with values for only four of those attributes, space is consumed only for those four attributes
- Stores multiple-value attributes and properties, which means that there can be multiple values for a single attribute or property, for example, the database can store multiple telephone numbers for a single user without requiring multiple telephone number attributes
- Communicates directly with individual records in the directory data store on the basis of the object's relative distinguished name attribute

Data Store

The database file NTDS.DIT is manipulated only by the Extensible Storage Engine database engine. You can administer the file by using the NTDSUTIL tool, located in the \Winnt\system32 folder on the domain controller.

NT File System (NTFS)

NTFS is a file system that is designed for Windows 2000 and supports many features, such as file system security, Unicode, recoverability, and long file names. The File Replication Service (FRS) for Windows 2000 requires NTFS; the Directory Service module does not.

Vocabulary

Review the following terms in preparation for the certification exam.

Term	Description
Active Directory	A new directory service implemented in Windows 2000 that represents a restructuring of the former network organization implemented by Microsoft and which lets any object on a network be tracked and located.
ADSI	Active Directory Service Interfaces provides several standard interfaces for open synchronization and application integration.
API	Application Programming Interface provides application developers with consistent rules for designing programs to interact with the TCP/IP stack.
ATM	Asynchronous Transfer Mode is a very fast packet-switching technology capable of quality real-time video transmission.
DACL	Discretionary Access Control List defines security groups, user accounts and associated permissions. DACLs define object permissions for resource security enforcement and access levels for each list member.
directory	An online storage location that contains objects that may have various kinds of structures and be related to one another in some way. For example, an online building directory of a mall contains names of businesses, locations, and telephone numbers.

Term	Description
distributed directory	The distribution of data across the network on many different computers in a manner that is transparent to the users.
DSA	Directory System Agent
ESE	Extensible Storage Engine
FRS	File Replication Service
HTTP	HyperText Transfer protocol is a computer language used for creating Web pages.
KDC	Kerberos Key Distribution Center.
Kerberos	The Kerberos protocol is the primary authentication procedure in Windows 2000. It is a security system that authenticates users. At logon, it establishes identity, which is used throughout the session. Kerberos does not provide authorization to services or databases.
kernel mode	Provides direct access to memory. Kernel mode consists of four components: Microsoft Windows 2000 Executive, Device Drivers, the Microkernel, and the Hardware Abstraction Layer (HAL).
LDAP	Lightweight Directory Access Protocol is used to access a directory service and is the primary access protocol for Active Directory.
LSA	Local Security Authority
MAPI	Messaging Application Programming Interface

Term	Description
multimaster replication	A feature of Active Directory that provides and maintains copies of the directory across multiple servers in a domain. The Active Directory replication system propagates the changes from a given replica to all other replicas. Replication is automatic and transparent.
NDS	Network Directory Services is available to administrators for managing directory objects.
NTFS	NT File System is a file system that is designed for Windows 2000 and supports many features, such as file system security, Unicode, recoverability, and long file names.
objects	A distinct named set of attributes that represent something concrete, such as user data, printers, applications, or servers. The attributes hold data describing the thing that is identified by the directory object.
OUs	Organizational Unit is an entity or group of entities organized in a logical manner by the system administrator according to business or system functions or policies. They also enable the delegation of administration to distinct subtrees of the directory.
QOS	Quality of Service
REPL	Replication. Active Directory DSAs connect to each other by using a proprietary RPC interface when they are replicating directories.
RFC	Request for Comments

Term	Description
RPC	Remote Procedure Call is a call by one program to a second program on a remote system.
SAM	Security Accounts Manager is an interface used by Windows clients that use Windows NT 4.0 or earlier to connect to the DSA. In addition, replication from backup domain controllers in a mixed-mode domain goes through the SAM interface.
schema	The definition of all objects that can be created in Active Directory. This includes their characteristics or attributes. For each object class, the schema defines what attributes an instance of the class must have, additional attributes it may have, and what object class can be a parent of the current object base.
services	The useful actions that can be performed on the resources in the directory. For example, the contents of the directory can be queried, listed, and printed. Active Directory is the directory service included in Windows 2000
SSL	Secure Sockets Layer is a protocol that creates a secure connection, or channel, over which all data between a Web client and a secure Web server are encrypted.
UNC	Universal Naming Convention
URL	Uniform Resource Locator is a standardized addressing system for locating Internet resources.

In Brief

If you want to...	Then do this...
Identify the layers and layer components in the Windows 2000 operating system architecture	Review the material on user mode and kernel mode. User mode has two different types of components: environmental subsystems, which allow Windows 2000 to run applications written for different operating systems and integral systems which perform essential operating system functions. The kernel mode layer has access to system data and hardware and provides direct access to memory.
Explain the purpose of Active Directory	Remember that Active Directory is the directory service included with Windows 2000 Server. It stores information about network resources (user data, printers, servers, groups, etc.).
Explain the objects and schema in Active Directory	Review the material on objects and try drawing some of your own. A good example would be a computer object. Make a list of its attributes. This is the material that would be contained in the schema.
Identify an OU	Recall that an organizational unit is a container used to organize objects within a domain into logical administrative groups that reflect your organization's structure. An OU can contain objects such as user accounts, contacts, groups, computers, printers, applications, and other OUs from the same domain.

Lesson 1 Activities

1. Describe a domain tree.
2. Define schema as it relates to the Active Directory.
3. Explain the difference between a directory and a directory service.
4. Explain the difference between implicit two-way transitive trusts and explicit one-way transitive trusts.
5. Explain the purpose of the Global Catalog in Active Directory
6. List and define the logical structure elements in Active Directory.
7. Explain the organization of the logical structure elements and the relationships they form in Active Directory.
8. Describe what LSA does for the users.
9. Describe the two types of trusts.
10. Name the component within Windows 2000 architecture that holds Active Directory.

Answers to Lesson 1 Activities

1. In Windows 2000, one domain can be a child of another domain, e.g. child.domain.com is a child of domain.com (a child domain always has the complete domain name of the parent in it), and a child domain and its parent share a two-way transitive trust.

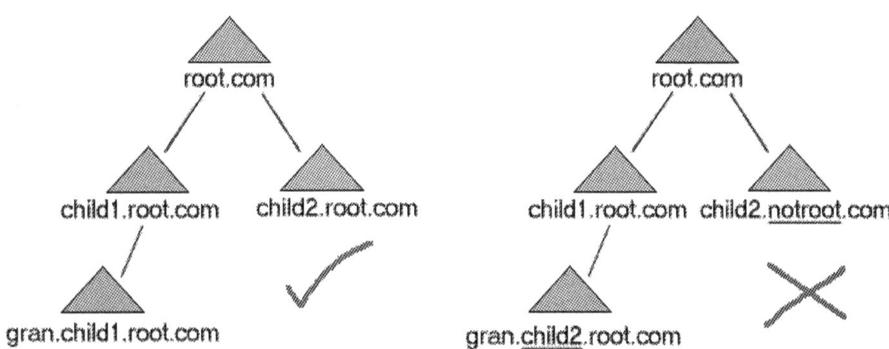

When you have a domain as a child of another, a domain tree is formed. A domain tree has to have a contiguous namespace. The name of the tree is the root domain name, so in the example, the tree would be referred to as root.com. Since the domains are DNS names and inherit the parent part of the name, if a part of the tree is renamed, then all of its children will implicitly also be renamed. For example, if parent ntfaq.com of sales.ntfaq.com was renamed to backoffice.com the child would be renamed to sales.backoffice.com.

2. The schema contains a formal definition of the contents and structure of Active Directory, including all classes, attributes, and class properties.

3. The terms directory and directory service refer to the directories found in both public and private networks. A directory provides a means of storing, managing, and retrieving information related to the network resources. A directory service identifies all the resources in a network and makes them available to users and applications.

4. An implicit two-way transitive trust is a trust between Windows 2000 parent and child domains in a tree and between the top-level domains in a forest. These trust relationships make all the objects in all the domains of the tree available to all the other domains in the tree.

   An explicit one-way trust is a relationship between domains that are not part of the same tree. One way trusts support connections to existing pre-Windows 2000 domains to allow configuring trust relationships with domains in other trees.

5. The central repository for information about objects in a tree or a forest is called the Global Catalog. A Global Catalog is created initially on the domain controller and is known as the Global Catalog server. It stores a full replica of all object attributes in the directory for its host domain and a partial replica for all object attributes contained in every domain in the forest. The partial replica stores attributes most frequently used in search operations. Object attributes replicated in the Global Catalog inherit the same permissions as in the source domains, ensuring the Global Catalog is secure.

   The Global Catalog performs two key directory roles:
   It enables network logon by providing universal group membership information to a domain controller when a login process is initiated.
   It enables finding directory information regardless of which domain in the forest actually contains the data.

6. The logical structure elements in Active Directory are: objects, which are concrete items that share a common set of attributes and can be organized by classes; attributes (also referred to as properties), which are categories of information that define the characteristics of all objects; and object classes, which are logical groupings of objects. The schema is the set of definitions for Active Directory objects. It is the definition of all object attributes, classes, and class properties.

7. Elements are organized into OUs within a domain. Domains link together to form trees. Trees join to create a forest.
   In Active Directory, a tree is a hierarchy of multiple domains connected by trust relationships. They share a common schema, configuration, and Global Catalog server.

8. In Active Directory, a tree is a hierarchy of multiple domains that are connected by trust relationships that share a common schema, configuration, and Global Catalog server.

9. When domains are created and linked to a tree, transitive trusts are created. Transitive trusts are two-way trusts between domains.
   Explicit trusts are one-way relationships that limit access to the member domain that is explicitly trusted. Explicit trusts are created manually.

10. Active Directory is the directory service included in Windows 2000 Server and part of the component called the security subsystem. Active Directory includes the directory, which stores information about network resources such as user data, printers, servers, databases, groups, computers, and security policies. The directory can scale from a small installation with a few hundred objects to large installations with millions.

Lesson 1 Quiz

These questions test your knowledge of features, vocabulary, procedures, and syntax.

1. What is a Domain?

   A. A container of objects that share security requirements, replication processes, and administration
   B. An object
   C. A hierarchical structure based on a company's administrative model
   D. A collection of one or more trees

2. What is the function of a DACL?

   A. Translates a name into some object or information the name represents
   B. Determines who can see an object and what actions a person can perform on an object
   C. Allows users in one domain to gain access to resources and information through a forest
   D. Delegates authority to administrators to manage a specific container or subtree

3. Which of the following is NOT one of the functions of the Windows 2000 Security infrastructure?

   A. A directory service store for security policies and account information
   B. Authenticates Active Directory access.
   C. Stores trust information for Active Directory
   D. It is a Global Catalog

4. Which of these would you use to view users in a logical, hierarchical format?

   A. The DSA
   B. The LDAP
   C. The LSA
   D. The DNS

5. What are the two processes that take part in the flow of information through the Active Directory?

    A. Forests and Trees
    B. Replication and Queries
    C. Delegation and Access Rights
    D. Transitive Trusts and Explicit Trusts

6. What does the Kernel Mode of Windows 2000 contain?

    A. The Active Directory
    B. HAL
    C. Plug and Play Manager
    D. The Security Subsystem

7. What is the definition of a Schema?

    A. A group of one or more Active Directory trees that trust each other.
    B. A partial replica of every Windows 2000 domain in the directory.
    C. Contains users and global groups from any domain in the forest universal groups and other domain local groups.
    D. The definition of an entire database. The universe of objects that can be stored in a directory.

Answers to Lesson 1 Quiz

1. Answer A is correct. A domain is a group of computers that are part of a network and share a common directory database. It is given a unique name, organization levels and administers as a unit with common rules and procedures. It is a container of objects that share security requirements, replication processes and administration.

   Answer B is incorrect. An object represents something concrete and is part of a domain.

   Answer C is incorrect. An OU (organizational Unit) is the hierarchal model.

   Answer D is incorrect. A forest is a collection of trees.

2. Answer B is correct. A Discretionary Access Control List (DACL) defines security groups, user accounts and associated permissions. This includes determining who can see an object and what actions a person can perform on an object.

   Answer A is incorrect. A name resolution is used to translate a name into some object or information the name represents.

   Answer C is incorrect. Trust relationships allow users in one domain to gain access to resources and information through a forest.

   Answer D is incorrect. Delegation is giving authority to administrators to manage a specific container or subtree.

3. Answer A is correct. A security structure is the directory service store for security policies and account information.

   Answer B is correct. The security structure authenticates Active Directory access.

   Answer C is correct. The security structure stores trust information for Active Directory.

   Answer D is incorrect. To make information widely available to users, it is centralized and stored in a Global Catalog.

4. Answer A is correct. The Directory System Agent allows you to view users in a logical, hierarchal manner.

   Answer B is incorrect. The Light Weight Directory Protocol is used to access a directory service.

   Answer C is incorrect. Active Directory is part of the Local Security Authority.

   Answer D is incorrect. A DNS is a Domain Name System.

5. Answer B is Correct. Information flows through your Active Directory using two processes, Replication and Queries. With replication each domain controller is updated on a regular basis. The Global Catalog contains information about every object in the Active Directory. You can query the global catalog about information on any object.

   Answer A is incorrect. Forests and trees are part of the Active Directory schema.

   Answer C is incorrect. Delegation and access rights are part of Active Directory security.

   Answer D is incorrect. Trust relationships allow users in a domain to gain access to resources and information in the forest.

6. Answer B is correct. The Hardware Access Layer is part of the Kernel Mode.

   Answers A, C and D are incorrect. They are all part of User Mode, not Kernel Mode.

7. Answer D is correct. A Schema is the definition of all objects that can be created in Active Directory. This includes their characteristics, or attributes. For each object class, the schema defines what attributes an instance of the class must have, additional attributes it may have and what object class can be a parent of the current object base.

   Answer A is incorrect. It is a forest.

   Answer B is incorrect. It is a global catalog.

   Answer C is incorrect. It is a Domain Local Group.

8. Answer C is correct. Windows 2000 security features provide directory services store for policies and account information, implements security models for all objects, authenticates Active Directory access, and stores trust information for Active Directory.

   Answer A is incorrect. These four items are part of maintaining security.

   Answer B is incorrect. These four items are part of the services domain controllers perform.

   Answer D is incorrect. DACLs apply to these four items.

9. Answer A is correct. Using domains, you can structure your network to match your organization.

   Answer B is correct. Domains are neither restricted to a single site or single location, but can span multiple sites and locations.

   Answer C is correct. If you want to lower administrative overhead, a single domain is the least costly.

   Answer D is incorrect. It describes organizational units, not domains.

10. Answer D is correct. A child domain contains the name of the parent domain. Looking at the grandchild domain, the correct name for the child domain is Seattle.MyCompany.com.

    Answer A is incorrect. MyCompany.Seattle.com is in the wrong order. MyCompany is the root domain not the child domain. Seattle is the child domain not the root domain.

    Answer B is incorrect. Admin is the name of the grandchild domain and the root domain is missing.

    Answer C is incorrect. It is missing the root domain MyCompany.

Lesson 2

Designing an Active Directory Naming Strategy

Active Directory makes it possible to configure or model the enterprise in many ways. Since no two enterprises are identical, successful design and implementation is based on understanding how to use Active Directory's flexibility, scalability, and granularity to your advantage.

Active Directory's directory service contains information about all the objects in the network. This lesson addresses the standards naming conventions, and structure needed to provide access to this information for qualified users. These standards are flexible enough to allow the user to use various naming strategies for the objects in the directory, based on the Domain Name System (DNS).

After completing this lesson, you should have a better understanding of the following topics:

- Active Directory naming conventions
- Domain Name System (DNS) components
- Name resolution process
- DNS naming strategies
- Active Directory domain names
- DNS deployment strategies for Active Directory
- Designing an Active Directory naming strategy

Active Directory Naming Conventions

Active Directory's naming conventions enable the client to reference network resources. Since these clients must be able to use various directory services, Active Directory addresses this issue by supporting standardized naming conventions.

Understanding Naming Convention Standards

Since the Domain Name System (DNS) and Lightweight Directory Access Protocol (LDAP) work together in Active Directory, the designer of the system must adhere to naming conventions of both. DNS, with its role of storing and managing records, must agree in naming conventions with LDAP and its role of querying and retrieving records.

Names should be simple and use standard DNS characters and Unicode characters. Windows 2000 supports the following standard DNS characters: A-Z, a-z, 0-9, and the hyphen (-) as defined in Request for Comment (RFC) 1035. The Unicode character set includes additional characters not found in the American Standard Code for Information Exchange (ASCII) character set, which are required for some languages other than English.

Warning: The set of characters described above does not include the underline underscore (_).

Names must be unique within the parent domain.

Domain Name System (DNS)

The DNS is the hierarchical distributed database used for name/address translation and client-server rendezvous. Domain Name System is also the namespace used on the Internet to translate computer and service names into TCP/IP addresses. Active Directory uses DNS as its location service, and so clients find domain controllers via DNS queries.

Although Active Directory and DNS are closely related, they have distinct roles that you must understand.

- DNS servers store and manage resource records
- Active Directory is used to store domain objects

You identify Active Directory domains by the DNS names you assign them. Because Active Directory and DNS domain names are identical, each Active Directory domain requires a corresponding DNS domain. However, each DNS domain does not require a corresponding Active Directory domain.

Note: You must install and configure the DNS service before you begin adding and naming objects. This installation allows Active Directory and associated client software to function correctly.

Lightweight Directory Access Protocol (LDAP)

LDAP is a protocol used to access a directory service. LDAP support is currently being implemented in Web browsers and e-mail programs, which can query an LDAP-compliant directory. LDAP is a simplified version of the Directory Access Protocol (DAP), which is used to gain access to X.500 directories. It is easier to code the query in LDAP than in DAP, but LDAP is less comprehensive. For example, DAP can initiate searches on other servers if an address is not found, while, in its initial specification, LDAP cannot. Lightweight Access Directory Protocol is the primary access protocol for Active Directory.

In Active Directory, the namespace is based on the Domain Name System (DNS) naming scheme, which allows for interoperability with Internet technologies and the Lightweight Directory Access Protocol (LDAP), which Active Directory uses to reference, locate, and retrieve the information in Active Directory. All access to directory objects occurs through LDAP.

In addition to searching, an LDAP directory server supports the following four types of update requests:

- Add an object to the directory
- Modify (add, delete, or replace) attribute values of an object in the directory
- Move an object by changing the name or parent of the object
- Delete an object from the directory

To make all this possible, the objects must be named according to LDAP naming standards, which are defined in RFC 1779 and RFC 2247.

Note: Active Directory supports LDAP versions 2 and 3.

An LDAP name contains the information necessary for an LDAP client to retrieve an object's information from the directory. The categories of these LDAP names are:

- LDAP distinguished name
- LDAP relative distinguished name
- User principal name
- NetBIOS Name

Understanding the LDAP Distinguished Name

This name shows the full path to the object from the directory root. The LDAP distinguished name is composed of common names (CN), organizational units (OU), and domain components (DC). An example of an LDAP distinguished name is:
JohnSmith@MyCompany.com.

The LDAP Distinguished Name is composed of the Common Names (CN), Organizational Units (OU), and Domain Components (DC). For example:

CN=JohnSmith, CN=Users, DC=MyCompany, DC=com makes up the following LDAP Distinguished Name:

JohnSmith.MyCompany.com

Understanding the LDAP Relative Distinguished Name

This is a shorthand version of the LDAP distinguished name and is known as the *friendly* name. Depending on where you are in the pathway, the LDAP relative distinguished name will vary. For example, in the preceding case, it is the name of the object itself separated from the path to the object. For example, if you started your search at CN=Users, DC=MyCompany, DC=com, the LDAP relative distinguished name would be CN=John Smith.

Assigning a User Principal Name

This is shorter than the LDAP relative distinguished name and is even easier to remember! Windows 2000 users and groups have principal names. For example, the user John Smith in MyCompany.com might have the user principal name ofJohnS@MyCompany.com, where JohnS is the logon name and MyCompany.com is the name of the domain tree in which the JohnS user object resides.

Using a NetBIOS Name

The NetBIOS name is concatenated with the Security Accounts Manager (SAM) account name. For example, users on computers running Microsoft Windows NT or Microsoft Windows 98 log on with NetBIOS names. The SAM name is the old format and must be unique throughout the organization.

Tip: To log on while using earlier versions of Microsoft Windows, you can use the NetBIOS domain name combined with a user name, such as seattle\Dougs.

Domain Name System (DNS) Components

Since the DNS database is indexed by name, each domain must have a name. As you add domains to the hierarchy, the name of the parent domain is appended to its child domain (called a sub-domain). In Figure 2.1, the domain name *publishing.ibidpub.com* identifies the publishing domain as a sub-domain of the *ibidpub.com* domain and *ibidpub* as a sub-domain of the *com* domain.

Figure 2.1 A Domain Hierarchy

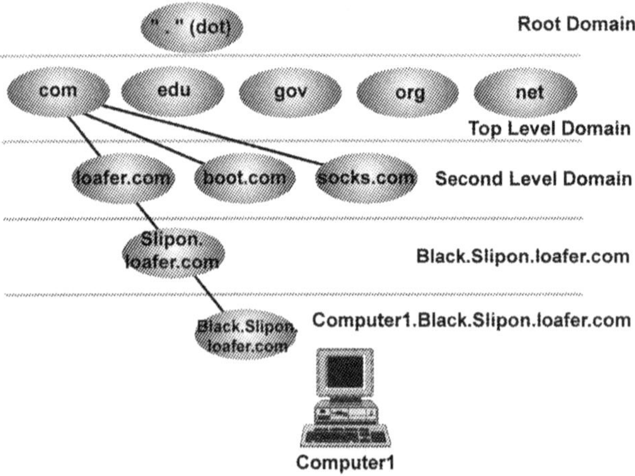

Understanding Domain Namespace

Like any directory service, Active Directory is primarily a namespace in which a name can be resolved or translated into some object or information that the name represents. This namespace is hierarchically structured and provides rules that allow the namespace to be partitioned. A namespace is also defined as a name or group of names that are defined according to some naming convention; any bounded area in which a given name can be resolved.

The naming scheme, called a *domain namespace*, provides the hierarchical structure for the DNS database that Active Directory uses. This structure is represented by nodes, or domains, which represent partitions of the DNS database. This hierarchy typically consists of:

- Root-Level domain
- First-Level domain
- Second-Level domain
- Sub-domains
- Host names

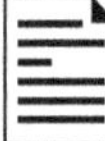

Note: In the context of DNS, the term *domain* is not related to domain as used in Windows 2000 directory services, which refers to computers and devices that are administered as a unit.

Root-Level Domain

The root domain is at the top of the hierarchy and is represented by a period (.). The Internet root domain is managed by several organizations.

First-Level Domain

These domains are organized by organization type or geographic location and are standardized, but not mandated, by the groups that manage the root domain. Table 2.1 provides examples of the most common first-level, or top-level, domains.

Table 2.1 First Level Domain Names

First-Level Domain Name	Description of Use
com	Commercial organizations
org	Non-commercial organizations
edu	Educational institutions
gov	Government
net	Networks

Note: These domains may also contain individual country names, such as *uk* for United Kingdom.

Second-Level Domain

A second-level name has two name parts: a top-level name and a second-level name, which must be unique. To ensure that this name is unique, it must be registered.

Table 2.2 provides a few examples of second-level domain names.

Table 2.2 Second-Level Domains

Second-Level Domain Name	Description of Use
friends.edu	Friends University
amazon.com	Amazon online bookstore
w3.org	World Wide Web Consortium
pm.gov.uk	Prime Minister of United Kingdom

Note: The gov.uk domain seems to contradict the rules for First-Level Domains, but it depends on the way the name is structured. If the name is structured as company.uk, then uk is First-Level.

Sub-domains

These child domains are created within the domain tree. These should be modeled according to your business needs and structure.

Warning: Remember that you lose these sub-domains, if you change the name of your root domain.

Host Names

A host name refers to a specific computer that is located on the Internet or a private network. A host name is the leftmost portion of a *Fully Qualified Domain Name (FQDN)*, which describes the exact location of the host within the domain.

Note: The host name does not have to conform to the computer name, the NetBIOS protocol, or any other naming protocol.

Understanding Zones

Each zone represents a discrete portion of the domain namespace. In addition, a zone must encompass a contiguous domain namespace.

The following concepts are necessary to understand the way zones work:

- Reasons for dividing a namespace into zones
- Zone database files

Reasons for Dividing a Namespace into Zones

Zones let the administrator partition the domain namespace into manageable sections. The structure and names of the zones should reflect the structure of the organization.

Zone Database Files

The zone database files store the name-to-IP-address mappings for the zone. Each zone is anchored to a specific domain, referred to as the zone's *root domain*. This database file does not contain information for all sub-domains of the zone's root domain, but only those sub-domains within the zone.

Understanding Name Servers

A DNS name server stores the zone database file. These name servers can store data for one or more zones. A name server is said to have authority for the domain namespace that the zone encompasses.

Two concepts are important:

- Primary zone database file
- Secondary zone database file

Primary Zone Database File

This is the master zone database file. Changes to a zone, such as adding domains or hosts, are performed on the server that contains the primary zone database file.

Secondary Zone Database File

These files serve as backup to the name server containing the primary zone database files, and they exist on multiple name servers. These multiple name servers provide important advantages:

- They perform zone transfers by obtaining a copy of the zone database file from the name server that contains the primary database zone file; these name servers periodically query the name server containing the primary zone database file for updated zone data
- They perform redundancy, providing added fault tolerance
- They improve access speed for remote locations across slow Wide Area Network (WAN) links
- They reduce the load on the name server containing the primary zone database file

Name Resolution Process

Name resolution is the process of translating a name into some object or information that the name represents. A telephone book forms a namespace in which the names of telephone subscribers can be resolved into telephone numbers. Similarly, Active Directory forms a namespace in which the name of an object in the directory can be resolved into the object itself.

With name resolution, which is provided by DNS, users can access servers by name rather than having to type in an IP address, which would be difficult to remember. Active Directory clients locate Active Directory services on the network by querying DNS domains for the SRV (Service Resource Records), which provide hostnames or IP addresses for domain controllers providing the requested services.

To find an object in Active Directory, the following resolution processes must be completed:

- Resolving services
- Resolving Active Directory objects

Resolving Services

The client performs DNS queries to resolve which computers are hosting Active Directory LDAP services.

Resolving Active Directory Objects

LDAP queries the domain controllers to locate the object.

Locating Active Directory Objects

Sometimes the first domain controller cannot return the object but can provide the name of a domain where the information may be. It is, in effect, saying, "I don't have it, but I can tell you where you might find it." This is known as an *LDAP referral.* Sometimes the client will receive multiple referrals from domain controllers until one of them responds with the object. This response is known as an *authoritative answer.*

Following is a typical process:

1. The client queries DNS for an LDAP server in the publishing.ibidpub.com domain.
2. DNS responds with a domain controller for the domain.
3. The client queries the returned domain controller for information about the user Jdoe using LDAP.
4. The client receives an LDAP referral to sales.ibidpub.com.
5. The client queries DNS for an LDAP server in the sales.ibidpub.com domain.
6. DNS responds with a domain controller for the domain.
7. The client queries the returned domain controller in the sales.ibidpub.com domain for information about the user Jdoe using LDAP.
8. The client receives an LDAP referral to east.sales.ibidpub.com.

9. The client queries DNS for an LDAP server in the east.sales.ibidpub.com domain.
10. DNS responds with a domain controller for the domain.
11. The client queries the returned domain controller in the east.sales.ibidpub.com domain for information about the user Jdoe using LDAP.

The client receives a response to the query, known as an *authoritative response.* The domain controller that responded contained a full replica of the queried information.

Locating IP Addresses

Active Directory clients locate Active Directory objects and services on the network by querying DNS domains for the SRV (Service Resource Records), which provide hostnames of IP addresses for domain controllers that provide the requested service. DNS can translate an IP address into a domain name. For example, a numeric address like 293.452.120.54 can become something like abc.com.

Understanding Lookup Queries

DNS name servers can only resolve a query for a zone for which it has authority. If it cannot resolve the query, it passes it to other name servers. The name server caches the query results to reduce the DNS traffic on the network. Lookup queries are categorized as:

- Forward lookup query
- Reverse lookup query

Forward Lookup Query

A forward lookup query resolves a name to an IP address. To resolve a forward lookup query, a client passes a query to a local name server. The local name server either resolves the query or passes it to another name server.

Reverse Lookup Query

A reverse lookup query resolves an IP address to a name. Troubleshooting tools, such as the NSLOOKUP command-line utility, use reverse lookup queries to report host names. Because the DNS database is indexed by name and not by IP address, this approach is much more difficult and requires more supporting tools.

DNS Naming Strategies

With Active Directory, you design a directory structure and scope that mirrors your organizational structure and scope.

Defining Your Active Directory Scope

Before implementing Active Directory, you need to examine your organization's business structure and operations. Your plan of the domain structure, domain namespace, OU structure, and site structure will reflect the way your organization functions. When you determine the scope of Active Directory, make it as broad as possible to avoid having to fix it later.

Among other considerations, scope should include:

- Internal organization, including all geographical locations
- External presence, such as the Internet

Table 2.3 provides a checklist for implementing such a plan.

Table 2.3 Implementation Checklist

Step	Process
1	Determine the number of forests
2	Create a change control policy for each forest
3	Determine the number of domains in each forest
4	Choose a forest root domain
5	Assign a DNS name to each domain
6	Plan DNS server deployment
7	Optimize authentication with shortcut trust relationships
8	Create OUs to delegate administration
9	Create OUs to hide objects
10	Create OUs for group policy
11	Define sites and site links
12	Place servers in sites

Figure 2.2 shows the directory after the plan has been implemented.

Figure 2.2 An Implemented Plan

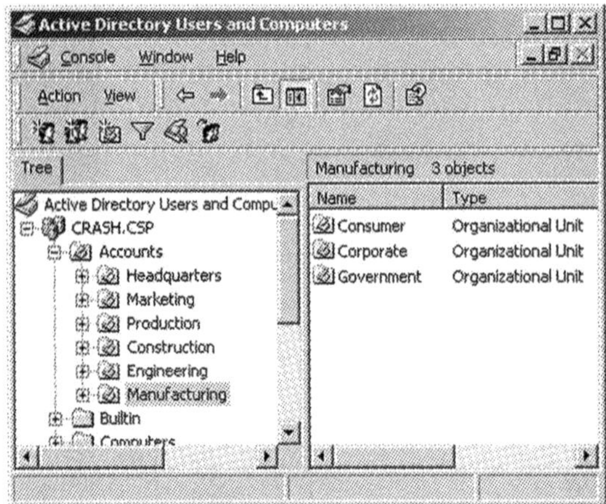

After the initial planning phase, you must complete the following:

- Choose a DNS root name
- Register your DNS root name with InterNic
- Create a domain name hierarchy
- Choose a DNS service
- Understand the way DNS zone data is stored

Choosing a DNS Root Name

When you set up your DNS server, you should begin by choosing and registering a unique parent DNS name that can be used for hosting your organization. Each organization can have only one DNS root name; therefore, you should choose this name very carefully. It should represent your entire organization and allow all users to access information and resources.

Active Directory can exist within the scope of the Internet DNS structure. If this is the case, you must register your DNS root name with an Internet Registrar such as InterNIC.

Registering a DNS Root Name with InterNIC

Registration has these benefits:

- Ensures that all DNS names are unique
- Provides assignment of network addresses that are recorded in the global DNS database

After registering your DNS name with InterNIC and receiving confirmation from them, you will have the authority to manage your own hierarchy of child domains, zones, and hosts within your DNS root domain.

A search of the Internet using the string *InterNIC* will lead you to the InterNIC site, where you will receive instructions for registering your name. InterNIC will check to see if your name is in use and recommend alternative names, if a conflict is found.

Note: Remember that your DNS root name must be unique and not in use by any other organization.

Creating a Domain Name Hierarchy

The number of domains will reflect the structure and services of your organization. For example, if your organization is located in diverse geographical areas, you may want to configure a domain for each location. Within each domain, each service, such as sales, publishing, etc., may need its own domain.

Domains in Active Directory are arranged in a hierarchical structure that reflects their relationships to each other. Since this hierarchy is visible to the users, it should be carefully organized and easy to use. These take the form of a tree structure and are organized as follows:

- Root domain
- Domains derived from the root domain

Root Domain

This is the top of the hierarchy and provides the basis for all the other domains that will be derived from it. It uses only one name. If you plan an Internet presence using this root name, you need to register it to be sure that it is unique. Do this before you add any child domains to it. Careful planning at this point will save hours of corrections later.

Warning: You cannot change the name of the root domain in your Active Directory forest without removing Active Directory and creating a new forest.

Domains Derived from the Root Domain

Once you have established your root domain and have confirmed that its name will not change, you will start adding child domains to it to mirror the structure, services, and objects within your organization. For example, if an educational institution named friends.edu needs to divide its network into three domains, KC (for Kansas City), Topeka, and Wichita, the domains could be kc.friends.edu, topeka.friends.edu, and wichita.friends.edu. Each domain name is separate, but maintained within the same Active Directory tree.

Choosing a DNS Service

In choosing a DNS service, be sure that it does the following:

- Supports SRV records
- Supports the dynamic update protocol
- Supports incremental zone transfers (recommended)
- Is compatible with recommended protocols

SRV Records

SRV records are DNS records that map to the name of a server offering that service. Support of SRV records is mandatory.

Dynamic Update Protocol

This enables the servers and clients in your environment to add records to the DNS database automatically, thus reducing administration costs. This is optional but highly recommended. See RFC 2136 for more details. On the network, this information is stored in systemroot\System32\Config\Netlogon.dns.

Incremental Zone Transfers

This allows only new or modified resource records to be replicated between DNS servers rather than the entire zone database file. It is optional but recommended.

See RFC 2135 for more details.

Note: Windows 2000 DNS Server service provides support for all of these features.

Storing DNS Zone Data

You can choose between two ways to store DNS zone information:

- Standard text files
- Active Directory

Text Files Storage

If you choose this method for DNS zone information storage, you must designate a server as a primary server for the text files. You can provide redundancy for fault tolerance by designating additional DNS name servers or secondary servers to store read-only copies of the zone database file.

Zone database information is transferred to the secondary servers using a process known as zone transfer. In a zone transfer, the originating server is referred to as the master server. Either a primary or a secondary server can act as a master server, depending on how you define your DNS replication topology.

Note: This approach means that you must manage your own zone transfer.

Active Directory DNS Zone Data Storage

You can store zone data in Active Directory. Here the zone object is replicated automatically as part of domain replication. All name servers act as primary servers. This means that changes can originate at any domain controller that has the DNS service installed. Administrators can remove the DNS service from a domain controller after integration, but as long as the DNS service is installed on at least one domain controller, the zone data is always replicated to all domain controllers.

Note: If you decide to store DNS zone information in Active Directory, you can designate secure update, which means that only authorized users can perform dynamic updates to the DNS resource records.

Active Directory Domain Names

Remember that Active Directory naming follows the standard DNS format. Therefore, Active Directory names must conform to DNS naming guidelines.

Note: RFC 1034, RFC 1035, RFC 1039, and RFC 2052 contain valuable information on DNS character standards.

Selecting a Domain Name

Access to the Internet determines a DNS naming strategy. If you are planning an Internet presence, you must register your DNS domain that you designate as the root Active Directory domain with an Internet registering authority.

Using a Registered DNS Domain Name

If your company already has a registered DNS hierarchy, you can use this as your Active Directory root domain name. Just be sure that your internal DNS server supports SRV resource records. Then you can use the existing DNS zone and create the root of the Active Directory forest using the existing DNS name.

Using a Delegated DNS Sub-Domain Name

This is an alternative to using the organization's registered DNS domain name. Here you delegate a DNS child domain that exists in a separate zone and then designate it as the Active Directory root domain. With this configuration, you only expose the zone containing the DNS root domain to the Internet.

Note: One disadvantage of this approach is a longer name structure, since naming starts at a third-level domain.

Using a Reserved Private DNS Domain Name

The local domain is a first-level name that InterNIC reserves for private use. The Active Directory root can be a second level domain below the reserved top-level domain of .local. These private DNS names are similar in purpose to the ranges of IP addresses that are reserved for private use as specified in RFC 1918.

This private reserved name cannot be registered for use on the Internet. Here are some reasons for using this approach:

- You do not have a registered DNS domain name
- You do not foresee an Internet presence in the future
- You want to differentiate between Active Directory and your Internet presence

Warning: Be careful with this decision! If you decide to establish an Internet presence later, you must obtain a registered DNS name and completely reinstall the forest.

Using a Single DNS Domain Name for Public and Private Networks

You may want to retain a single DNS domain name but wish to ensure that its internal network is kept separate from the Internet. You can retain a single DNS domain name for both internal and external use by the following strategies:

- Separate DNS zones by using a firewall
- Allow Internet access to internal clients

Separate DNS Zones by Using a Firewall

This approach uses two DNS zones with the same name on either side of a firewall. You then manage the contents of those zones so that the appropriate records are present in each. Here, the DNS server on the public network would maintain records only for hosts to be accessed by means of the Internet. The DNS server on the internal network would have the resource records that will be available to all internal hosts, including all Active Directory-related resource records.

If you choose this solution, be aware that it requires administration of the SRV resource records. You must be careful to ensure that only the appropriate resource records are available to external requests.

Allow Internet Access to Internal Clients

This solution also requires two DNS servers, one on either side of the firewall. The difference between this and the previous solution is that the internal clients can access the Internet. If an internal host attempts to connect to an external host, they will resolve the host name to an external IP address and the connection attempt will be passed through the firewall.

This solution requires administration of resource records on two DNS servers. However, it eliminates the need for mirroring Internet resources on the private network, since users have direct access to the Internet.

Note: This apparent advantage is counterbalanced by the need for extensive planning for the firewall to specify exactly what types of traffic from internal clients will be allowed through it.

Choosing Public and Private Network Domain Names

Yet, another alternative is available for domain naming. You can use different domain names for the public and private networks.

Note: This solution makes is easy to separate public and private resources. A disadvantage is that you cannot access internal resources from the Internet. In addition, some users may be confused by the different name.

DNS Deployment Strategies for Active Directory

Active Directory provides methods for designing a directory structure that meets the needs of your organization. When you plan for Active Directory, you are defining a significant part of the network infrastructure for your organization.

Planning for Active Directory

In the plan, you create a set of structures that best reflects your organization. The structures you create will determine:

- The network usage characteristics of directory clients and servers
- How efficiently you can manage the contents of the directory
- The availability and fault tolerance of the directory
- The way users view and interact with the directory
- The ability of your directory structures to evolve as your organization evolves

To have cost effective deployment, a plan is essential. Time invested in the planning phase will help you avoid spending time and money in the future reworking structures that you have already put in place.

To create your directory structure plans, follow the sequence of planning steps as presented in this chapter. Complete the following tasks, while you create your plans:

- Learn the key Active Directory concepts that influence structure planning and adjust the suggested planning steps as necessary to best suit your organization
- Identify the people in your organization who should participate in structure planning
- Understand how existing business practices might need to change or evolve to take full advantage of Active Directory
- Understand the flexibility of the structures you create and determine how easy or difficult it will be to change your choices in the future

The following four basic components make up the Active Directory structure: forests, domains, organizational units, and sites.

Creating A Forest Plan

A forest is a collection of Active Directory domains. Forests serve two purposes—to make user interaction and management of domains simpler. Forests have the following characteristics:

Schema—An object class and its attributes can be created in a directory. The schema exists as a naming context that is replicated in every domain controller in the forest.

Configuration Container—A naming context that is replicated to every domain controller in the forest. Sharing the configuration across domains of a forest eliminates the need to configure domains separately.

Trusts—Active Directory creates transitive two-way trust relationships between the domains of a forest. Users and groups from any domain can be recognized by any member computer in the forest and included in groups or ACLs (Access Control Lists). When you add a domain to the forest, it is automatically configured with a two-way transitive trust. This eliminates the need to create additional trusts with domains in the same forest.

Global Catalog—Contains a copy of every object from every domain in the forest but only a selected set of attributes from each object. This allows for fast searching through the entire forest. The global catalog makes directory structures within the forest transparent to users.

Note: In most situations, a single forest is sufficient. You may need to create an additional forest, if your network is distributed among many autonomous divisions. Because forests have shared elements, it is necessary for all participants in a forest to agree on content and administration of those shared elements. It may be necessary to create more than one forest, if individual organizations want to limit the scope of the trust relationship. In order for a user in one forest to use resources in another, additional configuration will be required.

Creating a Domain Plan

Because the core unit of the logical structure in Active Directory is the domain, it is essential to plan the domain structure carefully (Figure 2.3). When you plan your domain structure, you must assess the following aspects of your company:

- Logical environment structure
- Physical environment structure

- Administrative requirements
- Domain organizational needs
- Domain requirements

Assessing the Logical Environment

You need to understand how the company conducts daily operations to determine the logical structure of your organization.

Figure 2.3 Domain Model Echoes the Business Model

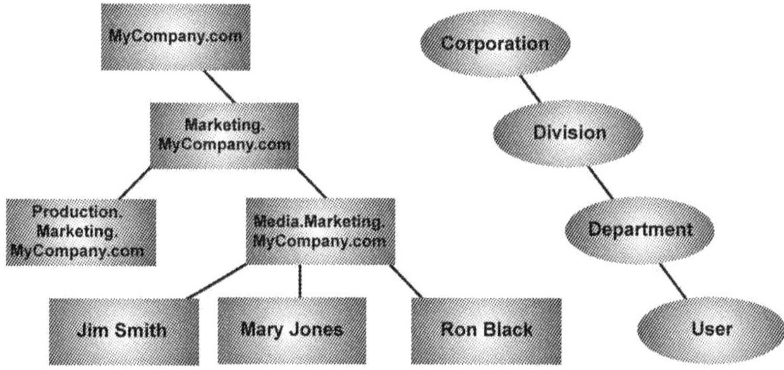

Assessing the Physical Environment

By assessing the company's physical environment, you can ascertain the technical requirements. You need to determine the following factors:

- Number of employees
- The growth rate
- Plans for expansion

To assess the requirements for each of the business models, you need to have the following information:

- How the network connections are organized
- Network connection speed
- How the network connections are utilized
- TCP/IP subnets

Accessing the Administrative Requirements

Accessing how your company's network resources are managed can help you to plan your domain structure. You will need to identify the method of network administration used by your company:

- Centralized administration
- Decentralized administration
- Customized administration

Domain Organizational Needs

After you have ascertained the logical, physical environment structure, and the administrative requirements for your company, you can decide on the domain needs in your organization. You may determine that your company requires more than one domain. If so, you must organize the domains into a hierarchy that fits the needs of your organization.

Domain Requirements

The easiest domain structure to administer is a single domain. When planning you should start with a single domain and add to it when the single domain no longer meets your needs.

Tip: One domain can span multiple sites, geographic locations and millions of objects. Keep in mind that site and domain structures are separate and flexible.

The possible reasons for creating additional domains are:
Decentralized network administration

- Replication Control
- Different password requirements between organizations
- Massive numbers of objects
- Different Internet domain names
- International requirements
- Internal political requirements

Assigning DNS Names to Create a Domain Hierarchy

The first domain created in Active Directory is the starting point or root. All other domains are derived from this initial domain. Only one name can be used for this root domain.

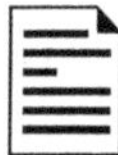

Note: You cannot change the name of the root domain in your active directory forest without removing Active Directory and creating a new forest.

Active Directory domains are named with DNS names. Because DNS is the predominant system on the Internet, DNS names are globally recognized and have well known regulation authorities. DNS names are hierarchical and can be partitioned along the lines of the hierarchy. Internet mail, which manages DNS in a similar manner to Active Directory, is an example of how DNS as locator mechanism can maneuver through extraordinarily large networks such as the Internet.

Here are several recommendations for assigning domain names:

- Use names relative to a registered Internet DNS name (names registered on the Internet are globally unique)

- Use Internet standard characters—A-Z, a-z, 0-9 and the hyphen (-), which ensures that your Active Directory will comply with standards-based software
- Use names that are distinct and never use the same name twice for different domains, even if the domains are on unconnected networks with different DNS namespaces because if, for example, both an intranet and an Internet domain in the same company have the same domain name, when a user connects to both the intranet and the Internet simultaneously, the directory that answers first during the locator search would be displayed and it would be difficult to determine if this is the correct one
- Use the fewest trees possible because after you own a particular DNS name, you own all the names that are subordinate to that name; thus, the fewer trees created, the fewer DNS names you will own
- Use names that are short enough that you can remember all the components

Creating an Organizational Unit Plan

An Organizational Unit (OU) is the container you use to create structure within a domain. The following are important to consider during this process:

OUs can be nested—They can contain child OUs, allowing you to create a hierarchical structure within a domain.

OUs can delegate—Administration and control access to directory objects.

OUs are not security principles—Since OUs are used for delegation of administration, the parent of the OU user object indicates who manages the object but does not indicate which resources a user can access.

In versions of Windows NT earlier than Windows 2000, delegation of administration within a domain was limited to the use of built-in local groups. These groups had predefined capabilities, and sometimes these capabilities did not fit the needs of the organization. In Windows 2000, delegation is more powerful and flexible. This flexibility is achieved through a combination of Organizational Units, per attribute access control and access control inheritance.

Deciding Which OUs to Create

The OU structure you create will depend entirely on how administration is delegated in your organization. There are three ways to delegate administration:

- By physical location
- By business unit
- By role or task

The three dimensions can be combined. Creating OUs, moving OU sub-trees within a domain, moving objects between OUs in the same domain, and deleting OUs are simple tasks.

Creating a Site Topology

An Active Directory site topology is a logical representation of a physical network. Site topology is defined on a per-forest basis. Active Directory clients and servers use the site topology of a forest to route query and replication traffic efficiently. A site topology also helps you decide where to place domain controllers on your network. Keep the following key concepts in mind when designing your site topology:

- A site is a set of networks with fast, reliable connectivity
- A site is defined as a set of IP subnets connected by fast, reliable connectivity; networks with LAN speed or better are considered fast networks
- A site link is a low-bandwidth or unreliable network that connects two or more sites
- Site links are used to model the amount of available bandwidth between two sites and, as a general rule, any two networks connected by a link that is slower than LAN speed is considered to be connected by a site link, however, a fast link that is near capacity has a low effective bandwidth and can also be considered a site link
- Site topology information is stored in the configuration container

Sites, site links, and subnets are all stored in the configuration container, which is replicated to every domain controller in the forest. Every domain controller in the forest has complete knowledge of the site topology. A change to the site topology causes replication to every domain controller in the forest.

Note: Site topology is separate and unrelated to domain hierarchy. A site can contain many domains, and a domain can appear in many sites.

Site Topology Planning Process

To create a site topology for a forest, use the following process:

- Define sites and site links using your physical network topology as a starting point
- Place servers into sites
- Understand how changes to your site topology after deployment will impact end users

When creating the site topology plan, you will most likely need to consult:

- Teams that manage and monitor the TCP/IP implementation on your network
- Domain administrators for each domain in the forest

Designing a Site Structure

Designing a site structure that consists of a single local area network is simple. Because local connections are fast, the network can be a single site. A separate site with its own domain controller can be set up when the domain controllers are not responding fast enough to meet the needs of the users. Determining what is fast enough depends on your organization's criteria for network performance. Inadequate performance usually occurs when deploying over a wide geographic range.

Follow these steps to design a site structure for an organization with multiple sites:

1. **Assess the physical environment.** Review the information that you have gathered when determining domain structure, including the locations of the sites, the TCP/IP subnets, the speed of the various networks, how those network connections are organized, and how the networks are utilized.

2. **Determine the physical locations that form the domains.** Determine which physical locations are involved in each domain.

3. **Determine which of the areas of the network should be sites.** If the network area requires workstation logon controls or directory replication, the area should be set up as a site.

4. **Identify the physical links connecting the sites.** Identify the link types, speeds, and utilization that exist so the links can be determined as site link objects.

5. **For each site link object, determine the cost and the schedule.** The lowest cost site link performs replication; determine the priority of each link by setting the cost (default cost is 100; lower cost provides higher priority).

6. **Provide redundancy by configuring a site link bridge.** A site link bridge provides fault tolerance for replication.

Lab A: Designing a Naming Strategy

Objective

After completing this lab, you will be able to:

- Configure a computer as a member of the MyCompany domain
- Create a custom Microsoft Management Console (MMC)
- Evaluate a naming strategy
- Create a naming strategy

Exercise 1—Configuring your Computer to be Part of a Domain

In this exercise, you will configure your computer as a member of the MyCompany domain.

Note: If your computer is a domain controller, you cannot change the identification.

To join the **MyCompany Domain:**

1. **Log on** to your computer as **Administrator** with the appropriate **password**.
2. Right click on **My Computer** and then click **Properties**.
3. Click the **Network Identification** tab.
4. Click **Advanced**. The **Identification Changes** dialog box appears.
5. Click **Domain**.
6. In the Domain box type **MyCompany.msft** and click **OK**.
7. The Domain **Username and Password** box will open, welcoming you to the MyCompany.msft domain and click **OK**.
8. Click **OK** when the **Network Identification** information box appears telling you the computer must be rebooted.
9. Click **OK** to close the System Properties, then **Yes** to restart your computer.

Exercise 2—Creating a Custom MMC Console

Microsoft Mangement Console (MMC) contains the administrative tools that you can use to administer networks, computers, services, and other system components.

As an Administrator, you will need tools to manage DNS and Active Directory, this exercise will help you to create a custom MMC console for the Administrator account.

1. **Log on** to your computer as **Administrator**.
2. To start the Console, click **Start** and then click **Run**.
3. Type **MMC** in the Open dialog. The **Console** window will open.
4. On the **Console** menu, click **Add/Remove Snap-in** (Ctrl-M).
5. Ensure your domain (MyCompany) is displayed in the snap-ins added to dialog. Click **Add**. The **Add Standalone Snap-in** window is displayed.

6. Click **Active Directories Domains and Trusts** and then click **Add**. Active Directories Domains and Trusts will now be displayed in the Add Remove Snap-ins window.
7. Click **Active Directories Users and Computers** and then click **Add**. Active Directories Users and Computers will now be displayed in the Add Remove Snap-ins window.
8. Click **Computer Management** and then click **Add**. Computer Management will now be displayed in the Add Remove Snap-ins window.

To save an MMC Console File

Saving an MMC console to a file keeps the list of loaded snap-ins for the console, the arrangement and contents of console windows in the main MMC window, the default mode, and information about permissions.

All the configuration settings for the tools and controls are saved with the console and restored when the console file is opened. You can open a console file on different computers or even different networks and restore the saved settings for all the tools.

Console files have an .msc (management saved console) extension. When you create console files, save them in Administrative Tools folder (in Windows 2000, located at *systemdrive*\Documents and Settings\user\Start\Menu\Programs\ Administrative Tools). They will be available to you from the Administrative Tools folder on the **Programs** menu. The console files will not be available for other users of the computer.

After you save a console, you can distribute it by using a floppy disk, e-mail, or your network.

If you are working with a console in author mode, you can save changes to the console by using the **Save** command on the **Console** menu. If you are working with a console in one of the user modes, saving changes to the console is determined by whether the **Do not save changes to this console** check box (available by clicking **Options** on the **Console** menu) was selected when the console was configured. If this check box was not selected, changes to the console are automatically saved when you close MMC; if it was selected, changes to the console are discarded when you close MMC.

To save the Console you have created:

1. In an MMC console opened in author mode, on the **Console** menu, click **Save**.

2. If a console is saved to the per-user Administrative Tools folder (in Windows 2000, located at *systemdrive*\Documents and Settings*user*\Start\ Menu\ Programs\Administrative Tools), it is then available in the Administrative Tools folder on the **Programs** menu for that user.

Renaming an Item on the Console Tree

To rename an item on the console tree of an MMC console:

1. Open a saved console in author mode by doing one of the following: right-click the .msc file, and then select **Author**, or choose **Start**, **Run**, then type **mmc path\filename.msc /a**, and then click **OK**.
2. In the console tree, choose the item you want to rename.
3. On the **Action** menu, choose **Rename** and then type the new name.

Note: Not all items in the console tree can be renamed. If the **Rename** command does not appear on the **Action** menu, you cannot rename the item.

Exercise 3—Evaluate a Naming Strategy

In this exercise, you will examine the naming strategy for an organization and evaluate its design.

MyCompany is a potholder manufacturer based in Kansas with four office locations based around the world. Virtual private networks and high-speed connections to the Internet connect the offices.

The company has registered the DNS name MyCompany.com with the appropriate Internet authorities. Separate DNS servers are used in each location and a single DNS server responds to the public inquiries on the public side of the firewall.

Information about the four offices is in the following table:

Table 2.4 Exercise 3 Table

Region	City	DNS domain	Number of Users
United States	Kansas	Us.MyCompany.com	600
Canada	Edmonton	Ca.MyCompany.com	80
England	Portland	Uk.MyCompany.com	300
Asia	Singapore	Sg,MyCompany.com	250

Business Requirements

The business requirements include:

The existing Internet Web site and applications will need to be preserved with minimal reconfiguration or down time

The Systems Information Group in Kansas City will manage all users centrally

Employees who travel will need to be able to log on at any Windows 2000 computer in the network with a username and password

Proposed Naming Strategy

Design Element	Proposed Implementation
Active Directory root domain name	MyCompany.com
Additional Active Directory Domains	None
(NetBIOS) Name	MYCOMPANY
User Principal Name suffix	MyCompany.com
Internal DNS Name	MyCompany.cmsft hosted by Windows 2000 service on all MyCompany.com domain controllers using Active Directory integrated zones.
External DNS Name	MyCompany.com hosted by existing DNS server.

To evaluate the solution, consider the following questions:

1. Which of the following statements about this solution are true?
   a. All the user accounts can be managed by the Systems Information Group in Kansas.
   b. Users can log on to any Windows 2000 computer in any location with a username and password.
   c. The MyCompany can continue to use their existing DNS name on the Internet.
2. Which of the following features of DNS must be supported by the DNS server that supports Active Directory?
   a. Service (SRV) resources
   b. Dynamic update protocol
   c. Secure dynamic updates
   d. Active Directory-integrated zones
   e. Incremental zone transfers
3. Which DNS Server must support the use of SRV resource records?
   a. Internal DNS server (domain controllers)
   b. External servers (On the Internet)

Explain your answer.

Exercise 3—Answers

1. The correct answer is c. There is not enough information given to asume either a or b would be correct.
2. A, b, c and e are correct.
3. A only. The servers on the Internet do not need to respond to queries for SRV records.

Exercise 4—Create a Naming Strategy

In this exercise, you will devise a naming strategy for an organization.

Scenario

Enterprise Partners is a company based in Portland, Oregon. The company also has locations in Mazatlan, Mexico and Madras, India. A subsidiary, Endeavor Ltd., is based in Calgary, Canada. A virtual private network and high-speed connections to the Internet connect the offices.

Enterprise Partners has a presence on the Internet using the registered name Enterprise.com. Endeavor uses Endeavorltd.com as its registered DNS domain name. The two DNS servers that host both the internal and external Enterprise.com domain for the internal and public networks use an earlier version of BIND that does not support the use of SRV resource records. A separate Information Technology (IT) group manages the servers and the servers will not be upgraded. The company has decided that five domains will make up the Active Directory.

Business Requirements

The business requirements include the following:

Computers on the internal network need to be able to resolve the names of the company's servers on the Internet

Employees who travel need to be able to log on to any Windows 2000 computer with a username and password

Proposed Naming Strategy

Using the following diagram to resolve the questions.

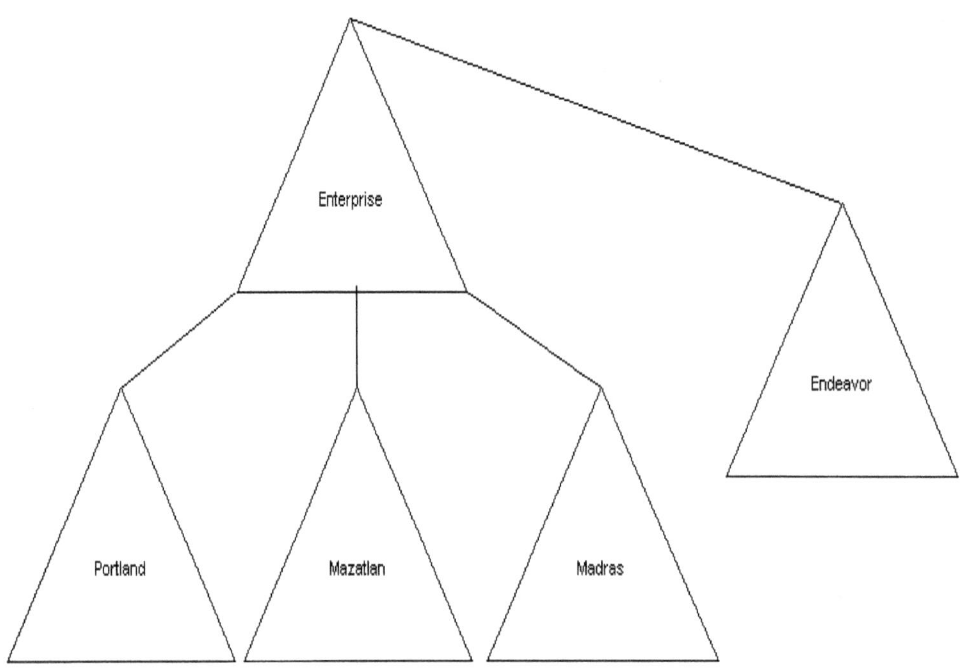

What will be the name of your Active Directory Root Domain?

What will be the fully qualified domain names (FQDN) of the other names in the Active Directory?

What DNS zone must be available on the internal network?

How will you provide DNS support for the Enterprise.com and Endeavorltd.com Active Directory domains?

Vocabulary

Learn the following terms in preparation for the certification exam.

Term	Description
DNS	Domain Name System is an industry standard name resolution service that allows clients to locate Active Directory services. DNS can translate an IP address into a domain name. For example, a numeric address like 232.452.120.54 can become something like xyz.com.
firewall	An electronic boundary that prevents unauthorized users from accessing certain files on a network; or, a computer used to maintain such a boundary.
FQDN	The full computer name is a Fully Qualified Domain Name for the computer. In addition to these, a computer might also be identified by the FQDN comprised of the computer (or host) name and a connection-specific domain name, where one is configured and applied for a specific network connection on the computer. The full computer name is a combination of both the computer name and the DNS domain name for the computer.
LDAP	Lightweight Directory Access Protocol is used to access a directory service and is the primary access protocol for Active Directory.

Term	Description
LDAP Distinguished Name	This name allows you to see where in the Active Directory hierarchy the object is located by showing the full path to the object from the directory root. The LDAP is composed of the Common Names (CN), Organizational Units (OU), and Domain Components (DC), for example, CN=JohnSmith, CN=Users, DC=MyCompany, DC=COM
LDAP Relative Distinguished Name	This is a short version of the LDAP distinguished name. It is the name of the object itself separated from the path to the object. Depending on where you are in the pathway, the LDAP relative distinguished name will vary, for example, if you started your search at CN=Users, DC=MyCompany, DC=COM, the LDAP relative distinguished name would be CN=JohnSmith.
root domain	The first domain created in Active Directory. All other domains derive from this initial domain. Only one name can be used for the root domain.
snap-in	A type of tool you can add to a console supported by Microsoft Management Console (MMC). You can add a stand-alone snap-in or an extension snap-in to extend the function of another snap-in.
SRV	Service Resource Records are DNS records that map to the name of a server offering that service. Support of SRV records is mandatory.
User Principal Name	Windows 2000 users and groups use principal names. For example, the user John Smith in MyCompany.com might have the user principal name of JohnS@MyCompany.com, where JohnS is the logon name and MyCompany.com is the name of the domain tree in which the JohnS user object resides.

In Brief

If you want to...	Then do this...
Create a custom MMC console for the Administrator	1. Choose **Start**, **Run**, type **MMC**, and then click **OK**. 2. On the **Console** menu, choose **Add/Remove Snap-in**, and then select **Add**. 3. Under **Snap-in**, double-click the item you want to add, and do one of the following: 4. Choose **Local computer:** (the computer this console is running on), and then click **Finish**. 5. Or, if a wizard appears, follow the instructions on your screen. 6. To add another item to the console, repeat step 3.
Create a planning list for designing the active directory structure	1. Determine the number of forests. 2. Determine the number of domains in each forest. 3. Choose a forest root domain. 4. Assign a DNS name to each domain. 5. Plan DNS server deployment. 6. Optimize authentication with shortcut trust relationships. 7. Create OUs to delegate administration. 8. Define sites and site links. 9. Place servers in sites.

If you want to...	Then do this...
When setting up namespace planning for DNS	1. Decide how you intend to use DNS naming and what goals you are trying to accomplish in using DNS. 2. If you have previously chosen and registered a DNS domain name for use on the Internet, this can be the basis for your DNS namespace. 3. Determine if you are going to set up DNS servers on a private network or the Internet and if you are going to use DNS to support your use of Active Directory. 4. Determine what naming requirements you need to follow when choosing DNS domain names for computers.
If you want to keep your internal and external namespaces easily identifiable	1. Use a differing set of distinguished names that do not overlap as the basis for your internal and external DNS use. 2. For example, if your organization's parent domain name is "alberta.mycompany.com", for internal DNS names usage, you could use a name such as "internal.alberta.mycompany.com" and for external DNS names usage, you could use a name such as "external.alberta.mycompany.com" 3. By keeping your internal and external namespaces separate and distinct, you enable simplified maintenance of configurations such as domain name filter or exclusion lists.

Lesson 2 Activities

Complete the following activities to prepare for the certification exam.

1. While Active Directory is integrated with DNS and shares the same namespace structure, it is important to note the difference between them.
   Define this difference.

2. Your company has registered the domain name MyCompany.com with the appropriate internet authorities. The company has separate divisions for Kansas, Alberta and Oregon. You have defined the scope of the active directory to be a single domain for Alberta only. What should the name of the domain be?

3. Outline a basic DNS namespace plan for Active Directory.

4. You need to evaluate whether your existing DNS server can support Active Directory. What must you know about your current DNS server?

5. You have decided that you want to use the same DNS domain name for both your company's internal network and the portion of your network that is connected to the Internet. You want to ensure that information about Active Directory servers is not available to users on the Internet. What can you do?

6. To create a custom MMC:
   To view the currently configured options, click on Options on the Console menu. MMC displays the Options dialog box with the Console tab active. How does a console that is saved in User mode differ from one that is saved in Author mode?

7. To use a reconfigured MMC:
   From the Start menu, choose Programs, Administrative Tools, and then select Event Viewer.
   Windows 2000 displays the Event Viewer console, which gives you access to the event files on your computer. You can use the Event Viewer to monitor various hardware and software activities.
   Looking at the console tree, what logs are listed?
   Can you add snap-ins to this console? Why or why not?

8. You need to design a site structure for an organization with multiple physical locations. What are the six steps you would use for the design?

9. There are advantages to using the Active Directory integrated zone types. Explain why you use zones.

10. Explain the DNS name resolution process.

Answers to Lesson 2 Activities

1. DNS is a name resolution service. DNS clients send DNS name queries to their configured DNS server. The DNS server receives the name query and either resolves the name query through locally stored files or consults another DNS server for resolution. DNS does not require Active Directory to function.

   Active Directory is a directory service. It provides an information repository and services to make information available to users and applications. Active Directory clients send queries to Active Directory servers using the Lightweight Directory Access Protocol (LDAP). In order to locate an Active Directory server, an Active Directory client queries DNS. Active Directory requires DNS to function.

   Active Directory uses DNS as a locator service, resolving Active Directory domain, site, and service names to an IP address. To log on to an Active Directory domain, an Active Directory client queries their configured DNS server for the IP address of the LDAP service running on a domain controller for a specified domain.

2. MyCompany.com would encompass more than the scope of the Active Directory and could conflict with future Active Directory deployments by the main office. Alberta.MyCompany.com would match the intended scope of the directory but would require reinstallation if a MyCompany.com were created in the future and the Alberta division wanted to be part of the same enterprise. It is also possible to use another name entirely that is different from the public name used on the Internet. This would avoid a future conflict with a MyCompany.com enterprise but would require reinstallation of the existing domain to participate in it.

3. In Windows 2000, Active Directory domains are given DNS names. When choosing DNS names to use for your Active Directory domains, start with the registered DNS domain name suffix that your organization has reserved for use on the Internet, such as "MyCompany.com," and combine this name with either geographical or divisional names used in your organization to form full names for your Active Directory domains.

   For example, the Oregon test group at MyCompany might call their domain "wintest.oregon.mycompany.com." This method of naming ensures that each Active Directory domain name is globally unique. You use existing names as parents to create additional sub-domains and further grow the namespace to accommodate new departments within your organization.

4. Determine whether it supports SRV records. Optionally, you may also want it to support dynamic update.

5. Maintain two separate DNS servers, one behind the firewall, and one outside the firewall. Manage the contents of the zones on these two servers separately so that information about Active Directory servers is never replicated to the external servers.

6. You can modify consoles that are saved in Author mode. You cannot modify consoles that are saved in User mode after they have been saved. Different levels of User mode restrict the degree of user access.

7. The logs listed are Applications Log, Security Log, and System Log.
   No, you cannot add snap-ins. This is a preconfigured console and saved in User mode. You cannot modify consoles saved in User mode.

8.
   1. Assess the physical environment.
   2. Determine the physical locations that form the domains.
   3. Determine which of the area of the network should be sites.
   4. Identify the physical links connecting the sites.
   5. For each site link object, determine the cost and the schedule.
   6. Provide redundancy by configuring a site link bridge.

9. Each zone represents a discrete portion of the domain namespace. In addition, a zone must encompass a contiguous domain namespace.
   The following concepts are necessary to understand the way zones work:
   Reasons for Dividing a Name Space into Zones - Zones let the administrator partition the domain namespace into manageable sections. The structure and names of the zones should reflect the structure of the organization.
   Zone Database Files - The zone database files stored the name-to-IP-address mappings for the zone. Each zone is anchored to a specific domain, referred to as the zone's *root domain*. This database file does not contain information for all subdomains of the zone's root domain, only those subdomains within the zone.

10. Name resolution is the procedure of relating a 32 bit numeric IP address to a name that is easier to remember. This is comparable to using a telephone book – where a name is connected to a number. For example, to connect to MyCompany.com website, you use the address MyCompany.com and the DNS relates it to its IP address 293.452.120.54.

Lesson 2 Quiz

These questions test your knowledge of features, vocabulary, procedures, and syntax.

1. What standard DNS characters does Windows 2000 support?

   A. Unicode characters and Uncials
   B. A-Z, a-z, 0-9 and the hyphen (-) and Unicode characters
   C. A-Z, a-z, 0-9 and the Number sign (#) and the ampersand (&) and Unicode characters
   D. All the Characters on the standard keyboard.

2. You have just created a user in the Users container in the MyCompany.com domain. The user name of the user is JohnS.
   What is the LDAP distinguished name of the user object in Active Directory?

   A. CN=JohnS, DC=MyCompany
   B. CN=JohnS, CN=Alberta, DC=MyCompany, DC=com
   C. CN=JohnS, CN=Users, DC=MyCompany, DC=com
   D. JohnS@mycompany.com

3. Which of the following features of DNS must be supported by DNS server?

   A. SRV resource records
   B. Dynamic Update Protocol
   C. Active Directory MMC
   D. Incremental Zone Transfers

4. If you have a currently registered DNS domain name, you can use this as your Active Directory root domain name.
   To use the existing DNS name for the root domain in Active Directory, which of the following would you not do?

   A. Use the existing DNS.
   B. Create a new DNS Zone in a new domain.
   C. Create the root of the Active Directory forest using the existing DNS name.
   D. Ensure that your internal DNS server supports SRV resources.

5. Domains are an integral part of Windows 2000 and Windows NT. Which of the following statements about domains applies to Domains in Active Directory?

   A. Domains derived from the root domain form a hierarchal tree.
   B. Domains determine the scope of Active Directory in your organization.
   C. Domain names represent your Internet name.
   D. DNS naming conventions have nothing to do with your domains.

6. Microsoft Windows 2000 Active Directory Service contains information about all objects in your network and uses standard naming conventions. Which of the following are correct?

   A. DNS and LDAP
   B. MMC and SRV
   C. DHCP and DAP
   D. FDQN and CN

7. An internal namespace is only used by users within an organization. Which of the following are the disadvantages to using the same internal namespace externally?

   A. It results in a more complex proxy configuration.
   B. Care must be taken not to publish internal resources on the external public Internet.
   C. There will be a duplication of efforts in managing resources.
   D. Even though the namespace is the same, users will get a different view of internal and external resources.

8. Which of the following do you need to take into consideration when planning a domain structure for your organization?

   A. Use the country name in your namespace.
   B. Divide your organization into a public and an internal zone.
   C. Examine your organization's logical and physical structure, administrative requirements, need for multiple domains, and domain organization need.
   D. Define all the objects in your directory and what attributes those objects have.

9. Which of the following are first level domain names in the international DNS naming system?

   A. Com, org, edu, gov, net
   B. Any extension that you register.
   C Com, org, edu, gov, net plus Country Codes such as .ca (Canada)
   D. RFC, HTTP, UNC, URL, LDAP.

10. Network basic input/output or NetBIOS is an application programming interface used on a LAN. NetBIOS provides programs with a set of commands for managing names. In Active Directory, how are NetBIOS names used?

    A. NetBIOS names are never used.
    B. They are connected with SAM.
    C. NetBIOS names are used on computers using Windows NT or 98.
    D. You use NetBIOS names for domain names

Answers to Lesson 2 Quiz

1. Answer A is incorrect. Unicode characters are part of the standard DNS characters, but uncials are a type of font.

   Answer B is correct. The following standard DNS characters: A-Z, a-z, 0-9, and the hyphen (-) as defined in Request for Comment (RFC) 1035. The Unicode character set includes additional characters not found in the American Standard Code for Information Exchange (ASCII) character set, which are required for some languages other than English.

   Answer C is incorrect. The Number sign (#) and the ampersand (&) are not part of the standard DNS character set.

   Answer D is incorrect. The Keyboard character set can vary, depending on the keyboard and the language.

2. Answer A is incorrect. CN=JohnS, DC=MyCompany is missing the CN= Users and DC=com entries.

   Answer B is incorrect. CN=JohnS, CN=Alberta,DC=MyCompany,DC=com has CN=Alberta instead of CN=Users.

   Answer C is correct. CN=JohnS,CN=Users,DC=MyCompany,DC=com.

   Answer D is incorrect. JohnS@MyCompany .com is an email address.

3. Answer A is correct. SRV resource records are a feature of DNS supported by DNS server.

   Answer B is incorrect, however, support for Dynamic Update Protocol is a highly recommended feature.

   Answer C is incorrect. MMC is the Microsoft Management Console.

   Answer D is incorrect. Incremental Zone Transfers allows only new or modified resource records to be replicated between DNS servers, rather than the entire zone database file.

4. Answer A is correct. You use the existing DNS.

   Answer B is incorrect. In DNS, a zone is a contiguous section of the DNS tree managed as a single unit by a DNS server. The zone contains all the resource records for the names within the zone.

   Answer C is correct. You create the root of the Active Directory forest using the existing DNS name.

   Answer D is correct. You need to ensure that your internal DNS server supports SRV resources.

5. Answer A is correct. Use the existing DNS If you have multiple domains in your Active Directory, a naming hierarchy is formed.

   Answer B is incorrect. Create a new DNS Zone in a new domain. Your organization determines the domain structure. Creating a new domain is unnecessary.

   Answer C is incorrect. Create the root of the Active Directory forest using the existing DNS name. Domain names can have a relationship with your internet name but they are separate and do not need to become the root of your structure.

   Answer D is incorrect. If your company already has a registered DNS hierarchy, you can use this as your Active Directory root domain name. Just be sure that your internal DNS server supports SRV resource records. Then you can use the existing DNS zone and create the root of the Active Directory forest using the existing DNS name.

6. Answer A is correct. DNS (Domain Name System and LDAP (Lightweight Directory Access Protocol.

   Answer B is incorrect MMC is the Microsoft Management Console and SRV is Service Records.

   Answer C is incorrect DHCP is Dynamic Host Configuration Protocol and DAP is Directory Access Protocol.

   Answer D is incorrect FDQN is Fully Qualified Domain Name and CN is Common Name.

7. Answer A is correct. Using the same namespace internally and externally results in a more complex proxy configuration.

   Answer B is correct. You must take care not to publish internal resources on the external – public Internet.

   Answer C is Correct. There is a great deal of duplication in your efforts to managing your resources.

   Answer D is correct. Even though the name is the same, users will get a different view when they are looking at internal resources from looking at external resources.

8. Answer A is incorrect. The country name can be used in your name space but does not have anything to do with planning your domain structure.

   Answer B is incorrect. You can divide your domains into public and internal zones for security.

   Answer C is correct. Examine your organization's logical and physical structure, administrative requirements, need for multiple domains, and domain organization need.

   Answer D is incorrect. You do not need to define all the objects or their attributes.

9. Answer A is incorrect. It does not include the Country codes.

   Answer B is incorrect. There are specific top-level domains that are managed internationally and must be registered.

   Answer C is correct. Com is commercial organizations, org is non-commercial organizations, edu is educational institutions, gov is government organizations, net is commercial sites or networks, plus Country Codes such as .ca (Canada).

   Answer D is incorrect. RFC is Request for Comments, HTTP is Hypertext Transfer Protocol, UNC is Universal Naming Convention, URL is Uniform Resource Locator, and LDAP is Lightweight Directory Access Protocol.

10. Answer A is incorrect. The NetBIOS name is concatenated with the Security Accounts Manager (SAM) account name. For example, users on computers running Microsoft Windows NT or Microsoft Windows 98 log on with NetBIOS names. The SAM name is the old format and must be unique throughout the organization.

    Answer B is correct. The NetBIOS name is concatenated with the Security Accounts Manager (SAM) account name.

    Answer C is correct. Users on Windows NT and Windows 98 log on with NetBIOS names.

    Answer D is incorrect. To log on while using earlier versions of Microsoft Windows, you can use the NetBIOS domain name combined with a user name, such as seattle\Dougs.

Lesson 3

Administrative Authority Delegation

Early views of network administration, centered on a single-source administrative model—the network formed a ring and the administrator stood in the center, equally responsible to each direction. The model defined both figuratively and literally how all the parts of a network relied on a central authority.

As networks have mushroomed in size and their scale has extended even more widely, centralized administration has become inefficient and impractical.

Active Directory solves this problem by applying domain-based hierarchical structure to the directory administration. The network model is the administrative model. Administration is distributed throughout the network using the same access control and permissions and any other network resource in the same hierarchical fashion. While administrative control originates at the top of the domain tree, local control can be granted all the way down the chain.

Active Directory is optimized for distributed administration; any user authorized by a higher administrative authority can perform administrative duties in their designated area of the domain tree. For example, users could have limited administrative control over their workstations and the department manager might have the administrative rights to create new users on his area of the domain. This administrative control is highly specific. Permissions can be controlled not only in a specific area of the network but also by object type. This model provides control over who performs what administrative functions on the network, while also allowing administrators to distribute responsibility very widely. This distributed administrative model works hand-in-glove with the network security model.

Microsoft Windows 2000 Active Directory permissions provide security for resources by allowing you, the administrator, to control who can gain access to individual objects or object attributes and the type of access you will allow. An administrator or the object owner must assign permissions to the object before users can gain access to the object.

After completing this lesson, you should have a better understanding of the following topics:

- Active Directory Security
- Administrative Authority Delegation
- Delegation Methods
- Delegation Tools
- Administrative Control Implementation

Active Directory Security

The tight integration of the directory service and security subsystem services (Figure 3.1) is key to the implementation of Windows 2000 distributed systems. Access to all directory objects first requires proof of identity (authentication). This is performed by components of the security subsystem in conjunction with the security reference monitor.

Figure 3.1 Location of Active Directory within Windows 2000

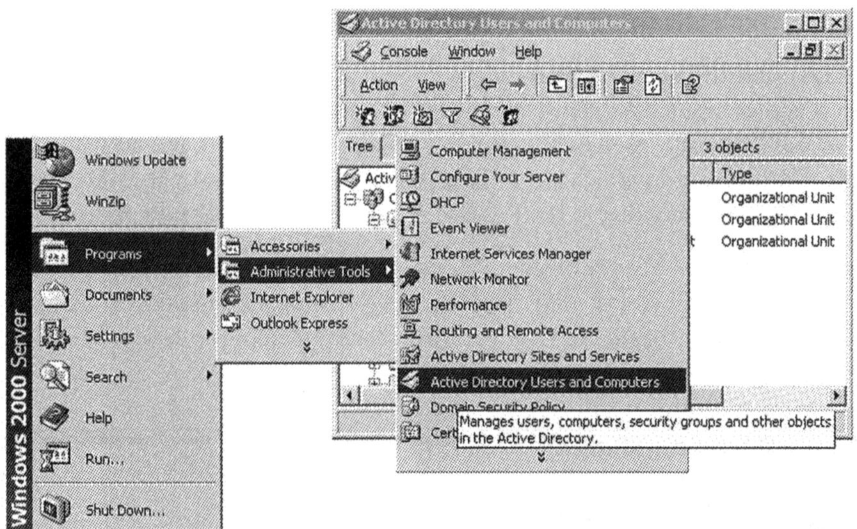

Storage of user account and group information is protected in Active Directory by using access control on objects and user credentials. Because Active Directory stores user credentials and access control information, users who log on to the network obtain both authentication and authorization to access system resources. Access to Active Directory information can be controlled down to the object attribute level. Each object and object attribute has a unique identifier that allows it to be individually secured.

When planning for delegation of authority, you need to understand how security works in Active Directory. This includes understanding the components of Active Directory security and the concepts of ownership of objects and how objects can inherit permissions and user rights.

Understanding Active Directory Security Principals

Storing security account information in Active Directory means that users and groups are represented as objects. Security information can be controlled at the object and object attribute level. Security principles, security identifiers, and security descriptors are basic components of Active Directory security.

Security Principles receive permissions—They are users, groups and computers. Access control permissions can only be assigned and granted to security principles. Group memberships, security policy profiles, and security identifiers define security principles.

Security Identifiers (SIDs) identify security principles—These are exclusive, alphanumeric identifiers for users and group and computer accounts. A unique SID is issued to every account on the network when it is created. SIDs are only used by the system and are transparent to the user. The first part of the SID identifies the domain in which the SID was issued. The second part identifies an account object within the issuing domain, that is, the Relative Identifier (RID). SIDs are never reused.

Security Descriptors protect objects—Every object in Active Directory has a security descriptor. It is a set of information attached to an object that specifies the permissions granted to users and groups, as well as the security events to be audited. In brief, the security descriptor defines the access permissions for an object.

Note: Users obtain permissions according to the SIDs they have, which, in turn, are a function of their group memberships. For controlling delegation after users are logged on, they are identified by their SID, not their username.

Granting Permissions

Granting permissions involves deciding who may or may not have access to an object and its contents, as well as the type of access a person is given. Permissions define the type of access granted to a user or group for an object or object property. For example, the Marketing group can be granted Read, Write, and Delete permissions for the file *ideas.dat.* The permissions attached to an object depend on the type of object. For example, the permissions that can be attached to a file are different from those that can be attached to a registry key. Some permissions, however, are common to all types of objects.

Note: In controlling access to Active Directory objects, there are two things to consider: the permissions that you are allowed to attach to the object and the ways in which you can attach these permissions to delegate administrative responsibility for Active Directory objects.

Standard and Special Permissions

You can set standard and special permissions on objects. Standard permissions are the most frequently assigned permissions and are composed of special permissions. Special permissions allow you to have a finer degree of control over objects. For example, the Write permission is composed of the Write All Properties, Add/Remove Self as Member, and Read special permissions.

The following table lists the standard permissions available for most objects and the type of access that each permission allows.

Table 3.1 Standard Permissions

Object Permission	Allows the User to
Full Control	Change permissions and take ownership, as well as perform all the tasks specified in the other permissions.
Read	View objects and object attributes, the object owner, and the Active Directory permissions.
Write	Change object attributes.
Create All Child Objects	Add any type of child object to an OU.
Delete All Child Objects	Remove any type of object from an OU.

Warning: Avoid assigning permissions for specific properties of objects because this can complicate system administration. Errors can result in preventing users from completing tasks.

The goal of delegating the ability to grant permissions is to conserve administrative efforts and cost. Ways to achieve this goal include:

- Delegating the ability to grant access control permissions for objects to users and groups of users
- Controlling who can gain access to individual objects or object attributes and the types of access they have for them; the object type defines the available permissions and varies from one object type to another
- Using inheritance to allow access control permissions to flow to child objects

Inheriting Permissions

Careful planning of permissions on OUs (Organizational Unit) can minimize granting permissions to individual objects in Active Directory. Objects that are created in OUs inherit the permissions that are granted to the parent object. When you assign permissions, you can apply the permissions (Figure 3.2) to the child objects, which propagates all the permissions to all of the child objects for a parent object. For example, you can assign Full Control permissions to a group for an OU that contains printers and then transmit this to all the child objects. The result is that all group members can administer all printers in the OU.

Figure 3.2 Inheritance of Permissions

Objects inherit existing permissions and inheritance can be blocked.

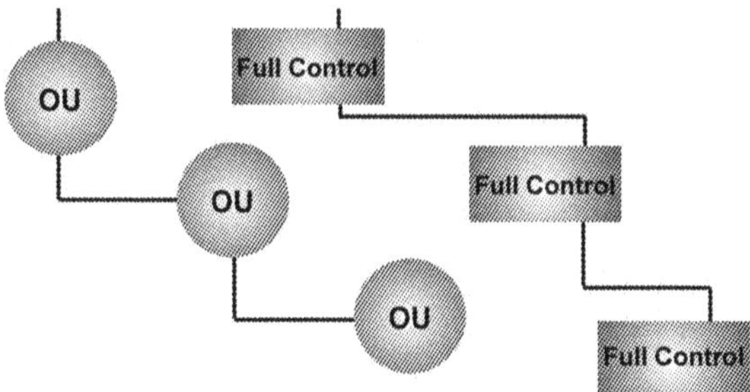

This allows an administrator to manage all the child objects. When permission is granted to a container, it can be applied to the object (container) only, the object (container) and all child objects, child objects only, or specific types of child objects (computers, users, groups, etc.). Objects inherit permissions on directory objects that are stored as attributes of the objects.

Permissions can be applied to any object in Active Directory or on a local computer, but the majority of permissions should be applied to groups, rather than individual users. This eases the task of managing permissions on objects. You can assign permissions for objects to:

- Groups, users, and special identities in the domain
- Groups and users in that domain and any trusted domains
- Local groups and users on the computer where the object resides

Tip: To change the permission on an entire OU or OU hierarchy, change the permission on the top OU and specify that the change should also affect child objects. The permissions will be automatically added to the access control list of every object in the hierarchy.

Preventing Permission Inheritance

You can also prevent permission inheritance to the child objects by clearing the **Allow Inheritable Permissions From Parent to Propagate To This Object** check box. When you prevent inheritance, only the permissions that you explicitly assign to the object apply. When you prevent permission inheritance, Windows 2000 allows you to:

Copy previously inherited permissions to the object—The new explicit permissions are a copy of the permissions that it previously inherited from its parent object. Then, according to your need, you can make the necessary permissions to the object.

Remove previously inherited permissions from the object—No permissions will exist for the object and you can assign any permissions for the object.

Understanding Security Descriptors and Identifiers

Permissions are defined within an object's security descriptor. Permissions are associated with, or assigned to, specific users and groups. For example, for the file ideas.dat, the Marketing group could be assigned Read, Write, and Delete permissions and the Sales group might be assigned Read and Write permissions only.

Each allocation of permissions to a user or group is known as a permission entry, or Access Control Entry (ACE) The entire set of permission entries in a security descriptor is known as a permission set. Using the above example, for ideas.dat, the permission set includes two permission entries: one for the Marketing group and one for the Sales group.

Security Descriptors

Every container and object on the network has a set of access control information attached to it. Known as a security descriptor, this information controls the type of access allowed by users and groups. Windows 2000 automatically creates the security descriptor when a container or object is created. A typical example of an object with a security descriptor is a file. Each security descriptor stores the following information:

- Owner SID
- Group SID
- Access Control Lists

Owner SID

The Security Identifier of the owner of the object is known as the Owner SID. The owner of an object is responsible for granting access permissions and granting rights for the object. An ownership is a security principle and is also identified by a SID.

Group SID

The Group SID is used for integration with non-Microsoft operating systems. Each group that you create has a unique, non-reusable identifier (SID). Windows 2000 uses the SID to identify the group and the permissions that are assigned to it. When you delete a group, Windows 2000 does not use that SID for that group again, even if you create a new group with the same name as the group that you deleted. Therefore, you cannot restore access by recreating the group.

Access Control Lists

Access control is the process of authorizing users and groups to access objects on the network. This is a list of users or user groups with access permissions. An owner is a security principle and is identified by its SID. NT File System (NTFS) stores an Access Control List (ACL) with every file and folder.

The ACL contains a list of all user accounts and groups that have been granted access to the folder, as well as the type of access they have been granted. When a user tries to gain access to a resource, the ACL must contain an Access Control Entry (ACE) for the user account or group to which the user belongs. The entry must allow the type of access that is requested for the user to gain access. If no ACE exists in the ACL, the user cannot gain access to the resource.

Discretionary Access Control Lists (DACLs)—The DACL contains the access control permissions for an object and its attributes and the SIDs which determine who can use the object. The permissions and rights that a user has are referred to as Access Control Entries (ACEs). The ACEs apply to an object class, an object, or an object attribute and can be inherited by a specific object type.

System Access Control List (SACL)—The SACL contains a list of events that can be audited for an object. For example, an administrator could audit all attempts to create a user object in a given Organizational Unit (OU) by creating an auditing entry for the OU. If the audit directory service access policy is enabled on a domain controller, access to the audited objects appears in the security log of the domain controller.

Access Control Entries

ACEs are part of the DACL and the SACL. The ACEs define the line-by-line entries that exist in either a DACL or SACL. ACEs can apply to an object class, object, or object property and can be inherited by specific object type. Access is granted through ACEs. Access can be:

Denied—The Deny Access ACE can control access to an object, an attribute of an object, or a set of attributes.

Granted—The Grant Access ACE can control access to an object, an attribute of an object, or a set of attributes.

Both denied and granted ACEs contain a:

- Set of access rights
- Globally Unique Identifier (GUID) that identifies the type of object or attribute
- SID that identifies the security principle to whom Active Directory will deny access
- Set of flags that control inheritance of the ACE by child objects

Taking Ownership

Every object has an owner. The owner controls how permissions are set on an object and to whom permissions are granted. When an object is created, the person creating the object automatically becomes its owner. Administrators will create and own most objects in Active Directory and on network servers (when installing programs on the server). Users will create and own data files in their home directories and some data files on network servers. Ownership can be transferred in the following ways:

- The current owner can grant the *Take Ownership* permission to other users, allowing those users to take ownership at any time
- An administrator can take ownership of any object under his or her administrative control, for example, if an employee leaves the company, the administrator can take control of the employee's files

Although an administrator can take ownership, the administrator cannot transfer ownership to others. This restriction keeps administrators accountable for their actions.

When you delete a group, you delete only the group and remove the permissions and rights associated with it. Deleting the group does not delete the user rights of the group.

Warning: You cannot delete a group if one of the members has its group as their primary group.

Administrative Authority Delegation

You can delegate authority down to the lowest level of your organization by creating a tree of OUs within each domain and delegating authority for parts of the OU subtree to other users or groups.

By delegating administrative authority, you can eliminate having most users log on regularly to accounts that have sweeping authority over an entire domain. Although you will still have an

Administrator account and a Domain Administration group (with administrative authority over the entire domain), you can keep these accounts reserved for occasional use by a very limited number of highly trusted administrators.

When you decide how to structure your OUs and in which OUs to put each user, consider the hierarchy of administration. For example, you may want to create an OU tree that enables you to grant a user the administrative rights for all branches of a single organizational department, such as the Accounting department. Alternatively, you may want to grant administrative rights to a subunit within an Organizational Unit, such as the Accounts Payable section of an Accounting OU. Another possible delegation of administrative rights would be to grant an individual the administrative rights for the Accounting OU, but not to any OUs contained within the Accounting OU.

Defining OU Administrator Access

Delegation of administration is the process of decentralizing the responsibility for OU ownership and administration from a central administrator to other people or groups. The ability to establish separate access to individual OUs is an important security feature in Active Directory. You can control access down to the lowest level of your organization without having to create a large number of domains.

- When you develop a plan to delegate administrative authority, you need to:
- Define what type of access administrators will have to OUs
- Examine the methods by which you can delegate OU authority
- Understand the tools for delegating administrative authority

Levels of Administration

When you install Windows 2000, a number of built-in groups are created. Belonging to a group gives a user rights and abilities to perform various tasks on their computer and on the network. You can add to the default set of groups (Table 3.2) and define your own parameters. The following table describes the built-in local groups created by Windows 2000.

Table 3.2 Groups and Properties

Title	Description
Administrators	Members of the Administrators group have full control over the computer. It is the only built-in group that is automatically granted every built-in right and ability in the system.
Backup Operators	Members of the Backup Operators group can back up and restore files on the computer, regardless of any permissions that protect those files. They can also log on to the computer and shut it down, but they cannot change security settings.
Power Users	Members of the Power Users group can create user accounts but can only modify and delete those accounts which they create. They can create local groups and remove users from local groups they have created. They can also remove users from the Power Users, Users, and Guests groups. They cannot modify the Administrators or Backup Operators groups, and they cannot take ownership of files, back up or restore directories, load or unload device drivers, or manage the security and auditing logs.
Users	Members of the Users group can execute most of the common tasks, such as running applications, using local and network printers, shutting down and locking the workstation. Users can create local groups, but can modify only the local groups that they created. Users cannot share directories or create local printers.

Title	Description
Guests	The Guests group allows occasional or one-time users to log on to a workstation's built-in Guest account and be granted limited abilities. Members of the Guests group can also shut down the system.
Replicator	The Replicator group supports directory replication functions. The only member of the Replicator group should be a domain user account used to log on to the Replicator services of the domain controller. Do not add the user accounts of actual users to this group.

Mapping Administrators and their Level of Authority

When you create a delegation plan, you need to define the type of access and the actions that can be performed on every object for every OU in a domain. This will be simpler if the OU structure accurately reflects your administrative model. Things to consider are:

Determine Information Technology (IT) management—You must decide at what level of administration and control you want IT management and at what level in the OU hierarchy you will delegate administration. The delegation plan should define what permissions a group of users has for an OU. A minimum of Read is required for an administrator to have knowledge of an OU. Without the Read permissions to an object, a user cannot view, search for or administer that object.

Determine who will administer which users and resources—This will help you to determine the ownership and permissions assigned to an OU that you create. The users receive access rights by being placed in a group that is in the DACL or the SACL, not by being an object within the OU. An administrator or the object owner must grant users access rights to an object in Access Directory before users can have access to that object.

Determine the ownership system of all the OUs—Each OU has an owner that is responsible for adding, modifying, and updating objects and for granting permissions.

Determine a permissions inheritance scheme—OU permissions can be inherited or propagated from a parent OU to a child OU.

Build in flexibility to your model—You can grant rights to an administrator to manage a small set of users within their area of responsibility and deny them permission to manage accounts in another area. You can also specify certain OU administrators to have Full Control access to specific OUs and objects and have other administrators restricted to the point where they may not even know that other OUs exist.

Map administrative roles to authority—Review the default Windows 2000 administrative groups and map their roles to the roles in your delegation of administration plan. Create new groups with the appropriate administrative rights as required.

Delegation Methods

You define delegation of responsibility to create new users or groups at the level of the OU, or container, where the accounts are created.

Delegating Administrative Control

Group administrators for one Organizational Unit do not necessarily have the ability to create and manage accounts for another OU within a domain. However, policy settings that are domain-wide and permissions that are defined at higher levels in the directory tree can apply throughout the tree by using inheritance of permissions.

You can delegate administration of a domain or OU by using the Delegation of Control Wizard available in **Active Directory Users and Computers.**

There are three ways to define the delegation of administration responsibilities:

- Delegate permissions to change properties on a particular container
- Delegate permissions to create, modify and delete objects of a specific type under an OU, such as users, groups, or printers
- Delegate permissions to update specific properties on objects of a specific type under an OU. For example, you can delegate the right to set a password on a User object.

You can delegate administration of particular resources to a specific individual or group, eliminating the need for multiple administrators to have authority over an entire domain or site. With appropriate delegation, the user or group who has been granted the appropriate permissions can, in turn, delegate administration of a subset of their accounts and resources.

You can configure the scope of delegated administrative responsibility in many different ways. Although you generally grant permissions at the OU level by applying inheritance, you can also delegate administration for an entire domain within a forest.

Administrators can view the delegation information that is defined for containers by using **Active Directory Users and Computers.**

You delegate administrative control of objects by assigning permissions to the object to allow users or groups of users to administer the objects.

The following permissions can be delegated to various users in your organization:

- Change container properties
- Create, change, and delete child objects
- Update attributes in a certain class
- Create new users and groups
- Manage small groups in an area of responsibility

Using Container Properties

It is much easier to delegate permissions at the container level than to track permissions on the individual objects or object attributes. Assigning permissions at the OU or container level allows you to delegate control for objects that are contained in the OU or container. To assign permissions at this level you would use the Delegation of Control Wizard.

Delegation Tools

You can delegate administration of a domain or OU by using the **Delegation of Control Wizard** available in **Active Directory Users and Computers**. The following tools can be used to manage the permissions on objects in Active Directory:

Delegation of Control Wizard—Use this Wizard to delegate administrative control of OUs and objects.

Security Tab of the Object Properties dialog box—Use this option to review or edit an object's permissions.

DSACLS.EXE—This command-line tool can be used to verify and refine object permissions. This tool is available in the Windows 2000 Resource Kit.

Using Control Wizard

The Delegation of Control Wizard steps you through the process of assigning permissions at the container or OU level. More specialized permissions must be manually assigned.

In Active Directory Users and Computers, choose the OU or container for which you want to delegate control, and on the Action menu, select Delegate Control to start the wizard. (See Lab A for a walkthrough of the entire process).

Table 3.3 describes the Delegation of Control Wizard options.

Table 3.3 Delegation of Control Wizard Options

Option	Description
Users of Groups	Choose the user accounts or groups to which you want to delegate control
Tasks to Delegate	Choose common tasks from a list or create common tasks to delegate
Active Directory Object Type (Available only when custom tasks are selected in Tasks to Delegate)	Choose the scope of the tasks you want to delegate: This Folder, Existing Objects in This Folder, or Creation of Objects in This Folder.
Permissions (Available only when custom tasks are selected in Tasks to Delegate)	Choose one of the following permissions to delegate: General – the most commonly assigned permissions that are available for the object Property Specific – the permissions that you can assign to the attributes of the object Creation/Deletion Of Specific Child Objects – the permission to create and delete child objects

Using Security Properties

The **Security** tab of an object's **Properties** dialog box is used for viewing or changing object or object attribute security permissions and rights. It is available when you have activated the **Advanced Features** view. This is the more advanced method for granting permissions and granting rights at the object level. It provides a method for defining access rights to Active Directory objects by an attribute set or by individual properties. It also supports defining inherited access rights that flow from OU objects to all child objects in that portion of the directory tree.

Using the DSACLS.EXE Tool

DSACLS.EXE is a command line tool in the Windows 2000 Resource Kits. It assists in the management of ACLs for directory services. DSACLS.EXE enables you to query and manipulate security attributes on Active Directory objects. It is the command line equivalent of the Security page on various Active Directory snap-in tools.

Administrative Control Implementation

This section helps you understand each administrative task.

Granting Access Permissions to Groups

Granting access permissions to users should be done at the group level rather than the individual level. This makes it easier to keep DACLs current on the networks that have many users, groups, and objects. Granting permissions becomes even more powerful when groups are nested within groups.

Granting OU Level Control

Granting control at the OU level takes advantage of the inheritance. Assigning control at the highest OU level, rather than to individual objects, makes managing permissions more efficient and easier. This procedure is simpler for administrators to audit, and there is less chance of major difficulties if an administrator makes a mistake when logged on to an administrator account. You should avoid granting permissions at the property level to simplify administration.

Working with Group Policy Inheritance Flow

Whenever possible, set a policy as high as you can in the hierarchy and let it flow down by inheritance. This will simplify administration and the logon process.

Using Group Policy, you can distribute a customized console to specific groups by one of two methods: publishing or assigning. Publishing a customized console presents the console to the members of a group specified in the Group Policy setting by adding the console to the list of available programs in **Add/Remove Programs**. The next time the members of the group open **Add/Remove Programs**, they have the option to install the new console. Assigning (as opposed to publishing) a console forces the console to be automatically installed for all specified accounts.

To publish or assign a console, create or modify a Group Policy object and apply it to the appropriate group of users. Then use the **Software Installation** extension of the **Group Policy** snap-in to either publish or assign the console.

Note: If a user is logged on to their computer at the time a Group Policy object is applied to their account, the user will not see the published or assigned console until they log off and then log on again.

Assigning Domain Administrators

The smaller the number of domain administrators you assign, the better. The Domain Admins group has special abilities within the domain, including the ability to take ownership of any object and define domain-wide security policies.

You can delegate administrative control to any level of a domain tree by creating OUs within a domain and delegating administrative control for specific OUs to particular users or groups.

To decide what OUs you want to create, and which OUs should contain accounts or shared resources, consider the structure of your organization. For example, you may want to create an OU that enables you to grant a user the administrative control for all user and computer accounts in all branches of a single organizational department, such as an Accounting department. You may instead want to grant a user administrative control only to some resources within the department, for example computer accounts. Another possible delegation of administrative control would be to grant a user the administrative control for the Accounting OU but not to any OUs contained within the Accounting OU.

By delegating administrative responsibilities, you can eliminate the need for multiple administrative accounts that have broad authority (such as, over an entire domain). Although you will probably still use the predefined Domain Admins group for administration of the entire domain, you can limit the accounts that are members of the Domain Admins group to highly trusted administrative users.

Windows 2000 defines many very specific permissions and user rights that can be used for the purposes of delegating or restricting administrative control. Using a combination of Organizational Units, groups, and permissions, you can define the most appropriate administrative scope for a particular person—an entire domain, all OUs within a domain, or even a single OU.

Use the Delegation of Control Wizard to choose the user or group to which you want to delegate control, the OUs and objects you want to grant those users the right to control, and the permissions to access and modify objects. For example, a user can be given the right to modify the Owner of Accounts property without being granted the right to delete accounts in that OU.

To create a new Group Policy object, follow these steps:

1. Open **Active Directory Users and Computers** to create a Group Policy object linked to a domain or an OU.

   or

   Open **Active Directory Sites and Services** to create a Group Policy object linked to a site.

2. In the console, right-click the site, domain, or OU to which the newly created Group Policy object will be linked. (It will be stored in the current domain.)

3. Choose **Properties** and then select the **Group Policy** tab.

4. Choose **New**, type a name for the Group Policy object, and then select **Close**.

To open **Active Directory Users and Computers**, choose **Start**, **Programs**, **Administrative Tools**, and then select **Active Directory Users and Computers**.

To open **Active Directory Sites and Services**, choose **Start**, **Programs**, **Administrative Tools**, and then select **Active Directory Sites and Services**.

The newly created Group Policy object is linked by default to the site, domain, or OU that was selected in the Microsoft Management Console when it was created. Therefore, its settings apply to that site, domain, or OU. You might want to unlink the Group Policy object from the site, domain, or OU, so that its settings do not apply.

Lab A—Step by Step Guide to Using the Delegation Control Wizard

This exercise assumes a server as a domain controller and a sample Active Directory service structure (Figure 3.3). Although the exercise uses the name MyCompany.com for the domain and has named the OUs, these are for example purposes only.

Figure 3.3 Sample Active Directory Structure

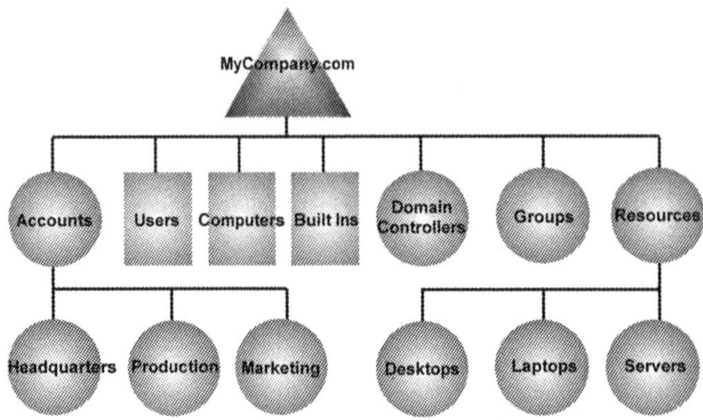

The domain is MyCompany.com. Circles represent the OUs: Accounts, Headquarters, Production, Marketing, Groups, Resources, Desktops, Laptops, and Servers. OUs exist for the delegation of administration and for the application of Group Policy and do not simply mirror a business organization.

Populating Active Directory

This portion of the exercise describes how to manually create the OUs, Users, and Security Groups outlined in the diagram above.

To **Create OUs and Groups**, follow these steps:

1. Choose **Start**, **Programs**, **Administrative Tools**, and then select **Active Directory Users and Computers**.
2. Choose the '+' next to MyCompany.com to expand it. Choose **MyCompany.com** to show its contents in the right pane.
3. In the left pane, choose MyCompany.com, **New**, and then select **Organizational Unit**.
4. Type **Accounts** in the name box, and choose **OK** (Figure 3.4).
5. Repeat steps 3 and 4 to create the Groups and Resources OUs. These three OUs now show up in the right pane.
6. Choose **Accounts** in the left pane. Its contents now display in the right pane (it is empty to start).
7. Choose **Accounts**, **New**, and then select **Organizational Unit**.
8. Type **Headquarters**, and choose **OK**.
9. Repeat steps 6 and 7 to create the **Production** and **Marketing** OUs under **Accounts**. When you have finished, the OU structure should look like the screen below:

Figure 3.4 OU Creation

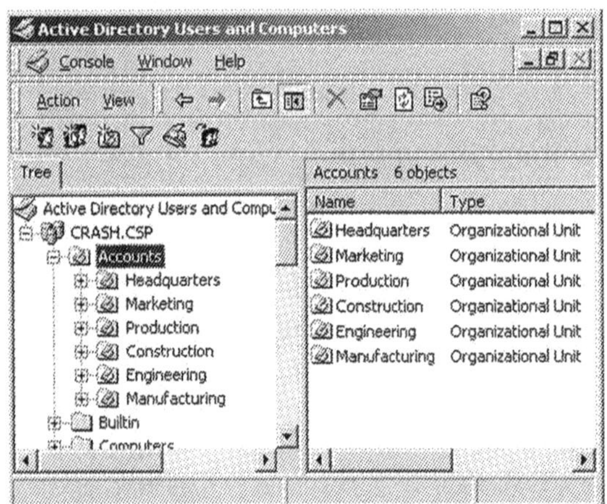

10. In the same way, create **Desktops**, **Laptops**, and **Servers** under the **Resources OU**.
11. Create the two security groups by right-clicking **Groups**, then selecting **New**, and then selecting **Group**. The two groups to add are **Management** and **Non-management**. The settings for each group should be **Global** and **Security**. Choose **OK** to create each group.

To **Create User Accounts** follow these steps:

1. In the left pane, choose the **+** next to the **Accounts** folder to expand it.
2. Choose **Headquarters** (under **Accounts**) in the left pane. Its contents now display in the right pane (it is empty at the beginning of this procedure).
3. Choose **Headquarters**, **New**, and then select **User** (Figure 3.5).
4. Type **`George`** for the first name and **`Arnold`** for the last name.

Note: The full name is automatically filled in at the full name box.

Figure 3.5 New Object User Window

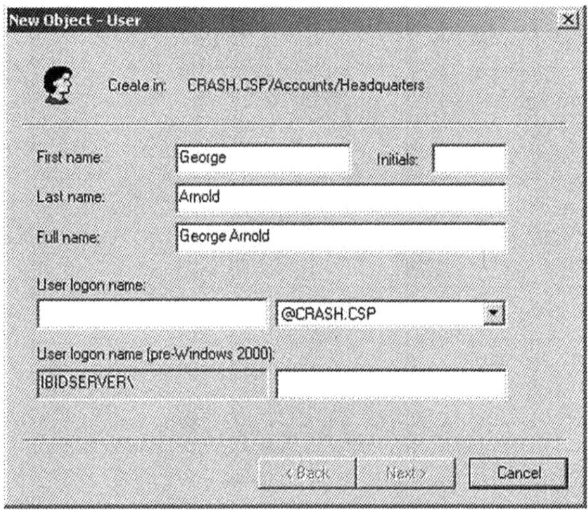

With the First Name George, Last Name Arnold, Full name George Arnold, User Logon Name George, @MyCompany.com, follow these steps to proceed:

1. Choose **Next**.
2. Choose **Next** on the **Password** page to accept the defaults.
3. Choose **Finish**. George Arnold now displays in the right pane as a user under MyCompany/ Accounts/Headquarters.
4. Repeat steps 1 through 8, adding the following names to the following OUs.

Table 3.4 User Accounts

OU	Full Name	Login Name	Group Membership
Headquarters	George Arnold	George	Management
	Bill East	Bill	Management
	Joan Royce	Joyce	Management
	Eric Flanders	Eric	Management
	John Lee	John	Management
	Miles Ham	Miles	Management
	Liz Rainer	Liz	Non-management
Production	Allen Bell	Allen	Management
	Cathleen Chablani	Cathleen	Non-management
	Jay Henkle	Jay	Non-management
	Brad Bates	Brad	Non-management
	Chris Van Staden	Chris	Management
	Cindy Franks	Cindy	Non-management
	Alex Gordon	Alex	Non-management
OU	**Full Name**	**Login Name**	**Group Membership**
Marketing	Raj Ayub	Raj	Management
	Kent Ertman	Kent	Non-management
	Suzanne Harris	Suzanne	Non-management
	Joni Maxwell	Joni	Non-management

To **Add Users to Security Groups**, follow these steps:

1. In the left pane, choose **Groups**.
2. In the right pane, double-click the **Management** group.
3. Choose the **Members** tab, and then select **Add**.
4. Choose the users in the upper pane as shown in the Figure 3.6 by holding down the **CTRL** key while selecting each name; select **Add** to add them all at once.
5. Their names will display in the bottom pane. Choose **OK** to accept.

Figure 3.6 Management Properties Window

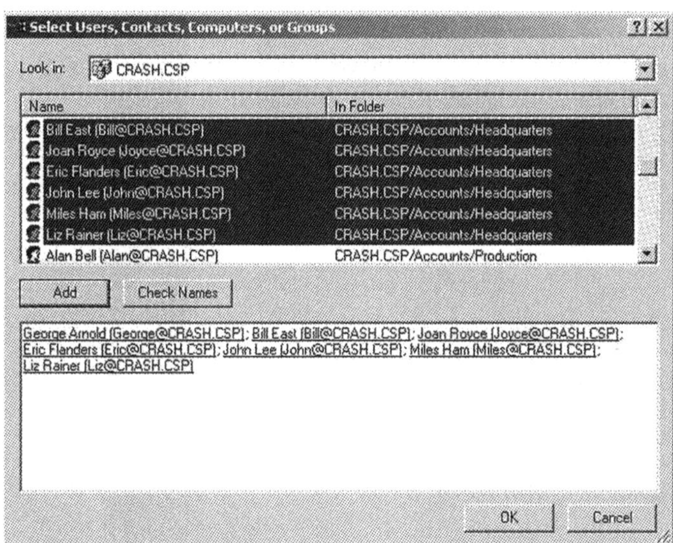

Note: The members of the Management group are drawn from three OUs

6. Repeat steps 2 through 4 to add members to the **Non-management** group.
7. Close the **Active Directory Users and Computers** snap-in.

Using the Delegation of Control Wizard

This portion of the exercise demonstrates a task that large organizations often perform—delegating complete control of an OU to another group of administrators, partitioning the control of the directory namespace. You will delegate complete control of an OU called *Independent Division* to a group within the Independent Division called *AUAdmins*. Delegate creation and deletion of users in an OU called *Divisions* to a group called *PeopleDept*. Delegate resetting of passwords for all users in an OU called *Sector* to a group called *HelpDesk*.

In this section of the exercise you will:

1. Add a new OU to the MyCompany root that is called Divisions
2. Add three new OUs to Sector called Operations, Independent Division, and Product Group
3. Add a new group to Operations called HelpDesk
4. Add a new group to Independent Division called IDSection
5. Add a new group to Product Group called PeopleDept

To add the MMC Snap-in after the sector OU is added, follow these steps:

1. Choose **Start**, **Programs**, **Administrative Tools**, and then select **Active Directory Users and Computers** (Figure 3.7). (This uses a MMC snap-in).

Figure 3.7 MMC Snap-in After Sector OU is Added

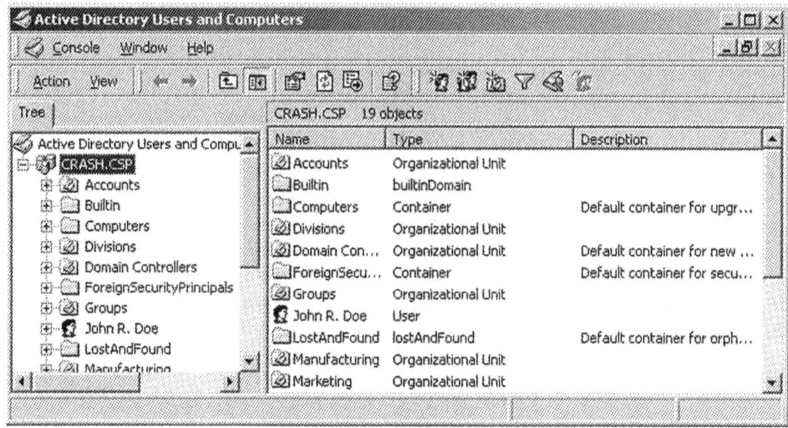

2. In the left pane, right-click **Divisions**, and then choose **Delegate control**. The **Delegation of Control Wizard** appears.
3. On the **Welcome** page, choose **Next**.
4. On the **Users or Groups** page, scroll to **IDSection**, choose **IDSection**, select **Add**, and then select **Next**.
5. On the **Tasks to Delegate** page, choose **Create a custom task to delegate**, and then select **Next**.
6. On the **Active Directory Object Type** page, choose **This folder**, and then select **Next**.
7. On the **Permissions** page, choose **Full Control**, to delegate complete control select **Next**, and then select **Finish**.

Verifying the Permissions Granted

You can check the access control settings for the **IDSection** group to verify that you set permissions appropriately.

1. In the **Active Directory Users and Computers** snap-in, on the **View** menu, choose **Advanced Features**.
2. Right-click **Independent Division**, and then select **Properties**.
3. On the **Security** tab, choose **Advanced**. On the **Permissions** tab (Figure 3.8), note the permission entries that apply to User objects. One of them is for **IDSection**.

Figure 3.8 ID Permission Selection Verification

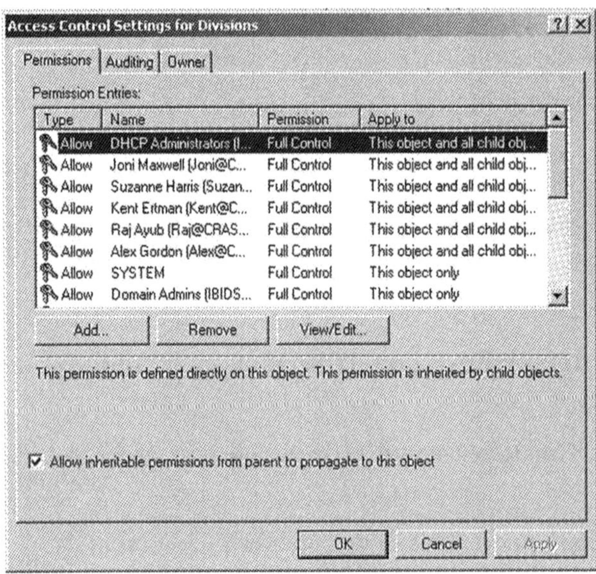

Access Control Settings for Independent Division

4. Double-click **IDSection**. Full control is granted for the OU and all its subobjects. This indicates that permissions were granted correctly.

Lab B—Examine Inheritance of Permissions on Directory Objects

In this exercise you will:

- Observe the inheritance of permissions when creating an OU
- Observe the inheritance of permissions when creating a child object

To **Observe the Current Permissions on an OU**, follow these steps:

1. Log on to your Windows 2000 computer as an administrator.
2. Open **MyConsole**.
3. Choose **Active Directory Users and Computers, View** menu, and then select **Advanced Features**.

Tip: This step is required to enable the **Security** tab to appear on the **Properties** page for Active Directory objects.

4. Expand **Active Directory Users and Computers**, and then expand your domain (if you have done the previous exercise you will have created MyCompany.com).
5. Expand an **OU** (PeopleDept), right-click the OU, and then choose **Properties**.
6. Choose the **Security** tab (Figure 3.9). Identify the current permissions on the OU for the **Domain Administrators,** ***MyComputer*** **Administrators**, and **Authenticated Users**.

Figure 3.9 Security Properties

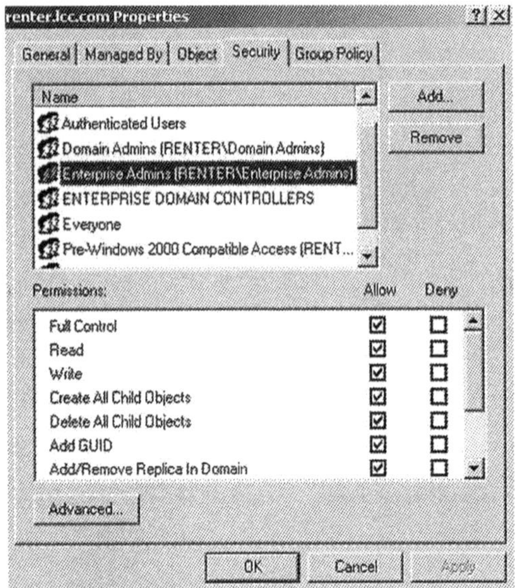

7. Choose **Cancel** to close the **Properties** box.

To **Observe the Inheritance of Permissions when Creating an OU**, follow these steps:

1. Right-click ***MyComputer*OU,** choose **New** and then select **Organizational Unit**.
2. In the **Name** dialog box, type ***MyComputer*Users**. For example, if your server name is MyCompany, type MyCompanyUsers.
3. Choose **OK**.
4. Expand ***MyComputer*** to display the newly created OU.

Tip: The **Create All Child Objects** permission allows you to create the OU as your account. Thus, it becomes a member of the *MyComputer*Admins group that has Full Control.

5. Right-click the ***yourserversname*****Users** OU. Choose **Properties**, and then select the **Security** tab (Figure 3.10).

What permissions were granted to yourserversnameADMINS on the new OU by default? (Figure 3.10.)

Figure 3.10 Inherited Permissions

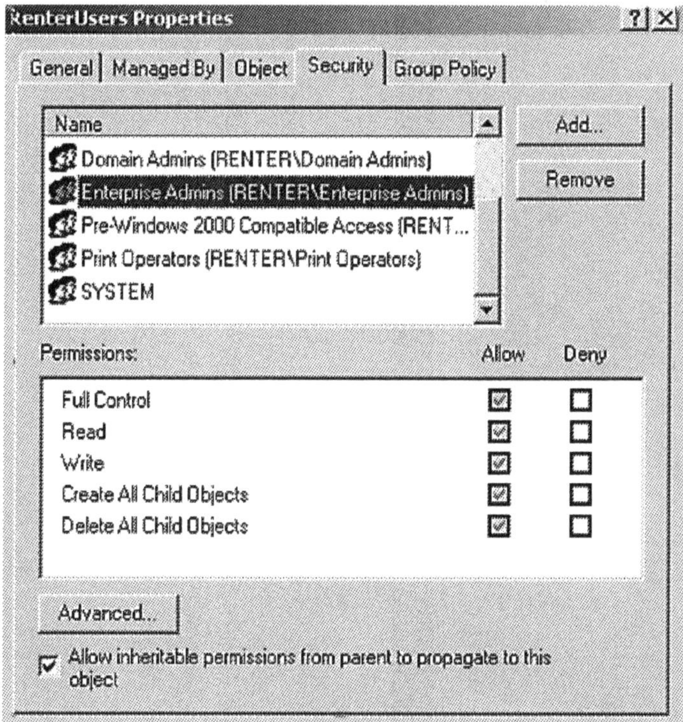

Note: The check boxes in the allow column are unavailable to indicate the permissions were inherited from the parent.

1. Choose **Cancel** to close the **Properties** box.

The Inheritance of Permissions when Creating a Child Object

1. Right-click ***MyComputer*USERS** OU, choose **New** and select **User**.
2. In the **First name** box, type ***MyComputer*User**.
3. In the **User logon name** box, type ***MyComputer*User**, and choose **Next** (Figure 3.11).

Figure 3.11 New Object—User

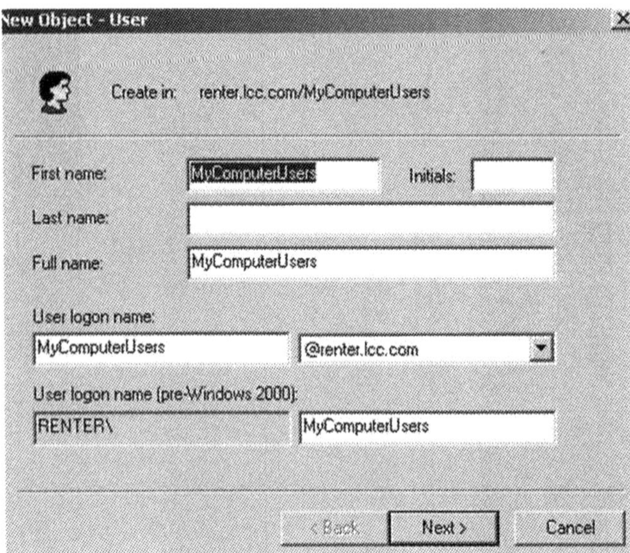

4. In the **password** box, type **password** and then again in **Confirm password**. Choose **Next** and then **Finish** to create the User.
5. Choose the ***MyComputer*Users** OU and in the details pane, right-click ***MyComputer*User**.
6. Choose **Properties** (Figure 3.12) and then select the **Security** tab.

Figure 3.12 New User Properties

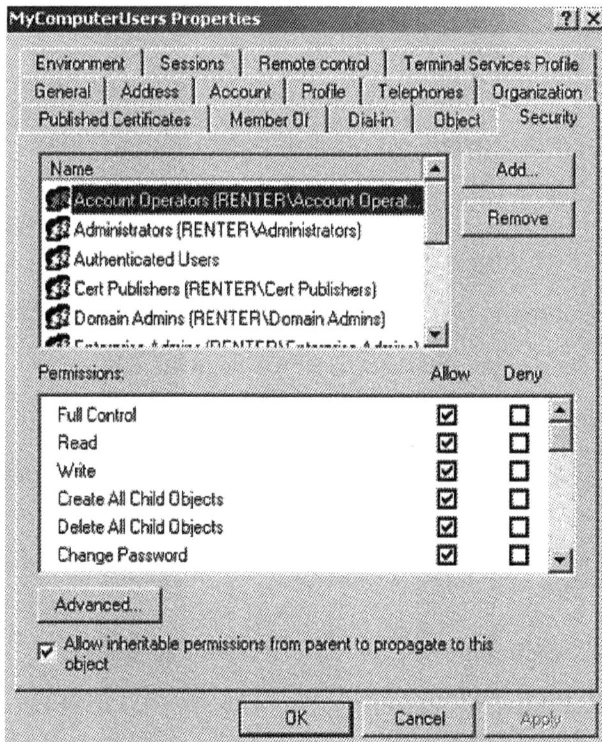

Note: Permissions are inherited from the parent object.

7. Choose **Advanced**, and then select the **Owners** tab.
8. You will see that the default Owner of the new Object is MyComputerAdmins.
9. Choose OK and OK again to return to Active Directory Users and Computers.

Lab C—Blocking Inheritance of Permissions

In this exercise, you will block inheritance in an OU hierarchy.

To **Block Inheritance on the Printers OU**, follow these steps:

1. Create a new child OU for **Printers** in **MyCompany** OU named **MyCompanyPrinters**
2. Right-click **MyCompanyPrinters**, choose **Properties** and then select the **Security** tab.
3. Clear the **Allow inheritable permissions from parent to propogate to the object** check box.
4. In the **Security information** box, choose **Copy**. All the inheritable permissions will be inherited from parent.
5. Choose **OK**. The **MyComputerPrinters** OU will no longer inherit permissions that are set on its parent OU, MyComputer.

To **Observe Inheritance when Permissions are Changed on the Parent**, follow these steps:

1. Right-click the **MyComputer OU**, choose **Properties**, select the **Security** tab, and then select **Add**.
2. Double-click the **Guests** group and then choose **OK**.
3. Choose **Advanced**.

4. In the **Permissions Entries** dialog box, choose the entries for the **Guests** group, and then choose **View/Edit** (Figure 3.13).
5. In the **Apply onto** box, choose **This object and all child objects**.
6. Choose **OK** and select **OK** again to return to the **Properties** dialog box.

Figure 3.13 View and Edit Permission Entry

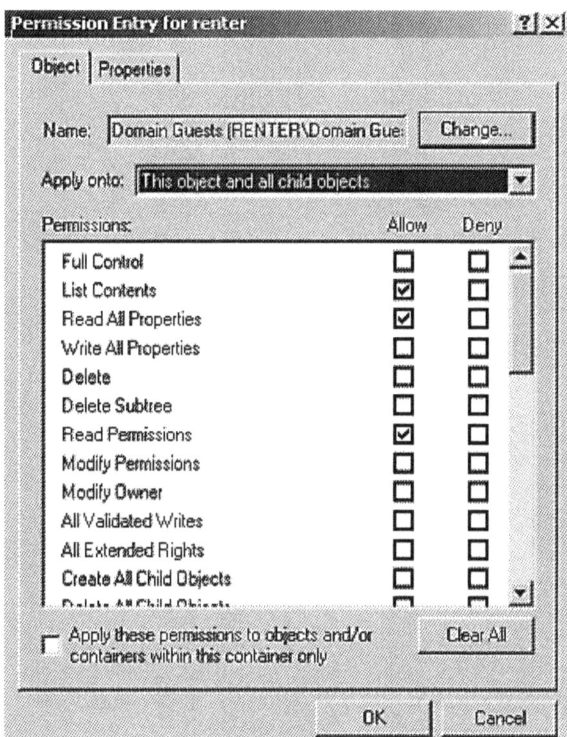

To **Cease the Blocking of Inheritable Permissions**, follow these steps:

1. Open the **Security** window for an object for which you have removed the inheritable permissions (in this set of exercises it is **MyComputer Printers**)
2. Choose the **Allow inheritable permissions from parent object** check box.
3. Choose **OK** to close the **MyComputer Printers Properties** dialog box.
4. Right-click the **MyComputer Printers** OU and then choose **Properties**.
5. Choose the **Security** tab. Notice that the **Guests** group has been granted **Read permissions through the inheritance from the parent**.
6. Choose **OK**.

Vocabulary

Review the following terms in preparation for the certification exam.

Term	Description
ACE	Access Control Entry or permission entry is the allocation of permissions to a user or group. It can be inherited by a specific object type. Each ACE contains a security identifier (SID), which identifies the principle (user or group) to whom the ACE applies and on what type of access the ACE grants or denies.
ACL	Access Control List is a list of all users or user groups with access permissions. It also contains the type of access they have been granted.
attribute	A single property of an object. An object is described by the values of its attributes. The term attribute is often used interchangeably with property. Attributes are also data items used to describe the objects that are represented by classes defined in the schema. Attributes are defined in the schema separately from the classes; this allows a single attribute definition to be applied to many classes.
child object	An object that resides in another object. For example, a file is a child object that resides in a folder (the parent object).
container object	An object that can contain other objects. For example, a folder is a container object.

Term	Description
delegation	Allows a higher administrative authority to grant specific administration rights for containers and subtrees to individuals and groups. This eliminates the need for domain administrators with sweeping authority over large segments of the user population. Access Control Entries (ACEs) can grant specific administrative rights on the objects in a container to a user or group. Rights are granted for specific operations on specific object classes through ACEs in the container's Access Control List (ACL).
DSACLS.EXE	DSACLS.EXE is a command line tool in the Windows 2000 Resource Kits. It assists in the management of ACLs for directory services. DSACLS.EXE enables you to query and manipulate security attributes on Active Directory Objects. It is the command line equivalent of the Security page on various Active Directory snap-in tools.
Group SID	Group Security Identifier is an alphanumeric structure for security principles that integrates with non-Microsoft operating systems.
GUID	Globally Unique Identifier identifies the type of object or attribute in remote installations. It is part of the Access Control Entry (ACE).
LDAP	Lightweight Directory Access Protocol is used to access a directory service and is the primary access protocol for Active Directory.

Term	Description
Owner SID	Security Identifier is an alphanumeric structure for security principles; an owner SID is the owner of an object, who is responsible for granting access permissions and granting rights for the object.
NTFS	NT File System stores an Access Control List (ACL) with every file and folder.
parent object	The object in which another object resides. A parent object can be the child of another object. For example, a subfolder that contains a file is both the parent of the file (child object) and a child object of the parent folder.
permission	A rule associated with an object to regulate which users can gain access to the object and in what manner.
permissions inheritance	A mechanism that allows a given Access Control Entry (ACE) to be copied from the container where it was applied to all the children in the container. Inheritance can be combined with delegation to grant administrative rights to a subtree of the directory in a single update operation.
RID	The Relative Identifier is the second part of a Security Identifier (SID). It identifies an account object within the issuing domain.

Term	Description
SACL	System Access Control List contains a list of events that can be audited for an object. An administrator can audit all attempts to create a user object in a given Organizational Unit (OU) by creating an auditing entry for the OU. If the audit directory service access policy is enabled on a domain controller, then access to the audited objects appears in the security log of the domain controller.
security descriptors	Access control information attached to every container and object on the network. This information controls the type of access allowed to users and groups. Windows 2000 automatically creates the security descriptor when a container or object is created, for example a file.
security principles	Users, groups and computers who are assigned or granted access control permissions. Group memberships, security policy profiles, and security identifiers define security principles.
SIDs	Security Identifiers (SIDs) are unique, alphanumeric structures for security principles. Every user, group or computer has a SID, which identifies the domain where the SID was issued and has an account object within the issuing domain. SIDs are transparent to the user, never reused, and are only used by the system.

In Brief

If you want to...	Then do this...
Delegate control	1. Open **Active Directory Users and Computers** 2. In the console tree, double-click the domain node. 3. In the console tree, right-click the folder that you want another user or group to control. 4. Choose **Delegate control** to start the Delegation of Control Wizard. 5. Follow the instructions in the Delegation of Control Wizard. *Note: To open Active Directory Users and Computers, choose* ***Start, Programs, Administrative Tools****, and then select* ***Active Directory Users and Computers****.*
View the inheritance of permissions when creating a child object	You can check the permissions for on object by: 1. In the **Active Directory Users and Computers** snap-in, on the **View** menu, choose **Advanced Features**. 2. Right-click the object you wish to view the permissions for, and select **Properties**. On the **Security** tab, choose **Advanced**. On the **Permissions** tab, note the permission entries that apply to the object.
Delegate control using the Delegation of Control Wizard	1. Open **Active Directory Sites and Services**. 2. Right-click the container whose control you want to delegate. 3. Choose **Delegate Control** to start the Delegation of Control Wizard. Follow the instructions in **the Delegation of Control Wizard**.

If you want to...	Then do this...
Block inheritance on an OU	After you create a new child OU: 1. Right-click the OU you have just created. Choose **Properties** and then select the **Security** tab. 2. Clear the **Allow inheritable permissions from parent to propagate to the object** check box. 3. In the **Security information** box, choose **Copy**. All the inheritable permissions will be inherited from parent. 4. Choose **OK**. The New OU will no longer inherit permissions that are set on its parent OU.
Set permissions for managing Group Policy	1. Open **Group Policy**. 2. In the **Group Policy** console root, right-click the Group Policy object for which you want to set permissions, choose **Properties**, and then select **Security**. 3. In the **Properties** dialog box, set the options you want to use, and then choose **OK.** **Add**: Opens the **Add Users and Groups** dialog box where you can specify the users and groups for whom to assign permissions. **Remove**: Removes users or groups and their associated permissions from this object. **Permissions**: Lists the standard permissions that you can allow or deny to users; for example, Full Control, Read, Write, and so on. **Advanced**: Use this option to set special permissions, auditing information, and owner information for the selected object. **Allow inheritable permissions from parent to propagate to this object**: Specifies whether security permissions for this object are affected by inheritance.

Lesson 3 Activities

Complete the following activities to prepare for the certification exam.

1. Explain the purpose of administrative authority delegation.
2. Describe how you would find the current permissions for the domain administrator.
3. Describe what permissions you need on a parent object to create an OU.
4. When you create a new child object, describe what permissions are granted by default and explain why.
5. Define OU Administrator access.
6. Explain the purpose for using container properties.
7. When you create a delegation plan, you need to define the type of access and the actions that can be performed on every object for every OU in a domain. Describe the things you need to take into consideration in building your delegation plan.
8. You have changed the permissions on an organizational unit and its child objects. However, when you examine the properties of one of the printer objects in the organizational unit, the permissions are unchanged. The permissions on the object remained the same. Explain why.
9. A division within your organization wants to manage the properties of their users in Active Directory. However, your organization's security policy dictates that only the Security group should create all new user accounts. Explain how you can delegate administrative authority to achieve this.
10. You need to restrict access to the accounting directories in your domain. Identify and explain the main factor you need to consider.

Answers to Lesson 3 Activities

1. By delegating administrative authority, you can eliminate the need to have people who regularly log on to accounts that have sweeping authority over an entire domain. Although you will still have an Administrator account and a Domain Administration group (with administrative authority over the entire domain) you can keep these accounts reserved for occasional use by a very limited number of highly trusted administrators.
   You can delegate authority down to the lowest level of your organization by creating a tree of OUs within each domain and delegating authority for parts of the OU subtree to other users or groups.

2.
   1. **Log** onto your Windows 2000 computer as an administrator.
   2. **Open MyConsole**.
   3. Choose **Active Directory Users and Computers** and then the **View** menu. Select **Advanced Features**.
   4. Expand **Active Directory Users and Computers** and then expand your domain (if you have done the previous exercise you will have created MyCompany.com).
   5. Expand an **OU** (PeopleDept), right-click the OU, and choose **Properties**.
   6. Choose the **Security** tab. Identify the current permissions on the OU for the **Domain Administrators.**

3. The **Create All Child Objects** permission allows you to create an OU when your account is a member of the *MyComputer*Admins group that has **Full Control**.

4. The same permissions as the parent. If you create the child object as an Administrator, the child object will have full permissions. This is because the permission is inherited from the parent object.

5. Delegation of administration is the process of decentralizing the responsibility for OU ownership and administration from a central administrator to other people or groups. The ability to establish separate access to individual OUs is an important security feature in Active Directory. You can control access down to the lowest level of your organization without having to create a large number of domains.

   When you develop a plan to delegate administrative authority, you need to:

   - Define what type of access to OUs administrators will have
   - Examine the methods by which you can delegate OU authority
   - Understand the tools for delegating administrative authority

6. It is much easier to delegate permissions at the container level than tracking permissions on the individual objects or object attributes. Assigning permissions at the OU or container level allows you to delegate control for objects that are contained in the OU or container. To assign permissions at this level, you would use the Delegation of Control Wizard.

7.
   - Decide at what level of administration and control you want Information Technology (IT) Management and at what level in the OU hierarchy you will delegate administration
   - Determine who will administer which users and resources, as well as the ownership system of all the OUs
   - Determine a permissions inheritance scheme
   - Build in flexibility to your model
   - Map administrative roles to authority

8. The printer object was set not to inherit permissions from its parent.

9. Create an OU for the division's users. Grant the Security group the Create Users permission. Grant the division's administrators the Modify Properties permission for user objects.

10. Permissions are defined within an object's security descriptor. Permissions are associated with, or assigned to, specific users and groups. For example, for the directory accounts, the Accounting group could be assigned Read, Write, and Delete permissions and the Payroll group might be assigned Read and Write permissions only.

Lesson 3 Quiz

These questions test your knowledge of features, vocabulary, procedures, and syntax.

1. When you create a new object, logged on as Admins, who is the owner of the object by default?

   A. Anyone who needs to see the object.
   B. Any object that is higher in the tree.
   C. The parent object.
   D. *MyComputer*Admins

2. Of the following, what tools are used for the delegation of access control?

   A. Security Properties
   B. DSACLS.EXE
   C. The Accessibility wizard.
   D. The Delegation of Control wizard.

3. What is the purpose of adding a group to another group?

   A. Adding groups to other groups (nesting) creates a consolidated group and can reduce the number of times you need to assign permissions.
   B. To simplify login processes for the users.
   C. Local groups do not appear in the Active Directory, and you must administer local groups separately.
   D. Groups multiply the amount of work required to assign rights to individual members.

4. How would you view a domain using the Active Directory Users and Computer console?

   A. Choose View menu, Users, Groups and Computers as Containers.
   B. Action menu, Connect to Domain.
   C. Expand active Directory Sites and Services.
   D. In the console tree, double-click the name of the domain you wish to view.

5. ACE is Access Control Entry and ACL is Access Control Lists. Which of the following statements is correct?

   A. An ACE is a list of ACLs.
   B. An ACL is a list of ACEs.
   C. An ACE is stored a binary value called a security descriptor.
   D. An ACL is a security identifier.

6. Which of the following statements about an OU (Organizational Unit) is correct?

   A. An OU is a container object that is an active directory partition.
   B. OUs can contain users, groups, resources and other OUs.
   C. OUs enable delegation of administration to distinct subtrees of a directory.
   D. A collection of information selected and applied to the interaction between a subject and an object.

7. Every container and object on the network has a set of access control information attached to it called the security descriptor. What information does the security descriptor store?

   A. ACEs and ACLs
   B. Parent SIDs, Child SIDs, and a Denied or Granted flag
   C. Owner SID, Group SID, DACL and SACL
   D. GUIDs

8. Inherited permissions have been blocked on a directory and you need to restore them. You are viewing the Security tab of the object that you originally blocked. What are the correct steps to take to restore the inherited permissions?

   A. Enable the **Allow inheritable permissions from parent object** check box.
   B. Clear the **Allow inheritable permissions from parent to propagate to the object** check box.
   C. Choose **Advanced**. From the Permissions Entries dialog box, select the entries for the Guests group, then **View/Edit.** In the **Apply onto** box, select **this object and all child objects.**
   D. The Security tab is not the correct place to change the blocked permissions.

9. What is the functionality of the DSACLS.EXE file?

   A. It eliminates the need for domain administrators with sweeping authority over large segments of the user population.
   B. It assists in the management of ACLs for directory services.
   C. Enables you to query and manipulate security attributes on Active Directory Objects.
   D. It is the command-line equivalent of the Security page on various Active Directory snap-in tools.

10. One of the tools to make administration easier is the Delegation of Control Wizard. What does it do?

    A. Manage small groups in an area of responsibility.
    B. Reviewing or editing an object's permissions.
    C. Verifying and refining object permissions
    D. Assigning permissions at the container or OU level.

Answers to Lesson 3 Quiz

1. Answer D is correct. When you create an object, you are the owner of the object and have full control over the object and its' permissions.

   Answer A is incorrect. Anyone who needs to view the object does not own the object.

   Answer B is incorrect. An object higher in the tree does not affect ownership.

   Answer C is incorrect. The parent object is not the creator of the object.

2. Answer A is correct. The **Security** tab of an object's **Properties** dialog box is used for viewing or changing object or object attribute security permissions and rights.

   Answer B is correct. DACLCLS.EXE assists in the management of ACLs for directory services. With it you can manipulate security attributes on Objects.

   Answer C is incorrect. The Accessibility wizard provides a minimum level of functionality to those users with special needs. Most users with disabilities need utility programs with higher functionality for daily use.

   Answer D is correct. The Delegation of Control wizard is used to delegate administration of a domain or organizational.

3. Answer A is correct. Nesting creates a consolidated group and reduces the number of times you need to assign permissions.

   Answer B is incorrect. Adding a group to another group does not affect login processes for the users.

   Answer C is incorrect. For this particular question, the statement is correct - local groups do not appear in the Active Directory, and you must administer local groups separately.

   Answer D is incorrect. Assigning rights to individual members is more work than assigning rights to groups.

4. Answer A is incorrect. This function allows you to manage a domain.

   Answer B is incorrect. This function connects you to a domain.

   Answer C is incorrect. This function is not available in Active Directory Users and computers.

   Answer D is correct. To view the domain, highlight it in the left hand pane and double-click. The contents of the domain can be viewed in the right hand pane.

5. Answer B is correct. An ACE contains a security identifier (SID) which identifies the principle (user or group) to whom the ACE applies, and information on what type of access the ACE grants or denies. An ACL is the set of data associated with a file directory, or other resource that defines the permissions that users and/or groups have for accessing it. In Active Directory, an ACL is a list of ACEs stored with the object it protects.

   Answer A is incorrect. A list of Access Control Entries (ACE) is contained in and Access Control List (ACL).

   Answer C is incorrect. The security descriptor defines the access permissions for an object and contains the ACLs.

   Answer D is incorrect. Security principles are exclusive, alphanumeric identifiers for users, group and computer accounts. A unique SID is issued to every account on the network when it is created.

6. Answer A is correct. An OU is a container object that is an active directory partition.

   Answer B is correct. OUs can contain users, groups, resources and other OUs

   Answer C is correct. OUs enable delegation of administration to distinct subtrees of a directory.

   Answer D is incorrect. A collection of information selected and applied to the interaction between a subject and an object is a made-up statement.

7. Answer C is correct. A security descriptor is made up of: Owner SID, Group SID, DACL and SACL.

   Answer A is incorrect. ACE is Access Control Entry, ACLs is an Access Control List.

   Answer B is incorrect. Parent SIDs, Child SIDs, and a Denied or Granted flag are access control entries.

   Answer D is incorrect. GUID is Globally Unique Identifier and is an Access Control entry.

8. Answer A is correct. Enable the **Allow inheritable permissions from parent object** check box.

   Answer B is incorrect. Clearing the check box blocks the inheritance of permissions.

   Answer C is incorrect. You would observe the inheritance when permissions have been changed on the parent object.

   Answer D is incorrect. The Security tab is the correct place to restore the blocked security.

9. Answer B is correct. DSACLS.EXE assists in the management of ACLs for directory services.

   Answer A is incorrect. Delegation eliminates the need for domain administrators with sweeping authority over large segments of the user population.

   Answer C is correct. DSACLS.EXE enables you to query and manipulate security attributes on Active Directory Objects.

   Answer D is correct. DSACLS.EXE is the command line equivalent of the Security page on various Active Directory snap-in tools.

10. Answer D is correct. The delegation of control wizard assigns permissions at the container or OU level.

    Answer A is incorrect. Managing small groups in an area of responsibility is how you would delegate control to other administrators.

    Answer B is incorrect. The Security tab of the Object Properties dialog box reviews or edits an object's permissions.

    Answer C is incorrect. DSCALS.EXE verifies and refines object permissions.

Lesson 4

Domain Structure Implementation

This lesson is about simplifying your ongoing tasks as an administrator of Active Directory. Planning how to organize objects in your domain makes your work easier and more efficient. Within domains, you can create a hierarchical structure of Organizational Units (OUs) and then group objects into these units.

Before you can start planning your structure, you must have a thorough understanding of the following:

- What a domain is
- What an OU is
- How you can control objects within domains and OUs

After completing this lesson, you should have a better understanding of the following topics:

- Organizational Units and domains
- Planning Organizational Units
- Security groups
- OU administration model
- Active Directory domain creation
- Active Directory installation verification
- Fault tolerance issues
- Native mode
- Object Management

Organizational Units and Domains

Understanding Domains

Microsoft Windows 2000 uses the domain as the core administrative unit. The domain has its own boundary for security and replication and is distinguished by a unique name. You use the domain to define how information and resources will be organized and stored. As you design your domain, you must decide what roles domains and OUs will play and plan the arrangement of OUs within the domains.

Understanding OUs

You can create a hierarchy of Organizational Units in a domain. Organizational Units can contain users, groups, computers, printers and shared folders, as well as other OUs.

Organizational Units are directory container objects. They are visually represented as folders in Active Directory Users and Computers.

Organizational Units simplify the view of directory objects in a domain, as well as the administration of those objects. Administrative control of each organizational unit can be delegated to specific individuals. This allows you to distribute domain administration among various administrators and lets you manage administrative responsibilities in a manner that more closely resembles assigned organizational responsibilities.

OUs can be used in different ways. For example, they can address an organization's technology and business requirements. You must understand the nature and role of OUs within a domain structure so that you can determine whether a series of OUs within a single domain is appropriate for your business, or whether you need additional domains. Understanding how to use Organizational Units and reviewing what they can contain will help get you started with your design of an OU structure within a domain.

Here are some reasons for creating a new domain:

- Physical location
- Network traffic
- Administrative considerations

Defining Physical Locations

Different locations may have unique security and administration policies which require separate domains. For example, vendors that are involved in joint ventures or partnerships with the company may not be permitted to have access to an organization's internal information.

Reducing Network Traffic

Creating multiple domains helps to reduce network traffic, because only changes to the Global Catalog are replicated instead of changes to the entire forest.

Considering Administrative Issues

Decentralized Information Technology (IT) divisions that are responsible for implementing different security policies might require separate domains. Otherwise, a single-domain model with multiple OUs will meet the needs of most organizations.

Planning Organizational Units

Figure 4.1 A Model for OU Structure

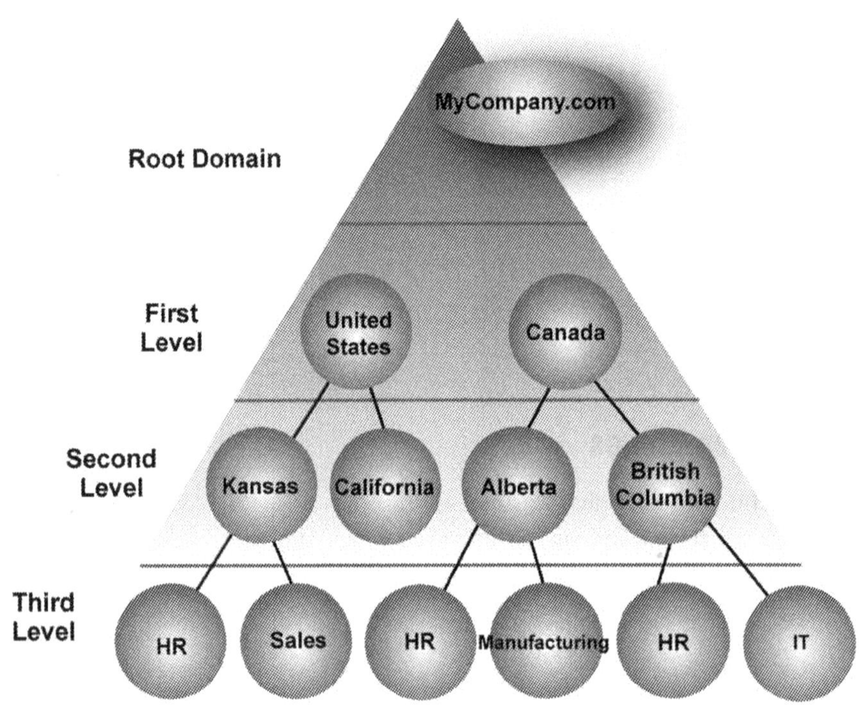

Each domain can implement its own OU structure. However, if you have multiple domains, your design process for each new domain should consider existing domains in the planned structure.

Following are the steps in planning an OU structure:

- Create a strategy for designing and implementing the OU structure
- Determine how many levels of OUs you will need in your domain
- Choose an OU delegation model
- Define how you will grant OU delegation permissions

Developing an OU Design Strategy

When you design an OU structure, you are defining your Active Directory administrative model. This administrative model defines who in your organization is responsible for managing specific users and resources across the network, and the level of control each administrator maintains.

You do not need to organize the OU hierarchy for ease of browsing because Active Directory contains a powerful query capability. Keep the design simple, as a complex OU structure requires more management. Your OU hierarchy should also remain relatively static to minimize management.

Identifying Administrative Tasks and Operations

You should interview the key people in your company to identify the administrative tasks that IT personnel have been performing in all areas of the organization. Next, decide whether you will change any aspect of the existing administrative operations design.

Selecting Administrative Features

Study the administration control features of Windows 2000 Server. These include delegation of administration, Group Policy, etc. If you have decided to use delegation or Group Policy, you need to plan the implementation of these features before proceeding.

Note: Delegation and Group Policy impact the structure and levels of OUs.

Establishing an Administrative Model

Be sure that your existing model accommodates the new features you have decided to implement. Then, determine if the existing administrative model requires alteration to accommodate new features or if you should avoid new features in order to retain existing structure.

Defining the Number of OU Levels

An OU hierarchy's purpose is to provide detailed administrative control. You can design a hierarchical Organizational Unit structure in which new OUs are nested within existing OUs. This helps you to accommodate your administration model. However, before you start to create nests, consider the following:

- Although Organizational Units can be administrated independently, when you create an OU within an existing OU, it inherits the properties of the parent OU by default
- You should nest OUs only when nesting provides meaningful administrative advantages because deep nesting can become more confusing then helpful
- Nested Organizational Units can have a negative impact on response time, as Group Policy is applied to objects in OUs from the domain root; an OU embedded within another OU will have two levels of logon policy to be applied and the response time implication of this is related to the number of policies to be applied and the size of those policies
- An OU cannot contain objects from another domain

First Level Organizational Units

Be careful when you design your first level of OUs because you want to avoid the problems associated with changing them later. Think about what would happen to the company structure if it were reorganized. If you have locations in different countries and differences in administrative policies for those countries, you most likely will want to have a different Organizational Unit for each country. As OU structures are unique to each domain, try to make them standard throughout an organization, regardless of whether an OU needs them or not. OUs do not have replication or hardware costs and this provides consistency for organization-wide support.

Additional OU Levels

To determine the additional OU levels, you need answer some key questions:

- Whether you will have a general-purpose administrators' group
- Whether administration will be resource-based
- Whether administrators will manage divisions or just a department
- What the nature of the objects is in the existing Organizational Unit in which you intend to nest the new OU

Organizational Unit Nesting and Performance

You can nest an OU structure to many levels. However, consider the advantages and disadvantages of deep OU nesting, as illustrated in Table 4.1.

Table 4.1 Advantages and Disadvantages of OU Nesting

Advantages	Disadvantages
Provides for greater control	Can have an impact on object discovery performance
Provides for easier management of OUs	Impacts performance when Group Policy must travel over slow links to be applied to computer or user objects
Reduces network traffic in a domain tree	
Simplifies administration	

To strike a balance between the advantages and disadvantages, plan for adequate administrative benefits without introducing unnecessary administrative complexity or confusion.

Deploying the OU Structure

The deployment should be based on careful planning. You should consider the following:

Develop administrative scenarios to test your proposed OU design—First draw them out on paper and then test them in a lab to compare the administrative model with your OU structure.

Create the Organizational Unit structure based on your evaluations—Choose OU names that will make sense to administrators. Remember that the OUs are for the administrator, not the user, and that you should not design your OU structure to facilitate user browsing. The OUs are not exposed in the result set of a query.

Update the existing administrative operations design—Update, if necessary, to reflect the new OU structure.

Remember—OUs are not part of Domain Name System (DNS) naming.

Security Groups

Groups organize individual user or computer objects and are used primarily for security purposes. Groups, rather than individual users, should be defined and placed in an OU level where security policies are administered. Group naming follows the same guidelines as those for naming an OU.

Understanding Group Types

The group type determines the group's function. Groups are stored in Active Directory, which permits them to be used anywhere in a network. Windows 2000 has the following group types:

- Security groups
- Distribution groups

Security Groups

These groups can be granted container object permissions and individual object and object attribute permissions. Computers, as well as users and other groups, can be added to security groups.

Distribution Groups

These groups are used for non-security related functions, such as e-mail, and cannot be used to grant permissions. A group of any scope can be nested in a distribution group.

Note: Security groups can be made members of distribution groups, but distribution groups can never be members of security groups.

Table 4.2 shows the membership in these groups and other possible membership for these group members.

Table 4.2 Security Groups

Group Scope	Group Members	Other Possible Membership for these Group Members
Domain Local Groups	User accounts, universal and global groups from any domain	Domain local groups in the same domain
Global Groups	User accounts and global groups from the same domain	Universal and domain local groups in any domain
Universal Groups	User accounts, universal and global groups from any domain	Domain local groups in any domain

Understanding and Planning Group Security

In your plans for group security, you must include the scope of each group. A group's scope dictates two things: who can belong to the group and where that group can be granted permissions. Windows 2000 has the following group scopes:

- Domain local groups
- Global groups
- Universal groups

Domain Local Groups

These groups grant permissions to users to enable them to gain access to network resources, such as folders, files, or printers, in a single domain. Domain local groups should be used when visibility is not required outside the domain.

Global Groups

These groups organize domain user objects. Place objects in domain local groups to grant permissions to resources in multiple trusted domains and use them for forest-wide visibility. While in native mode, security global groups can be nested within other global groups. When implemented as distribution groups, they can be nested in both native and mixed modes.

Universal Groups

These groups can contain any combination of user objects and global groups from any domain, but they cannot contain domain local groups. Security universal groups are only available in native mode.

Understanding Nesting Groups

Adding groups to other groups is called *nesting*. This process can reduce the number of times permissions are granted. You can create a hierarchy of groups to meet your business requirements. Nesting groups in a multiple-domain environment can reduce network traffic between domains and simplify administration.

Nesting Levels

Tracking permissions becomes very difficult with multiple levels of nesting. One level of nesting is most effective because it reduces the number of permission assignments and improves tracking.

Group Membership Permission Assignments

For example, if managers are organized by country and are further consolidated worldwide, you can use groups to administer them. Country groups can contain managers specific to that country. Then all of the country groups can be added to the worldwide group. Because all managers have identical access needs, permissions are granted once to the worldwide group.

Planning for these groups must include careful documentation. For example, a temporary consultant's groups can be created within a group for a short-term project. If the consultant's group were added to a group with access to confidential information, the consultants would also have access to company confidential information, which may not be acceptable. Documenting group memberships helps to prevent this.

You use security groups to secure resources. Deciding when to use each type of security group is one of the most important parts of planning resource security. At this point you need to review general concepts of group scope and understand some of the specific qualifications needed to use the following groups:

- Universal groups
- Global groups
- Domain local groups

Universal Groups

These groups can contain members from any domain in the forest and can be used in a Discretionary Access Control List (DACL) or System Access Control List (SACL) on any object in the forest. These are considerations for creating and updating universal groups in your organization:

- Universal groups should have a fairly static membership because you want to avoid constantly updating and modifying them; that causes replication to all of the other Global Catalog servers in the forest and this can create a large amount of replication traffic

- Do not add individual users to universal groups, but only nest other types of groups (global or domain local) inside universal groups
- Keep the total number of objects within a universal group small, as this will help reduce replication traffic

Global Groups

When planning for global groups, you should consider the following:

- These groups reduce inter-domain replication traffic because replication for global group membership takes place within a domain and not throughout the forest; only the group name is replicated to the entire forest, not the group membership
- Global groups are global in scope and appear in the Global Catalog
- All other trusted domains can view and access global groups for assignment to either domain local or universal groups for security purposes
- Global groups can only contain other global groups or individual users; you should never assign permissions to global groups
- To make membership management easier, keep group sizes to a maximum of a few thousand users; you can break large global groups into smaller global groups, and then you can nest the global groups as needed

Tip: You must convert a domain to native mode before you can nest global groups.

Domain Local Groups

These group memberships are local to the domain where they are defined and are not replicated to the Global Catalog. You can use domain local groups to combine individual users and global groups from your domain and other trusted domains as well as universal groups.

Following are some important considerations for planning domain local groups:

- Since these groups are replicated throughout a domain, you should keep membership size small and take advantage of nesting
- These groups can contain members from any domain but can only be referenced in DACLs or SACLs within the same domain

Developing an OU Delegation Plan

After you choose your Organizational Unit delegation model, your next step is to begin developing an OU delegation plan. This plan defines all aspects of how you will implement delegation of OU administration in your organization, including the level of control that administrators will need for an OU.

Planning for Delegation Using OUs

Like all other objects in Active Directory, OUs have Access Control Lists (ACLs). By managing the permissions on OUs, you can manage the ability of users to create or modify objects in those OUs. This lets you delegate administration of portions of Active Directory by placing objects in the appropriate OUs and then granting permissions to the OUs. At this point you must consider the following:

- Levels of delegation
- Delegation at the object and attribute level

Levels of Delegation

Three levels of delegation are available:

- Class level
- Object level
- Attribute level

These levels allow administrative flexibility where certain users need specific rights without full administrative control. For example, a user may need the ability to reset user passwords but should not have the ability to create new user accounts.

Delegation at the Object and Attribute Level

Here are some examples of delegation of administrative controls at the object and object attribute level in Active Directory:

- User rights that enable a user to read and write to all attributes
- User rights to a related group of attributes, such as user business information, to narrow the scope of usage
- User rights to specific properties, such as a group membership list, to permit restricted access to an attribute

Note: Consider administrative overhead in your planning. If administrators manage permissions on individual objects, this can take a lot of their time. A better solution is to create an OU and then manage the permissions on the OU. This approach reduces the number of objects whose permissions need to be managed and provides a simple way of duplicating permissions to multiple objects.

OU Administration Model

A delegation model for OU administration provides an organized way to delegate administrative authority in your organization. You need to consider geography, business requirements, and technology infrastructure as you decide which tasks will be performed centrally, locally, or a in a hybrid of central and local.

The OU model you design can reflect a:

- Centralized administration model
- Distributed administration model
- Model that is a combination of centralized and distributed administration models

Designing a Centralized Administration Model

This kind of model allows you to administer permissions from a central group, such as the IT group within an organization. This model would be suitable for organizations that need to restrict access to highly sensitive information and resources. Delegation of OU administration would be rare in this model.

Designing a Distributed Administration Model

This type of model allows delegation of permissions to groups according to business requirements. Organizations using a decentralized administration model may be very large and have multiple levels. Delegating control of the OU to separate administrators reduces administration time and costs by distributing administrative control closer to its point of service.

Designing a Model that is a Combination of Centralized and Distributed Administration Models

You can combine aspects of both of the above models by delegating routine tasks to subsidiaries or branches and control the principal tasks centrally from headquarters.

Note: Members of the built-in Administrators group have ultimate authority over a domain. They can override any OU owner's authority.

Recommended Best Practices

To help you get started, here are some recommended best practices for planning your domain structure in Active Directory:

- Consider using a single domain since this lowers administrative and hardware costs and can accommodate company reorganizations more easily; add domains only as a last resort when an OU does not meet your needs

- Your centralized IT organization should provide first-level OU support
- Assign control at the OU level rather than the object level whenever possible for easier tracking of permissions
- Document the delegation of administration assignments

Tip: Document, document, and document some more throughout the planning and implementation process. Remember that this is a complex process that will be difficult to remember at a later time.

Active Directory Domain Creation

By implementing a domain structure in Active Directory, you create an administrative structure for your network. The placement of your OUs and objects should mirror your network administrative model. You will need to do the following:

- Create a domain
- Create and structure Organizational Units within the domain
- Create and place user, group, and resource objects within the OUs

Creating the First Domain

To create a new domain, you must:

- Promote a server to a domain controller
- Verify server promotion and connectivity
- Verify the installation of Active Directory
- Perform optional post-installation configurations

Using the Active Directory Installation Wizard

To install Active Directory on the first server, use the Active Directory Installation Wizard. Understanding each step of the wizard is important from a troubleshooting and preparation perspective. You can launch the Active Directory Installation Wizard by running DCPromo.exe, which brings up the screen in Figure 4.2.

Figure 4.2 Opening Screen for Active Directory Installation

Using the Installation Wizard to Promote a Server

Figure 4.3 shows the second screen you see when installing Active Directory. It gives you information about promoting a server to a domain controller.

Figure 4.3 Specifying a Domain Controller Type

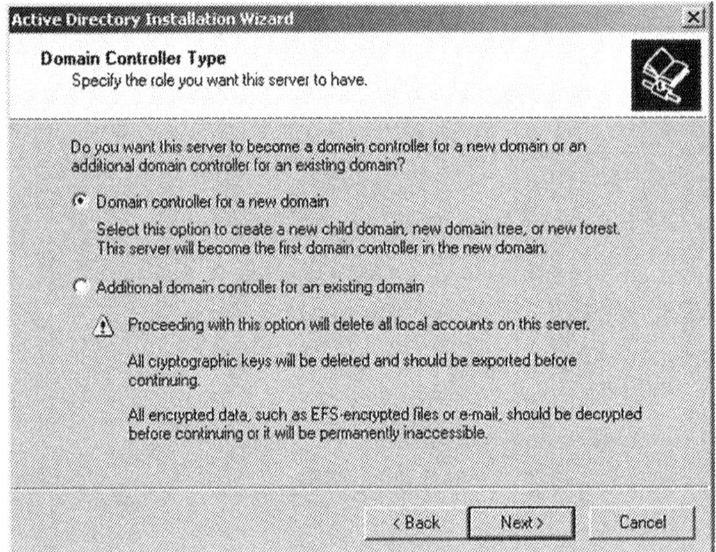

Promoting a Server to a Domain Controller

As indicated in the above figure, during the installation process the server will be promoted to a domain controller. During promotion the following processes take place:

Transmission Control Protocol/Internet Protocol (TCP/IP)—TCP/IP installation and configuration is verified. The wizard will not continue if TCP/IP cannot be detected. However, you can install it manually and resume the wizard.

Domain Name System (DNS)—DNS installation and configuration is verified. If DNS client is not running on the first domain controller or if it cannot find a DNS server, the wizard will prompt you to continue with an automatic installation and configuration of DNS Server. The DNS root is created with a forward lookup zone. A reverse lookup zone can be manually created.

DNS domain name—A valid DNS domain name is requested. The wizard will not continue without a valid name.

Network basic input/output system (NetBIOS) name—The NetBIOS name generated from the DNS domain name is displayed. You can change the name, but the wizard must then verify that the NetBIOS name is unique in your network.

Administrator credentials are validated—To create the first domain controller, you will need an administrative account and password. The account used to create additional domains must have sufficient permissions to create a new domain:object in the forest.

Note: Dynamic updates should be configured for each DNS zone. The Active Directory Installation Wizard will provide an opportunity to enable dynamic updates for each zone it configures, or you can manually configure dynamic updates in DNS on the **General** tab in the **Properties** dialog box for the particular DNS zone. Although it is possible to deploy Active Directory without using a DNS server that supports dynamic update, you must manually synchronize the Service (SRV) Resource Records when you add or remove domain controllers.

Active Directory Installation Wizard

The next screen allows you to decide whether to create a new domain tree or a new child domain in an existing domain tree.

Figure 4.4 Create Tree or Child Domain Decision Screen

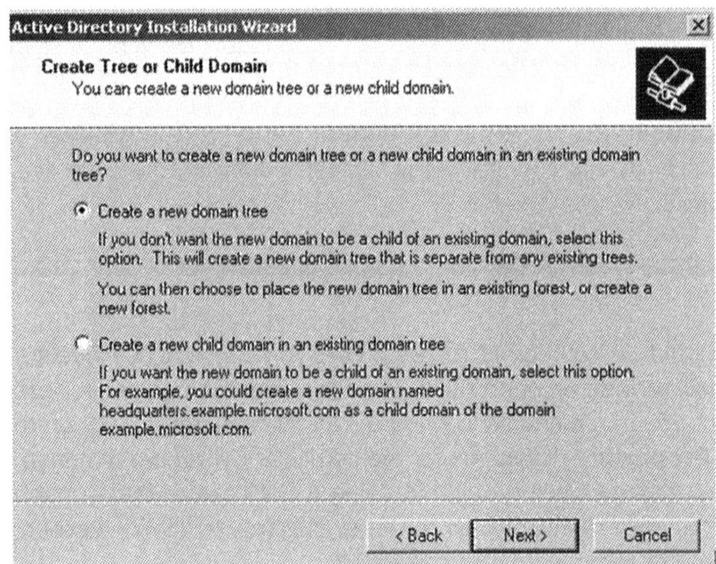

At this point, active server checks the network. Although you may think that you are installing for a standalone server, you MUST have your modem connected.

Warning: Check to be sure that your modem is functioning properly because Active Directory has to go out on the network and verify locations even for stand-alone installations. The installation will fail if the modem is not connected.

Creating the First Active Directory Domain

The next screen, Figure 4.5, gives you a choice of creating a new forest of domain trees or placing the tree in an existing forest. Choose the first option to create your first Active Directory domain.

Figure 4.5 Choosing a New Forest or Joining an Existing Forest

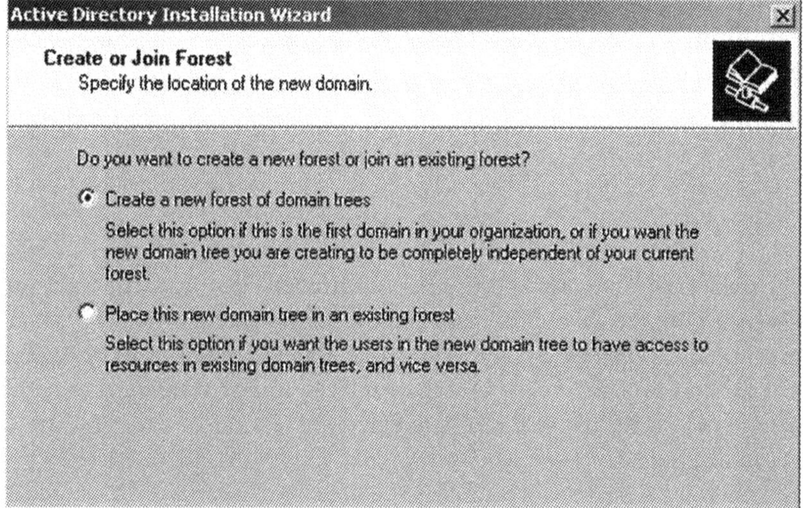

Verifying Server Promotion

To verify a server promotion, check to be sure that the following items are present on the domain controller after promotion:

- Database
- Shared system volume

- Default first site name
- Global Catalog server
- Root domain
- Default containers
- Default domain controllers Organizational Unit

Database

The database file for your new domain is stored in Active Directory. The default location for the database and database log files is *systemroot*\Ntds, where *systemroot* represents the root name of your system. You may want to override this default and place this file on a separate hard disk to improve read-write access.

Shared System Volume

The shared system volume is hosted on all Windows 2000 domain controllers. It stores scripts that are part of the Group Policy objects for both the current domain and the enterprise network. The default location for the shared system volume is *systemroot*\Sysvol. The shared system volume must be located on an NT File System (NTFS) partition because Active Directory utilizes advanced unique sequential number journaling functionality in NTFS 5.0 to track replicated changes. Therefore, be very sure of yourself if you decide to override this default.

Default First Site

Active Directory automatically creates the first site when you install and promote the first domain controller. It is called **Default First Site Name** and it contains the first domain controller. You can create additional sites later.

Global Catalog Server

By default, the first domain controller in the forest becomes a Global Catalog server. You can configure additional Global Catalog servers using Active Directory Sites and Services.

Root Domain

Active Directory creates the forest root domain when it installs the first domain controller.

Default Containers

When Active Directory creates the first domain, it automatically creates the following default containers:

- **Built-in**—This container contains default security groups, such as Account Operators, Administrators, etc.

Figure 4.6 Default Built-in Container

- **Computers**—This container is the default location for domain computer objects
- **Users**—This container is the default location for domain user objects

Default Domain Controllers OU

This Organizational Unit contains the first domain controller and other domain controllers as they are added to the domain. As an OU, Group Policy can be applied to domain controllers within this OU.

Adding Domain Controllers

If you already have one domain controller in a particular domain, you can add additional domain controllers to that domain to improve the availability and reliability of network services. Having more than one domain controller in a domain makes it possible for the domain to continue to function if one domain controller fails or must be disconnected for some reason. Multiple-domain controllers can also improve performance by making it easier for a Windows 2000 client to connect to a domain controller when logging on to the network.

If your network is divided into sites, it is often good practice to put at least one domain controller in each site. When network clients log on to the network, they must contact a domain controller as part of the logon process. If the clients must connect to a domain controller over a slow network connection, the logon process may take an unacceptably long time. Placing a domain controller in each site allows client logon processes to be handled within the site without using the slower network connection between sites.

Active Directory Installation Verification

After you install Active Directory, you must verify that the necessary files and records have been created so that Active Directory works properly. You need the following:

- Directory database files, which are located in *systemroot*\Ntds\Ntds.dit
- System volumes, which are the security policies and files
- DNS SRV resource records

Verifying Active Directory Installation

The Active Directory Installation Wizard Log File is created when you install Active Directory. This file lists the results of each step in the installation procedure. You can find it in the *systemroot*\Debug folder. This provides an efficient tool for verifying correctness and completeness of your Active Directory installation.

Verifying SRV Resource Records

DNS zones are portions of a DNS naming hierarchy whose records are stored and managed in a single DNS database file. DNS zones created on a Windows 2000 domain controller can be:

- Standard primary
- Standard secondary
- Active Directory-integrated

After installation of Active Directory, each DNS database file will contain SRV resource records, which are pointers to DNS hosts running Active Directory services. You need to verify that the SRV resource records have been created for the domain controller after promotion. You can use DNS in Microsoft Management Console (MMC) to verify SRV resource records if you are using a server running the Microsoft DNS Server service.

If you are using a DNS Server service that does not support dynamic updates, you will need to manually register the SRV resource records.

To verify that SRV resource records were created for the domain controller, view the Netlogon.dns file that is located in *systemroot*\System32\Config on each Active Directory domain controller. The SRV resource records are listed in the standard DNS resource record text representation.

You will see the Lightweight Directory Access Protocol (LDAP) SRV record in the form: ldap.tcp.*Active_Directory_domain_name* In SRV 0 100 389 *domain_controller_name*.

After you have installed Active Directory, you can also use the NSLOOKUP command-line utility to verify that the domain controller registered its SRV resource records in the DNS database. Use the following 4-step process:

1. Choose **Start** and then select **Run.**

2. At the command prompt, type **`NSLOOKUP`** and then press the **`ENTER`** key.

3. Type **`set type=SRV`** and then press the **ENTER** key to set the DNS query type to filter for SRV records only.

4. Type **`_ldap.tcp.`*`Active_Directory_domain_name`*** and then press the **ENTER** key to send a query for the registered SRV record for a domain controller in your Active Directory domain.

Note: Active Directory will report time-outs when you first run NSLOOKUP if you do not have a reverse lookup zone configured. NSLOOKUP generates a reverse lookup to determine the host name of the DNS server based on its Internet Protocol (IP) address.

Integrating a DNS Zone

This is an optional post-installation task that you can do to enhance your domain capabilities. In this task, you integrate a DNS zone with Active Directory. This allows DNS to use Active Directory for storing and replicating DNS zone databases. Also, when you integrate a DNS zone with Active Directory, DNS runs on one or more domain controllers, saving you the trouble of setting up a separate DNS replication topology. Taking advantage of the Active Directory replication topology provides fault tolerance for DNS zone information.

Only DNS servers that run on domain controllers can load Active Directory-integrated zones. In this scenario, all name servers act as primary master servers. Stated another way, updates can occur at any domain controller, and zone transfer occurs automatically as part of Active Directory replication. You can configure member servers or non-Microsoft DNS servers to function as secondary DNS servers for the Active Directory-integrated zone. These DNS servers will receive zone updates using standard DNS zone transfers.

Note: You will need to explicitly specify IP addresses of the DNS servers to which the client computer may send queries, since the client will not send queries to any DNS servers other than those listed.

Delivering Secure Dynamic Updates

Secure dynamic updates are only available with Active Directory-integrated DNS zones. With secure dynamic updates, the server domain controller does not perform a dynamic update on behalf of the client unless it has authenticated the client and determined that the client has sufficient permissions to perform the dynamic update. Only those with appropriate authority can update or add resource records. This prevents unauthorized computers from adding or overwriting existing resource records.

Note: Windows 2000 implements secure dynamic updates in accordance with RFCs 2137 and 2078.

Fault Tolerance Issues

If one domain controller fails, Active Directory's replication feature recovers the failed data from the next domain controller in the same domain. Active Directory supports multimaster replication of directory data between all domain controllers in the domain. Some changes are impractical to perform in multimaster fashion, however. Therefore, only one domain controller, called the operations master, accepts requests for such changes. In any Active Directory forest, there are at least five different operations master roles that are assigned to one or more domain controllers.

Implementing Fault Tolerance

You must have a minimum of two domain controllers in a single domain to implement fault tolerance. Because all domain controllers in a domain replicate their domain-specific data to one another, installing multiple-domain controllers in the domain automatically enables fault tolerance for the data stored in Active Directory. Should one domain controller fail, the remaining domain controllers will provide authentication services and access to Active Directory objects, allowing the domain to operate as usual. When a new domain controller is added to a domain, replication takes place to ensure consistency in the directory.

Native Mode

By default, domains are created in *mixed mode*. This means that domain controllers can be running either Windows 2000 or Windows NT. You can switch to *native mode* when all domain controllers are running Windows 2000. Native mode has the following advantages over mixed mode:

- Universal groups
- Nested security groups
- Directories larger than 40 megabytes (MB)

One disadvantage is that you can no longer add Windows NT domain controllers to a domain in native mode. However, you can still have clients and member servers running other operating systems.

Switching to Native Mode

To change the domain mode:

1. Open **Active Directory Domains and Trusts** as follows: Choose **Start**, **Programs**, **Administrative Tools**, **Active Directory Domains, and Trusts**.
2. Right-click the domain node for the domain you want to administer, and then choose **Properties**.

3. On the **General** tab, choose **Change Mode**, select **Yes**, and then select **OK**.
4. Restart the computer.

 Warning: This is an irreversible operation! Remember that you can only change the mode from mixed mode to native mode. Once a domain is running in native mode, it CANNOT be changed back to mixed mode.

Object Management

You can manage objects the following ways:

- Locate objects
- Move and delete objects
- Publish objects
- Make information available in the Global Catalog

Locating Objects

As an administrator, you can locate an object in Active Directory by right-clicking a container and then selecting **Find**. The **Find** dialog box will then display. Another way of locating objects is through the **Find** command on the **Action** menu in MMC.

Figure 4.7. Right-Clicking an Object

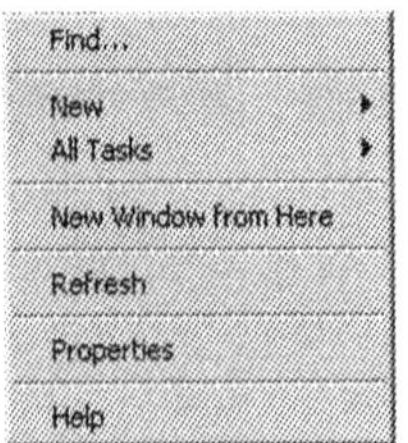

You can use the **Find** option with LDAP to query the Global Catalog server or a specific domain. This option provides many complex and helpful choices. They are:

- Find
- In
- Users, Contacts, and Groups tab
- Advanced tab
- Search criteria
- Results

Figure 4.8 The First FIND Dialog Box

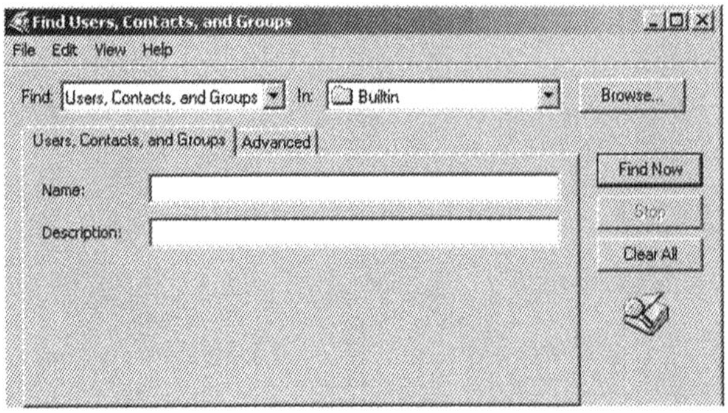

Find

Here you specify objects you want to find. These objects may be computers, printers, shared folders, OUs, or routers. You can customize a search to find any type of object.

In

This option lets you specify the location you want to search, which can be the entire directory, a specific domain, or an OU.

User, Contacts and Groups Tab

This specifies the name and description of users, contacts, and groups.

Figure 4.9 Object Attributes

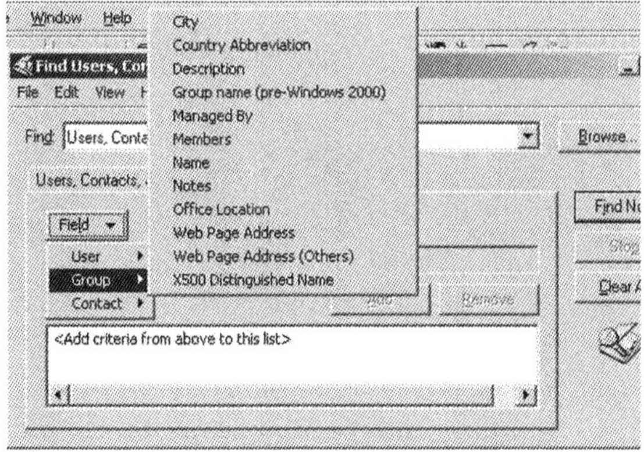

Advanced tab

Under this tab, you specify additional attribute criteria that you will use to locate the object. This includes the following:

Field—Lists object attributes for the object type.

Condition—Further defines the search for an attribute. These conditions include:

- Starts with
- Ends with
- Is (exactly)
- Is not
- Present
- Not present
- Value—The data for the condition of the attribute that you are trying to locate

Search Criteria

Search criteria—Lists criteria that you have defined under **Field**, **Condition**, and **Value** on the **Advanced** tab. Add or remove search criteria to narrow or widen your search.

Results

Results—Displays results of your search after you choose **Find Now**.

Figure 4.10 Advanced FIND Features

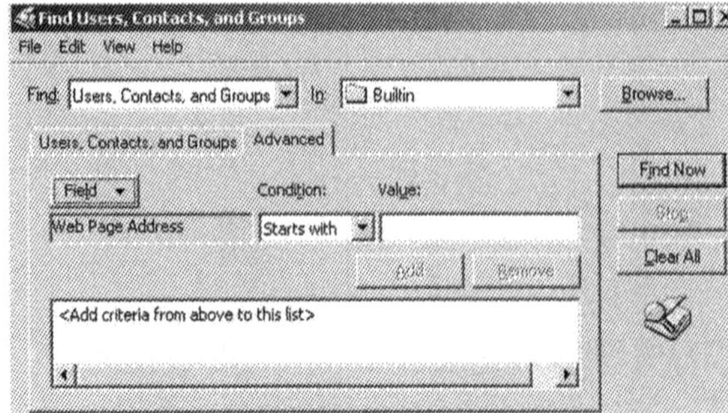

Moving and Deleting Objects

You use Active Directory Users and Computers to move and delete objects. By default, members of the Administrators group have the required permissions to move objects from one OU to another.

Reasons for moving or deleting objects include, but are not limited to, changing business requirements such as:

- Employees moving from one division to another
- Employees leaving the company
- General corporate restructuring

Moving Objects Between OUs Within a Domain

The following conditions apply when you move objects between OUs:

- Objects with explicitly defined permissions retain those permissions; permissions that are granted directly to an object remain the same
- Objects with inherited permissions inherit the permissions of the new parent container; permissions that were inherited from the old OU will no longer affect the objects

Deleting Objects from a Domains

The following occurs when you delete objects from a domain:

- In a process known as *tombstoning*, a marker is set on the objects, which are replicated to all domain controllers in a domain; this marker indicates that the object will be deleted after a specific interval
- The object's associated permissions are deleted
- The object no longer appears in queries

Note: If you want to recreate an object with the same name, you must reassign permissions because the object's identifiers have changed.

Publishing Objects

Publishing objects makes then visible in Active Directory and locatable by LDAP searches. Some information and resources are automatically published, but you must manually publish the following:

- File shares
- Printer shares created on computers not running Windows 2000

You must decide when to publish file and printer shares. You should publish information that needs to be readily accessible to a large number of users. For example, create a shared folder object for your organization's central application installation point. To publish existing file or printer shares, use Active Directory User and Computers to create shared folder or printer objects within your Organizational Unit structure.

Enabling Accessibility to Global Catalog Information

Each object and a subset of its attributes are replicated to the Global Catalog for forest-wide searches. You can choose to replicate additional attributes to the Global Catalog. However, remember that you should not add every attribute to the Global Catalog because Active Directory replicates the Global Catalog to all Global Catalog servers throughout the forest. The attributes that you choose to add to the Global Catalog should be:

- Relatively unique
- Easily available
- Relatively static
- Of reasonable size

Relative Uniqueness

The information should be relatively unique to the object, making it useful to a search. For example, employee last name, first name, or identification number are useful search items.

Easy Availability

The information should be easily available. For example, a user's last name or first name might be easily available, but their security clearance is not (implies weak security).

Static in Nature

Publish information that changes infrequently or never. For example, an employee's birth date is static information. The last name and address are subject to change.

Reasonable Size

Information should be of a reasonable size to minimize impact on replication traffic.

Note: You can use Active Directory Schema in MMC to define additional attributes to be included in the Global Catalog. But be careful when you do this. It is an advanced administrative task.

Vocabulary

Review the following terms in preparation for the certification exam.

Term	Description
ACL	Access Control List is a list of all users or user groups with access permissions. It also contains the type of access they have been granted.
DACL	Discretionary Access Control List defines security groups, user accounts and associated permissions. DACLs define object permissions for resource security enforcement and access levels for each list member.
DNS	Domain Name System is a hierarchical distributed database. DNS is the namespace used on the Internet to translate computer and service names into TCP/IP addresses. Active Directory uses DNS as its location service.
domain	The core administrative unit for Microsoft Windows 2000. The domain has its own boundary for security and replication, and is distinguished by a unique name. You use the domain to define how information and resources will be organized and stored. As you design your domain, you must decide what roles domains and OUs will play, and design the arrangement of OUs within the domains.
IP	Internet Protocol address is a unique 32-bit number that identifies a computer connected to the Internet to other Internet hosts for the purpose of enabling communication through the transfer of packets. Each IP address contains network and host ID information.
LDAP	Lightweight Directory Access Protocol is used to access a directory service and is the primary access protocol for Active Directory.
MB	Megabyte is 1,048,576 bytes of data storage.

Term	Description
mixed mode	Domain controllers can be running either Windows 2000 or Windows NT.
native mode	All domain controllers are running Windows 2000.
NetBIOS	Network Basic Input/Output System. NetBIOS provides a standard Application Programming Interface (API) for computer programs to communicate with other network protocols.
NTFS	NT File System is a file system that is designed for Windows 2000 and supports many features, such as file system security, Unicode, recoverability, and long file names. It also stores an Access Control List (ACL) with every file and folder.
OU	Organizational Unit is an entity or group of entities organized in a logical manner by the system administrator according to business or system functions or policies. They also enable the delegation of administration to distinct subtrees of the directory.
RFC	A Request for Comments is a formal proposal defining a new technology or an update to an existing technology.
SACL	System Access Control List contains a list of events that can be audited for an object. An administrator can audit all attempts to create a user object in a given Organizational Unit (OU) by creating an auditing entry for the OU. If the audit directory service access policy is enabled on a domain controller, then access to the audited objects appears in the security log of the domain controller.
SRV resource records	The Service Resource Records in DNS allow computers to search for servers in the DNS database based on the server's role in the network.

Term	Description
TCP/IP	Transmission Control Protocol/Internet Protocol. The most commonly used protocol suite, TCP/IP was originally developed by the military on UNIX computers to create very large, durable networks. The Internet is based on TCP/IP.
tombstoning	The process of setting a marker on objects to be deleted. This marker is replicated to all domain controllers in a domain, and indicates that the object will be deleted after a specific interval.

In Brief

If you want to...	Then do this...
Verify that the SRV resource records have been created for the domain controller after promotion (if you are using a server running the Microsoft DNS Server service)	Use Domain Name System (DNS) in Microsoft Management Console (MMC) to verify SRV resource records.
Verify that the SRV resource records have been created for the domain controller after promotion if you are using a DNS Server that does not support dynamic updates	Manually register the SRV resource records. View the Netlogon.dns file that is located in *systemroot*\System32\Config on each Active Directory domain controller or use the NSLOOKUP command-line utility to verify that the domain controller registered its SRV resource records in the DNS database.
Deliver secure dynamic updates	Configure Active Directory-integrated DNS.
Implement fault tolerance	Create a minimum of two domain controllers in a single domain to take advantage of Active Directory's replication feature.
Locate an object	Right-click a container in Active Directory, then select **Find** or choose **Find** on the **Action** menu in MMC.
Move or delete objects	Use Active Directory Users and Computers.

If you want to...	Then do this...
Publish existing file or printer shares	Use Active Directory User and Computers to create shared folder or printer objects within your OU structure.
Publish an object	Use Active Directory Users and Computers to create shared folder or printer objects within your OU structure.

Lesson 4 Activities

Complete the following activities to prepare for the certification exam.

1. Explain how to locate an object in Active Directory.
2. Discuss what you would do to reduce network traffic, and why this would be effective.
3. Name a few considerations for designing a first-level OU.
4. What are the advantages and disadvantages of OU nesting?
5. Name the types of objects that can be members of domain local groups, of global groups, and of universal groups.
6. List the three levels of delegation that are available in Active Directory.
7. Discuss what happens to permissions when you move objects between OUs.
8. List the steps in the process of tombstoning.
9. Name four characteristics of attributes you would add to the Global Catalog.
10. Give two examples of static information and two examples of information that is not static.

Answers to Lesson 4 Activities

1. To locate an object in Active Directory, right-click a container and then select.

2. To reduce network traffic, create multiple domains. This is effective because only changes to the Global Catalog are replicated instead of changes to the entire forest.

3. First-level OUs should be:
   - Unique to each domain
   - Standard throughout an organization
   - Named with names that are not likely to change

4. Advantages of OU nesting are:
   - Greater control
   - Easier management of OUs
   - Reduces network traffic in a domain tree
   - Simplifies administration

   Disadvantages:
   - Can degrade object discovery performance
   - Impacts performance when Group Policy must travel over slow links to be applied to computer or user objects

5. Membership of domain local groups:
   - User accounts, universal, and global groups from any domain
   - Domain local groups in the same domain

   Membership of global groups:
   - User accounts and global groups from the same domain
   - Universal and domain local groups in any domain

   Membership of universal groups:
   - User accounts, universal, and global groups from any domain
   - Domain local groups in any domain

6. The three levels of delegation available in Active Directory are:
   - Class level
   - Object level
   - Attribute level

7. The following happens to permissions when you move objects between OUs:
   - Objects with explicitly defined permissions retain those permissions
   - Permissions that are granted directly to an object remain the same
   - Objects with inherited permissions inherit the permissions of the new parent container
   - Permissions that were inherited from the old OU will no longer affect the objects

8. The process of tombstoning consists of the following steps:
   - A marker is set on the objects, which is replicated to all domain controllers in a domain; this marker indicates that the object will be deleted after a specific interval
   - The object's associated permissions are deleted
   - The object no longer appears in queries

9. Attributes you would add to the Global Catalog should be:
   - Relatively unique
   - Easily available
   - Relatively static
   - Of reasonable size

10. Examples of static information:
    - Social Security Number
    - Employee ID Number
    - Birth Date

    Examples of information that is not static:
    - Last Name
    - Address
    - Phone Number

Lesson 4 Quiz

These questions test your knowledge of features, vocabulary, procedures, and syntax.

1. Which command do you use to launch the Active Directory Installation Wizard?

   A. NSLOOKUP
   B. Netlogon.dns
   C. ActDir
   D. DCPromo

2. What feature of Active Directory do you use to configure additional Global Catalog servers?

   A. Routing and Remote Access
   B. Active Directory Sites and Services
   C. Telnet Server Administration
   D. Active Directory Users and Computers

3. What is the minimum number of domain controllers required in a single domain to implement fault tolerance?

   A. 2
   B. 1
   C. 5
   D. 10

4. What is the advantage of switching to native mode?

   A. It is easy to switch back to mixed mode.
   B. Your domain controllers can run other operating systems besides Windows 2000.
   C. You can nest global groups.
   D. You can add Windows NT domain controllers to a domain in native mode.

5. What is the disadvantage of switching to native mode?

   A. You cannot switch back to mixed mode.
   B. It disables Active Directory.
   C. You can have clients and member servers running other operating systems.
   D. You can have directories larger than 40 megabytes.

6. What happens when you delete objects from a domain?

   A. It is deleted immediately.
   B. A marker is set on the objects.
   C. It is sent to the Recycle Bin.
   D. It is sent to the Deleted Items container.

7. Why can nested OUs have a negative impact on response time?

   A. They take a long time to load.
   B. The administrator must load them manually each time they are used.
   C. Group policy is applied to objects starting at the domain root and travels until it finds the requested object.
   D. Contention for network objects can crash the computer.

8. Where are security universal groups available?

   A. Mixed mode
   B. Native mode
   C. Both mixed and native mode
   D. Neither mixed nor native mode.

9. At which level should you assign permissions?

   A. Global groups
   B. Universal groups
   C. Object and attribute level
   D. Site level

10. Which organization should provide first-level OU support?

    A. Information Technology
    B. Human Resources
    C. Comptroller's Office
    D. The organization that is responsible for administering the OU

Answers to Lesson 4 Quiz

1. Answer D is correct. DCPromo launches the Active Directory Installation Wizard.

   Answer A is incorrect. NSLOOKUP is used to verify SRV resource records.

   Answer B is incorrect. Netlogon.dns is a file, not a command.

   Answer C is incorrect. ActDir is not a command, nor does it exist anywhere within Active Directory.

2. Answer B is correct. You use Active Directory Sites and Services to configure additional catalog services.

   Answer A is incorrect. You use Routing and Remote Access to configure the Routing and Remote Access Service.

   Answer C is incorrect. You use Telnet Server Administration to view and modify telnet server settings and connections.

   Answer D is incorrect. You use Active Directory Users and Computers to manage users, computers, security groups, and other objects in Active Directory.

3. Answer A is correct. Active Directory requires at least two domain controllers for its automatic replication feature which enables fault tolerance.

   Answer B is incorrect. No replication can take place with only one domain controller.

   Answer C is incorrect. Five domain controllers, while acceptable, are more than the minimum required for fault tolerance.

   Answer D is incorrect. Ten domain controllers, while acceptable, are more than the minimum required for fault tolerance.

4. Answer C is correct. You can only nest global groups in native mode.

   Answer A is incorrect. You cannot switch back to mixed mode once you have switched to native mode.

   Answer B is incorrect. In native mode your domain controllers can only run Windows 2000.

   Answer D is incorrect. You can only add Windows NT domain controllers in mixed mode.

5. Answer A is correct. You cannot switch back to mixed mode once you have switched to native mode.

   Answer B is incorrect. Switching to native mode does not disable Active Directory. It just limits your domain controllers to Windows 2000.

   Answer C is incorrect. Having clients and member servers running other operating systems is not a disadvantage.

   Answer D is incorrect. Having directories larger than 40 megabytes is an advantage, not a disadvantage.

6. Answer B is correct. The object is marked for deletion after a specified interval.

   Answer A is incorrect. The object is not deleted immediately.

   Answer C is incorrect. Active Directory does not use the Recycle Bin to store deleted objects.

   Answer D is incorrect. Microsoft Outlook, not Active Directory, uses the Deleted Items container to store deleted items.

7. Answer C is correct. Group policy application must start at the top of the domain root and travel down the nested OU. This can slow down response time.

   Answer A is incorrect. The OUs are already loaded before any Group Policy application takes place.

   Answer B is incorrect. OUs are loaded when the computer is booted.

   Answer D is incorrect. There is no contention for network objects in traversing nested OUs.

8. Answer B is correct. Security universal groups are only available in native mode.

   Answer A is incorrect. Security universal groups are not available in mixed mode. They are only available in native mode.

   Answer C is incorrect. Mixed mode does not accommodate security universal groups.

   Answer D is incorrect. Native mode accommodates security universal groups.

9. Answer C is correct because the object and attribute levels provide the best place to assign permissions. This can include:

   - Read permissions to attributes
   - Write permissions to attributes
   - User rights to a related group of attributes
   - User rights to specific properties, such as a group membership list, to permit restricted access to an attribute

   Answer A is incorrect. Permissions at the global level increase replication traffic. Also, not every user or object at this site will require the same permissions.

   Answer B is incorrect. Permissions at the universal level increase replication traffic. Also, not every user or object at this site will require the same permissions.

   Answer D is incorrect. Permissions at the site level increase replication traffic. Also, not every user or object at this site will require the same permissions.

10. Answer A is correct. IT has the technical knowledge to provide this level of support.

    Answer B is incorrect. Although HR knows a lot about organizational structure, these employees do not have the necessary technical skills or tools.

    Answer C is incorrect. Although the Comptroller's Office knows a lot about business practices, these employees do not have the necessary technical skills or tools.

    Answer D is incorrect. Although the administrative organization has a lot of the necessary technical skills, they still need first-level support.

Lesson 5

Multiple-Domain Structures

Forests, trees and domains are delimited units that can share resources but can be administered separately. They differ in how they communicate with one another and how replication traffic flows between them. If your organization requires more than one domain, tree or forest, you will need to understand the interactions across the replication borders and administrative borders. In this lesson you will learn how to structure more intricate domains than a single domain and make effective decisions about the structures and administrative models required for these more complex networks.

After completing this lesson, you should have a better understanding of how to perform the following tasks:

- Identify criteria for determining whether a single- or multiple-domain structure is necessary to meet business needs
- Describe the trust relationships inherited in multiple-domain structures
- Plan a multiple-domain tree
- Plan a multiple-tree forest
- Plan multiple forests

Multiple-Domain Tree

A single domain is the smallest domain in Windows 2000 Active Directory. Knowing when you need to expand beyond a single domain and when you should create child domains to add to your domain tree is a critical decision-making process. Not only does expansion impact on hardware costs, but replication and resource access also need to be considered.

By default, a single-domain tree is created when the first server is promoted to a Domain Controller (DC). You can construct a larger tree by adding more domains to the existing tree. Additional domains, or child domains, form a hierarchical structure.

Understanding the Multiple-Domain Tree Model

In Windows 2000, a tree is a set of one or more domains with contiguous names. If more than one domain exists, you can combine the multiple domains into hierarchical tree structures. If a division of your organization has its own registered DNS name and runs its own registered DNS name and runs its own DNS servers, you will probably need more than one tree in your forest. One domain can be the child of another domain, (for example, child.domain.com is a child of domain.com) and a child domain and its parent are a two-way transitive trust. An Active Directory tree hierarchy is a Domain Name System (DNS) naming hierarchy. Child domains derive their names from the parent domain.

Note: A child domain always has the complete name of the parent domain in it.

Figure 5.1 Multiple-Domain Tree

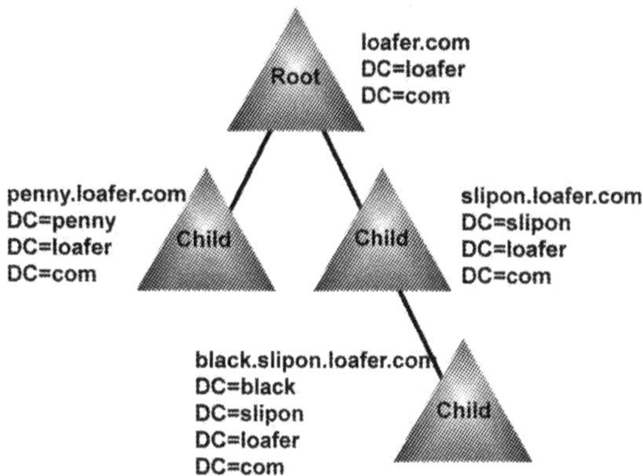

Sharing a Single Tree Root

When you have a domain as a child of another, a domain tree is formed. A domain tree has to have a contiguous namespace. The name of the tree is the root domain name; in Figure 5.1, the root would be loafer.com.

The parent-child relationship between domains in a domain tree is a naming relationship and a trust relationship only. Administrators in a parent domain do not automatically apply to child domains. Each domain in a tree is directly related to the level above and the level below it.

Note: After a tree root has been established, you cannot add a domain with a higher-level name in a forest. You cannot create a parent of an existing domain; you can only create a child.

Infrastructure Models Requiring Multiple Domains

The most flexible, least expensive and easiest model to administer is a single domain in Active Directory. However, you may consider adding domains if your business requires any of the following:

Distinct domain-level policies—The user account policy is applied at the domain level, which allows you to create separate domains that contain sets of users, each with a distinct policy, such as a password policy.

Reduced replication traffic—Between domains, only changes to the global catalog server, configuration information, and schema are replicated.

Tighter administrative control and decentralized administration—Domain administrators cannot cross domain boundaries to manage other domains without explicit permissions. Each domain can maintain administrative control of their hardware.

Separation and control of affiliated relationships—Domains can isolate shared resources and external users for administrative and security purposes. This can help with administration in large corporate partnerships or joint ventures. Because information and resources are often managed and accessed differently between domains than within a domain, replication traffic can differ as well. You will need to examine how these processes differ to help you decide if a multiple-domain model meets your organization's needs.

Sharing Information with Automatic Trusts

All domains within an Active Directory share a common directory schema, configuration information, and Global Catalog and there are a number of advantages to placing domains in a tree. The first and most useful is that all the members of the tree have Kerberos transitive trusts with its parent and all its children. These transitive trusts have the added advantages that any user or group in a domain tree can be granted access to any object in the entire tree and that a single logon can be used at any workstation in the domain tree.

Tip: If your Active Directory infrastructure requires domains that are administered separately, consider using the multiple-domain model.

Establishing Inter-Domain Trusts

A trust relationship is a relationship established between two domains that allow users in one domain to be recognized by a domain controller in the other domain. Trusts let users access resources in the other domain and let administrators manage user rights for users in the other domain. A relationship established between two domains allows users in one domain to be authenticated in another domain. All domain trust relationships have only two domains in the relationship, the trusting domain and the trusted domain.

Figure 5.2 Domain Trusts

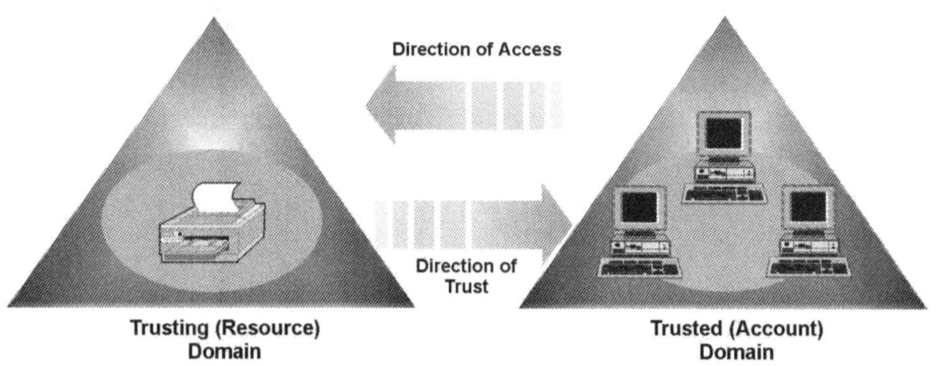

LDAP Queries

Active Directory uses Lightweight Directory Access Protocol (LDAP) to locate objects. The LDAP search begins in the domain where the search was initiated. Because each domain is aware of all of the other domains in the tree, the LDAP query can be referred from domain to domain until the query is resolved. Although each domain is aware of other trees in the forest, the maximum scope of LDAP referrals is the current tree.

Transitive Trusts

One of the headaches in administering enterprise NT 4.0 environments was trying to manage trust relationships between domains. In the worst-case scenario of a complete trust environment, a company will have N*(N-1) trust relationships to manage, where N is the number of domains they have. For a company with 20 domains they will need to have to up to 380 domains (20*(20-19)). Simply put: a headache.

Windows 2000 goes a long way towards solving this problem by using transitive Kerberos trusts. Transitive means that if A trusts B and B trusts C, then A trusts C.

Windows 2000 automatically configures trusts when you create domains. However, this only happens between Windows 2000 domains. If you have NT 4.0 domains that you want to be able to communicate with Windows 2000 domains, you will have to manually configure trusts between the domains.

Transitive trusts make information accessible to all the domains in the tree. Once a user is authenticated, Discretionary Access Control List (DACL) entries grant or deny resources to users or groups.

Note: It is important to remember that these trust relationships with NT 4.0 domains are not transitive.

Cross-Link Trusts

Before an account can be granted access to resources by a domain controller of another domain, Windows 2000 must determine whether the domain containing the desired resources (target domain) has a trust relationship with the domain in which the account is located (source domain). To make this determination for two domains in a tree or a forest, Windows 2000 computes a trust path between the DCs for these source and target domains. A trust path is the series of domain trust relationships that must be traversed by security to pass authentication requests between any two domains. Computing and traversing a trust path between domain trees in a complex tree or forest can take time. Creating cross-link trusts can reduce this time.

Cross-link trusts are two-way transitive trusts that enable you to shorten the path. You create a cross-link trust between domains in the same tree or forest.

Figure 5.3—Cross-link Trusts

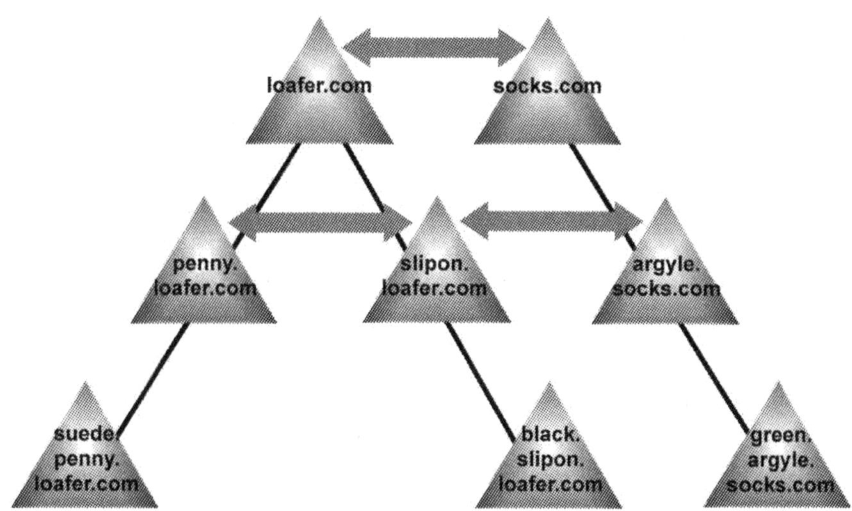

As shown in the illustration, you can create a cross-link trust between mid-level domains within a domain or between two domain trees to shorten the trust path between two domains in a forest and optimize the authentication process.

Note: If necessary, you can create multiple cross-link trusts between domains in a forest.

The following describes a cross-link trust:

- Can be established between any two domains in the same tree or forest
- Must be set up manually in each direction
- Must be transitive

Implementing Domains in a Tree

Plan Each New Domain Individually

When you have determined that multiple domains are required, you should plan the structure within each domain individually, then, as each new domain is added, consider all existing domains when planning the next domain.

Only members of Enterprise Admins can add domains to a tree—To control naming, only members of the Enterprise Admins group can add domains to a tree. To create a new domain, you promote a server to be the first domain controller in the new domain. During Active Directory installation on the new DC, you must choose to join the existing tree and then use the **Create New Child Domain** option to add domains to a tree.

A DNS server is necessary for the root domain—Each additional Active Directory requires a DNS subdomain. The subdomains can be implemented within the same parent DNS zone or in a separate DNS zone. If you use a DNS server that supports dynamic updates, these DNS subdomains will be automatically generated during the process of promoting a server to a domain controller.

Tip: Members of the Enterprise Admins group can add new domains using the NTSUTIL command-line utility. Administrators who are not part of the Enterprise Admins group can create a domain controller but cannot create a new name for the domain.

Multiple-Tree Forest

A collection of one or more Active Directory trees, organized as peers and connected by two-way, transitive trust relationships between the root domains of each tree, is a forest. The trees in a forest share information, a common configuration, schema, and Global Catalog. This sharing of data and the trust relationships between their roots differentiate a forest from a collection of unrelated trees.

The DNS name of the first domain created in a tree is unique in the forest and identifies that particular tree. Each tree forms a separate naming hierarchy that is based on different DNS root domain names. The forest itself is identified by the DNS name of the initial tree that was created in the forest (the root domain).

Figure 5.4—The Multiple-Tree Forest

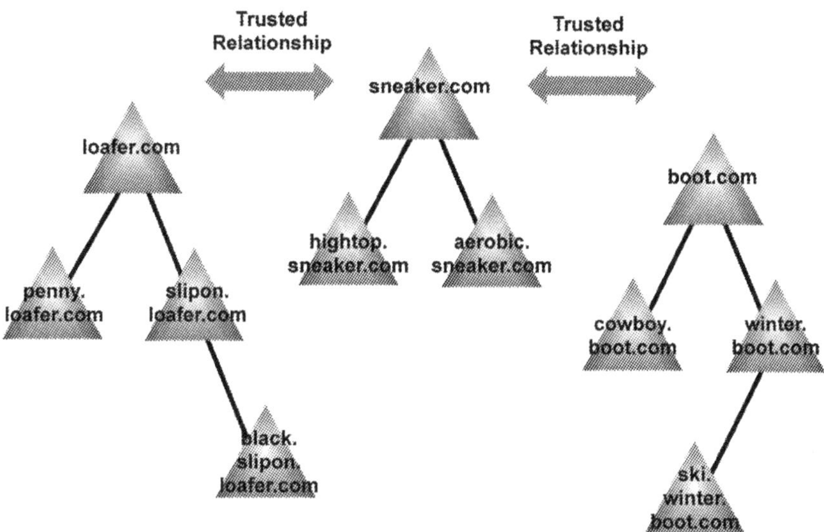

As shown in Figure 5.4, the roots of the separate trees have non-contiguous names. The trees are part of a single overall hierarchy because the same Active Directory can still resolve names of objects within the forest.

The process for designing a multiple-tree forest involves:

- Examining the multiple-tree structure to ensure that it meets your needs
- Determining whether you need a multiple-tree forest

- Ensuring that inter-domain searches and access of resources meet your needs
- Implementing trees in a forest

Unifying Multiple Trees into a Single Forest

You should consider using a multiple tree forest when you need:

- Distinct DNS names
- Tightly controlled access

Trees offer significant partitioning between domains that need to share resources. A major reason to implement more than one tree is to accommodate distinct DNS names. This may apply to companies that are:

- Acquired enterprises that want to base Active Directory naming on their Internet presence and maintain distinct Internet names
- Involved in partnerships
- Made up of different business divisions
- Multiple trees can be combined into a single forest and each tree will have its own root name. Defining additional trees may be appropriate if you need:

To maintain multiple, distinct DNS names—For example, your company's Active Directory is called sneakers.com and you acquire another company, The Boot Company. They have an established Internet presence. To accommodate both companies in the same forest and maintain each DNS name, each would have their own tree. In this case, sneakers.com would be the root directory of the Active Directory forest and boot.com would be the new tree.

To facilitate but tightly control partner resource access—Large corporations involved in partnerships can use trees to control shared resources and external users for administrative and security reasons.

You are not limited to only two domain trees in a forest—You can add as many trees as you want and all the domains in the forest will be able to grant access to objects for any user within the forest. This cuts back on having to manually manage the trust relationships.

Figure 5.4 shows one forest with three domain trees. The three root domains are not contiguous with each other, but loafers.com and boot.com are child domains of sneaker.com.

Note: It is not possible to create a forest containing only parts of a domain.

Distinct DNS Names

A domain is identified by a DNS name. You use DNS to locate the DC servers for a given domain. DNS names are hierarchical, and the DNS name of an Active Directory domain indicates its position in the forest hierarchy. For example, MyComputer.com might be the name of a domain. A domain named Edmonton.MyComputer.com can be a child domain of MyComputer.com in the forest hierarchy.

Controlled Access

Multiple-domain trees within a single forest do not form a contiguous namespace; they have non-contiguous DNS domain names. Although trees in a forest do not share a namespace, a forest does have a single root domain, called the forest root domain. The forest root domain is the first domain created in a forest. The two forest-wide predefined groups—Enterprise administrators and Schema administrators—reside in this domain.

Locating Resources between Trees

Because the standard LDAP query is limited to locating objects within a tree, global catalog query mechanisms are used to locate directory objects between trees. By default, there is only one Global Catalog server in the forest, located on the first domain controller in the forest.

You can designate additional DCs to be Global Catalog servers by using Active Directory Sites and Services. If you anticipate a high volume of cross-tree searches, you may want to designate additional Global Catalog servers to ensure adequate search performance.

Accessing Resources between Trees

When you create a new tree during the promotion of a server to a domain controller, you specify the root domain of the initial tree in the forest. A trust relationship is then established between the root domains of the new tree and the initial tree. Creating a third tree establishes a trust relationship between the root of the forest and the third tree. As this trust is transitive and bi-directional, resources can be shared between the three trees with no further configuration of trusts.

Implementing Trees in a Forest

To implement a tree in a forest, you must first resolve its structure according to the following parameters:

Determining the DNS name of the new tree—Each tree has a distinct DNS domain name. When you have chosen the name, you can create the new domain. A minimum of two domain controllers is required for fault tolerance.

Determining additional domains—It may be necessary to determine additional domains in the tree, as well as which domains would be child domains.

Identifying the root domain of the initial tree in the forest—This establishes a trust between the new tree's initial domain and the root domain of the forest. Trees are added to the forest when you use the Active Directory Installation Wizard to promote a DC and use the Create New Domain Tree in an Existing Forest option.

DNS Domain Name of the New Tree

Domains that form a single-domain tree share a contiguous namespace (naming hierarchy). Following DNS standards, the Fully Qualified Domain Name (FQDN) for a domain that is part of a contiguous namespace is the name of that domain appended to the names of the parent and root domains using the dot (.) character format. For example, a domain with a NetBIOS name of "skiboot" that has a parent domain named winter.boot.com would have a Fully Qualified DNS Domain Name of skiboot.winter.boot.com.

Domain trees in a forest share the same directory configuration, directory configuration, replication, and schema but do not share a contiguous DNS domain namespace.

Both contiguous and non-contiguous DNS namespaces can be included in your directory. Using a combination of domain trees and forests will provide you with flexible domain naming options.

Domain Organization in the Tree

Domains are used to accomplish network management goals such as structuring the network, delimiting security, applying Group Policy, and replicating information. A domain provides you with a number of benefits:

- Organizing objects
- Using Organizational Units (OUs), you can manage the accounts and resources in the domain
- Publishing resources and information about domain objects
- Using multiple directories, you can scale the Active Directory directory service to accommodate your requirements
- By creating multiple domains, you can partition or segment the directory to serve a dissimilar user base, whereas a domain only stores information about the objects located in that domain
- Applying a Group Policy object to the domain combines resource and security management

A domain defines a scope or a policy. A Group Policy object sets up how domain resources can be accessed, configured, and used. Policies are applied only within the domain and not across domains. Delegating authority eliminates the need for a number of administrators with broad administrative authority. By delegating authority in conjunction with Group Policy objects and group memberships, you can assign administrator rights and permissions to manage objects in an entire domain or in one or more OUs within the domain.

Multiple Forests

All Windows 2000 domains in all of the domain trees in a forest adhere to the following characteristics:

- Have transitive trust relationships among the domains within each tree
- Have transitive trust relationships among the domain trees in a forest
- Share common configuration information

- Share a common schema
- Share a common global catalog

Note: Adding new domains to a forest is easy. However you cannot move existing Windows 2000 Active Directory domains between forests. You can remove a domain from a forest only if it has no child domains.

Creating a New Domain in an Existing Forest

To create a domain, you must promote one or more computers running Windows 2000 Server to be domain controllers. A DC provides the Active Directory directory service to network users and computers, stores directory data, and manages user-domain interactions, including user logon processes, authentication, and directory searches. Every domain must contain at least one DC.

Creating a Replica Domain Controller

Windows 2000 supports multi-master replication—all domain controllers of a domain can receive changes made to objects and can replicate those changes to all other DCs in that domain. By default, the first DC created in a forest is a Global Catalog server and contains a full replica of all objects in the directory for its domain and a partial replica of all objects stored in the directory of every other domain in the forest.

Replicating Active Directory data among domain controllers provides benefits for information availability, fault tolerance, load balancing, and performance. Installing multiple-DCs ensures that the Active Directory remains available, even if a single-DC stops working.

Users and services should be able to access directory information at any time from any computer in the forest. To make this possible, additions, modifications, and deletions of directory data must be relayed to other domain controllers. For example, if you change your account's password in your organization's Kansas office, your new password must be valid when you log on with the same account at the Edmonton office. Replicating the directory changes to other DCs makes this possible.

Directory information must be widely distributed, but you must balance this with network performance. Updates constantly distributed to all other domain controllers in the domain will consume network resources. Although you can manually add or configure connections or force replication over a particular connection, you should allow replication to be automatically optimized by the Active Directory knowledge consistency checker, based on information you supply to Active Directory Sites and Services about your operation.

Sites enable the replication of directory data both within and among sites. Active Directory replicates within a site more frequently than across sites. This means the best-connected domain controllers receive updates first. DCs in other sites receive all changes to the directory less frequently, thus reducing network bandwidth consumption.

A site is delimited by subnet and is usually geographically bounded. A site is separate in concept from Windows 2000-based domains. A site can span multiple domains, and a domain can span multiple sites. Sites are not part of the domain namespace. Sites are used to control replication of your domain information to help determine resource proximity. For example, a workstation will choose a DC within its site with which to authenticate.

Windows 2000 uses sites and replication change control to optimize replication in the following ways:

- By occasionally re-evaluating which connections are used, Active Directory uses the most efficient network connections
- By using multiple routes to replicate changes, fault tolerance is provided
- By only replicating changed information, the process is optimized

How Replication Works

To visualize Active Directory replication, imagine an organization with one site in Portland, Oregon and one in Edmonton, Alberta, each with one domain controller. They are one domain that spans a multi-site Wide Area Network (WAN); each city has one DC.

The domain controllers keep track of how many changes they have made to their copy of the directory, and how many changes they have received from the DCs that are their replication partners. If the Portland DC finds it does not have all the changes from the Edmonton DC, the Portland DC can request the new changes, and only the new changes, from the Edmonton DC.

If a domain controller has been disconnected from the network, updating is easy. It is clear which directory information has changed and, as a result, needs to be replicated. Changes are tracked by a numerical sequence, not by time, so the need for synchronized clocks is eliminated in all but the most unusual cases, such as when resolving conflicting changes.

Querying the Global Catalog Server in a Forest

By default, a Global Catalog is created automatically on the initial domain controller in the forest. It contains a replica of all the objects in the directory for its host domain and a partial replica of all objects contained in the directory of every other domain in the forest.

The replica is partial because it stores some, but not all, of the property values for every object in the forest. The Global Catalog performs two key directory roles:

Logon—Provides universal group membership information to a domain controller when a logon process is started. This is not just for users. Every object authenticating to Active Directory must reference the Global Catalog server, including every computer at boot-up. In a multi-domain setup, at least one DC that contains a global catalog must be available.

Querying—It enables finding directory information regardless of which domain in the forest actually contains the data, without having to search each domain individually. The global catalog makes individual directory structures within forests transparent to users seeking information. Queries occur more frequently than updates to the directory. Assigning more than one domain controller to be a global catalog server improves response time for users seeking directory information. You must balance this advantage against the fact that doing so increases replication traffic on your network.

Resource Access between Domains

The root domain of each domain tree in the forest establishes a transitive trust relationship with the forest root domain. In Figure 5.4, sneaker.com is the root domain. The root domain and the other domain trees boot.com and loafer.com, have transitive trust relationships with sneaker.com. This establishes trust across all the domain trees in the forest.

Creating One-Way Trusts between Domains

When you create explicit trusts, you create one-way trust domains.

Creating Explicit Trusts

To create an explicit trust, you must know the domain names and a user account with permission to create trusts in each domain. Each trust is assigned a password that must be known to the administrators of both domains in the relationship.

To connect to a forest:

1. Open Active Directory Sites and Services.
2. Right-click **Active Directory Sites and Services**, and choose **Connect to Forest**.
3. In **Root domain**, type the root domain of the forest. This is the root domain of the first domain tree created in the forest.

Note: To open Active Directory Sites and Services, choose **Start**, **Programs**, **Administrative Tools**, and then select **Active Directory Sites and Services**. To use Active Directory Sites and Services on a computer that is not a domain controller, install the Windows 2000 Administration Tools.

Active Directory Sites and Services views a single forest. Change forests to view and configure Active Directory Sites and Services settings for a forest of your choosing.

To manage properties of a shared folder, follow these steps:

1. Open **Shared Folders**.
2. From the console tree, choose **Shares**.
3. Right-click the shared folder you want to manage properties for, and choose **Properties**.
4. On the **General** or **Security** tab, make the changes you want, and then choose **OK**.

Note: To open Shared Folders, choose **Start**, **Settings**, and then select **Control Panel**. Double-click **Administrative Tools**, double-click **Computer Management**, and then double-click **Shared Folders**.

Defining Domain Boundaries

As domains are a security boundary, administrative permissions for a domain are limited to the domain by default. For example, an administrator with permissions to set security policies in one domain is not automatically granted authority to set security policies in any other domain in the directory.

Accessing Resources in an Active Directory Forest

All the domain controllers in a forest host a copy of the forest Configuration and Schema containers in addition to a domain database. A domain database is one part of a forest database. Each domain database contains directory objects, such as security principle objects (users, computers, and groups) to which you can grant or deny access to network resources.

Exercise A. Creating a New Domain

This exercise explains how to set up the common infrastructure network for Active Directory. Follow the procedures to configure a computer running Windows 2000 Server as the first domain controller of a child domain of the parent domain. This requires that, in addition to the first DC in the network, you have two more computers running Windows 2000 Server that can be promoted to DCs. This entails installing Windows 2000 Server on those computers.

In this exercise, the root domain DNS name is MyComputer and the child you will be installing is Vancouver. You can replace these names for your own exercise if you wish.

Configuring a Child Domain

To configure a child domain, follow these steps:

Warning: Run this only on the computer that is the first domain controller for your network.

1. Run the **Configure Your Server Wizard**.
2. Choose **Start**, **Programs**, **Administrative Tools**, and then select **Configure Your Server**. The Configure Your Server Wizard will open.
3. Choose **One or more servers are already running in my network**, and select **OK**.
4. On the next wizard page, choose **Active Directory** from the list of services on the left. On the Active Directory information page, scroll to **Start the Active Directory Installation Wizard**, and choose **Start**. (To make this server a DC, you must install Active Directory.)

Note: Since your partition must be formatted with New Technology File System (NTFS) to host Active Directory, you might receive a message asking you to convert the file system on your computer to NTFS. Choose **Yes**. The process of converting the partition to NTFS begins, which includes disk check, processing files on the volume, and converting the file system. When the conversion is complete, you can return to step 4 and choose **Start** to start the **Active Directory Installation Wizard**.

5. Choose **Next**, **New**, and **Next** again.
6. Choose Create a new child domain in an existing domain tree, and select Next.

7. In the Network Credentials box, type the username as Administrator; do not enter a password. Type the domain name as MyComputer, and select Next.
8. On the Child Domain Installation page, type the parent domain as MyComputer.com, and the child domain as Vancouver.

Note: The complete DNS name of the new domain is displayed. In this example, **Vancouver.MyComputer.com**.

9. Choose **Next**.
10. Accept the defaults on each of the following pages of the wizard: NetBIOS Domain Name, Database and Log on Locations, and Shared System Volume.
11. If your network will contain computers running pre-Windows 2000 operating systems, choose **Permissions compatible with pre-Windows 2000 servers**. If you plan to have a Windows 2000-only configuration, select **Permissions compatible only with Windows 2000 servers**. Select **Next**.
12. When prompted to **Restore Mode Administrator Password**, choose **No**, and then select **Next**.
13. On the **Summary** page, you can review your selections, then choose **Next**. The wizard will configure **Active Directory**.
14. Choose **Finish** on the **Completing Active Directory Installation** page.
15. Before the wizard restarts Windows, the **Completing the Active Directory Installation** page appears, which confirms that Active Directory is installed on this computer and specifies that it is a domain controller assigned to the site, "Default-First-Site." Sites, which are configured with the Active Directory Sites and Services tool, determine how replication occurs.

Exercise B. Creating a Replica Domain Controller

In this exercise, you will create a replica domain controller for your domain. As you have started to define in the previous exercise.

To configure an additional DC as a replication partner, follow these steps:

1. Choose **Start**, **Programs**, **Administrative Tools**, and then select **Configure Your Server**.
2. On the first wizard page, choose **One or more servers already running in my network**, and select **Next**.
3. Choose **Active Directory** in the list on the left, scroll to **Start the Active Directory Wizard**, and select **Start**.
4. On the **Active Directory Installation Wizard** welcome page, choose **Next**.
5. On the **Domain Controller Type** page, choose **Additional domain controller**.

Note: This creates the domain controller as a replication partner.

6. On the **Network Credentials** page, log on as administrator, type the domain name **MyCompany**, and choose **Next**.
7. Accept the defaults on each of the following pages: Additional Domain Controller, Database and Log Location, and Shared System Volume, and choose **Next**.
8. Leave the **Restore Mode Administrator Password** page blank, and choose **Next**.
9. On the **Summary** page, choose **Next**.
10. The wizard will now configure Active Directory.
11. Choose **Finish** and **Restart Now** to restart Windows 2000.

Exercise C. Searching the Global Catalog

Note: Perform this procedure on your test computer setup in the previous exercise with two domain controllers. Do not start the exercise on either DC until the replica DC has been rebooted.

To search the Global Catalog server in a forest:

1. Log on to your domain as **Administrator**.
2. Open **My Console** on your desktop.
3. Expand **Active Directory Users and Computers**.
4. From the console tree, right-click your domain, and then choose **Find**. The **Find Users, Contacts, and Groups** dialog box appears.
5. From within the **Find** box, choose **Computers**.
6. In the **In** box, verify that your domain is selected, and choose **Find Now**.
    a. Which computers are listed in the result and why?
    b. Which domain controller(s) can satisfy this query?
7. In the **In** box, choose **Entire Directory**, and choose **Find Now**.
    a. How many computers are listed in the result?
    b. What domain controller(s) can satisfy this query?

Answers:

6.a. All the computers in the domain because the search was initiated at the domain level.

6.b. Only domain controllers for the domain.

7.a. Answers will vary based on the number of computers in the domain. All computers in the domain should appear.

7.b. Only global catalog servers for the forest.

8. Close the **Computers** box.
9. Close **My Console** without making changes.
10. Log off as **Administrator** of your domain.

Exercise D. Create an Explicit Domain Trust

A domain trust is a relationship established between two domains that enables users in one domain to be authenticated by a domain controller in another domain. All domain trust relationships have only two domains in the relationship: the trusting domain and the trusted domain.

1. Open **Active Directory Domains and Trusts**
2. From the console tree, right-click the domain node for the domain you want to administer, and then choose **Properties**.
3. Choose the **Trusts** tab.
4. Depending on your requirements, choose either **Domains trusted by this domain** or **Domains that trust this domain**, and then select **Add**.
5. If the domain to be added is a Windows 2000 domain, type the full DNS name of the domain. Or, if the domain is running an earlier version of Windows, type the domain name.
6. Type the **password** for this trust, and confirm the **password**.
7. Repeat this procedure on the domain that forms the other part of the explicit trust relationship.

Note: To open **Active Directory Domains and Trusts**, choose **Start, Programs, Administrative Tools,** and then select **Active Directory Domains and Trusts.**

The password must be accepted in both the trusting and trusted domains.

Exercise E. Identify Trust Relationships between Domains

In this exercise, you will identify the trusts that exist between your domain and other domains in the forest.

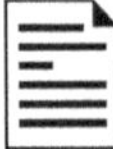

Note: Perform this procedure at your test system set up in the previous exercises with two domain controllers. Do not start the exercise on either DC until the replica DC has been rebooted.

1. Log on as **Administrator**.
2. Start **My Console**.
3. Expand **Active Directory Domains and Trusts**.
4. Expand **MyComputer.com**.
    a. How many domains now appear in your forest?
5. In the console tree, **Right-click** your domain and choose **Properties**.
    a. Which domain(s) are trusted by your domain?
    b. Which domain(s) trust your domain?
    c. What is the direction of the trust?
6. In the **Domains trusted by this domain** box, choose **MyComputer.com**, and then select **View/Edit**.
    a. Is the trust between your domain and MyComputer transitive? Why or why not?
7. Choose **OK** and then select **OK** again to return to **Active Directory Domains and Trusts**.
8. Right-click **MyComputer.com**, choose **Properties**, and select the **Trusts** tab.
    a. Which domains are trusted by MyComputer.com?
    b. Which domains trust MyComputer.com?

9. Choose **OK**.
10. Exit **MyConsole**. If prompted, do not save the changes.

Answers:

4 a. At least two—your domain and MyComputer.com.

5 a. MyComputer.com.

5 b. MyComputer.com.

5 c. Bi-directional two-way.

8 a. All the domains that have joined the forest.

8 b. All the domains that have joined the forest.

Vocabulary

Review the following terms in preparation for the certification exam.

Term	Description
DACL	Discretionary Access Control List defines security groups, user accounts and associated permissions. DACLs define object permissions for resource security enforcement and access levels for each list member.
DC	Domain Controller
DNS	Domain Name System is a hierarchical distributed database. DNS is the namespace used on the Internet to translate computer and service names into TCP/IP addresses. Active Directory uses DNS as its location service.
domain	Used to accomplish network management goals, such as structuring the network, delimiting security, applying Group Policy, and replicating information.
domain boundary	As domains are a security boundary, by default, administrative permissions for a domain are limited to the domain. For example, an administrator with permissions to set security policies in one domain is not automatically granted authority to set security policies in any other domain in the directory.
forest	A collection of one or more Active Directory trees that trust each other. All of the trees in a forest share a common schema, configuration, and global catalog. When a forest contains multiple trees, the trees do not form a contiguous namespace. All trees in a given forest trust each other through transitive trust relationships. Unlike a tree, a forest does not need a distinct name.

Term	Description
Global Catalog (GC)	Built automatically by the Active Directory replication system, it contains a partial replica of every Windows 2000 domain in the directory. When given one or more attributes of the target object, the GC allows users and applications to find objects quickly, without knowing what domain they occupy. The attributes in the global catalog are those used most frequently in search operations, and those required to locate a full replica of the object.
IPSec	Internet Protocol Security supports network-level authentication, data integrity, and encryption to secure intranet, extranet, and Internet Web communications.
Kerberos	A security system that authenticates users. Kerberos does not provide authorization to services or databases; it establishes identity at logon, which is used throughout the session. The Kerberos protocol is the primary authentication mechanism in the Windows 2000 operating system.
LDAP	Lightweight Directory Access Protocol is used to access a directory service and is the primary access protocol for Active Directory.
NTFS	NT File System is a file system that is designed for Windows 2000 and supports many features, such as file system security, Unicode, recoverability, and long file names. It also stores an Access Control List (ACL) with every file and folder.
OU	Organizational Unit is an entity or group of entities organized in a logical manner by the system administrator according to business or system functions or policies. They also enable the delegation of administration to distinct subtrees of the directory.

Term	Description
parent-child trust relationship	The two-way, transitive trust relationship established when you add a domain to an Active Directory tree. The Active Directory installation process automatically creates a trust relationship between the domain you are creating (the new child domain) and the parent domain.
resource	Any part of a computer system or a network, such as a disk drive, printer, or memory, that can be allotted to a program or process while it is running or shared over a local area network.
root domain	The domain at the top of the hierarchy.
site	A site is separate in concept from domains, is delimited by a subnet and is typically geographically bounded. A site can span multiple domains, and a domain can span multiple sites. Sites are not part of the domain namespace. Sites control replication of your domain information and help to determine resource proximity.
transitive trust	A trust relationship among domains, where if domain A trusts domain B and domain B trusts domain C, then domain A trusts domain C.
tree	A set of Microsoft Windows 2000 domains connected together via a transitive two-way trust, sharing a common schema, configuration, and global catalog.
WAN	A Wide Area Network that spans a large geographical area and consists of multiple LANs and leased lines from telephone carrier service providers.

In Brief

If you want to...	Then do this...
Connect to a forest	1. Open **Active Directory Sites and Services**. 2. Right-click **Active Directory Sites and Services**, and select **Connect to Forest**. 3. In Root domain, enter the root domain of the forest. This is the root domain of the first domain tree created in the forest.
Manage properties of a shared folder	1. Open **Shared Folders**. 2. In the console tree, choose **Shares**. 3. Right-click the shared folder for which you want to manage properties, and choose **Properties**. 4. On the **General** or **Security** tab, make the changes you want, and then choose **OK**.

If you want to...	Then do this...
Configure a child domain (Run this only on the computer that is the first domain controller for your network)	1. Start **dcpromo** and choose **Next**. 2. On the **Domain Controller** page, choose **Create a new child domain in an existing domain tree**, and select **Next**. 3. In the **Network Credentials** box, enter: User name (Administrator) Password (as required) Domain (as required), and choose **Next**. 4. On the **Child Domain Installation** page, enter: The parent domain name The child domain (The complete DNS name will be child.parent.extension), and choose **Next**. 5. Accept the defaults on each of the following pages of the wizard: NetBIOS Domain Name, Database and Log on Locations, Shared System Volume, and choose **Next**. 6. When prompted to **Restore Mode Administrator Password**, choose **No**, and select **Next**. 7. On the **Summary** page, review your selections, then choose **Next**. The wizard will configure Active Directory. 8. Choose **Finish** on the **Completing Active Directory Installation** page.

If you want to...	Then do this...
Configure an additional domain controller as replication partner	1. Choose **Start**, **Programs**, **Administrative Tools**, and then select **Configure Your Server**. 2. On the first wizard page, choose **One or more servers already running in my network**, and select **Next**. 3. Choose **Active Directory** from the list on the left, scroll **to Start the Active Directory Wizard**, and select **Start**. 4. On the **Active Directory Installation Wizard** welcome page, select **Next**. 5. On the **Domain Controller Type** page, choose **Additional domain controller**. 6. On the **Network Credentials** page, log on as administrator, type your domain name, and choose **Next**. 7. Accept the defaults on each of the following pages: Additional Domain Controller, Database and Log Location, Shared System Volume, and choose **Next**. 8. Leave the **Restore Mode Administrator Password** page blank, and choose **Next**. 9. On the **Summary** page, choose **Next**. 10. The wizard will now configure **Active Directory**. 11. Choose **Finish** and **Restart Now** to restart Windows 2000.

If you want to...	Then do this...
Set a computer as a Global Catalog server	1. Open **Active Directory Sites and Services**: choose **Start**, **Programs**, **Administrative Tools**, and then select **Active Directory Sites and Services**. 2. In the console tree, right-click **NTDS Settings**. Sites - your applicable site Servers - your applicable server 3. Choose **Properties**. 4. On the **General** tab, choose the **Global Catalog Server** check box.

Lesson 5 Activities

1. You will design a domain structure for a large, international trading company (MyCompany) that has corporate offices in Houston, Texas, with six different regional offices in various parts of the world and 42,000 employees.

   MyCompany has a Web site managed by the Information Technology (IT) group in Texas. The domain name that they have registered is MyCompany.com. There is very little travel between regions. However, users often need to access files and services located in different offices. Each region has its own IT group responsible for administering user accounts, network security and managing their own servers.

   While each region has high-speed links between offices in the same region, MyCompany wants to limit the traffic on the slower Wide Area Network (WAN) between regions to maximize bandwidth for critical applications. The company plans to implement IPSec and Kerberos group policies in Active Directory. Each region will have different requirements because of the specific needs of the local offices and because of different security requirements in different countries. These policies will be implemented at the local level.

   A small group of administrators in the corporate office will need to have security over the entire network to solve critical problems and audit company-wide security.

   To plan a domain tree structure:

   a. What domain name will be used for the root of the Active Directory Forest?

   b. Can MyCompany use a single domain for the enterprise (why or why not)?

   c. If multiple domains are used, what factors affect where domain boundaries are defined?

      - The number of Users.

      - The speed of the WAN between the locations.

      - The volume of changes to Active Directory information at a location.

      - The desired delegation of administrative authority.

      - The desired use of domain wide policies.

   d. MyCompany has decided to use multiple domains to limit the amount of replication traffic across the WAN. Should domain boundaries be determined by location (regions) or by company organization (divisions or departments)? Explain your answer.

   e. Does this create a contiguous or non-contiguous namespace? Explain your answer.

2. Explain the benefit to using trees.

3. Describe why you would use cross-link trusts.

4. What processes need to be taken into consideration when implementing trees in a forest?

5. There are three pieces of information that all the domains within a single- domain share. Describe these.

6. You have a requirement to allow users to access resources in an Active Directory of a different forest. What should you do?

7. You can create a cross-link shortcut trust between mid-level domains in two domain trees. What would the purpose of this be?

8. Replication is one of the benefits of Active Directory. Explain how this functions in a domain.

9. Transitive trusts are created by default between a child and its parent in an Active Directory forest. How does this type of trust impact authentication?

10. Based on what you know about the trusts that exist in a forest, from which domains can your computer authenticate users?

Answers to Lesson 5 Activities

1.
   a. MyCompany.com

   b. Multiple domains are needed to use IPSec and Kerberos policies and in order to localize replication of directory data within the regions.

   c. All of the listed factors can play a role in determining domain boundaries and in optimizing replication of domain information. The use of different domain-wide policies *requires* separate domains. It is more important to use domains as administrative boundaries than to use domain boundaries to enhance directory service performance.

   d. Domain boundaries should be set by region (rather than by divisions and departments). This optimizes replication of domain information using high-speed WAN links in each region. Divisions and departments could be spread geographically, and the current network infrastructure could cause latency issues.

   e. A contiguous namespace. All domains within a single tree share a hierarchical naming structure. The first domain in a tree is called the root of the tree. Additional domains in the same tree are called child domains. The domain name of a child domain is the relative name of that child domain; it is added to the beginning of the parent name.

2. There are a number of advantages to placing domains in a tree. All domains within an Active Directory share a common directory schema, configuration information, and global catalog. The first and most useful is that all the members of the tree have Kerberos transitive trusts with its parent and all its children. These transitive trusts mean that any user or group in a domain tree can be granted access to any object in the entire tree. This also means that a single logon can be used at any workstation in the domain tree.

3. A trust path is the series of domain trust relationships that must be traversed by security to pass authentication requests between any two domains. Computing and traversing a trust path between domain trees in a complex tree or forest can take time. This time can be reduced by creating cross-link trusts.

   Cross-link trusts are two-way transitive trusts that enable you to shorten the path. You create a cross-link trust between domains in the same tree or forest. You can create a cross-link trust between mid-level domains within a domain or between two domain trees to shorten the trust path between two domains in a forest and optimize the authentication process.

4. When implementing trees in a forest, the following processes need to be taken into consideration:

   The DNS name of the new tree must be determined. Each tree has a distinct DNS domain name. When you have chosen the name, you can create the new domain. Two domain controllers at a minimum are required for fault tolerance.

   The organization of a domain is defined in the tree. This can include determining if additional domains in the tree may be necessary and determining which domains would be child domains.

   Trees are added to a forest, when you use the Active Directory Installation Wizard to promote a domain controller and use the Create New Domain Tree in an Existing Forest option. You need to identify the root domain of the initial tree in the forest. This establishes a trust between the new tree's initial domain and the root domain of the forest.

5. All domains within an Active Directory tree share a common directory schema, configuration information, and global catalog.

6. To allow any sort of access between forests, you must create one-way explicit trusts between domains of different Active Directory directories.

7. Before an account can be granted access to resources by a domain controller of another domain, Windows 2000 must determine whether the domain containing the desired resources (target domain) has a trust relationship with the domain in which the account is located (source domain).

   To make this determination for two domains in a forest, Windows 2000 computes a trust path between the DCs for these source and target domains. A trust path is the series of domain trust relationships that must be traversed by Windows 2000 security to pass authentication requests between any two domains. Computing and traversing a trust path between domain trees in a complex forest can take time, which can be reduced with shortcut trusts.

   Cross-link or shortcut trusts are two-way transitive trusts that enable you to shorten the path in a complex forest. You explicitly create cross-link trusts between Windows 2000 domains in the same forest. This kind of trust is a performance optimization and shortens the trust path for authentication purposes. You can create multiple shortcut trusts between domains in a forest.

8. A replication service distributes directory data across a network. All domain controllers in a domain participate in replication and contain a complete copy of all directory information for their domain. Any change to directory data is replicated to all DCs in the domain.

9. Users from the trusted domain can authenticate in the trusting domain, and users from the trusting domain can authenticate in the trusted domain.

10. It can authenticate users from all the domains that have joined the forest, because the trusts between all of the domains are transitive.

Lesson 5 Quiz

These questions test your knowledge of features, vocabulary, procedures, and syntax.

1. In a domain tree, what administration privileges do administrators have?

   A. Domain administrators in a parent domain do not automatically apply to child domains.

   B. As each domain is related to the one above and the one below, domain administrators at a higher level automatically have a relationship with the one below.

   C. Any domain administrator has all rights to all domains.

   D. Domain administrators cannot cross domain boundaries to manage other domains without explicit permissions.

2. Which of the following choices best describes a forest?

   A. A collection of one or more Active Directory trees, organized as peers and connected by two-way transitive trust relationships between the root domains of each.

   B. A collection of one or more Active Directory trees that share information, a common configuration, schema, and global catalog.

   C. A collection of one or more Active Directory trees with a separate naming hierarchy based on different DNS root names.

   D. A collection of one or more Active Directory trees that are made up of different business divisions and want to share information.

3. In which instances should you consider creating multiple trees within a single forest?

   A. When domains need to be administered separately.

   B. When you want to maintain multiple distinct DNS names and facilitate, but tightly control, partner resource access.

   C. When you wish to reduce replication traffic.

   D. When you want to control hardware costs.

4. What is true about the Enterprise Admins group?

   A. To control naming, only members of the Enterprise Admins group can add domains to a tree. To create a new domain, you promote a server to be the first domain controller in the new domain. During active Directory installation on the new DC, you must choose to join the existing tree and then use the **Create New Child Domain** option to add domains to a tree.

   B. The parent-child relationship between domains in a domain tree is a naming relationship only. Administrators in a parent domain can automatically create child domains.

   C. Members of the Enterprise Admins group can add a new domain using the NTSUTIL command-line utility. Administrators who are not part of the Enterprise Admins group can then create a domain controller but cannot create a new name for the domain.

   D. Multiple-domain trees within a single forest do not form a contiguous namespace; they have noncontiguous DNS domain names. Although trees in a forest do not share a namespace, a forest does have a single root domain, called the forest root domain. The forest root domain is the first domain created in a forest. The two forest-wide predefined groups—Enterprise administrators and Schema administrators—reside in this domain.

5. Why would you want to create a cross-linked trust?

   A. So that any user or group in a domain tree can be granted access to any object.

   B. In order to use Lightweight Directory Access Protocol (LDAP) to locate objects.

   C. To shorten the search path in a complex forest.

   D. For performance optimization and because it shortens the trust path for authentication purposes.

6. Which of the following choices best describes a domain trust?

   A. A relationship established between two domains that allows users in one domain to be authenticated in another domain.

   B. The process by which the system validates the user's logon information.

   C. All domain trust relationships have only two domains in the relationship, the trusting domain and the trusted domain.

   D. Two-way, one-way, transitive and non-transitive.

7. Which of the following choices best describes a child domain?

   A. Domains located in the namespace tree directly beneath another domain name.

   B. A directory (logical grouping of related files) within another directory.

   C. Domains located in the namespace tree directly above other derivative domain names

   D. The object in which another object resides.

8. What type of query process does Windows 2000 use to find things?

   A. Transitive trust

   B. DNS

   C. Cross-link trust

   D. LDAP

9. Which of the following statements about forests is not correct?

   A. Numerous domain trees within a forest do not form an adjoining namespace. Although trees in a forest do not share a namespace, a forest does have a single root domain. The forest root domain is the first domain created in the forest.

   B. A forest is a distributed database made up of many partial databases spread across multiple computers. The forest's database partitions are defined by domains, that is, a forest consists of one or more domains.

   C. You can narrowly delegate administrative authority for individual organizational units as well as for individual domains, which reduces the number of administrators needed with wide administrative authority.

   D. The root domain of each domain tree in the forest establishes a transitive trust relationship This establishes trust across all the domain trees in the forest.

10. Which of the following would be the correct naming hierarchy for this figure?

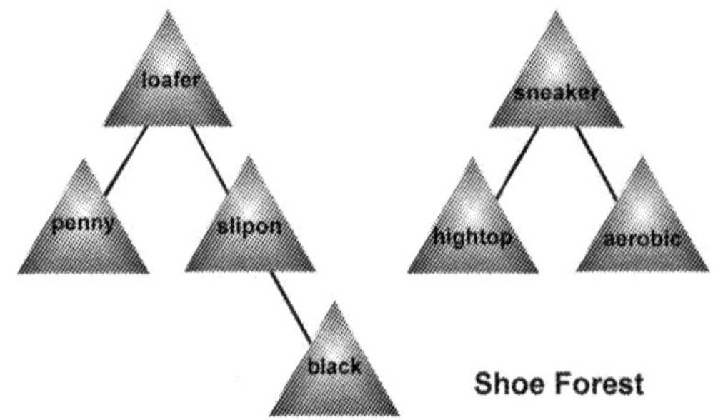

A. Black.hightop.sneaker.com

B. Black.slipon.loafer.com

C. Black.penny.loafer.com

D. Black.aerobic.loafer.com

Answers to Lesson 5 Quiz

1. Answers A and D are correct. The parent-child relationship between domains in a domain tree is a naming relationship and a trust relationship only. Each domain can maintain administrative control of its own hardware.

   Therefore, answers B and C are incorrect.

2. Answers A and B are correct. This sharing of data and the trust relationships between their roots, differentiate a forest from a collection of unrelated trees.

   Answer C is partly correct. The DNS name of the first domain in a tree identifies that particular tree. This name is unique in a forest and separates the trees in the forest. Each tree forms a separate naming hierarchy that is based on different DNS root domain names; the forest itself is identified by the DNS name of the initial tree that was created in the forest.

   Answer D is incorrect. It does not describe a forest, but it is one of the reasons why you would want to create a forest of different trees.

3. Answer B is correct.

   Answer A is incorrect. When domains need to be administered separately, you have a reason to consider a multiple-domain model.

   Answer C is incorrect. Reduction of replication traffic is not a reason to consider a multiple-domain model.

   Answer D is incorrect. Hardware costs are a reason to keep everything in a single domain.

4. Answer A is correct. To control naming, only members of the Enterprise Admins group can add domains to a tree. To create a new domain, you promote a server to be the first domain controller in the new domain. During Active Directory installation on the new DC, you must choose to join the existing tree and then use the **Create New Child Domain** option to add domains to a tree.

   Answer C is correct. Members of the Enterprise Admins group can add a new domain using the NTSUTIL command-line utility. Administrators who are not part of the Enterprise Admins group can then create a domain controller but cannot create a new name for the domain.

   Answer D is correct. Multiple-domain trees within a single forest do not form a contiguous namespace; they have non-contiguous DNS domain names. Although trees in a forest do not share a namespace, a forest does have a single root domain, called the forest root domain. The forest root domain is the first domain created in a forest. The two forest-wide predefined groups— Enterprise administrators and Schema administrators—reside in this domain.

   Answer B is incorrect. The parent-child relationship between domains in a domain tree is both a naming relationship and a trust relationship. Administrators in a parent domain do not automatically apply to child domains.

5. Answers C and D are correct. Cross-link or shortcut trusts are two-way transitive trusts that enable you to shorten the path in a complex forest. You explicitly create cross-link trusts between Windows 2000 domains in the same forest. This kind of trust is a performance optimization and shortens the trust path for authentication purposes.

   Answer A is not correct. It relates to trees not forests. All the members of the tree have Kerberos transitive trusts with its parent and all its children. These transitive trusts also mean that any user or group in a domain tree can be granted access to any object in the entire tree. This also means that a single logon can be used at any workstation in the domain tree.

Answer B is not correct. It relates to trees not forests. The LDAP search begins in the domain where the search was initiated. Because each domain is aware of all of the other domains in the tree, the LDAP query can be referred from domain to domain until the query is resolved. Although each domain is aware of other trees in the forest, the maximum scope of LDAP referrals is the current tree.

6. Answers A, C and D are correct. A domain trust is a relationship established between two domains that allows users in one domain to be authenticated in another domain. All domain trust relationships have only two domains in the relationship, the trusting domain and the trusted domain. Domain trusts can be: two-way, one-way, transitive and non-transitive.

   Answer B is incorrect. Authentication is the process by which the system validates the user's logon information.

7. Answer A is correct. A child domain is located in the namespace tree directly beneath another domain name (the parent domain).

   Answer B is incorrect. A child directory is a logical grouping of related files within another directory.

   Answer C is incorrect. A domain located in the namespace tree directly above other derivative domain names is a parent domain.

   Answer D is incorrect. An object in which another object resides is a parent object.

8. Answer D is correct. LDAP (Lightweight Directory Access Protocol) is the primary access protocol for Active Directory.

   Answer A is incorrect. A transitive trust is a two-way relationship between domains in a forest.

   Answer B is incorrect. DNS is the Domain Name System, a hierarchical distributed database. DNS is the namespace used on the Internet to translate computer and service names into TCP/IP addresses. Active Directory uses DNS as its location service.

Answer C is incorrect. Cross-link trusts are two-way transitive trusts that enable you to shorten the path for authentication purposes. You create a cross-link trust between domains in the same tree or forest.

9. Answers A, B and D are correct.

   Answer C is incorrect. It is a management goal of a domain.

10. Answer B is correct. You must follow standard DNS naming structures.

    Answers A, C and D are incorrect. They show incorrect naming structures.

Lesson 6

Microsoft Active Directory Connector (MSADC)

Maintaining directories on both Microsoft Windows 2000 and Exchange Server can be cumbersome, time-consuming, costly, and difficult to manage. Microsoft now provides a tool, Microsoft Active Directory Connector, to manage this process.

Active Directory Connector (ADC) provides a method for replicating a hierarchy of directory objects between the Microsoft Exchange Server version 5.5 directory and the Microsoft Windows 2000 Server Active Directory. It also provides an efficient migration path for upgrading to future versions of Exchange. Additionally, it enables administrators to eliminate redundant steps by providing drag-and-drop synchronization services between the following products and services:

- Microsoft Exchange Server v5.0 and v5.5
- Other e-mail and Lightweight Directory Access Protocol (LDAP)-compliant directories
- Novell Directory Services (NDS)

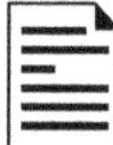

Note: Administrators can use Microsoft Directory Synchronization Services (MSDSS) to synchronize changes between Active Directory and NDS.

In comparison with former methods, Active Directory Connector makes it much easier for the administrator to maintain multiple directories, synchronize those directories, and perform other administrative tasks.

After completing this lesson, you should have a better understanding of the following topics:

- Active Directory Connector (ADC) structure
- Active Directory Connector (ADC) installation
- Connection agreement configuration
- Container synchronization
- ADC troubleshooting
- Recommendations

Active Directory Connector Structure

ADC is built upon the following structural components:

- Microsoft Windows 2000 Server
- Active Directory Connector (ADC)
- LDAP 3.0
- Exchange Server

Microsoft Windows 2000 Server

Before installing ADC, you need to consider the advantages and disadvantages of the installation options.

Table 6.1 Installation Options

Option	Advantage	Disadvantage
Domain controller	Reduces amount of network bandwidth consumed	Synchronizing large directories can consume considerable domain controller resources
Member server	Best for large directories	Increases requirements for network bandwidth

Active Directory Connector and LDAP 3.0

Active Directory accomplishes communication between Active Directory and the Exchange Directory by using LDAP 3.0.

Tip: ADC must be able to open a Transmission Control Protocol (TCP) port (389 by default) between itself and the servers defined in its Connection Agreements. Keep this in mind when you consider firewall and router configurations.

Exchange Server

No additional Exchange components are needed, since Exchange 5.5 natively supports LDAP 3.0.

Establishing and Maintaining Synchronization

Throughout this lesson, you will learn about a concept called synchronization. This does not necessarily mean replication. Two directories are synchronized when their databases contain equivalent, though not necessarily identical, content.

The Windows 2000 and Exchange Server directories must be synchronized with each other on a regular basis in an accurate and timely manner. You configure this synchronization between directories by defining *Connection Agreements* that are managed by the ADC service.

Connection Agreements

These agreements establish and maintain synchronization between containers within Active Directory and Exchange site containers. You can define multiple Exchange recipient containers to synchronize with a single Active Directory container, and you can define multiple Active Directory containers to synchronize with a single Exchange recipient container.

You can configure each Connection Agreement to synchronize multiple object types, or a single object type. For example, you can create two Connection Agreements that synchronize a single Active Directory container holding groups and users with two separate Exchange containers—one holding groups and the other holding users.

Starting and Stopping the MSADC Service

The administrator can start or stop Active Directory Connector service like any other service. It is displayed in Task Manager as MSADC. A Microsoft Management Console (MMC) snap-in can also be installed with the service. You use this snap-in to configure the service and Connection Agreements.

Active Directory Connector Installation

Windows 2000 has easy to use screens to facilitate installing the ADC. This is a straightforward process as long as you have gathered the pertinent information before you begin the process.

Obtaining Information before the Installation

Before you begin, you must ascertain the following:

- Locate your Windows 2000 CD
- Decide on an installation location for the ADC binary files; the default location is *systemroot*\Program Files\ADC
- Decide on a service account (ADC uses a service account and password); the installation program will assign this account to the **Logon As Service**, **Restore Files and Directories**, **Act as Part of the Operating System**, and **Audit Permissions**
- Ensure that Microsoft Exchange Server is running on your computer
- Know the name of your Microsoft Exchange Server
- Have the information on your organization's specific needs for connecting to and from the Microsoft Exchange Server

Tip: Microsoft Exchange Server must be running before you can fully configure ADC.

Installing the ADC

Note: ADC is not installed by default during Windows 2000 Server setup.

Before starting to install the ADC (Figure 6.1), close any applications you are running to avoid damaging system files or shared files, and follow these steps:

1. Insert the Windows 2000 Server CD into your CD-ROM drive.
2. In the **Windows 2000 CD ROM** window, choose **Browse This CD**.
3. Open the **Valueadd** folder, open the **MSFT** folder, open the **Mgmt** folder, open the **ADC** folder, and then double-click **SETUP.EXE**.
4. If your computer has Autoload turned off, go to My Computer to browse the CD to locate your CD drive.

Note: If this is a new ADC installation, the wizard skips the **Add/Remove/Reinstall** screen and displays the **Component Selection** screen.

Active Directory Connector Wizard

Figure 6.1 Opening Screen for Active Directory Connector

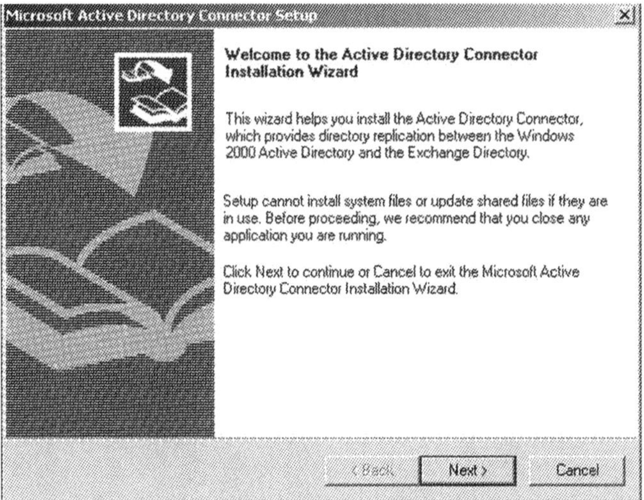

Choose an Installation Type

During this step, if the ADC Installation Wizard detects a previous installation of any ADC component, the ADC Installation Wizard adds, removes, or reinstalls those components.

You have the following three installation options to choose from:

- To add new ADC components or remove installed ADC components (Figure 6.2), choose **Add/Remove**. Select this option to display the **Component Selection** dialog box.
- To repeat the last installation and restore missing files and settings, choose **Reinstall**.
- To remove all previously installed ADC components, choose **Remove All**.

Warning: Choosing **Remove All** deletes the Connection Agreements hosted on this server. If you wish to preserve them, it is best to re-host the Connection Agreements on another server with ADC.

Figure 6.2 Component Selection Screen

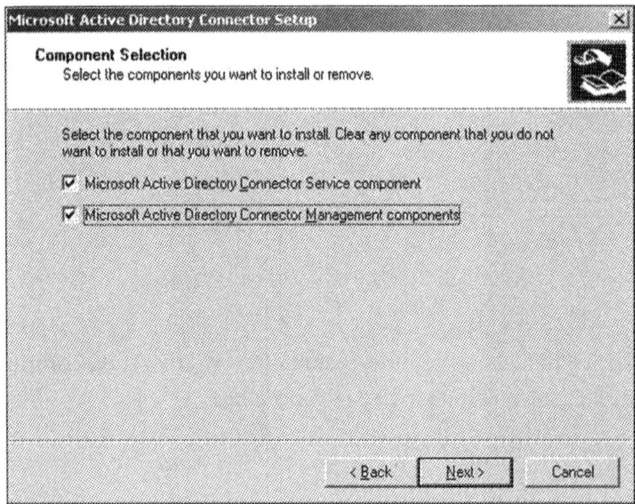

ADC contains the Active Directory Connector Sites and Services and the Active Directory Connector Management components. You should install only a single instance of the Active Directory Connector Sites and Services on the computer running Windows 2000 Server (Figure 6.3). However, you can install as many instances of the Active Directory Connector Management snap-in as are needed to provide adequate management.

1. Choose the **Microsoft Active Directory Connector Management components** check box to install the ADC Management components, or clear the check box to remove them.

Figure 6.3 Installation Location Screen

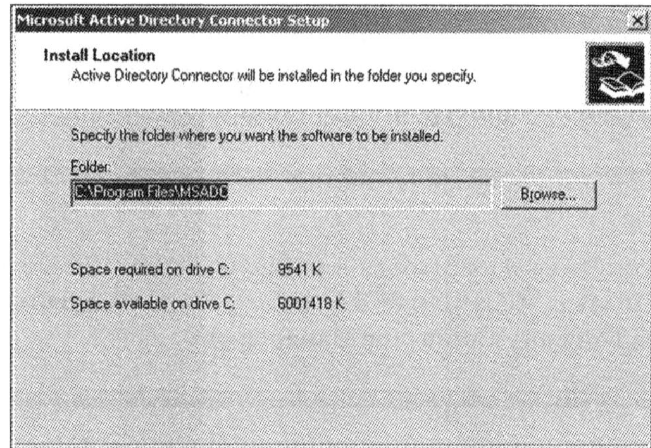

2. In the **Install Location** screen, specify a directory in which to install ADC. The default path is %SystemDrive%\Program Files\MSADC.

Note: The setup calculates the amount of space required to install ADC and the amount of space available on the current drive. If sufficient space is not available, ADC cannot be installed.

3. ADC requires a valid Windows 2000 Server account name and password.

4. In **Account name**, type the domain name and account name in the form <*Domain*>\<*Name*>, or choose **Browse** to select an account name from the list of accounts available on the domain controller for this computer.
5. In **Account password**, type the password.

Note: Workstations that you use to administer Active Directory users with mail attributes will need to have the Active Directory Connector management components installed. You can run Active Directory Setup to install just these components.

You can manage ADC using the Active Directory Connector Management snap-in in MMC. To open Active Directory Connector Management after it is installed, choose **Start**, **Programs**, **Administrative Tools**, and then select **Active Directory Connector Management**.

Tip: For more information about using ADC, in the console, choose the **Action** menu, and then select **Help**.

Connection Agreement Configuration

Connection agreements define the relationship between Active Directory and the Exchange Directory. In Active Directory, you can use Organizational Units (OUs) to group information. OUs are logical containers in which objects such as users, groups, and computers are categorized. For maximum scalability and reduced administration, you can organize your Exchange objects, such as mailboxes and distribution lists, into recipient containers that mirror the OU structure you create in Windows 2000 Active Directory.

For example, in Windows 2000 Active Directory, you would configure four Organizational Units: internal users, guests, groups, and computers. Then in Exchange, you would create only three recipient containers: internal users, guests, and groups, intentionally not creating a recipient container to correspond with the Windows 2000 computer's OU. Next, place all of your regular internal corporate users in the internal users container. Finally, place your custom recipients in the guests containers and your distribution lists in the groups container.

With this infrastructure in place, you can set up three Connection Agreements between the corresponding Windows and Exchange OUs. If you configure your Connection Agreement to replicate from Windows to Exchange, new internal users created in Windows would automatically be replicated to the correct Exchange recipient container.

Note: Windows 2000 has many group membership restrictions. For example, domain local groups cannot be members of global groups. If you do not respect the Windows 2000 limitations in Exchange 5.5, then the membership cannot replicate to Windows 2000.

To configure a Connection Agreement, follow these steps:

1. On the **Start** menu, choose **Programs**, **Administrative Tools**, and then select **Active Directory Connector Management**.
2. In the console tree, choose **Active Directory Connector**.
3. On the **Action** menu, choose **New**, and then select **Connection Agreement** to display the **Properties** dialog box.

Selecting Synchronization Direction and Service Location

The administrator has two choices for synchronization and two choices for service location. You have the following possibilities for synchronization direction:

- One-way
- Two-way

Two-Way Synchronization

This allows synchronization to flow both ways—changes in either directory are to be replicated to its directory synchronization partner. You should select this option when management will be divided between Active Directory administration and Exchange administration.

Note: During a two-way synchronization, the Windows directory is first updated with Exchange information.

From Exchange to Windows Synchronization

This allows only changes made in Exchange to be replicated to Active Directory. You should choose this option when you want all object administration to be done in Exchange.

From Windows to Exchange Synchronization

This allows only changes made in Active Directory to be replicated to Exchange. You should select this option when you want all object administration to be done in Active Directory.

Service Location

The service location is where the ADC service will reside.

Choosing a Synchronization Formula

When Active Directory becomes relatively static, after the upgrade from Microsoft Windows NT 4.0 and the integration with Exchange, only small amounts of data will be passed between directories. Changes to the Exchange Directory that are synchronized to Active Directory cause slightly more traffic than changes to Active Directory that are synchronized to Exchange. Synchronization traffic patterns can be summarized in the two following formulas:

- Active Directory synchronization formula
- Exchange synchronization formula

Active Directory Synchronization Formula

51 kilobytes (KB) bind + 14 KB per changed object

Exchange Synchronization Formula

61 KB bind + 26 KB per changed object

Configuring a Bridgehead Server

Bridgehead servers (Figure 6.4) are the contact point for exchange of directory information between sites. The Active Directory Connector service uses the directories on the bridgehead servers for synchronization between the directories. The administrator must define a bridgehead server in both directories for each Connection Agreement. In Active Directory, the bridgehead server must be a domain controller. In Exchange, the bridgehead server can be any Exchange Server.

Figure 6.4 Bridgehead Server Configuration Screen

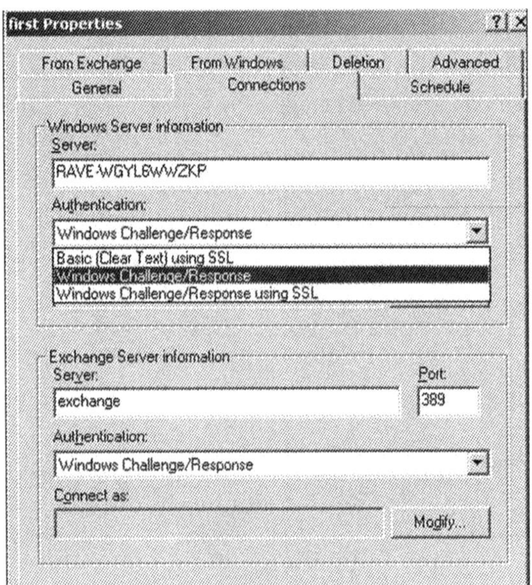

To configure the bridgehead server, choose the **Connections** tab. For each directory, you specify the server name, authentication method, and permissions account.

If the bridgehead server will be writing changes to this directory, the permissions account defined for each bridgehead server will only need Write permissions for its directory. For example, if you have selected two-way synchronization, the permissions accounts for both directories need Write permissions on their own directories. If you have selected one-way synchronization, only the permissions account for the target directory needs Write permissions.

Polling Bridgehead Servers

The polling process looks for changes made in each directory which are defined in the Connection Agreement. By default, polling takes place approximately every five seconds, which can result in an excessive load for some environments. To reduce server and network loads, set the following entries and values for the registry key

HKEY_LOCAL_Machine\System\CurrentControlSet\Services\MSADC\ Parameters:

Set the name as Sync Sleep Delay (Secs); type "**DWORD**"; and in the data field, specify the number of seconds you want the process to wait between cycles.

Exchange and Active Directory poll each other at regular intervals for configuration changes that affect partner relationships. The following events reset the polling interval:

- Adding a replica
- Deleting a replica
- Adding a connection
- Deleting a connection
- Changing a schedule
- Changing a file or folder filter

Container Synchronization

The administrator must specify the source and destination containers from each directory participating in the Connection Agreement. Use the **From Exchange** and **From Windows** tabs to configure the following:

- Which containers to poll for changes
- Which container receives the changes
- What type of objects to synchronize

The **From Windows** tab (Figure 6.5) also allows you to filter the objects that are replicated from Active Directory to Exchange based on the Discretionary Access Control Lists (DACLs) set on those objects.

Figure 6.5 From Windows Screen

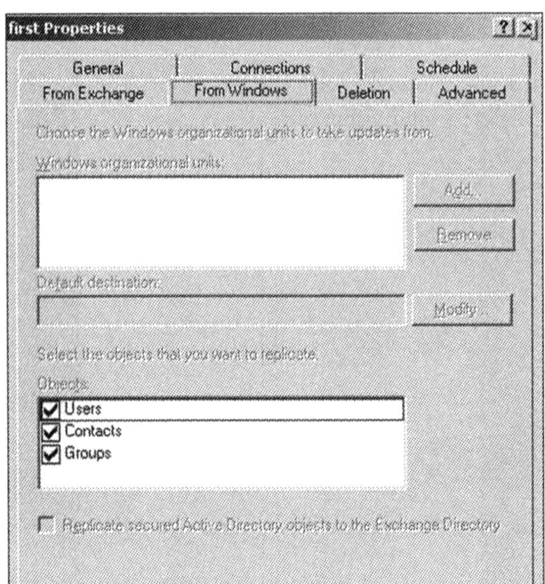

Selecting Source and Destination Containers

Once all objects in each container have been synchronized, changes to the object in one directory will be synchronized to the other directory if permitted by the synchronization direction setting. For example, if the **From Exchange** tab (Figure 6.6) specifies that two Exchange recipient containers will synchronize to a default destination in Active Directory and a synchronized custom recipient is changed in Active Directory, that change will synchronize back to the Exchange recipient container that hosts that custom recipient.

Figure 6.6 From Exchange Screen

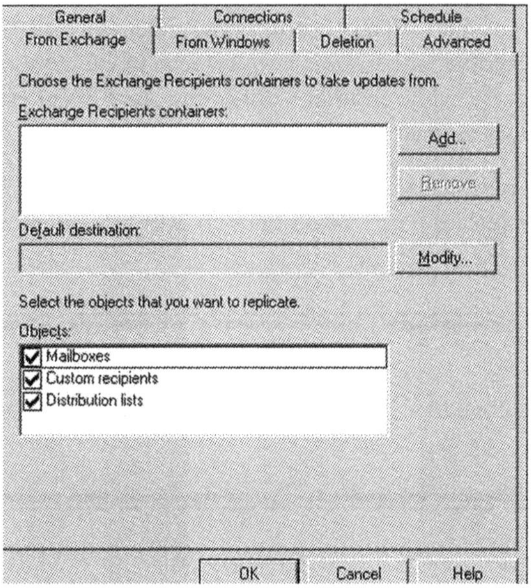

Table 6.2 shows the mapping between Active Directory objects and Exchange objects.

Table 6.2 Mapping between Objects

Active Directory Object	Exchange Object
User	Mailbox
Group	Distribution List
Contact	Custom Recipient

Synchronizing a Schedule

Although only one instance of the ADC can be installed on a single computer running Windows 2000 Server, multiple Connection Agreements can be established. Each Connection Agreement can be configured to perform unique replication tasks. For example, one Connection Agreement can continuously update the Windows 2000 Server Active Directory, while another Connection Agreement can update the Windows contacts to the Exchange Directory daily at 6:00 P.M.

You can set up individual Connection Agreements to perform replication on a defined schedule. You must determine the most appropriate times for each replication process. A network with a large number of users may require more frequent replication than a smaller network.

Note: Some networks may require specific objects to be replicated more frequently than other objects.

Following are some of the situations you must consider when planning a replication schedule:

- If you are replicating more than 500 users or mailboxes, you can improve performance by setting up multiple Connection Agreements to replicate different objects at different times
- If you make daily changes to either directory and do not need the changes to appear in the other directory until the next day, you should schedule replication nightly
- If there are times during the day when other replication occurs on either computer involved in the Connection Agreement, schedule the Connection Agreement around these times
- If directory manipulation is commonly done at a specific time or times of the week, customize the replication to occur soon after the changes are made and only after the changes are made

Use the Connection Agreement **Schedule** tab (Figure 6.7) to establish a replication schedule for each Connection Agreement.

Figure 6.7 Schedule Screen

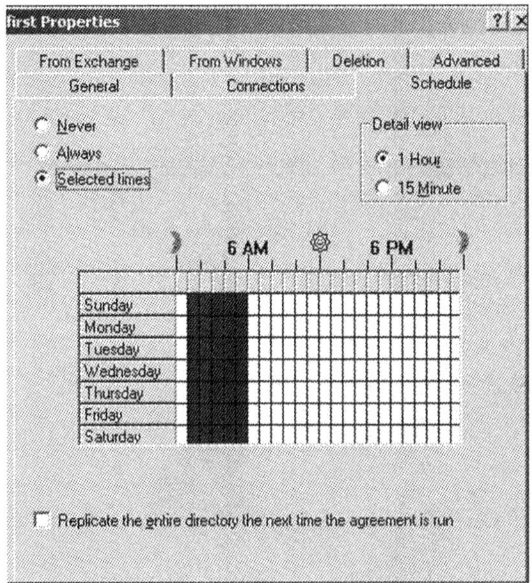

Complete the following steps to set a synchronization schedule:

1. In the details pane, double-click the Connection Agreement for which you want to schedule replication.

2. On the **Schedule** tab, choose a time specification. **Never** disables the Connection Agreement. **Always** enables automatic replication whenever the source directory changes. **Selected times** configures replication times.

3. To only replicate changes to the directory, clear the **Replicate the entire directory the next time the agreement is run** check box. If you want to replicate the entire directory, choose this option. The first time replication occurs, the entire directory is replicated by default.

4. For example, to schedule replication for every Wednesday at 6:00 P.M., choose **Selected times**, and then choose the schedule grid in the box that corresponds to 6:00 P.M. vertically, and Wednesday horizontally.

Tip: Under **Detail view**, choose **1 hour** to display the schedule in 1-hour intervals, or **15 Minutes** to display the schedule in 15-minute intervals.

Synchronizing Object Deletions

By default, objects deleted in one directory are not deleted in the partner directory. Instead, a record of the deletion is stored in a file on the server running the ADC service. The default location for this file is:

Systemroot\System32\MSADC*Connection Agreement Name**Filename*

Exchange Server deletions are recorded in the EX55.CSV file, and Active Directory deletions are recorded in the NT5.LDF file.

If needed, you can override this default and choose to have the corresponding object deleted.

Warning: Consider the consequences before you decide to synchronize deletions. For example, you may not want to automatically delete an Exchange mailbox when its corresponding Active Directory object is deleted.

To synchronize deletions, choose the **Deletion** tab to view object deletions (Figure 6.8).

Figure 6.8 Object Deletions

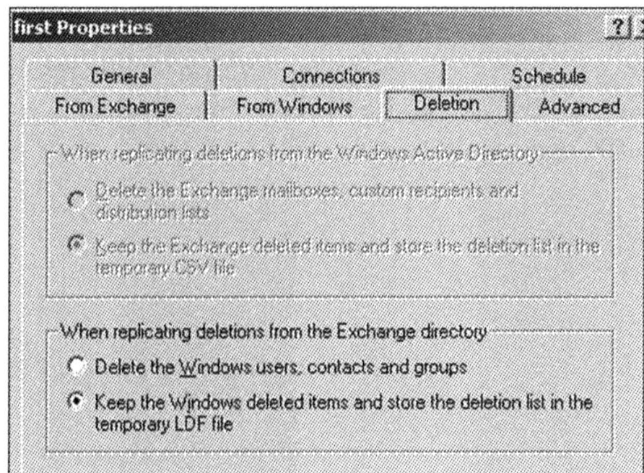

To replicate deletions from a Windows 2000 Server Active Directory to an Exchange Directory, choose one of the following methods for deleting the items:

Delete the Exchange mailbox—Choose this option to delete from the Exchange Directory any user account that was deleted in the Windows directory.

Keep the Exchange mailbox and store the deletion list in the temporary CSV file—Choose this option to store the list of deleted items in a common Comma-Separated Value (CSV) formatted file. Information is appended to this file as replication occurs. The log file is located in:

%SystemRoot%\Program Files\MSADC\MSADC\<*Connection Agreement name*>\ ex55.csv.

No checking or maintenance is performed on the LocalToRemote directory; therefore, you must ensure that adequate disk space is available for the file. If the file is no longer needed, you can remove it to increase the amount of space available on the disk.

To replicate deletions from an Exchange Directory to the Windows 2000 Server Active Directory, choose one of the following methods:

Delete the Windows account—Choose this option to delete from the Windows directory any user account that was deleted in the Exchange Directory.

Keep the Windows account and store the deletion list in the temporary LDF file—Choose this option to store the deletions performed in Exchange as a list of deletions in an LDF formatted file. Information will be appended to this file as replication occurs. The log file is located in: %SystemRoot%\Program Files\MSADC\MSADC\<*Connection Agreement name*>\ Win2000.ldf. No checking or maintenance is performed on the <*Connection Agreement name*> directory; therefore, you must ensure that adequate disk space is available for the file. If the file is no longer needed, you can remove it to increase the amount of space available on the disk.

Selecting Optimization Settings

Use the **Advanced** tab (Figure 6.9) to optimize your settings.

Figure 6.9 Advanced Tab Screen

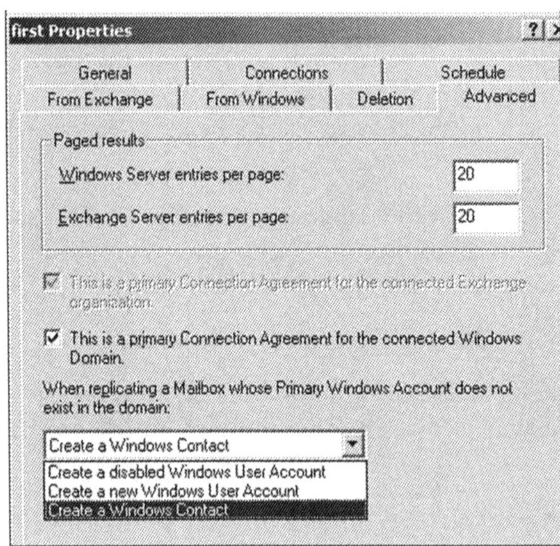

This screen lets you set the following options:

- Paged results
- Primary Connection Agreement for connected Exchange organization
- Primary Connection Agreement for connected Windows domain
- Options for replicating a mailbox whose primary Windows account does not exist in the domain

Paged Results

Here you can specify how many entries there are per page for synchronization. Following are the considerations for paged results:

- Larger page sizes provide more entries per page, thus require fewer requests
- Larger page sizes, on the other hand, require more memory
- The page size for Exchange should not exceed the LDAP search results specified in Exchange Server
- Setting the page size to zero will prevent synchronization from happening

Primary Connection Agreement for Connected Exchange Organization

Choose this option to specify which Connection Agreement will synchronize new Active Directory objects that are mail-enabled but do not have mailboxes. These objects are referred to as *non-homed.* These objects may be Active Directory mail-enabled contacts, groups, or users with e-mail addresses but no mailboxes. If this check box is not set, the Connection Agreement will not create any new objects in the Exchange Directory, but synchronization between existing objects will still occur.

If you have more than one Connection Agreement associated with a single Active Directory container, this primary Connection Agreement setting becomes very important. When you create a new non-homed object in the Active Directory container, the object will be synchronized to the Exchange recipient container specified as the primary Connection Agreement for the connected Exchange organization. If the Connection Agreements associated with the Active Directory container are both specified as primary Connection Agreements for the connected Exchange organization, then the non-homed object will synchronize to both Exchange recipient containers, creating duplicate Exchange objects.

Primary Connection Agreement for Connected Windows Domain

Choose this option to specify which Connection Agreement will synchronize new Exchange Directory objects to Active Directory. These new Exchange objects can be mailboxes, distribution lists, or custom recipients. If this check box is not selected, the Connection Agreement will not create any new objects in Active Directory, but synchronization between existing objects will still occur.

If you have more than one Connection Agreement associated with a single Exchange container, this primary Connection Agreement setting becomes very important. When you create a new object in an Exchange site recipient container, the object will be synchronized to the Active Directory container specified as the primary Connection Agreement for the connected Windows domain. If the Connection Agreements associated with the Exchange site recipient container are both specified as primary Connection Agreements for the connected Windows domain, then the object will synchronize to both Active Directory containers, creating duplicate Active Directory objects.

Options for Replicating a Mailbox Whose Primary Windows Account Does Not Exist in the Domain

This part of the screen provides a drop-down menu that lets you choose among the following options:

- Create a Windows contact
- Create a disabled Windows user account
- Create a new Windows user account

A mail-enabled contact is created by default. You may want to create a user object instead for those Microsoft Windows NT domains that are not scheduled for upgrade to Windows 2000.

Managing Directory Object Synchronization

ADC allows for centralized management of both Exchange and Active Directory objects. Depending on the synchronization direction of the Connection Agreement, you can manage synchronized objects from either Active Directory or Exchange Directory.

Managing Synchronization from Active Directory

You can manage Exchange recipient objects from Active Directory by using Active Directory Users and Computers. When the Active Directory Connector Management components are installed during ADC setup, mailbox-related property pages are added to the Active Directory Users and Computers console. The additional mailbox-related pages allow Active Directory administrators to manage the same mailbox attributes that can be managed by using the Exchange Administrator.

Even though mail recipients are administered from Active Directory, you must still manage the Exchange environment from the Exchange Administrator. This includes the management of queues, connectors, address book views, public folders, and monitors.

Note: Choose **Advanced Features** from Active Directory Users and Computers to see all the mailbox-related property pages.

Managing Synchronization from Exchange

You can manage additions, deletions, and changes to synchronized Active Directory objects in the Exchange Directory by using Exchange Administrator.

ADC Troubleshooting

When running ADC, you should monitor the activities of each Connection Agreement to ensure that proper directory replication is accomplished. Monitoring should be a part of regularly scheduled maintenance. Regular maintenance helps you keep directory replication performing optimally and can help you keep failures and errors to a minimum.

You perform maintenance by setting up the ADC diagnostic logging and monitoring in the Windows event log. You troubleshoot by reading and interpreting the ADC-related events written in the event log to determine appropriate repair activities. In addition, Performance Monitor counters can flag the need for additional resources.

Using Diagnostics Logging for Monitoring Events

ADC logs events to the application section of the event log. You can adjust the settings as follows:

Use the **Diagnostics Logging** tab on the **Active Directory Connector Properties** dialog box to change logging levels and choose logging categories for the Active Directory Connector service. Each logging category provides informational, warning, and error message types. Use the following procedure to configure diagnostic logging:

1. On the Start menu, choose **Programs**, **Administrative Tools**, and then select **Active Directory Connector Management** to start Microsoft Management Console.
2. In the left pane, highlight **Active Directory Connector**.
3. On the **Action** menu, choose **Properties** to view the **Active Directory Connector Properties** dialog box.
4. On the **Diagnostics Logging** tab, choose the logging category you want to configure, and then select the appropriate logging level from the **Category Logging Levels** list.

Table 6.3 describes the logging categories.

Table 6.3 Logging Categories

Category	Description
Replication	Messages indicating events that occurred during replication
Account management	Messages indicating events that occurred while attempting to write or delete an object during replication
Attribute mapping	Messages indicating events that occurred while mapping attributes between Active Directory and Exchange Directory
Service controller	Events that occurred while the service is started or stopped
LDAP	Events that occurred while accessing the directory using LDAP

The logging levels available are None, Minimum, Medium, and Maximum. These levels are described in Table 6.4.

Table 6.4 Logging Levels

Level	Description
None	This is the default logging level. Logs only critical events and error events, including starting and stopping the service and component installation.
Minimum	Logs events including the success or failure of adding or removing a user account, errors encountered when establishing Light Directory Access Protocol (LDAP) sessions, and errors updating the directory.
Medium	Logs events including those associated with the existence of specific objects in the directory and proxy error warnings.
Maximum	Logs all events and provides a complete record of the operation of the ADC service and the status of replication. Unless you are troubleshooting a problem, avoid using the Maximum logging level because it logs a large amount of information and can affect server performance.

Using Performance Monitor Counters

To start the Performance Monitor, take the following steps:

1. From the **Start** menu, choose **Programs**, **Administrative Tools**, and **Services**. Select **Performance Logs** and **Alerts**.
2. From ADC, choose the **MSADC performance** object. You can highlight each performance counter and choose **Explain** to view its definition.

To view the performance counters available for ADC, follow these steps:

1. Start **Performance Monitor**.
2. Choose the **Add button** on the toolbar to add counters.

You should also use existing network management tools to monitor network performance. You can observe the impact of Active Directory synchronization on your Exchange and Active Directory replication environments by using directory replication counters.

Technical Requirements and Recommendations

Planning an ADC implementation requires the following elements:

- Understanding deployment requirements and recommendations
- Examining test and production scenarios
- Choosing a scenario
- Additional deployment considerations

Ensuring a Successful Deployment

For a successful deployment of ADC, some features are required and some are merely recommended. All are desirable for maximizing the efficiency of the network.

Requirements

Observe the following technical requirements:

- Each Active Directory domain needs at least one ADC server and Connection Agreement
- The Exchange Server defined in the Connection Agreement must be running Exchange Server version 5.5
- Exchange Server 5.5 installed on a Windows 2000 Server requires Exchange Service Pack 2; to avoid TCP port contention when using Active Directory Connector with Exchange Server on Windows 2000, the Exchange Server LDAP port must be mapped to another port that does not conflict with Active Directory

Recommendations

Implementation of the following technical recommendations will facilitate a successful deployment:

Upgrade Primary Domain Controller (PDC)—Populate Active Directory with user accounts by upgrading the PDC to Windows 2000. Use ADC only to backfill directory data from the Exchange Directory to the pre-existing Active Directory accounts. This permits objects synchronized from Exchange to be mapped to security objects in Active Directory. It also prevents the creation of mail-enabled contacts in Active Directory for the Exchange objects. Such mail-enabled contacts would conflict with user objects when Microsoft Windows NT 4.0 accounts are migrated to Active Directory. Backup Domain Controllers (BDCs) need not be immediately upgraded.

Use connector servers—Connector servers are used to facilitate communications between Exchange sites with some Exchange implementations. If you have connector servers, use them as Exchange bridgehead servers for the Connection Agreement.

Place server hosting Active Directory Connector strategically—If possible, place the server hosting ADC on the same subnet as the Exchange Directory and Active Directory bridgehead. If ADC is being used in a Wide Area Network (WAN) environment, place it in a strategic location, such as the hub of a hub-and-spoke topology.

Plan carefully to avoid problems with Exchange recipient containers—Without careful planning, problems may occur with Exchange recipient containers that contain mailboxes associated with Active Directory accounts from multiple Active Directory domains. You may accidentally synchronize those mailboxes twice, through multiple Connection Agreements. This may cause multiple Active Directory objects for those mailboxes. You can avoid this by paying close attention to Connection Agreement direction and to primary Connection Agreement configuration.

Examining Test and Production Scenarios

Use ADC to evaluate your Active Directory design and Active Directory coexistence plan in your test environment. Your test environment should parallel your production environment by having the following elements:

- Multiple locations with suitable bandwidth between them
- Multiple servers and clients
- An Exchange Directory similar in size and complexity to your production directory

Your testing and evaluation should include performance monitoring, disaster recovery, and troubleshooting.

Tip: If you do not have a complete parallel test environment, here is a quick way to create one. You configure one-way Connection Agreements from your production Exchange Directory. This synchronizes Exchange Directory information from the production environment to the test environment. By using this method, you will create a test environment that will provide realistic replication and performance scenarios.

The following choices give you some possible test scenarios:

- Single-site, single-domain model scenario
- Single-site, multiple-domain model scenario
- Multiple-site, multiple-domain model scenario

Single-Site, Single-Domain Model Scenario

This model (Figure 6.10) contains a single Exchange site and a single Active Directory domain.

Figure 6.10 Single-Site, Single-Domain Model

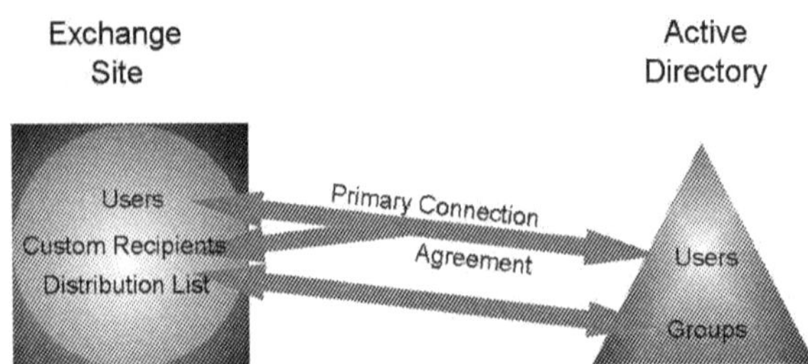

To configure a single-site, single-domain model, follow these guidelines:

- Configure a single Active Directory Connector
- Establish two Connection Agreements
- Synchronize Exchange users and custom recipients with the Active Directory users container.
- Synchronize the Distribution List recipient container with the Groups Organizational Unit (OU) in Active Directory

Table 6.5 Properties of the First Connection Agreement for a Single-Site, Single-Domain Scenario

Property	Value
Direction	Two-way
From Exchange	Exchange users and custom recipients container to Active Directory users
From Active Directory	Active Directory users to Exchange users recipient container
Primary Connection Agreement for the connected Exchange organization?	Yes
Primary Connection Agreement for the connected Active Directory domain?	Yes

Table 6.6 Properties of the Second Connection Agreement for a Single-Site, Single-Domain Scenario

Property	Value
Direction	Two-way
From Exchange	Exchange Distribution Lists to Active Directory Groups
From Active Directory	Active Directory Groups to Exchange Distribution Lists
Primary Connection Agreement for the connected Exchange organization?	Yes
Primary Connection Agreement for the connected Active Directory domain?	Yes

Single-Site, Multiple-Domain Model Scenario

This model (Figure 6.11) contains a single Exchange site and two Active Directory domains.

Figure 6.11 Single-Site, Multiple-Domain Model

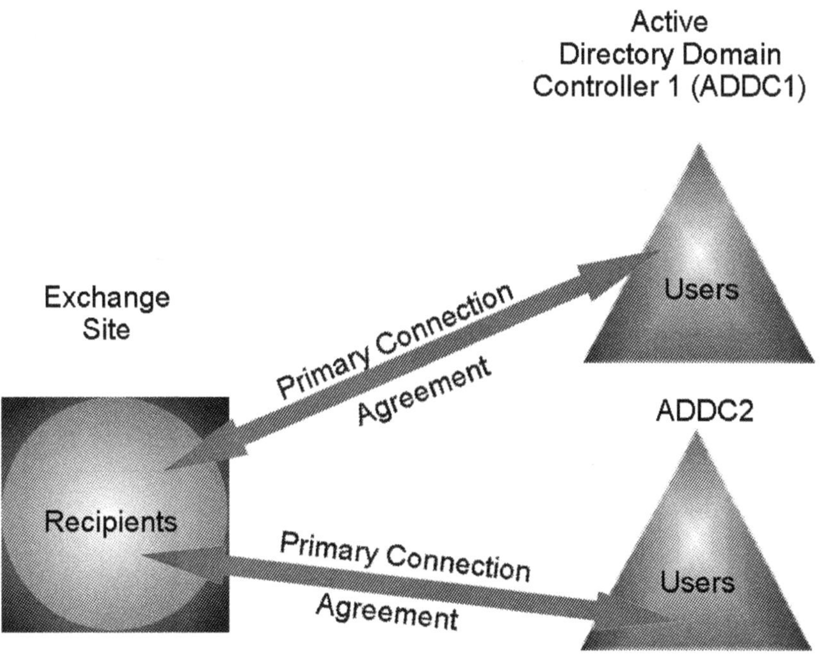

To configure a single-site, multiple-domain model, follow these guidelines:

- Configure a single Active Directory Connector
- Establish two Connection Agreements, one for each domain
- Ascertain that both Active Directory Domains and the Exchange site use only their default user and recipient containers
- Synchronize all of these containers
- Ascertain that the Exchange mailbox users are divided between both Active Directory domains

Table 6.7 Properties of the First Connection Agreement for a Single-Site, Multiple-Domain Scenario

Property	Value
Direction	Two-way
From Exchange	Exchange users and custom recipients to Active Directory users
From Active Directory	Active Directory users to Exchange users
Primary Connection Agreement for the connected Exchange organization?	Yes
Primary Connection Agreement for the connected Active Directory domain?	Yes

Table 6.8 Properties of the Second Connection Agreement for a Single-Site, Multiple-Domain Scenario

Property	Value
Direction	Two-way
From Exchange	Exchange recipient container to Active Directory users
From Active Directory	Active Directory users to Exchange recipient container
Primary Connection Agreement for the connected Exchange organization?	Yes
Primary Connection Agreement for the connected Active Directory domain?	Yes

Note: The configuration in this scenario will support the maintenance of separate Exchange and Active Directory administrative structures or consolidate most administration in Active Directory. All new Exchange objects will be synchronized across the first Connection Agreement.

Multiple-Site, Multiple-Domain Model Scenario

This model (Figure 6.12) contains a multiple Exchange site and multiple Active Directory domains.

Figure 6.12 Multiple-Site, Multiple-Domain Model

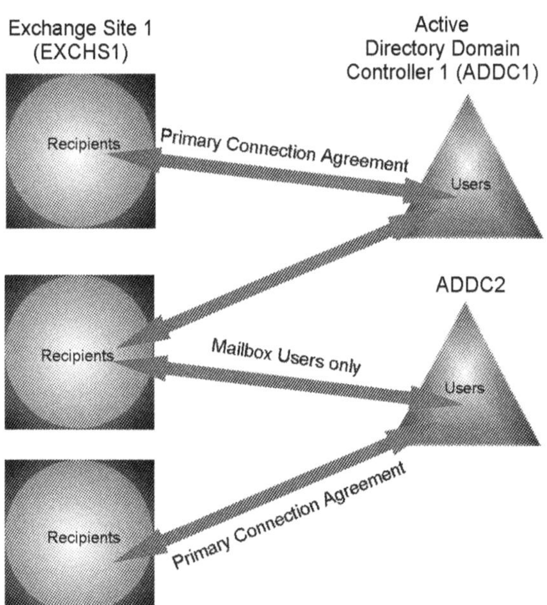

To configure a multiple-site, multiple-domain model, follow these guidelines:

- Ascertain that Exchange mailboxes in a given site are associated with Active Directory accounts in a given Active Directory domain (in the above model, the Exchange mailboxes of EXCH2 are associated with Active Directory accounts in either ADDC1 or ADDC2; mailboxes in EXCH1 are associated with Active Directory accounts from ADDC1; mailboxes in EXCH3 are associated with Active Directory accounts from ADDC2)
- Establish a single Active Directory Connector for each relationship between an Exchange site and a Windows 2000 domain
- Establish two Connection Agreements, one for each domain

Table 6.9 Properties of the First Connection Agreement for a Multiple-Site, Multiple-Domain Scenario

Property	Value
Direction	Two-way
From Exchange	Exchange recipient container to Active Directory users
From Active Directory	Active Directory users to Exchange recipient container
Primary Connection Agreement for the connected Exchange organization?	Yes
Primary Connection Agreement for the connected Active Directory domain?	Yes

Table 6.10 Properties of the Second Connection Agreement for a Multiple-Site, Multiple-Domain Scenario

Property	Value
Direction	Two-way
From Exchange	Exchange recipient container to Active Directory users (all objects)
From Active Directory	Active Directory users to Exchange recipient container
Primary Connection Agreement for the connected Exchange organization?	No
Primary Connection Agreement for the connected Active Directory domain?	Yes

Table 6.11 Properties of the Third Connection Agreement for a Multiple-Site, Multiple-Domain Scenario

Property	Value
Direction	Two-way
From Exchange	Exchange recipient container to Active Directory users (mailbox users only)
From Active Directory	Active Directory users to Exchange recipient container
Primary Connection Agreement for the connected Exchange organization?	No
Primary Connection Agreement for the connected Active Directory domain?	No

Table 6.12 Properties of the Fourth Connection Agreement for a Multiple-Site, Multiple-Domain Scenario

Property	Value
Direction	Two-way
From Exchange	Exchange recipient container to Active Directory users
From Active Directory	Active Directory users to Exchange recipient container
Primary Connection Agreement for the connected Exchange organization?	Yes
Primary Connection Agreement for the connected Active Directory domain?	Yes

Note: All new Exchange objects created in EXCH2 will be synchronized across the Connection Agreement between Site EXCH2 and ADDC1.

Choosing a Scenario

For maximum effectiveness and efficiency, your company should have a cross-functional team that chooses the production scenario. Collectively, this team will know enough about your Exchange site design, Active Directory design, and network topology to avoid costly mistakes. This team should consist of representatives from the following areas:

- Management
- Exchange administrators
- Active Directory administrators
- Network services group

Management's duties—These duties include defining and implementing high-level business requirements for the organization, coordinating and moderating meetings, arranging for needed technical personnel and training, and negotiating to obtain funding for all resources. Management must stay informed through regular status reports from all areas.

Exchange administrator's duties—The most important duty is to take inventory of your Exchange sites. You will need to know how many you have, how they are managed, and whether they are candidates for synchronization. For those sites to be synchronized, you will need detailed information on their recipient containers and the objects to be synchronized. Even though mail recipients are administered from Active Directory, the Exchange administrator must still manage the Exchange environment. This includes the management of queues, connectors, address book views, public folders, and monitors.

Active Directory administrator's duties—As Active Directory administrator you must examine your Active Directory structure and user mailbox locations. Identify where mailboxes reside for users in each domain. If recipient containers have mailboxes associated with Active Directory accounts from multiple domains, you must configure the Connection Agreement to synchronize objects only to the domain where the mailboxes belong.

Network Services Group's duties—These duties include providing input regarding general network topology, software, hardware, and configurations. You should be available as a resource for troubleshooting. You should also use existing network management tools to monitor network performance. Observe the impact of Active Directory synchronization on your Exchange and Active Directory replication environments by using directory replication counters.

Additional Considerations

Selecting bridgehead servers, identifying resource usage, and identifying initial synchronization strategies are important additional considerations for a successful Active Directory deployment.

Selecting Bridgehead Servers

Following are the requirements for Active Directory bridgehead servers:

- Adequate resources to support synchronization traffic and processing of incoming LDAP sessions
- Being well-connected to the network, for example, if an Exchange site spans multiple physical locations across a hub-and-spoke network, the bridgehead server for the site should be located at the hub
- If the bridgehead server is not a domain controller or Global Catalog server, it should be on the same Local Area Network (LAN) segment as a domain controller or Global Catalog server
- If the Exchange environment employs connector servers that do not host mailboxes, consider configuring these servers as ADC bridgehead servers

Identifying Resource Usage

The following processes consume network bandwidth:

- Replication with an Exchange site
- Replication within Active Directory
- Synchronization between an Exchange site and Active Directory

Identifying Initial Synchronization Strategy

Since synchronization of a large number of objects can consume large amounts of network resources, you should plan carefully for a convenient deployment schedule. You might consider staggering the deployment of ADCs and Connection Agreements across Exchange sites over an extended period. You might also consider using non-working hours and weekends for deployment.

Vocabulary

Review the following terms in preparation for the certification exam.

Term	Description
ADC	Active Directory Connector is a Microsoft software tool that simplifies synchronization between Active Directory and Exchange.
BDC	Backup Domain Controllers.
bridgehead server	Bridgehead servers are the contact point for exchange of directory information between sites. The Active Directory Connector service uses the directories on the bridgehead servers for synchronization between the directories.
Connection Agreement	A configuration that establishes and maintains synchronization between containers within Active Directory and Exchange site containers.
DACL	Discretionary Access Control List
LAN	Local Area Network
LDAP	Lightweight Directory Access Protocol is the primary access protocol for Active Directory.
MSDSS	Microsoft Directory Synchronization Services is a component of Microsoft's Services for Netware v.5 product that makes it easy for administrators to synchronize changes between Active Directory and Novell's Directory Services.
non-homed	New Active Directory objects that are mail-enabled, but do not have mailboxes.

Term	Description
PDC	Primary Domain Controller
polling	Procedure that checks for changes in each directory defined in the Connection Agreement.
synchronization	Two directories are synchronized when their databases contain equivalent, though not necessarily identical, content.
WAN	Wide Area Network

In Brief

If you want to...	Then do this...
Synchronize Active Directory and Exchange objects	Use Active Directory Connector (ADC).
Administer Active Directory users with mail attributes	Install ADC management components on all workstations that you plan to use to administer these accounts.
Find the Help files for Active Directory Connector	First, you must install ADC. Then, from the **Action** Menu on the console, choose **Help**.
Adjust the polling interval for a bridgehead server	Set the following entries and values for the registry key: **HKEY_LOCAL_Machine\System\CurrentControlSet\Services\MSADC\Parameters** • Name: Sync Sleep Delay (Secs) • Type: **DWORD** • Data: The number of seconds to wait between cycles
Configure a Connection Agreement	1. On the **Start** menu, choose **Programs**, **Administrative Tools**, and then select **Active Directory Connector Management**. 2. In the console tree, choose **Active Directory Connector**. 3. On the **Action** menu, choose **New**, and then select **Connection Agreement** to display the **Properties** dialog box.
Troubleshoot Active Directory Connector	Use diagnostics logging to monitor the activities of each Connection Agreement.

Lesson 6 Activities

Complete the following activities to better prepare you for the certification exam.

1. Name the building blocks necessary for coexistence between Active Directory and Exchange Directory services.

2. Name the important pieces of information that you should gather prior to installing Active Directory Connector.

3. Name the component that defines the relationship between Active Directory and the Exchange Directory.

4. Describe the configuration of the Connection Agreement if all objects are to be administered from Active Directory.

5. List the requirements for a bridgehead server.

   Activities 6-10 use the following scenario:

   Expanding U. is a university that has its principal location in Wichita, Kansas. In the past few years, Expanding U. has established satellite locations in Topeka, Kansas, Shawnee Mission, Kansas, and Independence, Missouri. Each location has the latest equipment and has the following products installed:
   Microsoft Windows 2000 Server
   Active Directory
   LDAP 3.0
   Exchange Server 5.3

   Expanding U. has always had the latest in Wide Area Network (WAN) technology. As recommended by the Active Directory project team, Expanding U.. has again upgraded its WAN service so there is ample bandwidth between each location and Wichita, based on a hub-and-spoke topology.

The following are the business requirements:

- Integrate the Windows directories and the Exchange directories
- Centralize administration by domain, so that the administrators in each domain administer both their Active Directory and Exchange users
- Administer all replication from the Windows environment

The following are the technical requirements:

- Each Active Directory user should have an Exchange mailbox and the objects in these two directories should be synchronized, regardless of the Active Directory domain in which they reside
- Synchronization latency between directories should be minimized

Exchange Server Information—Each physical location has at least one Exchange Server. Since there is only one Exchange site at Wichita, there are no Exchange site connectors. There is a single recipients' container containing all Expanding U users.

Each physical location is defined as an Active Directory site and has at least two domain controllers
Windows Information—Each physical location is defined as an Active Directory site and has at least two domain controllers, two Domain Name System (DNS) servers, and a Global Catalog server. Wichita hosts the domain controllers for the root domain (expanding.edu) as well as domain controllers for topeka.expanding.edu, shawneemission.expanding.edu, and independence.expanding.edu.

6. List any upgrades and installations that will be necessary before implementing the new requirements.

7. Name the locations where the Active Directory Connectors will reside.

8. In the topology diagram, draw the Connection Agreements and identify which of them would be Primary Connection Agreements.

9. State the direction of replication for each Connection Agreement.

10. Give your rationale for establishing a synchronization schedule.

Answers to Lesson 6 Activities

1. The following building blocks are necessary for coexistence between Active Directory and Exchange Directory services:
   - Microsoft Windows 2000 Server
   - ADC
   - Exchange Server 5.5
   - LDAP 3.0
2. The important pieces of information that you should gather prior to installing ADC are:
   - Installation location
   - Service account
   - Server names
3. The component that defines that relationship between Active Directory and the Exchange Directory is ADC.
4. If all objects are to be administered from Active Directory, the configuration of the Connection Agreement would be one-way replication from Windows to Exchange.
5. The requirements for a bridgehead server are as follows:
   - Adequate resources to support synchronization traffic and processing of incoming LDAP sessions
   - Well connected to the network, preferably at a hub location in a hub-and-spoke network configuration
   - Located on the same LAN server as a domain controller or Global Catalog, if the bridgehead server itself is not a domain controller or Global Catalog server
   - If the Exchange environment employs connection servers that do not host mailboxes, consider configuring these as Active Directory bridgehead servers

6. The Exchange Server must be upgraded to Version 5.5 and ADC must be installed.

7. Since all administration will be done from the Windows environment, ADC must reside on all workstations that will be administering changes in the following domains:

   - wichita.expanding.edu
   - topeka.expanding.edu
   - shawneemission.expanding.edu
   - independence.expanding.edu

8. In the topology diagram, a Primary Connection Agreement is necessary from each Active Directory domain to the Exchange Server.

9. All Connection Agreement directions will be from Windows to Exchange, since all administration is to be done from Active Directory.

10. Since the requirements stress minimizing latency and since the upgraded bandwidth would presumably support it, an initial schedule of once an hour during business hours would be feasible. Network traffic should be carefully monitored with performance counters, and the schedule adjusted accordingly. The administrator might also want to consider adjusting the polling interval.

Lesson 6 Quiz

These questions test your knowledge of features, vocabulary, procedures, and syntax.

1. What is a non-homed object?

   A. A new Exchange mailbox that does not have an associated Active Directory object.
   B. A new Active Directory object that is mail-enabled but does not have a mailbox in Exchange.
   C. A Connection Agreement that has not yet been established.
   D. An unsuccessful attempt at polling.

2. What are bridgehead servers?

   A. Exchange Servers only.
   B. Windows Servers only.
   C. Network Interface Cards (NICs).
   D. Contact points for exchange of directory information between sites.

3. What is a Connection Agreement?

   A. A management decision to network computers together.
   B. A synchronization configuration between directories in Windows and Exchange.
   C. A synchronization configuration between directories in Windows only.
   D. A synchronization configuration between directories in Exchange only.

4. What is Active Directory Connector?

   A. A hardware device for networking computers that use Active Directory.
   B. A software tool for synchronizing objects between Active Directory and Exchange.
   C. A software tool for connecting objects with Active Directory only.
   D. A software tool for connecting objects with Exchange only.

5. How do you change the default polling interval for a bridgehead server?

    A. Use the MMC console for DNS.
    B. Use the MMC console for Active Directory.
    C. Modify the registry key.
    D. Use the option on the Schedule dialog box.

6. What is the default process when an object defined in a Connection Agreement is deleted?

    A. The corresponding object in the partner directory is deleted.
    B. A record of the deletion is stored in a file.
    C. Corresponding objects are moved to a recycle bin or Deleted Items folder, depending on the end of the connection where the corresponding object resides.
    D. Only the original object is deleted.

7. What tool does the administrator of the Exchange environment use to synchronize additions, deletions, and changes with Active Directory?

    A. Exchange Administrator
    B. Active Directory Connector
    C. Windows Explorer
    D. Active Directory Main Console

8. What tools are available for monitoring and troubleshooting Active Directory Connector?

    A. Diagnostics logging
    B. Performance monitor counters
    C. The control panel
    D. The Settings tab on the dialog box for the monitor display

Answers to Lesson 6 Quiz

1. B is correct. A non-homed object is an Active Directory object that is mail-enabled.

   A is incorrect. It reverses the correct answer.

   C is incorrect. A Connection Agreement is not an object—it defines an association between objects.

   D is incorrect. Polling checks for changes in objects defined in a Connection Agreement.

2. D is correct. A bridgehead server is a point for exchange of directory information between sites.

   A and B are incorrect because bridgehead servers must reside on both ends of a Connection Agreement—one bridgehead server in Windows and one in Exchange.

   C is incorrect because a NIC is not a server.

3. B is correct. A Connection Agreement is a synchronization configuration between Windows and Exchange directories.

   A is incorrect. In this context, a Connection Agreement is not a management decision to network computers together.

   C and D are incorrect because a Connection Agreement is not confined to Windows or to Exchange.

4. B is correct. ADC is a tool for synchronizing objects between Active Directory and Exchange.

   A is incorrect because ADC is not a hardware device.

   C and D are incorrect because ADC does not connect objects within Exchange or within Active Directory.

5. C is correct. You must set the polling interval by modifying the registry key.

   A, B, and D are incorrect. You cannot set a polling interval for a bridgehead server from any console or dialog box.

6. B is correct. The results are stored in a file Ex55.csv for Exchange and in NT5.LDF for Active Directory.

   A is incorrect. By default, records of deletions are stored in a file. However, you can override the default so that the corresponding object in the partner directory is deleted when the original object is deleted.

   C is incorrect. These temporary holding containers are not used in this environment.

   D is incorrect. The idea of a Connection Agreement is to synchronize changes between directories.

7. A is correct. Use Exchange Administrator to manage synchronization of additions, deletions, and changes from the Exchange side.

   B is incorrect. The Active Directory Connector only defines connections.

   C is incorrect. Windows Explorer does not have this functionality.

   D is incorrect. Active Directory Main Console is not in Exchange.

8. A and B are correct. Diagnostic logging and performance monitor counters are available for monitoring and troubleshooting.

   C is incorrect. The Control Panel has no feature for monitoring and troubleshooting Active Directory Connector.

   D is incorrect. The dialog box for the monitor display has no feature for monitoring and troubleshooting Active Directory Connector.

9. A, B, C, and D are all correct. LDAP operations may also be logged.

10. C is correct. You must have Exchange Server v5.5 on the Exchange end of each Connection Agreement.

    A, B, and D are incorrect. Only v5.5 will work correctly.

Lesson 7

Active Directory Replication

Users and services should be able to access directory information at any time from any computer in the domain tree or forest. Replication ensures that changes to a domain controller are reflected in the domain controllers within a domain. Directory information is replicated to domain controllers both within and among sites. Windows 2000 Active Directory uses a multimaster replication model. This means that each domain controller in the network must have a current copy of the Active Directory. By understanding how Active Directory replication works, you can control replication traffic and ensure the reliability of your Active Directory data across your network.

After completing this lesson, you should have a better understanding of the following topics:

- Active Directory replication concepts
- Active Directory replication model
- Site replication
- Propagation dampening
- Conflict resolution
- Replication topology
- Replication traffic measurements
- Active Directory site roles
- New site creation and configuration

Active Directory Replication Concepts

Once you implement Active Directory, you will discover that your network relies heavily on its services. This reliance means that Active Directory must be available on multiple servers so that, if a server fails, users can contact a server with duplicate services and information. The replication component included with Active Directory services makes this a simple task for administrators. Adding domain controllers to an Active Directory domain is enough to start a replication process.

Since Active Directory uses multimaster replication, updates can occur on any Active Directory server. Each server keeps track of the updates it has received from the other servers and can request the necessary updates if there is a failure.

How Replication Works

Each Windows 2000 domain has one (or more) servers that act as domain controllers. Each of these domain controllers stores a complete copy of Active Directory for the domain and is included in the changes and updates to the directory.

Figure 7.1 Domains

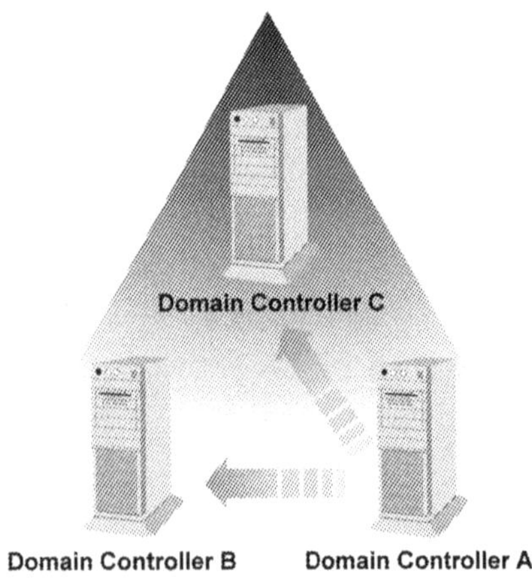

The Windows 2000 Active Directory uses a multimaster replication topology that allows you to use any domain controller to manipulate the domain database and pass the changes to its replication partners. Domain controllers use Update Sequence Numbers (USNs) to see if replication partners are up to date.

In the case of collisions (when the same attribute of the same object is affected on two domain controllers at the same time) the last writer wins. To decide last writer status, an algorithm checks the attribute version number, the attribute timestamp and then the Globally Unique Identifiers (GUIDs) of the domain controllers that performed the write operation. This process ensures the attribute value is determined consistently and locally, reducing communication between domain controllers.

Active Directory replicates information within a site more frequently than across sites. This balances the need for up-to-date directory information with the limitations imposed by your available network bandwidth.

Understanding Replication Terminology

Imagine an organization with one domain that spans a multi-site Wide Area Network (WAN). This WAN is comprised of one site in Hong Kong and the other in Seattle, each with a domain controller.

The domain controllers keep track of how many changes have been made in their copy of the directory and how many changes they have received from the domain controller that is their replication partner. If the Hong Kong controller finds that it does not have all of the changes that the Seattle controller has, then it can request the new changes from the Seattle controller.

This makes updating a domain controller that has been disconnected from a network easy. It is clear what directory information has changed and needs to be replicated. Since Active Directory tracks these directory changes by a numerical sequence and not time, the need for synchronizing clocks is eliminated—except in the most unusual cases.

Directory Replication

Users and services should be able to gain access to directory information at any time from any computer in the forest. To make this possible, additions, modifications, and deletions of directory data must be relayed to other domain controllers.

For example, if you change your account's password in your organization's Seattle office, your new password must be valid when you log on with the same account at the Hong Kong office.

By replicating the directory changes to other domain controllers, this is possible. Directory information must be widely distributed, but you must balance this with the need to optimize network performance. If directory updates are constantly distributed to all other domain controllers in the domain, they consume network resources. Although you can manually add, configure connections, or force replication over a particular connection, you should allow replication to be automatically optimized by the Active Directory Knowledge Consistency Checker (KCC) based on information you provide to Active Directory Sites and Services about your network.

Windows 2000 uses sites and replication change control to optimize replication in the following ways:

- By periodically re-evaluating which connections are used, Active Directory uses the most efficient network connections
- Active Directory uses multiple routes to replicate changes; this provides fault tolerance
- Replication costs are minimized as only changed information is replicated

Figure 7.2 Directory Replication

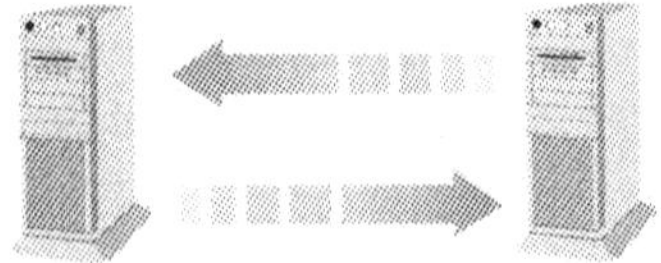

Windows 2000 Domain Controllers

When you are planning sites, you need to consider where the domain controllers and the network connections between the domain controllers will be located. Since each domain controller must take part in directory replication with the other controllers in its domain, you need to configure sites so that replication occurs at times and intervals that do not interfere with network performance.

Directory Synchronization

Directory synchronization occurs between different implementations of directory services. For example, implementations of Novell Directory Services (NDS) and Active Directory. A security principle to both parties performs mapping between the schemas that each directory uses.

Figure 7.3 Directory Synchronization

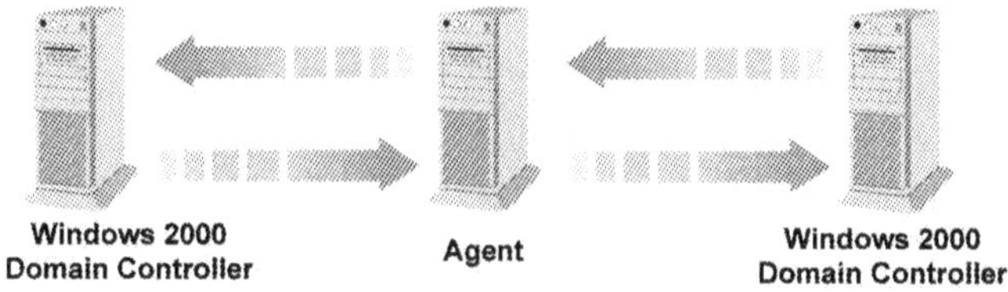

Active Directory Replication Model

The Active Directory replication model uses different methods to manage replication events. These include managing replication through different partitions, resolving the effect of update delays, enabling simultaneous updates of critical items to multiple-domain controllers, and attending to the effects of poor performance as the results of replication.

Replicating Partitions

The information stored in the directory is divided into three categories. Each of these information categories is referred to as a directory partition. These directory partitions are the units of replication. Table 7.1 explains the information that is contained in each directory.

Table 7.1 Replicating Partitions

Partition	Description
Schema information	Schema information defines the objects that can be created in the directory and what attributes those objects can have. This information is common to all domains in the domain tree or forest.
Configuration information	Configuration information describes the logical structure of your deployment. It contains information such as domain structure or replication topology. This information is common to all domains in the domain tree or forest.
Domain data	Domain data describes all the objects in a domain. This data is domain-specific and is not distributed to any other domains. This data is used to find information throughout the domain. It is stored in the Global Catalog.

The schema partition and the configuration directory partition are both enterprise partitions, that is, they are identical on all domain controllers in an enterprise (forest). As a result, they share the same replication topology because they must be replicated to all domain controllers.

Schema Partition

The **schema** container defines the objects, such as users, and attributes, such as telephone numbers, that can be created in the Active Directory, and the rules for creating and manipulating them. Schema information about what attributes are mandatory for object creation, what additional attributes can be set, and what attribute data types are used is replicated to all domain controllers to ensure that objects are created and manipulated in accordance with the rules.

Warning: Extensions to schema can have disastrous effects on large networks due to full synchronization of all domain data.

Configuration Partition

The configuration partition contains information about the Active Directory as a whole—what domains exist, what sites are available, what domain controllers are running in the particular sites and domains, and what additional services are offered. All enterprise domain controllers need this information to make operational decisions, such as choosing replication partners, so it is replicated to all of them.

Domain Partition

A domain partition holds objects such as users, groups, computers, and Organizational Units (OUs). A full domain-naming context replica contains a read-write replica of all information in the domain—all objects and attributes. A domain controller holds a full replica of its domain-naming context. A partial domain-naming context replica contains a read-only subset of the information in the domain—all objects, but only selected attributes.

A domain controller that is a Global Catalog (GC) server contains a partial replica of every other domain in the forest and a full replica of its own domain. A Global Catalog server cannot act as a replication source for any full domain directory partition other than its own. However, a Global Catalog server can act as a partial domain directory partition replication source for another catalog server.

Replicating Latency and Convergence

When servers replicate, there is a latency period or delay between the time an update is applied to the first replica, and the time it is propagated to all the other servers in the network. This latency period is called convergence, as the information at any given time may not be the same on all the domain controllers.

Replication Latency

The propagation of information over a network is not instantaneous. In distributed systems, as updates are replicated, different domain controllers will have different views of the Active Directory database at any given point in time. This is replication latency.

Replication Convergence

Active Directory replication manages the uncertainty of the system state by incorporating loose consistency and convergence. The replicas at each domain controller are not guaranteed to be consistent with each other at any particular time (loose consistency) because changes can be applied to any replica at any time. However, convergence is when the system reaches a steady state—no new updates are occurring, and all previous updates have been completely replicated—so that all replicas will have the same set of values.

Understanding Single Operations Masters

Active Directory supports multimaster replication of the Active Directory database among all domain controllers in the domain. However, some changes are not practical to perform in the multimaster fashion. One or more domain controllers can be assigned operations that are single master, which are not permitted to occur at different places in a network at the same time. The operations master functions are special. In any Active Directory forest, five operations master roles must be assigned to domain controllers. Some appear in every forest, others must appear in every domain in the forest. You can change the operations master roles after setup, but in most situations, this will be unnecessary.

Warning: You must be aware of the operations master roles assigned to a domain controller if problems develop with the controller or if it must be taken out of service.

Forest-Wide Operations Master Roles

Every Active Directory forest must have the following roles:

- Schema master
- Domain-naming master

These roles must be unique in a forest. This means that throughout the entire forest there can only be one schema master and one domain-naming master.

Schema Operations Master

The schema master domain controller controls all updates and modifications to the schema. To update the schema of a forest, you must have access to the schema master. At any time, there can only be one schema master in the entire forest.

Domain-naming Master

The domain controller holding the domain-naming master role controls the addition or removal of domains from the forest.

The domain-naming master is created in the first domain. It remains there no matter how large the forest becomes. The network is unaffected if this operations master is down. If the domain-naming master is to be permanently removed from the network, the role of domain-naming master can be transferred or it can be seized.

Domain Operations Master

Only the domain controller that is the domain operations master can add or remove existing domains from the directory or add or remove cross-references to external directory service. There can only be one domain operations master in the entire forest at the same time.

Primary Domain Controller (PDC) Emulator

If a domain contains computers operating without Windows 2000 or if it contains Microsoft Windows NT Backup Domain Controllers (BDCs), the PDC emulator acts as a Microsoft Windows NT Primary Domain Controller. It processes password changes from users and replicates updates to the BDCs.

Even after all systems have been upgraded to Windows 2000, and the Windows 2000 domain is operating in native mode, the PDC emulator receives preferential replication of password changes performed by other domain controllers in the domain. If a login authentication fails at another domain controller due to a bad password, that domain controller will forward the authentication request to the PDC emulator before rejecting the logon attempt.

Note: There can only be one domain controller acting as the PDC emulator in the forest.

Relative Identifier (RID) Operations Master

The Relative Identifier master distributes series of relative IDs to each of the different domain controllers in its domain. In each domain in the forest, there can only be one domain controller acting as the RID master at any time.

When a domain controller creates a user, group or computer object, it assigns the object a unique Security Identifier (SID), which is the same for all SIDs created in a domain, and a RID that is unique for each SID created in the domain.

To move an object between domains using MOVETREE.EXE from Active Directory Object Manager, you must initiate the move on the domain controller acting as the RID master of the domain that currently contains the object.

Note: There can only be one RID operations master per domain.

Infrastructure Operations Master

The infrastructure operations master is responsible for updating the group-to-user references whenever the members of groups are renamed or changed. When you rename or move a member of a group (and the member resides in a different domain than the group), the group may temporarily appear not to contain that member. The infrastructure operations master is responsible for updating the group so it knows the new name or location of the member.

Note: There can only be one infrastructure operations master per domain.

Site Replication

Within a site, Active Directory will automatically use a ring structure to generate a topology for replication among the domain controllers in the domain. The topology defines the path for directory updates to flow from one domain controller to another, until all domain controllers have received directory updates. The ring structure ensures that there are at least two replication paths from one domain controller to another. If one domain controller is down, replication continues to all other domain controllers. Active Directory periodically analyzes the replication topology within a site to ensure that it is still efficient. If you add or remove a domain controller from the network or a site, Active Directory reconfigures the topology to reflect the change.

Configure Inter-Site Replication

Inter-site replication occurs between two or more sites. Network connections are characterized by site links. By creating site links and configuring their cost, replication frequency, and replication availability, you provide the directory service with information about how to use these connections to replicate the directory data.

Site link connectivity can be maximized by linking overlapping existing site links into site link bridges, or you can bridge all site links. You can also designate a server, known as a bridgehead server, to serve as a contact point for the exchange of directory information between sites.

Note: You can manually schedule Inter-Site replication.

Understanding Intra-Site Replication

Intra-site replication occurs between domain controllers within a site. By introducing a change notification mechanism, Intra-Site replication prevents unnecessary network traffic. This replaces the usual polling of replication partners for updates. When a change is performed in the domain controller's database, the following processes take place:

- It waits a configurable interval (default 5 minutes)
- It accepts more changes during this time
- It sends a notification to its replication partners
- The replication partners pull the changes

Figure 7.4 Intra-Site Replication

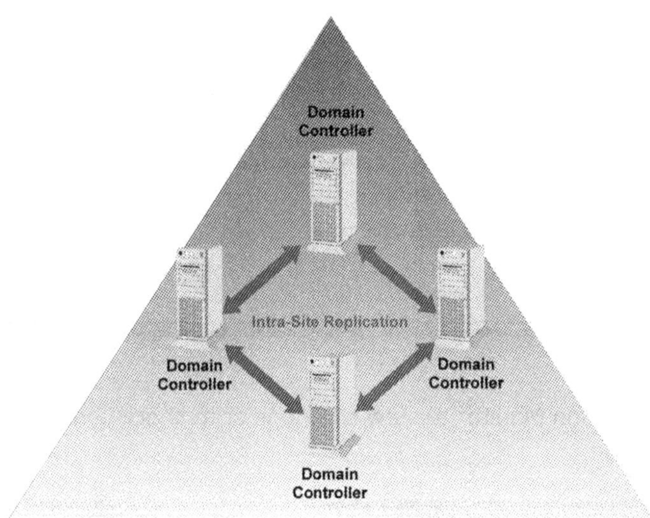

After a default period of 6 hours (configurable), the domain controller initiates a replication sequence to make sure that it did not miss anything. Attribute changes are considered security-sensitive and are immediately replicated. Intra-Site partners are notified. Some changes that could be security sensitive are: lockout of user accounts, change of domain trust passwords, some changes in the roles of domain controllers.

Intra-Site replication topology is a bi-directional ring built using domain controller GUIDs. Within a site, the Knowledge Consistency Checker (KCC) automatically generates a bi-directional ring topology for all domain controllers in the same domain. You provide the KCC with information on the site and subnets that belong to sites, the cost of sending data between the sites, and the network transports between the sites, and the KCC calculates the best connections between each domain controller. The KCC ensures there are no more than three hops from any domain controller in a site to any other domain controller in a site (by adding additional replication partners where necessary).

Intra-Site replication tries to complete in the fewest Central Processing Unit (CPU) cycles possible. Since domain controllers should be able to serve users quickly for logons, searches, etc., the network connection between them is assumed to have lots of available bandwidth and reliable connections.

Data should be as accurate as possible on all domain controllers. Since replication is a trade-off, this means that latency should be as short as possible. The best way to achieve this is with fast updates, which means frequent replication. Conversely, frequency does not always equal efficiency. For example, if there is a bulk import of directory objects, changes in a domain controller database will become out of date after 10 seconds. However, it makes no sense to replicate the changes until the database is stable, that is, until the bulk import is complete. Active Directory can automatically generate replication plus a replication topology for Intra-Site replication.

Tip: Use the Active Directory Replication Monitor to view site rings or to check connection objects and incoming replication.

Understanding Inter-Site Replication

Inter-Site replication topology is a spanning tree. The administrator decides which sites are connected, and can create a site link that allows domain controllers from any site to talk to domain controllers in any other site. Site links are based on the cost of replication and its schedule—the window when replication is allowed over the link.

Figure 7.5 Inter-Site Replication

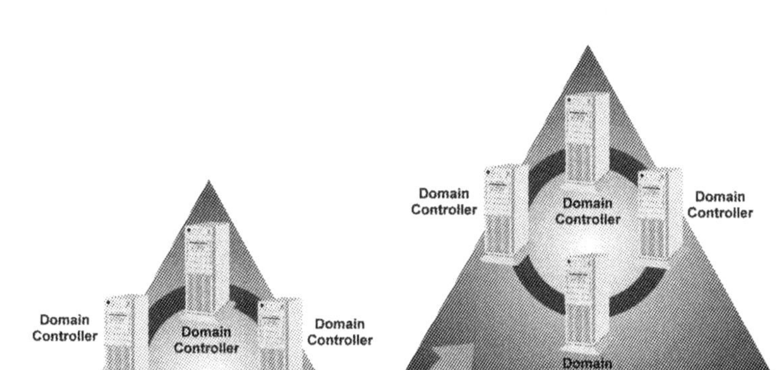

Unlike Intra-Site replication, Inter-Site replication does not use a notification process. Inter-Site replication can be scheduled by the administrator on a per site link basis. Since there is no notice between replication partners, a domain controller does not know which naming context was updated on the source replication partner. The domain controller has to check all existing naming contexts on the source machine.

A normal domain controller (one that uses a Global Catalog as replication partner) will check only the normal three naming contexts on the GC (schema, configuration, and its domain) but never the partial naming contexts of other domains. For that reason, the initial replication setup traffic is a little higher for Inter-Site. However, if many objects are replicated, a compression formula kicks in and makes this kind of replication more efficient.

While Intra-Site replication supports only replication based on Remote Procedure Calls (RPCs), Windows 2000 offers the following two methods for Inter-Site replication:

- Synchronous (scheduled) using RPC over TCP/IP
- Asynchronous using Simple Mail Transfer Protocol (SMTP) using the Collaborative Data Objects (CDO v2) interface and the SMTP component in IIS 5, included in Windows 2000

SMTP transport has limits. It can be used to replicate configuration and Global Catalog information. It cannot be used for replication between domain controllers that belong to the same domain and need to replicate the full domain-naming context. The reason for this restriction is some operations, for example, Global Policy, require the support of the File Replication Service (FRS) that does not yet support an asynchronous transport (like SMTP) for replication.

Updating Requests

Each Active Directory transaction creates an independent request that can either commit or not commit. A committed request is an originating update. After an update, the data must be replicated throughout the network. An update performed at a domain controller that did not originate the update is called a replicated update. Only changes are replicated.

Originating Updates

Table 7.2 shows the update request types that Active Directory supports.

Table 7.2 Update Request Types

Request	Description
ADD	Adding an object to the directory, for example, adding a new user.
MODIFY	Modifying an object's attribute values, for example, changing the personal information for an existing user account.
MODIFYDN	Changing the name or parent of an object and moving the object into a new parent domain, for example, changing 'sales' to 'marketing' and moving the object to the marketing domain.
DELETE	Deleting an object from the directory, for example, deleting an account for a user that no longer needs it.

Replicating Updates

A replicating update is a committed update carried out on one replica because of an originating update at another replica. Each originating update generates a stamp for each new or modified attribute value. This stamp is attached to the value of the update, so when the value is replicated, the stamp is also replicated. This new stamp is guaranteed to be different from any other stamps. In the case of an update, the new stamp is always greater than the stamp on the old values at the domain controller.

Note: A single replicated update might reflect a set of originating updates (or updates originating at several replicas) to the same object.

Update Sequence Numbers (USN)

The domain controller assigns an Update Sequence Number (USN) when an object is updated. USNs are stored in a table maintained by each domain controller and are incremented after each update. This happens with both originating and replicating updates. Each update is assigned its own 64-bit unique sequence number from a counter and is incremented whenever a change is made.

When a domain controller writes the change to the Active Directory, it also writes the USN of the change with the attribute. In this case, either both writes succeed, or both writes fail.

Timestamps involve precise synchronization among all the domain controllers. Using USNs for changes eliminates the need for timestamps. However, timestamps are still used in directory changes for tie-breaking purposes.

When a domain controller is brought back online, after it has failed or been off-line, it will request replication changes from the other domain controllers to bring it up to date. USNs simplify this process. The domain controller will only request changes with USNs greater than the last USN that it applied before the failure. Interrupted replication picks up exactly where it left off with no loss or duplication of updates.

Propagation Dampening

Replication topology is made up of a loop, so domain controllers have multiple paths for sending and receiving updates. These loops increase performance and provide fault tolerance. They could also result in the same update being replicated more than once to a controller by following the different replication paths. Active Directory uses a propagation-dampening scheme to prevent this.

For example, two domain controllers detect a change from a third domain controller. If the change has already been replicated to both from the third, the two others do not replicate the change.

To assist propagation dampening, each domain controller maintains a pair of vectors that are called the up-to-date vector and the high watermark vector.

Preventing Unnecessary Replication

Active Directory replicates data through automatically or manually created network connections detailed in the directory. This process gives fault tolerance. However Active Directory must also ensure that a single change is not replicated numerous times to the same domain controller by different sets of connections. For example, the Seattle domain controller has applied a change it has received from the Hong Kong domain controller. The Seattle domain controller must now indicate the new information should not be replicated back to the source, the Hong Kong domain controller. If it is not prevented, a cycle of replication back and forth from one domain controller to another would continue indefinitely and overwhelm your network.

Active Directory stops this from happening by tracking which attribute changed in the updated object and how many times the object's Originating Write property has been incremented. A change that increments an Originating Write property designates a change a client made to the object, as opposed to a change made by Active Directory when replicating updated directory information. When the Hong Kong domain controller is notified that an object in the Seattle directory has changed, it checks to see whether the change set the Originating Write property. If it is not set, no replication change is necessary for the Hong Kong directory.

Understanding the Up-to-Date Vector

Server-USN pairs that are held by each server make up the up-to-date vector and represent the highest originating update received from each domain controller.

For example, a user changes their password at the Hong Kong server and the Hong Kong server writes the change to the directory—this is considered an originating update. When the Hong Kong server replicates the change to the New York server and the New York server updates its copy of the directory, there is a replicated update at the New York server.

Note: An originating update is an update that is made to a directory object not caused by replication.

Understanding the High Watermark Vector

When an attribute is added or modified in the directory, the USN is advanced and stored as part of the replication metadata for that attribute. The highest attribute USN on an object is also stored as the object's **usnChanged** attribute. Each domain controller keeps track of the highest USN received from each direct replication partner. This is called the high watermark vector.

Conflict Resolution

Conflicts can occur during multimaster replication and must be resolved. It is possible for two different administrators to make changes to the exact same object property and to have these changes applied at two different domain controllers in the same domain before replication of either change can be completed. In this case, both changes are replicated as new changes to domain controllers and both have their Originating Write property incremented. When the updates are replicated, this will cause a collision. Active Directory both minimizes and resolves collisions.

Minimizing Collisions

To minimize collisions, Active Directory records and replicates changes to objects at the attribute level rather than the object level. Therefore, changes to two different attributes of an object, such as the users password and phone number at the same time, will not cause a collision.

Resolving Collisions

To resolve conflicts, the domain controller that receives conflicting changes examines the timestamp on each attribute change and accepts the change with the most recent timestamp, dumping the change with the older timestamp. If the timestamps are the same, the change with the highest GUID is accepted.

Active Directory maintains timestamps and version numbers as part of the metadata stored with an attribute. Unlike the USNs, the version number is not domain controller specific and follows the attribute through its life. When an attribute is written to an object, the version number is initialized. Each originating update increments the number.

A collision is detected when a domain controller receives a change to an attribute through the replication, and the replicated version number is equal to the locally stored version number. If the version number of the locally stored attribute or the replicated attribute is larger than the other, the one with the higher version number will be used.

The received and stored attribute values are different. The receiving domain controller applies the update only if the update has a later timestamp. This is the only time timestamps are used in Active Directory replication. If the version number and the timestamp are the same, the highest Active Directory GUID would be used. This ensures that the same update of the attribute wins.

For example, a conflict could arise in entering a user's name and address information. A user changes their personal information at the server in Hong Kong from Allen at 112 Street to Allan at 122 Street. An administrator changes the same mailing address at the Seattle server. A written value circulates until another value is chosen over that value by the collision reconciliation mechanism. As long as a value continues to win against other values in the collision resolution process, the value continues to propagate. Ultimately, the winning value will propagate to the Hong Kong server, the Seattle server and all other replicas if no other changes are made.

Replication Topology

Replication topology is the dynamic route replication travels through the network. A single domain controller may have different replication partners for different partitions. Your replication topology differs depending on whether you are considering schema, configuration, or domain replication. The links connecting replication partners are called connection objects.

Within the site, you can manually control these pathways, or Active Directory will do this automatically through the Knowledge Consistency Checker (KCC). Between sites, you must manually establish these pathways.

Figure 7.6 Replication Topology

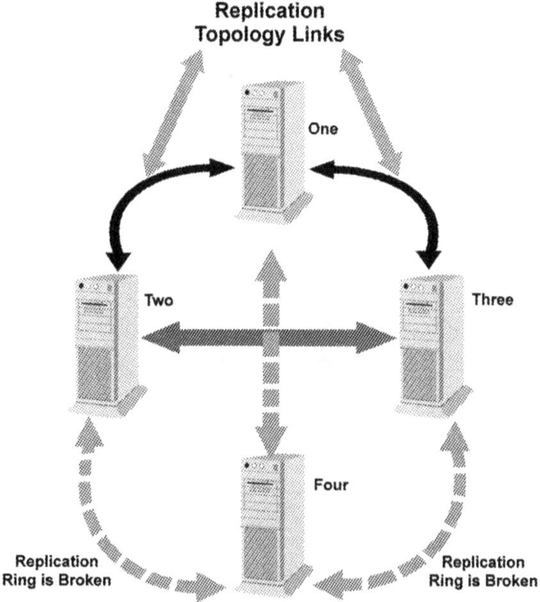

Connecting Replication Partners

Connecting replication partner is an important process for transmission of information through the Active Directory. This is accomplished by defining connection objects that you create automatically through wizards or set up individually. It is also important to note that all replication pathways are unidirectional.

Connection Objects

A connection object corresponds to a potential direct replication partner. Direct replication partners are domain controllers that are a direct source for Active Directory replication data. Active Directory determines, through a process called Knowledge Consistency Checker (KCC), whether to use the domain controller—represented by the connection object—as a direct replication partner. Through transitive replication partners, a domain controller can also receive Active Directory replication data. Transitive replication partners are domain controllers whose data is gained indirectly though a direct replication partner.

Connection objects are created in the following two ways:

- Through KCC running on the destination domain controller or
- Through a directory administrator

Unidirectional Replication Pathway

Connection objects are unidirectional. A domain controller's NT Directory Services (NTDS) settings object contains the connection object, which points to the replication source. Bi-directional replication is represented as two separate connection objects under two separate NTDS settings objects.

A single connection object between replication partners is enough to carry out any type of replication. There is never a need to create multiple connections linking the same two domain controllers in the same direction.

Replication is carried out between naming replicas. Two domain controllers in the same directory will always have at least two directory partitions in common: configuration and schema. If a connection exists from one domain controller to another it will be used for replicating as many partitions as needed.

Single Connection Object

All types of replication can use a single connection object. You can turn off the KCC for Inter-Site replication and manually define every connection object, however, it is not recommended. For most sites, you can just leave the site link transitivity turned on and you are done—without any other configuration needed.

Automating Topology Generation

Directory information needs to be distributed, but network performance also needs to be considered. If updates are always being distributed, to all other domain controllers, they use up your network resources. You can manually add, configure connections, or force replication over a connection, but you should let the Knowledge Consistency Checker do this automatically.

Knowledge Consistency Checker (KCC)

Replication value is improved by a flexible replication topology that can reflect the structure of an existing network. The Active Directory's replication topology generator runs as part of the Knowledge Consistency Checker (KCC). You enter information on the cost of sending data from one location to another and which domain controllers are running in the same location into the KCC. Using this, an Inter-Site replication topology is built that spans a tree, based on low-cost routing decisions between remote locations and a more strongly connected Intra-Site topology. You can disable the KCC topology generator and manually create the connection objects required for replication. During this process, the Active Directory logging mechanism identifies domain controllers that appear to be isolated from the enterprise-wide replication.

Note: Using the replication topology generator, which is part of the KCC, is strongly recommended: it simplifies a complex task, has a flexible architecture that reacts to failures and to changes you make later in the network topology and helps compute the lowest-cost topology.

The KCC then figures out the best connection between each domain controller. If replication within a site fails or has a single point of failure, the KCC automatically establishes new connection objects to resume Active Directory replication.

Default Bi-directional Ring

The default in a site is bi-directional ring replication topology. The ring is constructed with enough connections so that the average number of hops, which a change will make, is never more than three. When a change is applied to a specific replica, the replication engine is triggered. The replication engine waits for a configurable period of time—the default is 5 minutes—and notifies the first replication partner. Each additional partner is notified after a delay—the default is 30 seconds. Using the default configuration, the propagation delay within a site should be less than 15 minutes.

Modifying Replication Topology

An administrator can use Active Directory Sites and Services to modify a replication topology. You do this by establishing additional connection objects or removing connection objects. You only have to manually create connection objects if the connections that the KCC creates do not connect domain controllers that an administrator wants connected.

Before you create additional connections, it is important to consider the cost of additional connections compared with the default configuration. The cost of additional connections includes extra CPU cycles, disk reads, and network messages spent on replication.

Active Directory Sites and Services

You use Active Directory Sites and Services to modify replication topology in adding or removing connection objects and establishing connections that are beyond the KCC.

Tip: In addition to creating and modifying connection objects, Active Directory Sites and Services may be used to force replication and run KCC manually.

Modification Rules

When you modify the connection objects, the following rules apply:

- The KCC will never delete a connection object that has been manually created
- If you create a connection that is identical to one the KCC would create, it will not delete the connection that you created
- If the replication within a site fails, the KCC will step in and establish any necessary connections to resume Active Directory replication

Replication Traffic Measurements

You can adjust your replication topology based on traffic. To help you do this, you need to be able to view your replication traffic through your network. Windows 2000 gives you some tools for assessing network load:

Network Monitor—You can measure Remote Procedure Call (RPC) and Simple Mail Transfer Protocol (SMTP) replication traffic between domain controllers.

Performance Monitor—You can measure replication coming in and going out of a specific server.

Replication Monitor—You can view your Intra-Site replication topology.

Using Network Monitor

The Network Monitor measures replication traffic with a network "sniffer" to help you isolate network packets that belong to replication between domain controllers.

An easy way to detect replication traffic is to start Network Monitor and then force replication. You can do this by using the Sites and Services Administration snap-in in MMC or REPADMIN.EXE. This allows you to specify the particular naming context that has to be replicated. Once REPADMIN.EXE returns and reports that replication was successful, you can stop Network Monitor.

After you have done this, you will have measured all incoming and outgoing packets from the server machine. Some of these packets could have been sent by other services, such as NetLogon or the file server.

It can be hard to decide which of the packets measured belong to replication. One way of figuring this out could be to use the IP port that is used by replication. Replication uses dynamic RPC port mapping as a means of security. During this process the replication server requests an available port from the RPC port mapper interface. This tells the requesting client the port used by the replication interface, and the client then uses this port to communicate with the replication server. You can configure the IP port used on the replication server by typing this value into the registry:

HKEY_LOCAL_MACHINE \CurrentControlSet \Services \NTDS \Parameters \TCP/IP Port

You can set the port to 1349 (decimal), for example, to make 1349 the IP port, then find all replication-related packets by filtering on that port with Network Monitor.

Using Performance Monitor

The Windows 2000 Performance Monitor does not look the same as the versions available in Microsoft Windows NT. It is implemented as a Microsoft ActiveX control that can be used either as a Microsoft Management Console (MMC) snap-in or as a control in a Web page. This allows you to monitor servers and network traffic from a browser.

The Performance Monitor counters that are most frequently used to measure replication traffic appear under the NTDS object. Table 7.3 describes the counters.

Table 7.3 Performance Monitor Counters

Counter	Description
DRA inbound bytes total	Total number of bytes replicated. Sum of the number of uncompressed bytes (never compressed) and the number of compressed bytes (after compression).
DRA inbound bytes not compressed	Number of bytes replicated that were not compressed at the source, which typically implies that they arrived from other Directory System Agents (DSAs) in the same site.
DRA inbound bytes compressed (before compression)	Original size in bytes of inbound compressed replication data (size before compression).
DRA inbound bytes compressed (after compression)	Compressed size in bytes of inbound compressed replication data (size after compression).
DRA outbound bytes total	Total number of bytes replicated. Sum of the number of uncompressed bytes (never compressed) and the number of compressed bytes (after compression).
DRA outbound bytes not compressed	Number of bytes replicated that were not compressed, which typically implies that they were sent to DSAs in the same site or that less than 50,000 bytes of replicated data was sent.
DRA outbound bytes compressed (before compression)	Original size in bytes of outbound compressed replication data (size before compression).
DRA outbound bytes compressed (after compression)	Compressed size in bytes of outbound compressed replication data (size after compression).

You can also retrieve a subset of this information from the event log. The event log for directory service logging is set to the lowest level by default. This reduces the size of the log files and restricts logging to important events such as errors, lost connections to replication partners, etc. Activating higher levels of event logging consumes CPU time and can present you with the tedious task of finding the right information in huge log files.

Using Replication Monitor

The Replication Monitor graphically displays the replication topology of connections between servers on the same site. It enables administrators to view low-level status and the performance of replication between Active Directory domain controllers. It also includes functions that are Application Programming Interfaces (APIs) and make it easy to script replication with just a few lines of code.

With Active Directory Replication Monitor you can perform the following tasks:

- Display with whom the machine is replicating both directly and transitively
- Display each USN value, the number of failed attempts, reasons, and flags used for direct replication partners
- Poll the server at an administrator-defined interval to get current statistics and replication state and keep a log file history monitor
- Monitor the count of failed replication attempts; if the failures meet or exceed an administrator-defined value, it will be recorded in the event log and an e-mail message is automatically sent to the administrator
- Allow administrators to show which objects have not yet been replicated from a particular machine
- Allow administrators to synchronize between just two domain controllers
- Allow administrators to trigger the Knowledge Consistency Checker into recalculating the replication topology

The Replication Monitor utility can be run on any domain controller, member server, or standalone computer running Windows 2000.

Active Directory Site Roles

An Active Directory site is a set of TCP/IP subnets that are well connected.

Tip: Well-connected implies high-bandwidth LAN (10MB minimum) connectivity, possibly involving several hops through routers.

Sites, which are physical units, are not part of the Active Directory namespace, which is a logical construct. Sites may span multiple domains. Likewise, domains may span multiple sites.

Sites are used in Active Directory in the following way:

- Site A contains a domain controller (DC) from the root domain MyCompany and a DC from the child domain Edmonton.MyCompany.
- Site B contains a DC only from Kansas.MyCompany.
- Site C contains DCs from Edmonton.MyCompany and the root MyCompany.

Domains are logical structures and sites are physical structures.

Figure 7.7 shows graphically how site topology works.

Figure 7.7 Site Topology

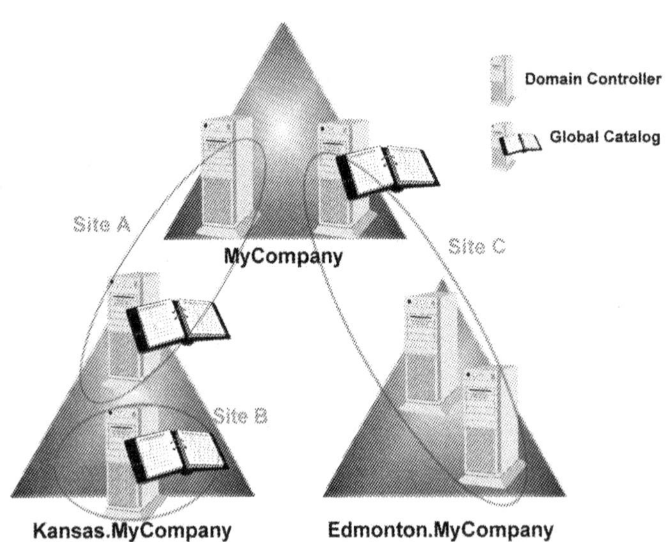

Sites serve three main purposes:

Service Location—Sites are used to locate services, such as logon and Distributed File System (DFS) services. When a client requests a connection to a DC login or to Global Catalog for universal group membership information, sites are used so that the client can connect to a domain controller within the same site. If there are no domain controllers in a site with users, then another site that does have domain controllers can provide coverage for the client site.

Logical Cost Assignment—Site links each have a logical cost assigned to them. If a user is searching for the closest DC to log on, he will first look for a DC and GC in his site. If none exists, he will search for a DC in the site with the lowest logical cost assigned to the site link. When a client requests a connection to a service, sites are used to locate and connect to a replica within the same site.

Replication—Sites are also used to control replication throughout a forest. The Active Directory automatically creates more replication connections between domain controllers in the same site than between domain controllers in different sites. This results in lower replication latency within a site and lower replication bandwidth between sites.

Replication between domain controllers in different sites is compressed 10-15%, resulting in less network bandwidth utilization over the slower links between sites.

Policy objects—Policy objects can be applied to sites as a group or, more specifically, to computer objects that reside in sites.

Using Sites Control

Sites help you to define the physical structure of your network. You can use sites to control the following:

Workstation traffic—When a user logs on, Microsoft Windows NT will attempt to find a domain controller in the same site as the workstation.

Replication traffic—When changes occur in Active Directory, you can use sites to control how and when the change is replicated to which domain controller and how and when the change is replicated to domain controllers in other sites.

Distributed File System (DFS) Topology—You can take advantage of the network's physical structure to provide fault tolerance, resource availability, and improved performance for the logical organization. The logical domain structure of an organization does not need to be the same as the network's physical structure. Sites are not tied in any way to the Active Directory namespace.

Establishing Site Parameters

A site can contain the following domain controllers:

- All domain controllers in a single domain
- Some of the domain controllers in a single domain
- Domain controllers from different domains

Understanding Site Server Objects

Sites consist of server objects. These are created for a computer when it is promoted to a domain controller using DCPROMO.EXE. Sites also contain connection objects that are used to configure replication.

Creating the First Site Automatically

Sites can be used to group servers into containers that mirror the physical topology of your network so that you can configure replication between domain controllers. TCP/IP subnets can also be mapped to sites to facilitate automatic joining of new servers to the correct site, which depends on their IP address, and to make it easier for users to find the domain controller closest to them.

When you create the first domain controller, a default site, Default First Site Name, is created, to which the domain controller is assigned. Subsequent domain controllers can be added to this site, however, you can then move these. This site can be renamed if necessary.

Sites are administered and created using the MMC snap-in **Active Directory Sites and Services Manager**. To create a new site, follow this procedure:

1. Start **Active Directory Sites and Services** MMC snap-in, choose **Programs**, **Administrative Tools**, and then select **Active Directory Sites and Services Manager**.
2. Right-click on the site branch and choose **New**. Select **Site** from the displayed context menu.
3. Enter a name for the site, such as Kansas. You must also select a site link (by default there will only be one, DEFAULTIPSITELINK) or type IP.

Note: The name must be 63 characters or less and cannot contain periods or space characters.

4. Choose **OK**.

Your new site has now been created and you can assign IP subnets to it.

Using Site Links

Sites are connected using site links. Active Directory site links are used to define replication connections between sites, and together they represent the physical network. A site link represents a set of sites that can communicate with one another.

For example, a single-site link might represent two sites that are connected with one another with a point-to-point T1. On the other hand, a set of buildings (each in their own site) that are connected to each other over an Asynchronous Transfer Mode (ATM) backbone might be represented by a site link that contains all of those buildings (sites). Similarly, a full mesh Frame Relay network might be represented with a single site link.

Site links are defined by the following components:

Transport—The networking technology that is used to transfer the data that is replicated.

Member sites—Two sites (or more) to be connected through a site link.

Cost—Which site link will be used for replication if there are multiple site links between two locations is determined by this value.

Schedule—The time replication will occur.

To create a site link follow this procedure:

1. Open **Active Directory Sites and Services**.
2. In the console tree, right-click the **Inter-Site transport protocol** you want the site link to use, and select **New Site Link**.
3. In **Name**, type the name to be given to the link.
4. Choose two or more sites to connect, and then select **Add**.
5. Configure the site link's cost, schedule, and replication frequency.

Warning: If you create a site link that uses SMTP, you must have an Enterprise Certification Authority (Enterprise CA) available and SMTP must be installed on all domain controllers that will use the site link.

Transport Site Link

Sites are connected by different network technologies, such as T1, network or dial-up links. Each site in a multiple-link environment must be connected to at least one site link. If not, the domain controllers in the site would not be able to communicate with other domain controllers in other sites. You create site links that use a specific transport—RPC over SMTP or RPC over TCP/IP. The RPC transport will appear as the IP transport option.

Site Link Cost Factors

It is important to calculate the cost of site links when you are figuring out replication. You configure site link cost by assigning a value for the cost of each available connection used for Inter-Site replication. If you have a number of redundant network connections, establish site links for each connection and assign costs to these site links that reflect their relative bandwidth.

For example, you have a high-speed T1 line and a dial-up network connection in case the T1 line is unavailable. Configure a lower cost for the T1 line and a higher cost for the dial-up network connection. Active Directory always chooses the connection on a per-cost basis, so the cheaper connection will be used when it is available.

Higher cost numbers represent lower priority replication paths. If there are multiple links between two sites, Active Directory replication will use the link with the lowest cost that is available.

Any number of site links can connect a site to other sites. Each site in a multi-site directory must be connected to at least one site link. You can control and schedule each topology independently.

Topology—You can control topology by setting the cost on site links. For example, you might set cost = 100 for site links for slow connections to branch office and cost = 1 for site links that are part of your backbone network. This way, branch offices will only replicate with a domain controller that is part of the backbone and not with a second branch office.

Replication—You can control frequency by setting the number of minutes between replication attempts on site links. For example, you might set the global default replication frequency for 15 minutes and a longer frequency for your branch offices. The longer frequency increases replication latency but makes more efficient use of the link.

Link availability—You can control link availability using the schedule on site links. You would use the default (100%) schedule on most links, but you can block replication traffic between peak hours on links to certain branches. By blocking replication, you give priority to other traffic but increase replication latency.

Site Link Replication Schedule

You can customize replication schedules so replication occurs during specific times to make replication more efficient. For instance, you can schedule your replication for when traffic is low.

To configure site link replication availability, follow this procedure:

1. Open **Active Directory Sites and Services**.
2. In the console tree, choose the Inter-Site transport folder that contains the site link whose schedule you want to adjust.
3. In the details pane, right-click the **site link** whose schedule you want to adjust, and choose **Properties**.
4. Choose **Change Schedule**.
5. Choose the block of time you want to schedule, and then select the desired frequency of replication for that block of time: **None**, **Once per Hour**, **Twice per Hour**, or **Four times per Hour**.

Warning: Since SMTP is asynchronous, it ignores all schedules. Do not configure site link replication availability on SMTP site links unless the site links use scheduled connections, or the SMTP queue is not on a schedule, and information is being exchanged directly from one server to another, and not through intermediaries.

Creating Site Link Bridges

Site link bridges are used to connect two or more sites together and define the routing activities of a network. By default, all site links will be considered transitive, or all the site links belong to a single site link bridge for that transport. Site link bridges are not needed in a fully routed IP network. If your IP network is not fully routed, the transitive site link feature for the IP transport can be turned off. The result is that all IP sites are considered intransitive and site link bridges will be needed to configure or model the actual routing of the network.

A site link bridge object for a specific Inter-Site transport (typically IP) is created by specifying two or more site links. For example:

- Site link AB connects sites A and B through an IP with a cost of 3
- Site link BC connects sites B and C through an IP with a cost of 4
- Site link ABC connects AB and BC
- The site link bridge ABC implies that an IP message can be sent from site A to site C with a cost of 7 (3+4)

Figure 7.8 Site Link Bridge

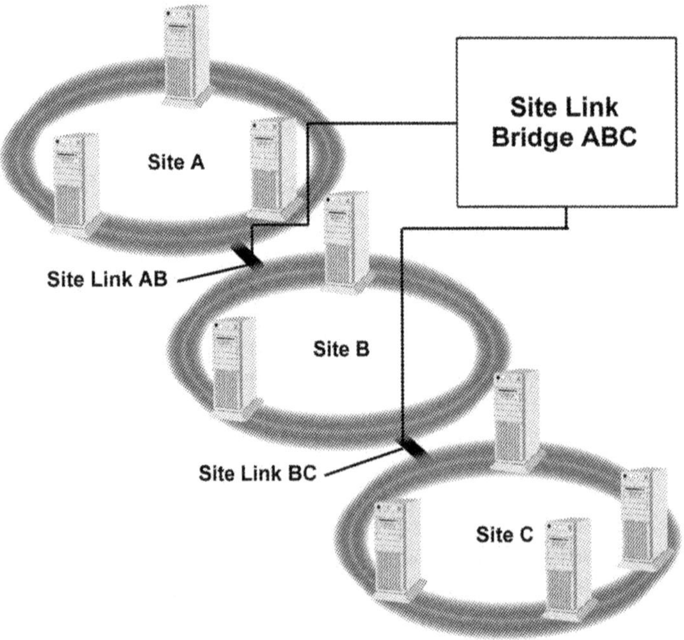

Each site link in a bridge needs to have a site in common with another site link in the bridge. If not, the bridge cannot compute the costs from sites in the link to the sites in other links of the bridge.

Multiple site link bridges for the same transport work together to model multi-hop routing. For example:

- Site link CD connects the sites C and D through an IP with the cost of 2
- Site link bridge BCD connects BC and CD
- The site link bridges ABC and BCD together imply that an IP message can be sent from site D to site A with a cost of 9 (2+3+4)

Any network can be described by a combination of site links and site link bridges can be described by site links alone.

Figure 7.9 Site Link Bridge Two

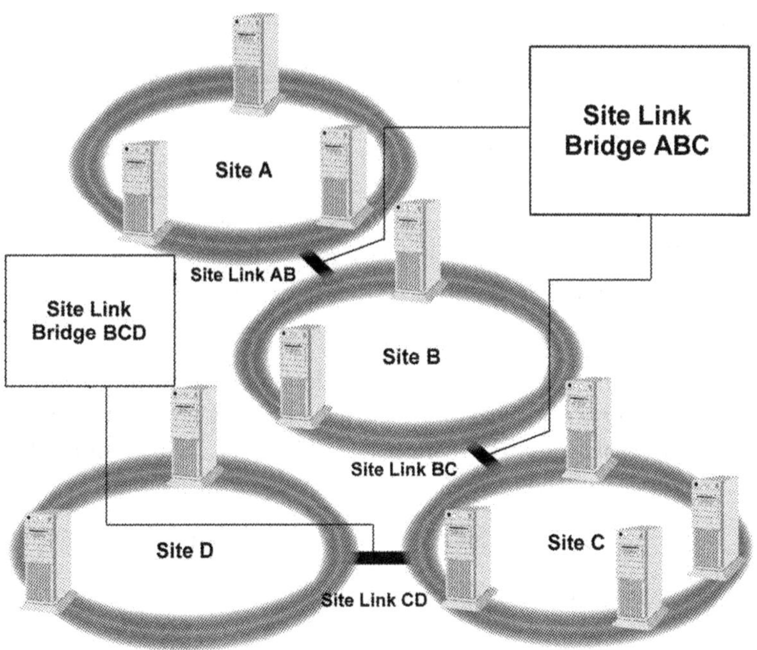

To create a site link bridge, follow this procedure:

1. Open **Active Directory Sites and Services**.
2. In the console tree, right-click the **Inter-Site transport folder** for which you want to create a new site link bridge, and then select **New Site Link Bridge**.
3. In **Name**, type a name for the site link bridge.
4. Choose two or more site links to be bridged, and then select **Add**.

Note: If you have enabled **Bridge all site links**, this procedure will have no effect. Creating a site link between two or more sites is a way to influence replication topology. By creating a site link, you provide Active Directory with information about what connections are available, which ones are preferred, and how much bandwidth is available. Active Directory uses this information to choose times and connections for replication that will afford the best performance.

Placing Domain Controllers in Your Network

Domain controller placement has an effect on network response time and application availability. For example, Microsoft Exchange depends on domain controllers for authentication, group policy, and user-specific information.

The first step in planning a site structure is to determine where a domain controller is required. With a domain controller at each site, all users will have a local computer that can service requests for each domain over LAN connections. To reduce replication traffic, an organization may choose not to place a domain controller at each site. Consider the following guidelines for placing domain controllers:

- A domain controller should be able to respond to client requests in a timely manner
- Configure your domain controllers so that they are able to support the number of objects in the domain where they are members

- For the best performance, put at least one domain controller in each site that contains users or computers of that domain
- The speed and the network bandwidth of the network connection is a determining factor in domain controller placement

Connectivity and Bandwidth

When grouping subnets into sites, you need to examine connectivity and net available bandwidth between locations. Only subnets that are connected by fast, inexpensive, and reliable means should be combined into a site. The definition of what is considered fast, inexpensive, and reliable is determined by your organization, as there are tradeoffs that each will take into consideration.

Available bandwidth is important in determining a site plan because a connection that is fast, inexpensive, and reliable may be heavily utilized. Your network connection between two locations may be fast, but if it has already reached 75% capacity—even without any Active Directory or logon traffic—you may want to control the replication traffic and logon requests to this location. Even though the connection may be fast, inexpensive, and reliable it may still be advantageous to create sites on either side of the connection.

Controlling Workstation Logon Traffic

You can use sites to control which domain controller each workstation should use to log on. When a user logs on, a workstation will attempt to find a domain controller in its local site. This is done using the TCP/IP address and subnet mask of the workstation and site information configured in Active Directory.

If you want a workstation to find a domain controller over a fast reliable connection, then sites can mirror the organization's topology of fast network connections. However, if you want specific workstations to log on to a particular domain controller or set of domain controllers, you define sites so only those specific domain controllers and not others in the same physical location are in the same site as the workstation.

You can define multiple sites at a single physical location, but there are potential disadvantages to doing so. If no domain controllers in the same site are available when a workstation logs on, the workstation will use another domain controller that could be anywhere on the network. Active Directory does not try to determine what other site is physically nearest to its own in terms of network connectivity.

Note: If a domain controller for the local site is not available when a workstation logs on, the workstation will periodically check whether a domain controller for the site has become available. If a domain controller has become available, the workstation will direct all subsequent requests to the local domain controller.

Controlling Replication Traffic

You can use sites to have greater control over how and when replication occurs. Replication within sites occurs automatically. Between sites, replication can be more closely controlled. For instance, you can schedule replication for off-peak times.

Inter-Site replication has the following advantages:

- You can specify the time when replication should occur
- Inter-Site replication is always compressed to reduce the data on the network by 10 to 15 percent of its original size
- You can specify the network transport

When you plan sites to control replication, it is important to determine how much replication traffic will be on the network. Active Directory works to minimize the amount of data to be replicated. It does this by replicating only the revised attributes of an object instead of the entire object.

The number of expected changes in an organization's directory will have an affect on the amount of data to be replicated.

Warning: How often users need to change their passwords has an impact on replication traffic. When users are required to change their passwords once a month, there will be more replication traffic than if they are required to change them every 60 days.

New Site Creation and Configuration

Site links need to exist for replication to occur between sites. Active Directory sites can be managed and configured using Active Directory Sites and Services. Site link resources can be managed through site link costs, and connections can be managed through site link bridges.

Creating a New Site

Active Directory Sites and Services are used to create and manage sites and site objects. You would use Active Directory Sites and Services for the following tasks:

- Create sites
- Create subnets
- Group subnets within sites
- Move servers within sites

Each server is represented as a server object in Active Directory. Server objects are children of site objects. A server's parent site should contain the server's subnet. When you promote a server to a domain controller, the newly created server object may not be placed in the proper site. You should move the domain controller to keep the servers' sites consistent with their IP subnet.

Create Site Links

When you create a site link you define the following elements:

- Transport protocol that will be used to transfer replicated data
- Sites that will be connected through the site link
- Cost information that determines which site link will be used for replication—if there are multiple links between sites
- Scheduled times for replication

Adding a Site to a Site Link

To add a site to a site link, follow these steps:

1. Open **Active Directory Sites and Services**.
2. In the console tree, choose the **Inter-Site transport folder** that contains the site link to which you are adding the site.
3. In the details pane, right-click the **site link** to which you want to add the site, and then choose **Properties**.
4. Choose the site you want to add to this site link, and then select **Add.**

Moving a Domain Controller between Sites

To move a domain controller to a new site, follow these steps:

1. Open **Active Directory Sites and Services**.
2. In the console tree, right-click the **domain controller** that you want to move to a different site, and then choose **Move**.
3. In the **Move Server** dialog box, choose the site to which you want to move the domain controller.

Tip: This procedure can be used to move servers, as well as domain controllers, between sites.

Exercise A—Transitive Sites

If you leave the site links as transitive, much of the work is done for you and this maximizes available connections between sites. However, this can cause problems in some environments and you can choose to remove this transitivity and instead manually create site link bridges that can communicate using a common transport. You must first disable the site link transitiveness with the following procedure:

1. Start the Sites and Services MMC snap-in (Start—Programs—Administrative Tools—Active Directory Sites and Services)
2. Expand the **sites branch**.
3. Expand **Inter-Site Transports**.
4. Right-click on the **relevant transport** (IP or SMTP) and choose **Properties**.
5. Unselect **Bridge all site links** and choose **OK**.

Now the sites are not all bridged by default.

You can manually group the site links by creating a site link bridge, however you must disable the bridge all site links first as follows, or this procedure will have no effect.

1. Start the **Sites and Services** MMC snap-in, Choose **Start**, **Programs**, **Administrative Tools**, and then select **Active Directory Sites and Services**.
2. Expand the **sites branch**.
3. Expand **Inter-Site Transports.**
4. Choose the **protocol**, for example, IP.

5. Right-click the **protocol** and choose **New Site Link Bridge**.
6. Choose at least two **site links** to be a part of the bridge and enter a name.
7. Choose **OK**.

Bridges are important. Suppose you have three sites: A, B and C, and you have two site links defined, A to B and B to C. If the site links are not transitive, A and C have no method to communicate.

By linking them into a site link bridge, they can now communicate through B.

You can completely turn off the KCC for Inter-Site replication and manually define every single connection object. For a large number of sites, this could be a time-consuming task, and the risk of errors would be high.

For most sites, you can just leave the site link transitivity turned on, and you are done without any other configuration needed.

Exercise B—Changing Replication Schedule between Two Domain Controllers in a Site

By default, domain controllers will replicate once an hour. However, this can be changed. The following exercise will step you through the process.

Warning: This is only for domain controllers in a single site; cross-site replication is configured differently.

1. Start the **Active Directory Sites and Services** MMC snap-in.
2. Expand the **sites branch** which will show the various sites.
3. The default site **Default First Site Name** may be your only site. Expand the site containing the domain controllers.
4. Expand the **servers**.

5. Choose the **server** you want to configure replication to and expand it.
6. Double-click on **NTDS Settings** for the server.
7. Right-click on the **server** you want to set replication from.
8. Choose **Properties** from the context menu.
9. Choose the **Active Directory Service connection** tab.
10. Choose **Change Schedule**.
11. Modify the replication as required.
12. Choose **OK**.

Figure 7.10 Schedule Window

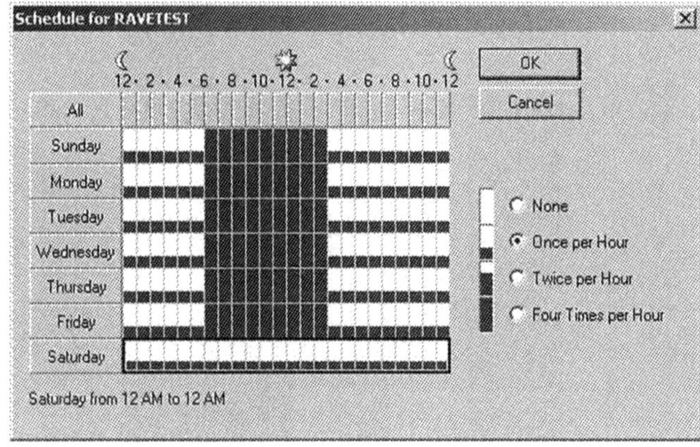

13. Choose **Apply**, then select **OK**.

Note: This replication schedule is one way. It would need to be repeated for the other direction.

Vocabulary

Review the following terms in preparation for the certification exam.

Term	Description
Global Catalog server	A Global Catalog server is simply a domain controller server that is also configured to act as a Global Catalog. Global Catalog servers are identified as such in DNS and can be located by users using DNS. The Global Catalog contains a partial replica (i.e. a subset of attributes) of all objects in the Forest. This means that some attributes of every object in every domain database in the forest are maintained in the Global Catalog. The Global Catalog is used for fast forest-wide searches of enterprise objects. The Global Catalog is also used during logon to determine universal group membership, since universal groups do not reside within any particular domain.
GUID	Globally Unique Identifier
KCC	The Knowledge Consistency Checker is a service that automatically generates a replication topology.
latency	The time lag between the beginning of a request for data and the moment it begins to be received. The time necessary for a packet of data to travel across a network.
multimaster replication	A replication model in which any domain controller accepts and replicates directory changes to any other domain controller. This differs from other replication models in which the computer stores the single modifiable copy of the directory and other computers store backup copies.

Term	Description
operations master roles	A domain controller that has been assigned one or more special roles in an Active Directory domain. The domain controllers assigned these roles perform operations that are single-master, which means they are not permitted to occur at different places on the network at the same time. The domain controller that controls that particular operation owns the operations master role for that operation. The ownership of these operations master roles can be transferred to other domain controllers.
REPADMIN.EXE	A command-line tool that enables replication consistency to be checked for a KCC recalculation. The switch /showreps displays a list of replication partners. The invocation ID is the database GUID and will also show reason for problems.
replication	The process of copying data from a data store or file system to multiple computers to synchronize the data. Active Directory provides multimaster replication of the directory between domain controllers within a given domain. The replicas of the directory on each domain controller are writeable. This allows the update to be applied to any replica of a given domain. The replication service automatically copies the changes from a given replica to all other replicas.
replication latency	Replication takes time. At any moment, all the domain controllers in your forest may not have equal replicas. The delay between an action and replication throughout your network is referred to as replication latency.
site	One or more well-connected TCP/IP subnets. A site allows administrators to configure Active Directory access and replication topology quickly and easily to take advantage of the physical network. When users log on, Active Directory clients locate Active Directory servers in the same site as the user.

Term	**Description**
site link	A link between two sites that allows replication to occur. Each site contains the schedule that determines when replication can occur between the sites that it connects.
site link bridge	The linking of more than two sites for replication using the same transport. When site links are bridges, they are transitive. All sites linked for a specific transport implicitly belong to a single site bridge for that transport.
TCP/IP	Transmission Control Protocol/Internet Protocol
topology	The relationship among a set of network components. In the context of Active Directory replication, topology refers to the set of connections that domain controllers use to replicate information among themselves.
USN	Update Sequence Number is assigned by the domain controller when an object is updated. USNs are stored in a table maintained by each domain controller and are incremented after each update. This occurs for both originating and replicating updates.

In Brief

If you want to…	Then do this…
Create a site link	1. Open **Active Directory Sites and Services**. 2. In the console tree, right-click the **Inter-Site transport protocol** you want the site link to use, and select **New Site Link**. 3. In **Name**, type the name to be given to the link. 4. Choose two or more sites to connect, and then select **Add**.
Configure site link replication availability	1. Open **Active Directory Sites and Services**. 2. In the console tree, choose the **Inter-Site transport folder** that contains the site link whose schedule you want to adjust. 3. In the details pane, right-click the **site link** whose schedule you want to adjust, and then select **Properties**. 4. Choose **Change Schedule**. 5. Choose the block of time you want to schedule, and then choose the desired frequency of replication for that block of time: **None**, **Once per Hour**, **Twice per Hour**, or **Four times per Hour**.

If you want to…	Then do this…
Move a domain controller to a new site	1. Open **Active Directory Sites and Services.** 2. In the console tree, right-click the **domain controller** that you want to move to a different site, and then select **Move**. 3. In the **Move Server** dialog box, choose the **site** to which you want to move the domain controller.
Identify and map your direct server connections	1. Open **Active Directory Sites and Services.** 2. Expand **Sites**. 3. Expand the **site** in which your server currently resides. 4. Expand **servers**. 5. Expand **yourservername**. 6. Choose **NTDS Settings** for your domain controller. 7. The connection objects for your server appear in the right pane.

Lesson 7 Activities

Complete the following activities to prepare for the certification exam.

1. Define the purpose of the Operations master roles.

2. Your Active Directory forest has 4 domains. A domain controller in one of the domains is a Global Catalog server. Define the naming contexts available on the Global Catalog server.

3. Your Active Directory domain has two domain controllers located on separate segments of the network. The router that connects the two networks fails and the two controllers cannot communicate for 36 hours. When the connectivity to them is restored, describe how much domain information will replicate between the two domains.

4. You change an attribute on a user in Active Directory on one domain controller. A short time later, the user changes his password on another domain controller. Explain what will happen to the two changes when they are replicated to domain controllers throughout the domain.

5. List at least four replication recommendations.

6. Explain collisions and how Active Directory handles collision resolution.

7. Explain how intra-site replication works in Windows 2000.

8. MyCompany has branch offices in Boston, Seattle, Paris and Honolulu. The company is divided into three divisions—West Coast, which includes Honolulu, East Coast and Europe. Each division has a headquarters. Explain the site link protocol you would use between sites.

9. You need to limit replication traffic between two domain controllers to the night hours. Describe the process you would follow.

10. Your office in Bellingham, WA is connected to the office in Seattle by a WAN. When large amounts of data are being transferred across the WAN, the users in Bellingham cannot log in. Explain what you can do to solve the problem.

Answers to Lesson 7 Activities

1. Since some changes are impractical to perform in multimaster fashion, one or more domain controllers can be assigned to perform operations that are single-master, which means they are not permitted to occur at different places in a network at the same time. Operations master roles are assigned to domain controllers to perform single-master operations.

2. The naming contexts available on the Global Catalog server are: a full replica of the Global Catalog server's domain, the configuration and schema for the forest, and partial replicas of the other three domains.

3. Only the changes, which have occurred since the last replication, will replicate.

4. The two changes will be replicated to all domain controllers. Since different attributes were updated, and replication occurs at the attribute level, no conflict occurred.

5. Here are some replication recommendations:

   a. Intra-Site replication assumes good network connectivity so that domain controllers can save CPU cycles for client logons, search operations, etc. by not compressing data for Intra-Site replication.

   b. Replication traffic is predictable. Use the tables in this chapter to find the data for your objects. If you set additional attributes on objects, add 100 bytes per attribute with a string size up to 10 characters.

   c. Partial replication (Global Catalog replication) is smaller than normal replication. The difference is bigger when more attributes are used on objects.

   d. Inter-Site replication adds compression. If there is a slow link between domain controllers, create a new site.

   e. Inter-Site replication is scheduled. This reduces communication between domain controllers.

   f. The SMTP transport creates more network traffic than the RPC Site connector. Use RPCs between sites whenever possible.

6. One problem in any multimaster replication scheme is that updates to a single object can occur in multiple places at the same time. For example, if an administrator in New York changes a user's name from "Curt" to '"Kurt" and an administrator in Hong Kong simultaneously changes that same user's name from "Curt" to "Kirk," a replication collision will occur. There are two problems to deal with when a collision occurs: detecting the collision and resolving the collision.

   Active Directory stores property version numbers to allow replication collision detection. These numbers are specific to each property of every object within Active Directory and are updated every time the property is modified. These numbers are propagated through Active Directory along with the change so that a server, which receives two different updates to the same property with the same property version number, can conclude that a replication collision has occurred.

   Active Directory servers resolve collisions by applying the update with the later timestamp. The server that initiated the change creates the timestamp, so it is very important to keep system time synchronized between Windows 2000 servers.

7. The KCC will automatically manage the replication within a site. A bi-directional ring topology is used intra-site using RPC over TCP/IP without any kind of compression. This is because domain controllers within a site are thought to be on a fast network, as per the definition of a site, and the extra processing required to compress/uncompress is undesirable.

   The KCC runs every 15 minutes adjusting the topology as needed and, as new domain controllers are created, they are automatically placed in the ring. You can view these links using the Active Directory Sites and Services MMC snap-in by expanding the site, expanding the servers container, and expanding the server. The created connection objects are under the NTDS Settings leaf.

   The rings are ordered by the domain controller's GUID to ensure convergence on a single topology as the KCC runs on all domain controllers. There is an exception to the ring rule. There can never be more than 3 hops between any two domain controllers within the ring and so if there are 7 or more domain controllers, extra links are added to protect the 3 hop rule.

8. IP is the only site link protocol that can be used between the West Coast and East Coast because these sites are in the same domain. Either SMTP, IP, or both could be used between Paris and the East Coast. If both protocols are used, a lower cost should be assigned to the SMTP site link because SMTP is a more efficient protocol than IP (RPC).

9. Put the domain controllers in separate sites and schedule replication appropriately.

10. Place a domain controller and Global Catalog server in the Bellingham office.

Lesson 7 Quiz

These questions test your knowledge of features, vocabulary, procedures, and syntax.

1. What utility allows you to view the status of replication on domain controllers in the domain?

   A. Performance Monitor
   B. Replication Monitor
   C. Network Monitor
   D. KKC

2. How can you choose between the two Inter-Site transports?

   A. You would use SMTP as the replication connector if the network connection is unreliable, or domain controllers have no direct network connection but are connected only through a messaging system.
   B. You would use multiple sites and RPC-over-IP replication connector if reduced network traffic is desired and the connection between domain controllers is fairly reliable.
   C. The SMTP transport creates more network traffic than the RPC site connector. Use RPCs between sites whenever possible.
   D. You would use only one site if good network connectivity is available and fast client logon is desired.

3. You are viewing the connection objects on a domain controller in your domain. Some of the replication partners are different than yesterday. Which of the following statements is correct?

   A. You have added or removed domain controllers from the network.
   B. There are network connectivity problems between domain controllers.
   C. You have added or removed a Global Catalog server.
   D. There has been a change in site topology.

4. What tools are available to monitor/change replication?

   A. REPLMON.EXE
   B. REPADMIN.EXE
   C. LSA
   D. Active Directory Sites and Services MMC snap-in

5. Replication is complex. Which of the following statements are correct?

   A. The fact that one domain controller uses another as a source for replication information is expressed as a connection object in the Active Directory. These define incoming replication only. Once a connection object has been created, it can be used to replicate information from all naming contexts.
   B. You cannot disable the KCC topology generator and manually create the connection objects required for replication.
   C. Intra-Site replication, replication between domain controllers in different sites, attempts to complete in the fewest CPU cycles possible.
   D. Attribute changes, such as lockout of user accounts, change of domain trust passwords, some changes in the roles of domain controllers, which are considered security-sensitive, are immediately replicated and intra-site partners are notified.

6. You can delegate a number of different controls and permissions using Active Directory Sites and Services. Of the following which are correct?

   A. Delegate control for the sites and subnets
   B. Delegate control for the Inter-Site transports, sites, and server containers
   C. Delegate control of Inter-Site transports and domain controllers.
   D. Delegate permissions for replication.

7. Can you identify the correct statements about the factors that influence replication topology?

   A. You replicate data through automatically or manually created network connections.
   B. Site links influence replication topology.
   C. Replication topology controls how and when replication will occur.
   D. Synchronizing your clocks influences replication topology.

8. How does Active Directory prevent updates on multiple-domain controllers for critical information such as the contents of the schema?

   A. Through the use of operations master servers, which ensure that these changes are made on only one server on the network.
   B. Through the use of directory synchronization.
   C. Through the use of up-to-date vector.
   D. Through the use of the PDC emulator.

9. To ensure that the Active Directory service in the Windows 2000 operating system can replicate properly, a service known as the KCC runs on all domain controllers and automatically establishes connections between individual computers in the same site. What are these called?

   A. Connection objects
   B. Containers
   C. Hierarchical namespace
   D. Organizational Unit

10. You administer a WAN with offices in Seattle and Hong Kong. You have changed a user's password in your organization's Seattle office, your user's new password must be valid when they log on with the same account at the Hong Kong office. What makes this possible?

    A. This is made possible by creating a site bridge.
    B. This is made possible if the two locations are in the same site.
    C. This is made possible by replicating the directory changes to other domain controllers, including that in the Hong Kong office.
    D. This is made possible by creating an explicit trust.

Answers to Lesson 7 Quiz

1. Answer B is correct. The Replication Monitor graphically displays the replication topology of the connections between the servers on the same site.

   Answer A is partly correct. The Performance Monitor replication counters measure the size and efficiency of Active Directory replication traffic.

   Answer C is partly correct. The Network Monitor helps you isolate network packets that replication traffic between domain controllers.

   Answer D is incorrect. The KCC is a service that automatically generates a replication topology.

2. Answer A is correct. SMTP replication connector is used for inter-site transport if the network connection is unreliable or the domain controllers have no messaging system.

   Answer C is correct. You would use RPC connectors as often as possible for inter-site transport as SMTP connectors create more network traffic.

   Answer D is correct. To have the fastest connectivity, use one site.

   Answer B is incorrect. It is a replication recommendation.

3. Answers A, B, C and D are all correct. Your replication partners can be different from one day to the next through adding or removing domain controllers or Global Catalog servers from the network, network connectivity problems, and changes in site topology.

4. Answer A is correct. REPLMON.EXE is a GUI tool used to display and monitor replication status on selected domain controllers.

   Answer B is correct. REPADMIN.EXE is a command-line tool that enables replication consistency to be checked for a KCC recalculation, etc.

Answer D is correct. The Active Directory Sites and Services MMC snap-in enables the viewing/creation/deletion of connection objects.

Answer C is incorrect. LSA is the Local Security Authority.

5. Answer A is correct. When one domain controller uses another for incoming replication information, that process is expressed as a connection object.

   Answer D is correct. Specific attribute changes that are security-sensitive are replicated immediately.

   Answer B is incorrect. You can disable the KCC topology generator and manually create the connection objects required for replication.

   Answer C is incorrect. Intra-Site replication, replication between domain controllers in the same site, attempts to complete in the fewest CPU cycles possible.

6. Answers A and B are correct. In Active Directory Sites and Services, you can delegate control for the subnets, inter-site transports, sites, and server containers. Delegating control of an object allows you to specify who has permissions to access or modify that object or its child objects

   Answer C is incorrect. You can delegate control for inter-site transports but not domain controllers.

   Answer D is incorrect. You cannot delegate permission for replication.

7. Answer B is correct. Creating a site link between two or more sites is a way to influence replication topology. By creating a site link, you provide Active Directory with information about what connections are available, which ones are preferred, and how much bandwidth is available. Active Directory uses this information to choose times and connections for replication that will afford the best performance.

   Answer A is incorrect. You do not replicate through network connections.

   Answer C is incorrect. Replication topology does not control replication.

   Answer D is incorrect. Clock synchronization does not influence replication topology.

8. Answer A is correct. The domain controllers assigned operations master roles perform operations that are single-master, which means they are not allowed to happen at different places on the network at the same time.

   Answer B is incorrect. Directory synchronization occurs between different implementations of directory services, such as Novell Directory Services and Active Directory.

   Answer C is incorrect. The up-to-date vector consists of server-USN pairs, which are held by each server, and is used in the prevention of unnecessary replication.

   Answer D is incorrect. The PDC emulator is a domain controller that can act as a PDC for requests from Microsoft Windows NT clients.

9. Answer A is correct. A connection object uses the actual network connections to exchange directory information. Active Directory uses site links as indicators for where it should create connection objects. Without site links, connection objects that use network connections to connect sites will not be created, and domain controllers will be isolated within their sites.

   Answer B is incorrect. A container is like other directory objects in that it has attributes and is part of the Active Directory namespace. However, unlike other objects, it does not usually represent something concrete. It is the container for a group of objects and other containers.

   Answer C is incorrect. A hierarchical namespace, such as DNS namespace and the Active Directory namespace, are hierarchically structured.

   Answer D is incorrect. An Organizational Unit (OU) is a container object that is an Active Directory administrative partition. OUs can contain users, groups, resources, and other OUs.

10. Answer C is correct. Replication ensures that directory changes are updated at other domain controllers.

    Answer A is partly correct. It is possible if the two sites are connected by a site link bridge. After updates are replicated the user will be able to log on.

Answer B is partly correct. If the two domain controllers are in the same site, the two domain controllers will be updated automatically during the inter-site replication.

Answer D is partly correct. Trusts are relationships established between domains to allow pass-through authentication, in which a trusting domain honors the logon authentications of a trusted domain. User accounts and global groups defined in a trusted domain can be given rights and permissions in a trusting domain, even though the user accounts or groups do not exist in the trusting domain's directory. Your user may have access to some things but not to others.

Lesson 8

Active Directory Schema Modifications

The Microsoft Windows 2000 Active Directory directory service schema contains the definitions of all objects that are stored in Active Directory such as computers, users, and printers. Managing the schema has network-wide implications. Deciding when and whether to modify the schema is one aspect of managing the schema. Schema modification includes adding or changing object class definitions to fit the needs of your network. This is a powerful feature of Active Directory that can also have a large impact throughout the network.

It is important to understand both schema management and Sschema modification, and to understand the implications of each. A carefully designed strategy is needed for managing the schema that includes controlling when and how you implement sSchema modifications.

After completing this lesson, you should have a better understanding of the following topics:

- Active Directory Schema
- Schema Modifications
- Schema Attributes
- Schema Object Identifiers
- Schema Admin Group
- Schema Modification Policy

Active Directory Schema

In Windows 2000, there is only one schema for the entire forest, and it is stored on every domain controller. All objects created in Active Directory (Figure 8.1) conform to the same rules because the schema is maintained forest-wide. When changes are made to the schema, those changes are replicated from the schema operations master to every other domain controller in the forest.

Figure 8.1 Active Directory Schema

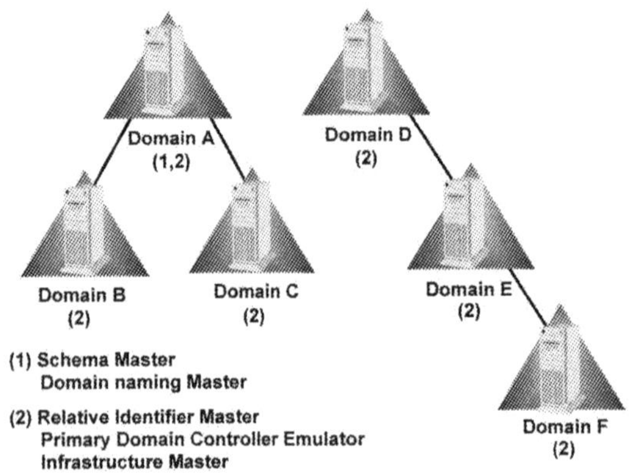

The Active Directory schema is stored in a database. Storing the schema in a database means that it has the following features:

- It is dynamically available to user applications
- It is dynamically extensible
- It can use Discretionary Access Control Lists (DACLS) to protect all classes and attributes

Tip: You can use Active Directory Schema in Microsoft Management Console (MMC) to view or modify the schema. Additionally, Active Directory Services Interface (ADSI) Edit, another MMC snap-in, is available in the Windows 2000 Server Resource Kit to view the schema.

Logically, the schema is stored in a directory partition of the Active Directory database. Within the database, a directory partition is a unit of replication. The schema is treated as an Active Directory object and has the following distinguished name:

CN=Schema, CN=Configuration, DC=Domain_name, DC=Domain_root

When you install Active Directory on the first domain controller in your network, a default schema is created that contains most of the object definitions that an enterprise would need. This schema is stored in the Active Directory database. The Active Directory database, in addition to the schema, contains all the information stored in Active Directory. The file of this database file is NTDS.DIT, and it is located in *systemroot*\Ntds\Ntds.dit.

Note: The Active Directory Installation Wizard uses a configuration file called SCHEMA.INI to preload the schema, which is contained in the NTDS.DIT. The SCIHEMA.INI file sets up the default Active Directory objects.

The Active Directory Schema is a list of definitions. These definitions describe both the kinds of objects that can be stored in Active Directory and the types of information that can be stored about those objects. The definitions are themselves objects that are stored. This allows Active Directory to manage the schema objects with the same object management operations used for managing the rest of the objects in Active Directory.

There are two types of definitions in the Active Directory schema: attributes and classes,classes, also referred to as schema objects or metadata.

In the Active Directory schema, attributes are defined separately from classes. Each attribute is defined only once. However, an attribute can be used in multiple classes. For example, the Description attribute is used in many classes, but is defined once in the schema. The single definition of the attribute assures consistency throughout the schema.

Active Directory objects that can be created are described in Classes. Classes are also referred to as object classes. Each class defines an object as a collection of attributes. When you create a new object, it is attributes that store the information that describes the object. For example, the User class is composed of many attributes, including name, logon name, network address, home directory, and so on. A set of basic classes and attributes is shipped with Windows 2000 Server.

Tip: Every object in Active Directory is an instance of an object class.

Understanding Schema Components

Before you begin to modify schema components, it is important to understand the nature of those components. The components (Figure 8.2) of a schema are classes, attributes, and attribute syntax.

Figure 8.2 Active Directory Components

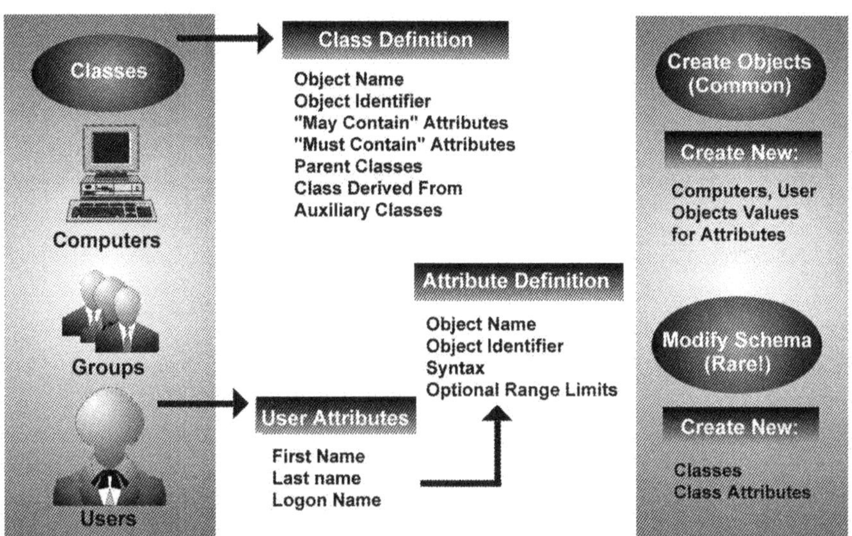

Classes and Attributes

Classes are definitions for groups of objects that share a common set of characteristics, called attributes (Figure 8.3). Users are a class because all Uusers share common attributes such as a first and last name. Every user has a first and last name, which means that they share attributes, but that does not mean that each and every user has the same first and last name. Each user's name can be unique. Printers would be Aanother example of a class. would be Printers.

Note: When you create a new user in Active Directory, you create an object of the class User. Do not confuse this with schema modification, which involves creating or modifying the class definitions themselves.

Figure 8.3 Active Directory Classes

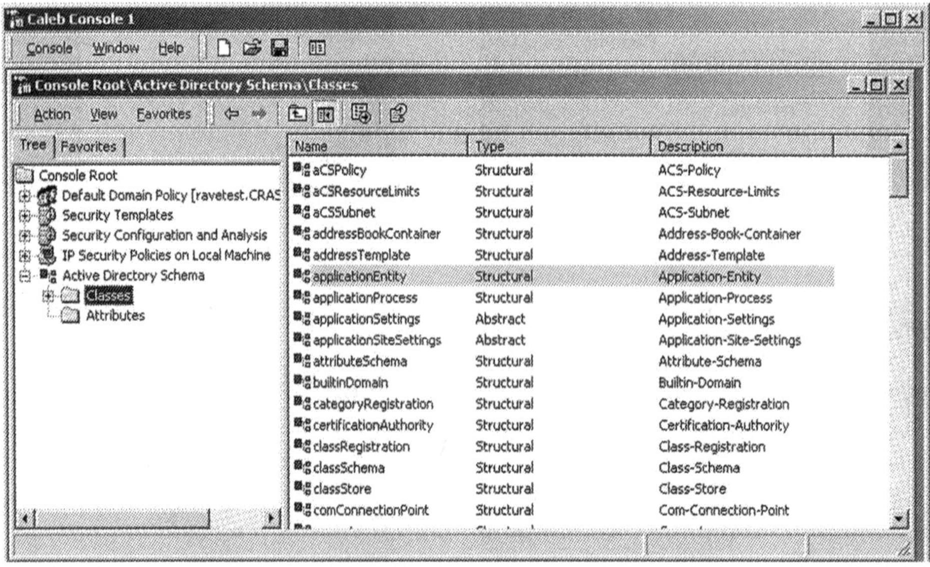

Attribute Syntax

Syntax rules determine the specific types of information attributes can hold. An attribute can have limits upon its definition,; it might require an integer, or a date-formatted value. For example, when you create a User user object, is created, only numeric values are acceptable for the attribute Telephone-Number. This is known as a syntax rule.

Object and Attribute Naming

Objects and attributes both have common and display names. These names can be viewed in the Active Directory Schema. These names do not necessarily map to the labels exposed on dialog boxes.

Schema Modifications

The schema may be dynamically extended. By defining new classes or new attributes for existing classes, the schema can be modified to fit your organization's needs. You must plan and prepare before extending the schema. There are some very valid reasons for modifying the schema. For example, if you need to maintain information about users that is not currently defined in the schema, you must extend the schema definition for the Users class.

Modifying the Schema

Modifying the schema should only be performed by experienced developers and network administrators. Extending the schema is an advanced operation with possible serious consequences

---

Warning: When you change the schema, it is automatically replicated. The new schema cannot be deleted; it can only be deactivated.

The schema defines the structure and relationships of your Active Directory classes and attributes. Using the Schema Active Directory MMC snap-in (Figure 8.4) or using the Active Directory Services Interface (ADSI)), you can add classes and attributes to your Active Directory schema. The ADSI is a set of Application Programming Interfaces (APIs) for programmatically accessing the Active Directory and other directory services.

Figure 8.4 Schema Snap-In

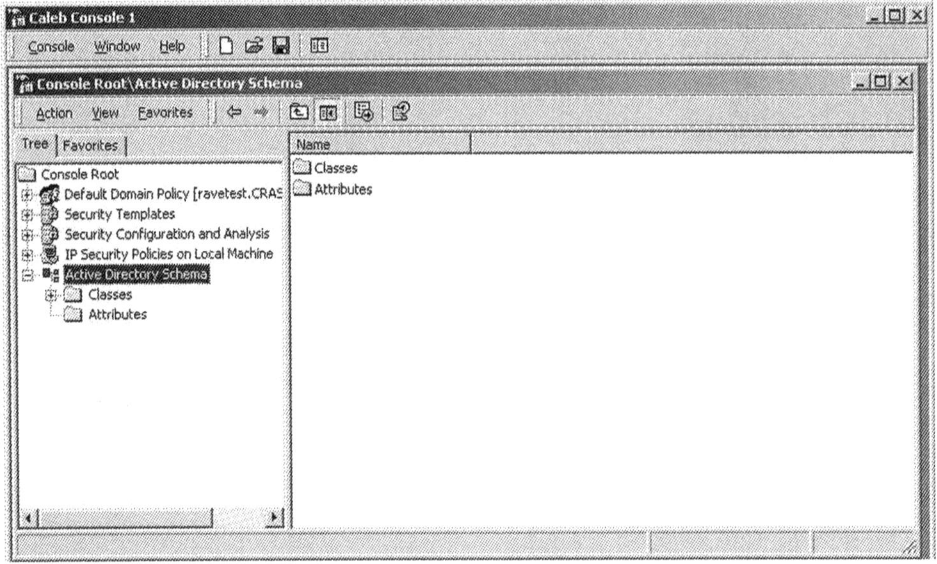

The concept of Active Directory schema modification works well if you have total control of your Active Directory environment, but it can present problems as your organizationsorganization, expands or contracts. This is because you can only have one Active Directory schema per forest. As you define your forest, the schema in place on the first domain is replicated to all other domains in the tree and to all subsequent trees that are made part of the forest.

After you determine that schema modifications are necessary, you must prepare to implement your modifications. While extending the schema is not procedurally difficult, it is an involved process with many steps. BecauseSince there is only one schema for the entire forest and the modifications you make affect the entire network, Windows 2000 has safety features that control modification of the schema. These features must be disabled for modification to occur.

Schema modification involves the following procedures:

- Obtaining an Object Identifier for each new class or attribute
- Preparing the schema operations master for modification
- Creating and modifying classes
- Creating and modifying attributes
- Indexing and replicating attributes
- Deactivating a class or an attribute

Schema modification must be well-planned and executed. There are several safeguard tasks thatSeveral safeguard tasks, which are designed to help prevent unauthorized modification, must be completed before modification can occur. One of these is installing Active Directory Schema in an MMC Console (Figure 8.5).

Figure 8.5 Active Directory Schema in MMC

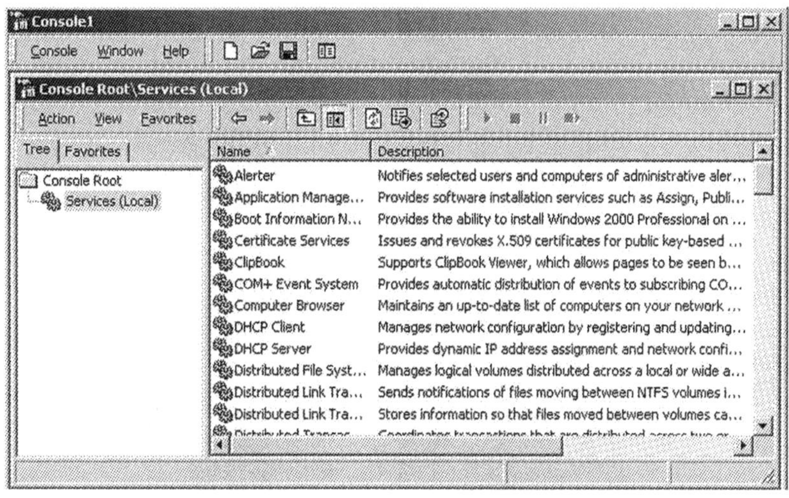

Installing Active Directory Schema in an MMC Console

The default Windows 2000 installation does not include the Active Directory Schema in MMC. You can install Active Directory Schema in MMC by following these steps:

1. Manually register the schema management Dynamic Link Library (DLL) (Figure 8.6) and at the command prompt, type: **`regsvr32 systemroot\system32\ schmmgmt.dll.`**
2. Install the support tools from the Windows 2000 Resource Kits separately from the compact disc.

Figure 8.6 Schema Management Dynamic Link Library Registration

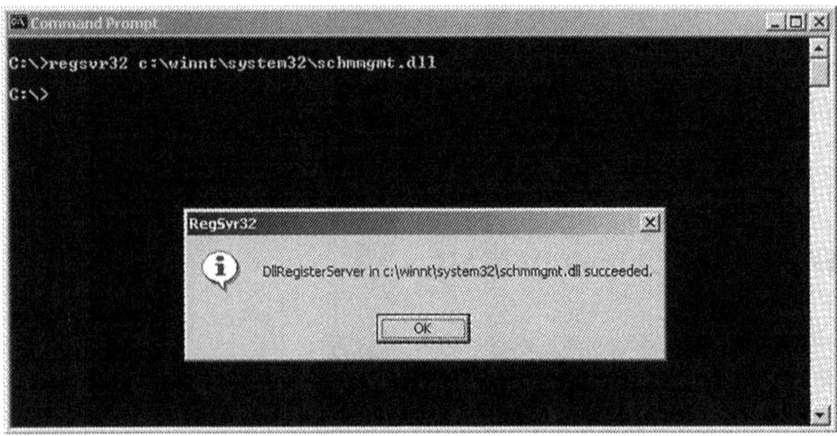

After installing Active Directory Schema, you can add it to a customized MMC console.

Processes for Modifying the Schema

You can use the following methods to modify the schema. You can modify the schema by::

- Using Active Directory Schema in MMC
- Using scripting with ADSI
- Installing software applications

Using Active Directory Schema in MMC

Members of the Schema Admins Group can use the Active Directory Schema in MMC to manage the schema by creating, modifying, or deactivating classes and attributes.

Using Scripting with ADSI

You can write a script with ADSI (Figure 8.7) calls to the schema. These calls can be used to create, modify, or deactivate classes and attributes. The scripting method should be used when you want to automate schema modifications.

Figure 8.7 Active Directory Services Interface Snap-In

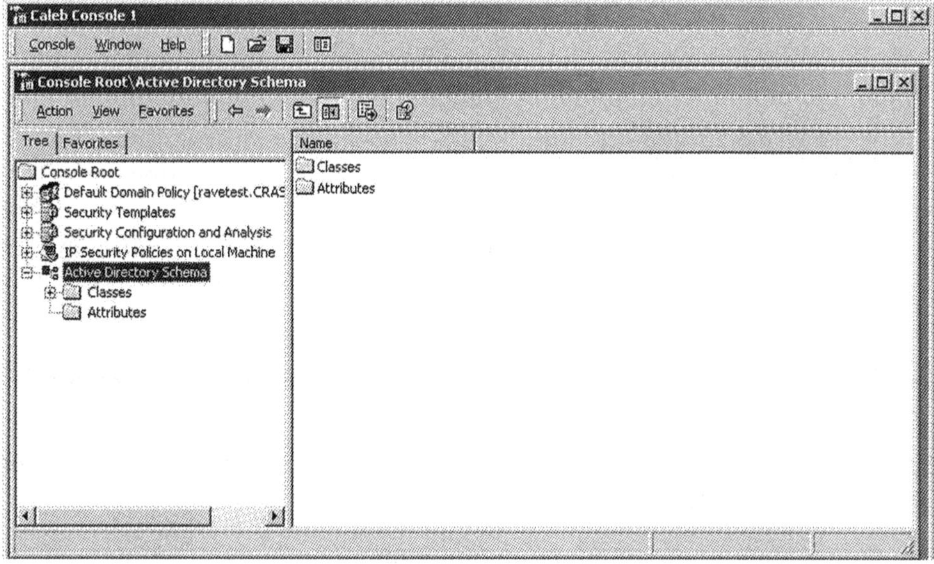

Tip: For sample scripts, see the Windows 2000 Server Resource Kits.

Installing software applications

Active Directory—enabled applications are software applications that add classes or attributes during the application installation process. Active Directory—enabled enabled applications should have the following two phases of installation:

- In phase one of the installation, the schema is modified;. only members of the Schema Admins Group are allowed to run the part of the software application installation that modifies the schema
- In phase two of the installation, the traditional application installation proceeds; a. nyone with appropriate permissions can run this part of the installation

Not all schema objects can be modified or deactivated. Classes and attributes that are defined as systems cannot be modified or deactivated. Modifications are also subject to certain restrictions. These restrictions are enforced by Active Directory. Whether the classes or attributes were part of the default schema or were added after the original installation often determines the restrictions. The directory service recognizes a set of valid attribute syntaxes that are hard-coded and cannot be changed.

Note: For more information about what can and cannot be modified in the schema, see the Windows 2000 Resource Kits.

Schema Modification Decisions

Every domain controller in the forest stores a replica of the schema and each of those replicas is updated whenever you make modifications to the schema. Schema modification impacts your entire network.

Even though Windows 2000 replication uses a multimaster replication model, changes to any single network-wide item must be single-mastered to avoid write conflicts. Replication timing depends on the size, structure, and connectivity of the network. Delays in replication can lead to inconsistencies between schema replicas on domain controllers.

Classes inherit the properties of the classes from which they are derived. You must consider the concept of inheritance when you plan to modify the schema. The definition of the class from which you choose to derive a new class definition will affect all future objects of that class type that you create.

Replication Latency and Recovery

Schema modifications are performed on a single domain controller. These modifications are then replicated across all domain controllers in the forest. To ensure schema and object integrity and to expedite convergence, the schema replication process is separate from the process of normal directory replication.

During schema replication, there is the potential for temporary inconsistencies in the schema. It is possible that an instance of an object of a newly- created class may be replicated to a domain controller prior to the arrival of the new schema class. In this case, Active Directory on the target domain controller cannot recognize the new object instance because it does not yet have the class definition for that object.

For example, you create a new class called Company-Cars at a domain controller. You then create an instance of this class, Van #001, at the same domain controller. When the changes are replicated to another domain controller, Van #001 is replicated before the new class, Company-Cars. The replication of the instance will fail on the second domain controller because the second domain controller is not yet aware of the class Company-Cars.

If a replication failure occurs, Active Directory will automatically replicate the schema from the schema operations master. This triggers an immediate schema cache update on the target domain controller. Using our example, this brings in the Company-Cars class and puts it into the target domain controller's schema cache. Once the target domain controller's schema has been updated, Active

Directory then invokes a new replication cycle and replicates the object(s) that failed to the target domain controller. This replication cycle will successfully bring in Van #001.

Note: Active Directory automatically corrects the target domain controller's schema when an object instance replication fails.

Write Conflict Prevention

Windows 2000 Server maintains two copies of the schema (Figure 8.8): one stored in cache and one stored on disk in the Active Directory. The cached schema is used for read purposes and to maintain consistency with any running threads.

Figure 8.8 Two Copies of the Schema

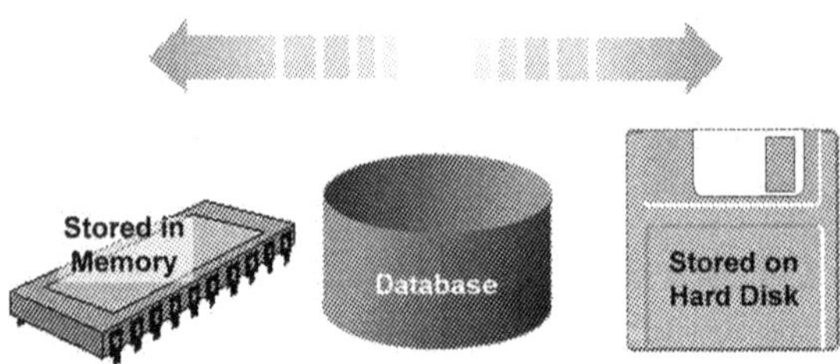

When an administrator writes to the schema, (Figure 8.9) the schema writes are first recorded in the disk copy. After a schema write, Active Directory waits five minutes before it copies the schema from the disk to the cache. Once this occurs, the updated Active Directory schema is then replicated to all domain controllers throughout the forest. During this five-minute interval, no objects that use a new or modified class or attribute can be added to the schema. This behavioraction keeps the cache consistent.

Figure 8.9 Administrative Schema Modifications

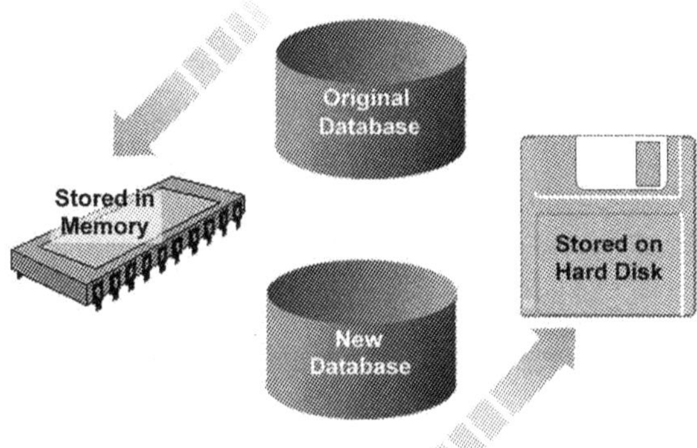

A new cache is built from the schema database each time you update the schema cache (Figure 8.10). However, the old cache remains in memory and existing threads under the old cache continue to use the old cache until their work is finished. When the new cache is built, all new threads refer to it.

Figure 8.10 Schema Cache

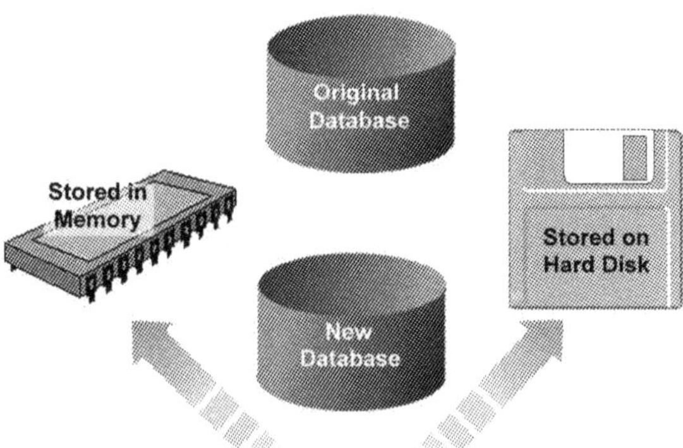

Tip: You can also force a schema cache update to start immediately. However, this should be done only once per editing session, and only after all required schema updates are finished. If multiple cache updates are forced, it is possible to have multiple versions of the schema cache in memory at once, causing a temporary memory drain on the server. For more information on forcing a schema cache update, see Windows 2000 Help.

For In some operations, for example, for schema modifications, (Figure 8.11) Windows 2000 uses a single-master of operations model. Having a schema operations master prevents potential conflicts by designating a single domain controller in the forest to store the write- enabled copy of the schema. By default, the first domain controller installed in the forest is the schema operations master. However, you can change the domain controller that serves as the schema operations master at any time.

Figure 8.11 Schema Modifications

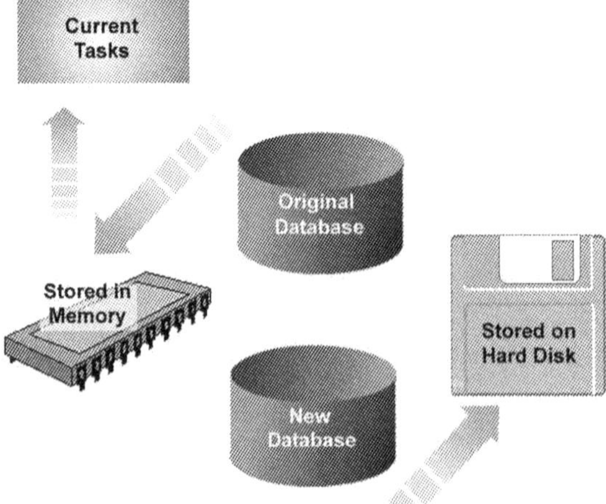

AlsoIn addition, by default, the first schema operations master is not enabled for schema modification. You must manually enable schema modification. As a best practice, you should reset this to the default after completing any schema modifications.

Creating Class Definitions

The ability of a subclass (child class) created from an existing class (parent class) to take on the attributes and rules of the parent class is called inheritance. Before creating new classes, you must be aware of how they are defined (Figure 8.12).

Figure 8.12 Class Definitions

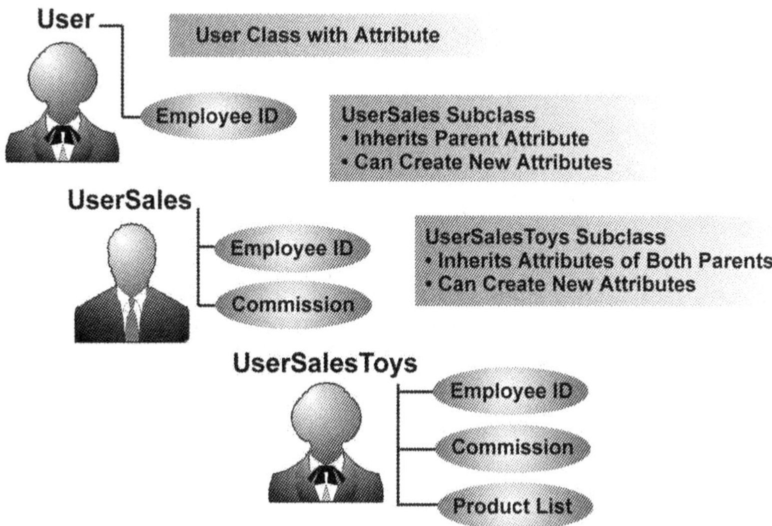

When creating new classes, you should consider the following:

- When new classes need to be created, you can save work if you choose the parent class carefully. By selecting If you choose the correct parent class, you will only need to add or modify attributes as needed for the child class. You will not need to define the existing parent attributes for the child class.

- Child classes inherit parent rules. However, if you modify a child class, those changes are not reflected in the parent class. The parent class does not change.

For example, you may want to create a Salesperson class that defines information about the salespeople in your company. In addition to the normal user data, you may want to include specialized information such as commission rates and territories. If you specify the Salesperson class as a child class of the User class, then the Salesperson class would inherit all the mandatory and optional attributes of the User class, as well as its parent classes. You would only need to create the attributes for the unique data of the Salesperson class: the commission rate and the territories.

Note: You cannot alter the class of an object after it has been created. It is almost alwaysusually better to add new attributes to the User class rather than to create a new a child class.

If you need to alter the class after the objects of that class have been created, you must delete all the existing objects and then recreate them as instances of the new class. In addition, you must also recreate all security assignments for each object. If the object belonged to the User class or a child class thereof, you must also notify the former user that their password has changed.

Using our example, you could alternatively add the commission rate and territories attributes to the User class and then use Groups to manage the Salesperson group. With this method, you need not modify the schema, but you can still have a separate logical grouping of Salesperson users.

Creating a New Class

Classes are treated as objects and are stored in Active Directory. You use Active Directory Schema to create or modify classes.

When you create a new class, you may have attributes that you want to set as mandatory. Setting an attribute as mandatory means that the attribute must have a value when an object instance is created. These mandatory attributes must be included in the class's **Must-Contain** attribute list at object creation. Because of this rule, these attributes will need to be created prior to creation of the class. (Figure 8.13).

Figure 8.13 New Schema Class Creation

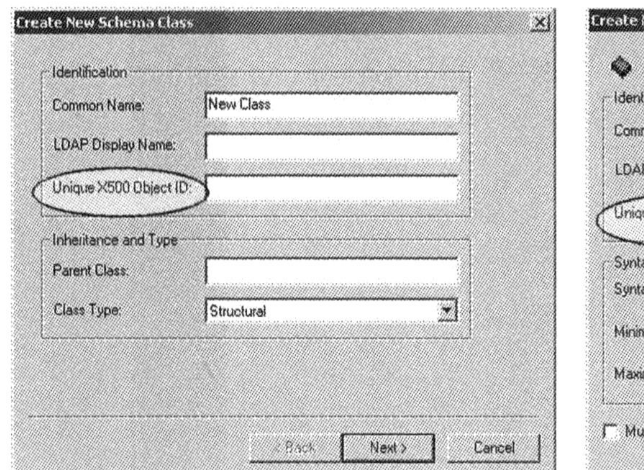

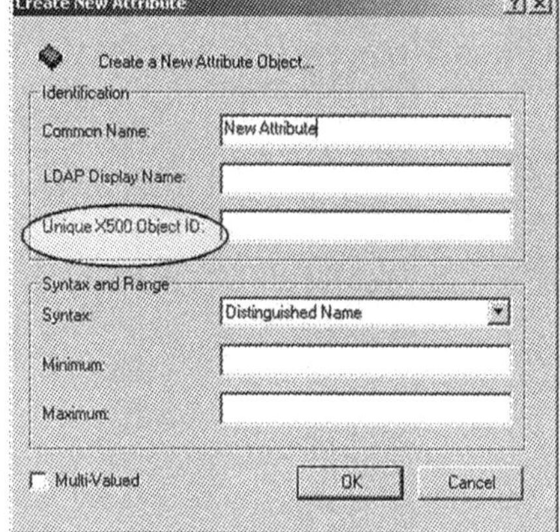

Always complete the following steps in sequence:

1. Add new attributes to the schema.
2. Add new classes to the schema.
3. Add attributes to classes.

Note: The contents of the Must-Contain attribute list cannot be modified once you have created the class definition.

You must provide the following mandatory information when you create a new class (Figure 8.14):

Figure 8.14 Class Properties Attribute Property Page

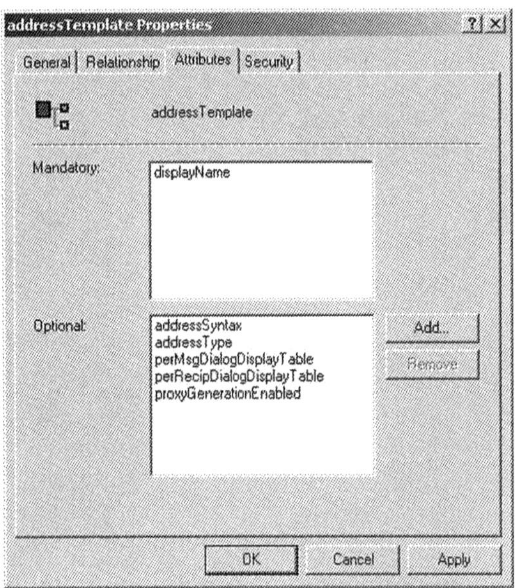

Common name—This is the name displayed in Active Directory.

LDAP display name— Lightweight Directory Access Protocol (LDAP) display names are used in Active Directory searches.

Unique X.500 Object Identifier—This . is the Object Identifier that is issued by a name registration authority and probably extended by your organization.

Parent class—The parent class defines what attributes the new class inherits, and the location in which objects of the new class are created.

Class type—You . must choose one of the following types: structural, abstract, auxiliary, or 88.

Class Types

Structural class type—Can be derived from another structural class or an abstract class. It can include auxiliary classes in its definition. It is the only type of class from which Active Directory objects can actually be created.

Abstract class type—Is a template class that is used to create new abstract, auxiliary and structural classes.

Auxiliary class type—Is a list of attributes and can be derived from existing auxiliary or structural classes. Adding an auxiliary class to the definition of a structural or abstract class adds the attributes defined by the auxiliary class to the structural or abstract class.

88 class type—Is special class type for classes defined prior to 1993 and based upon the 1988 X.500 specification.

Note: For more information on choosing the appropriate class type, see Windows 2000 Help.

Modifying an Existing Class

You can only modify a class by adding optional attributes. You cannot change the class definition. Adding attributes to a class further defines that class. For example, several of your user objects represent temporary employees and a new management policy requires that the billing rate of the supplying temporary agency be stored in Active Directory. The user objects already exist and you cannot change an existing object's class. Therefore, it would not do any good to create a new class. The way to solve this problem is to create an attribute—for example, a new attribute could be called BillingRate. The new attribute is then added to the user class definition.

In a larger organization, a class might already exist whose members are temporary employees. This class would be a child class of the uUser class. In this caseinstance, you would simply add the new attribute to the child class. The benefit in this case is that not all of your new users will be temporary employees and thus not all of your new users will need an associated billing rate.

Schema Attributes

Attributes, like classes, are treated as objects and are stored in Active Directory. You use Active Directory Schema to create or modify attributes.

Creating and Modifying Attributes

Attributes are characteristics of objects. Attributes help define a class, that is, attributes place associations on classes and help to categorize them. For example, the class that represents a user associates the user's name and an attribute, with the user instance. This means that the user object instance for Fred Jones has ana name attribute with the value of Fred Jones." Another attribute of the User class might be the department in which the user works. In this case, the department attribute helps categorize the instance. This means that all user object instances with the attribute value of Sales can be categorized as working in sales.

Creating a New Attribute

As attributes define classes by defining characteristics, Attributes also have characteristics that define them. Some of these characteristics are common to all attributes and thus are required. When you create a new attribute (Figure 8.15), you will be required to supply values for these characteristics:

Figure 8.15 New Attribute Creation

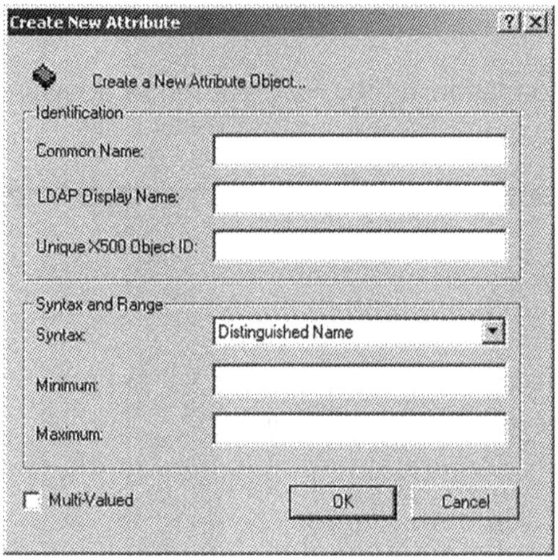

Common name—This is the name displayed in Active Directory.

LDAP display name—LDAP names are used in Active Directory searches.

Unique X.500 Object Identifier—This . is the Object Identifier that is issued by a name registration authority and probably extended by your organization.

Syntax—The syntax specifies the type of attribute value, such as a Distinguished Name, an Object Identifier, or a Case Sensitive String. Optionally, you can set a minimum or maximum range for the value held in the attribute.

Being either multi- or single-valued—A multi-valued attribute can be assigned more than one value. For example, an attribute such as SalesHistory may contain multiple dates representing a sales-person's sales history. Only aan object whose class is of the structural type can have multi-valued attributes.

Note: Multi-valued attributes do not display information in the order that the values were entered.

Modifying an Existing Attribute

You can modify an existing attribute by changing one of its properties (Figure 8.16). For example, an attribute called Zip-Code that holds only 5 integers may be modified to hold 9 integers.

Figure 8.16 Attribute Properties

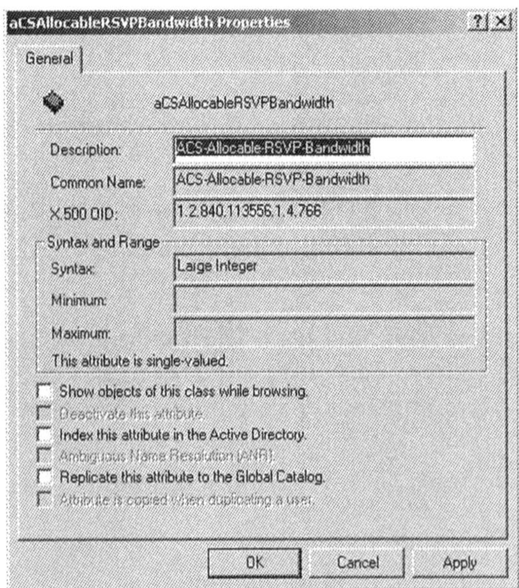

Indexing and Replicating Attributes

You can improve query performance by modifying the following attribute property specifications (Figure 8.17):

Figure 8.17 Attribute Property Specifications

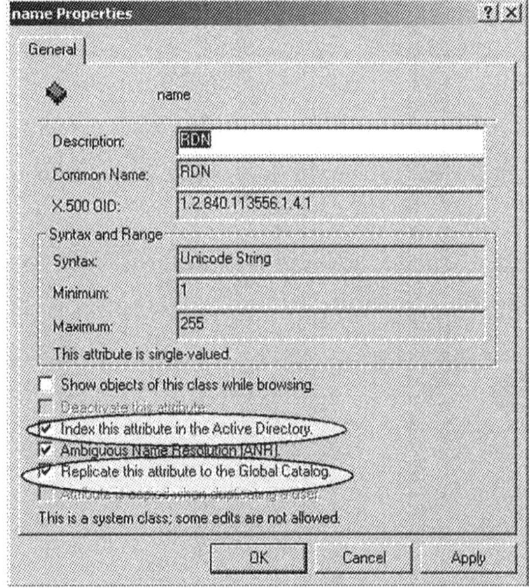

Query performance can be improved by modifying the schema to:

- Index attributes in Active Directory.
- Replicate attributes to the Global Catalog.

Indexing Attributes in Active Directory

When you want to specify an attribute that searches can sort by, you index the attribute in Active Directory. Indexing the attribute speeds up search performance when a search is performed on that attribute. Additionally, this also gives you the ability to create reports that are sorted on the indexed attribute. When you are determining which attributes to index, consider the following:

- Choose single-valued attributes. ; multi-valued attributes can also be indexed, but b. ear in mind that the cost to build the index for multi-valued attributes is larger in terms of storage, update, and search time
- Choose attributes that are likely to be unique to an object instance; . for example, if your company has a single facility and all the employees work at that facility, indexing the St (state) attribute would not be helpful
- As you add more indexed attributes to a class you increase the time it takes to create new instances of the class
- When you identify an attribute to be indexed, all instances of the attribute are indexed as well; t. he index is not limited to just the instances that are members of a particular class
- When you choose the **Index this attribute in the Active Directory** check box in the Name **Properties** dialog box for an attribute in Active Directory Schema, an index is dynamically generated in the Active Directory. (the index is built automatically by a background thread on the domain controller)

Replicating Attributes in the Global Catalog

You can choose attributes to be replicated in the Global Catalog (GC) (Figure 8.18). Attributes stored in the Global Catalog can be retrieved directly by searching the Global Catalog. The attributes you select will be replicated to all Global Catalog servers in the enterprise and,. because of this replication, you should select attributes of the following types:

Figure 8.18 Global Catalog Replication

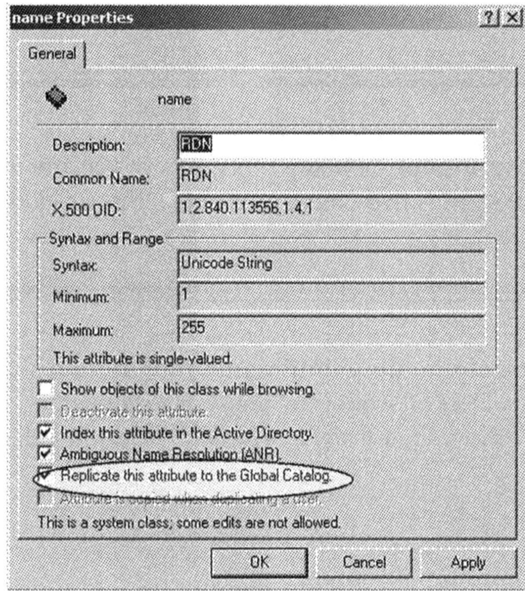

- Attributes that are required to locate objects that may be found anywhere in the forest
- Attributes for which read access is valuable even if the full object is not accessible
- Attributes whose values are relatively stable, since r eplication occurs only when the attribute value changes
- Attributes that have values whose sizes are relatively small; t he larger the attribute, the higher the impact on replication.

When you add an attribute to the Global Catalog, you are trading increased replication and disk storage on Global Catalog servers for potentially faster query performance.

Note: If the **Replicate this attribute to the Global Catalog** check box is selected in the **Properties** dialog box for an attribute in Active Directory Schema, the attribute is replicated to the Global Catalog.

A user may want to search for an attribute that is not stored in the Global Catalog. In this case, the user must first search the Global Catalog to locate the object of interest by using an attribute that is stored in the Global Catalog. Then, the user can retrieve the desired attribute from a domain controller within the domain in which the object resides.

Deactivating Classes and Attributes

Classes or attributes are never really removed from the schema. To prevent irreversible mistakes, they are deactivated instead of deleted. This also improves performance because time—consuming cleanups of deleted objects are not required. Deactivation and reactivation of a class or attribute can be accomplished by using the **Properties** dialog box for that object in Active Directory Schema.

You can only deactivate schema objects (Figure 8.19) that have been added to the schema after schema installation.

Figure 8.19 Schema Object Deactivation

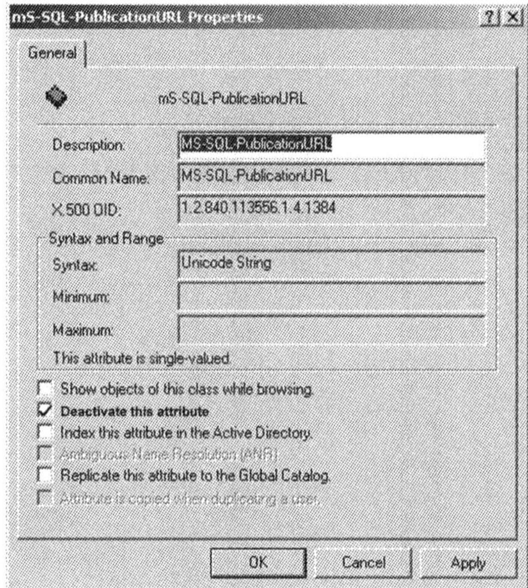

You cannot deactivate the following elements:

- Classes in the subclass-Of, auxiliary-Class, or poss-Superiors list of existing active classes.
- Attributes in the must-Contains or may-Contains of existing active classes.

Tip: For more information about class lists, use Windows 2000 help.

When you deactivate a class or attribute, it is no longer replicated throughout the network or to the Global Catalog server. You cannot create new objects from a deactivated class.

Note: Existing objects of the deactivated class type are not deactivated.

Objects from deactivated classes and deactivated class attributes (Figure 8.20) will appear in searches.

Figure 8.20 Class Deactivation

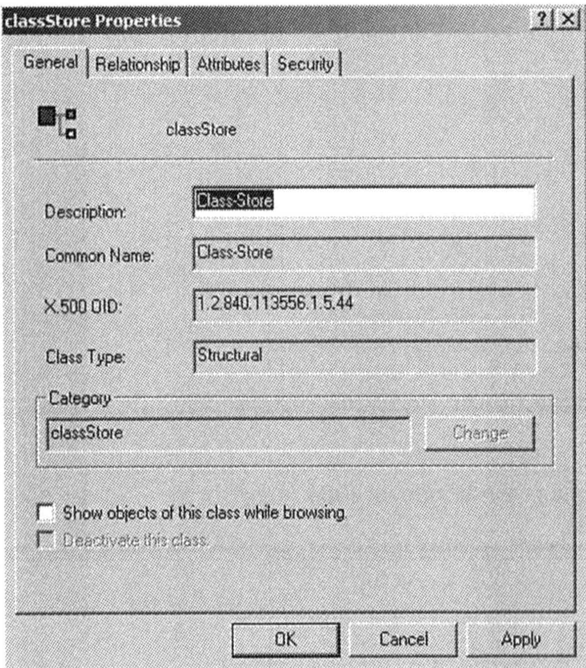

If you are certain that you no longer need objects of a given class, you can perform any or all of the following procedures:

- Deactivate the class
- Search for all objects that are instances of that class
- Delete those objects from Active Directory

If you determine that you no longer need an attribute, then after deactivating an attribute you can perform either or both of the following procedures:

- Search for all objects that have values for that attribute
- Delete the attribute value

Warning: You cannot use deactivated attributes in new or existing classes.

You cannot create new classes or attributes that have the same common name, Object Identifier, or LDAP display name as a deactivated class or attribute.

Note: Use Active Directory Schema to deactivate or reactivate classes and attributes.

Schema Object Identifiers

Each schema object must have a globally unique number, known as an Object Identifier or the X.500 OID (Figure 8.21). Object Identifiers are hierarchical, with the root controlled by the International Standards Organization (ISO). ISO allocates a branch of the Object Identifier tree to subordinate vendors or to name registration authorities.

Figure 8.21 X.500 OID Frame

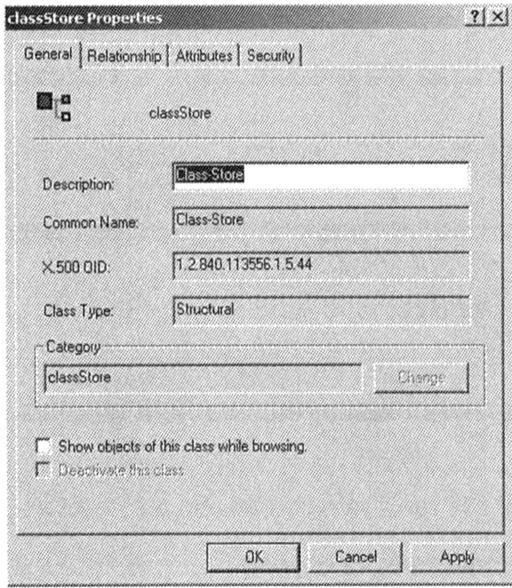

Understanding the Object Identifier Format

An Object Identifier is expressed as a string of numbers delimited by decimal points; for example, 1.2.840.w.x.y.z. The name registration authority issues the leading digits 1.2.840. The remaining digits, w, x, y and z, are reserved for your organization to extend as necessary.

Obtaining and Extending Object Identifiers

The Object Identifier is obtained from a name registration authority. The Object Identifier can be extended to logically represent the branches of objects in your Active Directory schema. You can subdivide the Object Identifier space by appending values to 1.2.840 replacing the values of w.x.y.z. These subspaces can then be assigned to various divisions of the organization. Each division of the organization can, in turn, further subdivide this subspace and so on as needed. An internal issuing authority within the company could then allocate Object Identifiers to requests for new attributes and classes added to your Active Directory schema.

Tip: The Windows 2000 Resource Kits includes the command-line utility OIDGEN.EXE that generates valid Object Identifiers.

Schema Admins Group

The Schema Admins Group exists only in the root domain of the forest. Only members of the Schema Admins Group can make schema modifications. By default, the only member in the Schema Admins Group is the Administrator account in the root domain of the forest. You must add other accounts explicitly.

Adding Members to a Schema Admins Group

You use Active Directory Users and Computers (Figure 8.22) to add a member to the Schema Admins Group.

Figure 8.22 Active Directory Users and Computers

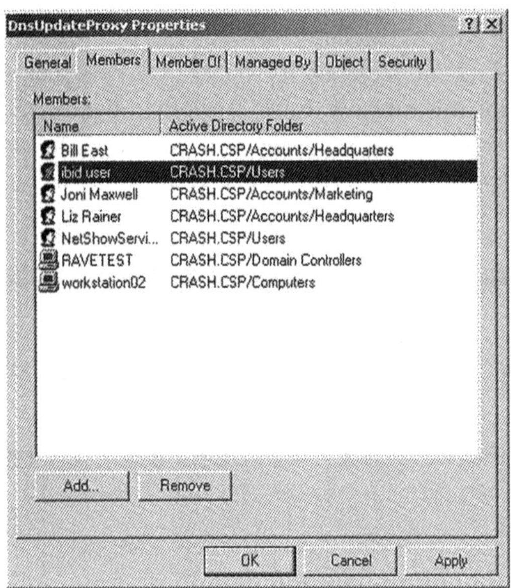

To add a member to the Schema Admins Group follow these steps

1. Open **Active Directory Users and Computers**.
2. In the console tree, double-click the appropriate **domain node** and then choose **users** or select the **folder** that contains the desired user.
3. In the details pane, right-click the **user account** that you want to add, and then choose **Properties**.
4. Choose the **Member of** tab, and then select **add**.
5. In the **Select Groups** dialog box, choose **Schema Admins** and then select **add**.

Warning: Membership in the Schema Admins Group should be carefully managed to prevent unauthorized access to the schema.

Enabling Write Access to the Schema

Schema modification is disabled on all domain controllers. This includes the initial schema operations master. You must first enable write access to the schema before Youyou can modify the schema. You do this by running **Active Directory Schema** and making sure that **The Schema may be modified on this server** check box (Figure 8.23) is selected in the **Change Operations Master** dialog box.

Figure 8.23 Schema Modification on a Server

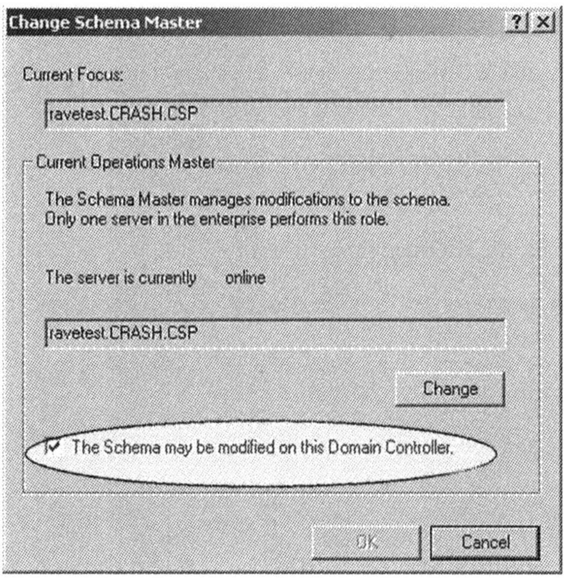

Schema Modification Policy

You should plan and implement schema modifications with care by adhering to the following guidelines:

- Modify the schema only when necessary
- Plan, document, and implement a schema modification strategy
- Take the simplest approach by using. existing attributes when you create new classes
- Avoid large, multi-valued attributes because t. hey are costly to store and retrieve and, while. Active Directory includes an LDAP extension to allow incremental reads of large, multi-valued attributes, not all LDAP clients will know how to use this extension
- Choose parent classes carefully and d. etermine where you want users to be able to create objects of the new class
- If you use scripting for large-scale modifications, require intensive testing of the script before the actual implementation

You should do your best to prevent unnecessary confusion when implementing schema modifications by applying the following recommendations:

- Use meaningful names for new classes or attributes and a. lways use distinctive prefixes to distinguish them from existing classes and attributes
- Do not move the role of the schema operations master unless you need to take the current master offline
- Use the common name for the LDAP display name. because this name is used for searches and this will make searches more efficient

Prevent unauthorized schema modifications by taking the following precautions:

- Keep **The Schema may be modified on this server** check box cleared on your schema operations master
- Closely guard Schema Admins Group membership

Note: If schema updates are performed remotely from a workstation, the setting has to be enabled at the schema operations master, not at the workstation.

Developing a Schema Modification Policy

Always thoroughly plan and prepare before making schema modifications. Significant problems that impair or disable Active Directory network-wide can be caused by inconsistencies in the schema. Some schema inconsistency problems may become evident immediately, but others. might not become evident until later on.

It may be desirable to appoint a committee of individuals who have expertise with directory services to take full responsibility for all schema changes. Members of this committee should have a thorough understanding of how the schema works, what the effects of schema modification are or can be, and how to avoid potential problems.

Regardless of the method, it is very important to establish a schema modification policy prior to any schema modifications. Your schema modification policy should provide guidelines for schema modifications.

Schema Modification Policy Guidelines

At a minimum, your schema modification policy should include guidelines for the following procedures:

- Initiating schema modifications
- Planning schema modifications
- Modifying the schema

Initiating Schema Modifications

Policies for initiating schema modifications should include the following points:

- Submitting schema change requests to a committee for approval
- Validating the need for requested schema changes
- Approving requested changes

Planning schema modifications

Policies for planning schema modifications should include the following points:

- Ensuring that the proposed schema modifications meet the specifications of the needed change
- Ensuring that an effective recovery plan is in place

Modifying the schema

Policies for modifying the schema should include the following points:

- Supervising and testing changes.
- Ensuring directory integrity.

Best Practices

As a best practice, you should always observe the following guidelines:

- Test schema modifications in an isolated test environment, which. should not be part of your forest
- Only use thoroughly tested scripts to avoid typographical errors when the modifications are applied to a production environment
- Remember that you can only deactivate classes or attributes that you have added to your schema, but you cannot delete them

Vocabulary

Review the following terms in preparation for the certification exam.

Term	Description
88 Class type	A special class type for classes defined prior to 1993 and based upon the 1988 X.500 specification.
Abstract Class type	A template class that is used to create new abstract, auxiliary, and structural classes.
ADSI	The Active Directory Services Interface.
attribute	Characteristics of objects.
Auxiliary Class type	A list of attributes, which can be derived from existing auxiliary or structural classes.
class	Definition for groups of objects that share a common set of characteristics, called attributes.
DACL	A Discretionary Access Control List is used to protect all classes and attributes.
inheritance	The ability of a child class to take on attributes of the parent class.
metadata	Another term for attributes and classes.
MMC	Microsoft Management Console.
object classes	Another term for Classes within the schema.
partition	A unit of replication within the database.

Term	Description
recovery	If a replication failure occurs, Active Directory will automatically replicate the schema from the schema operations master. This triggers an immediate schema cache update on the target domain controller. Once the target domain controller's schema has been updated, Active Directory then invokes a new replication cycle and replicates the object(s) that failed to the target domain controller.
replication latency	It is possible that an instance of an object of a newly created class may be replicated to a domain controller prior to the arrival of the new schema class. If this occurs, it is called replication latency.
schema	Contains the definitions of all objects that are stored in Active Directory.
schema object	Another term for attributes and classes.
schema operations master	Designates a single domain controller in the forest to store the write-enabled copy of the schema and thus prevents potential conflicts.
Structural Class type	Can be derived from another structural class or an abstract class. It can include auxiliary classes in its definition. It is the only type of class from which Active Directory objects can actually be created.
syntax	Specifies the type of attribute value, such as a Distinguished Name, an Object Identifier, or a Case Sensitive String.

In Brief

If you want to…	Then do this…
Install Active Directory Schema in an MMC Console	You can install Active Directory Schema in MMC by following these steps: 1. Manually register the schema management Dynamic Link Library (DLL). 2. At command prompt, type: **regsvr32 systemroot\system32\schmmgmt.dll** 3. Install the support tools from the Windows 2000 Resource Kits separately from the compact disc. 4. After installing Active Directory Schema, you can add it to a customized MMC console.
Create an attribute	When you create a new attribute, you will be required to supply values for the following characteristics: • Common name • LDAP display name • Unique X.500 Object Identifier • Syntax • Being either multi- or- single-valued
Index an attribute	Choose the **Index this attribute in the Active Directory** check box in the Name **Properties** dialog box for an attribute in Active Directory Schema.

If you want to…	Then do this…
To add a member to the Schema Admins Group	1. Open **Active Directory Users and Computers** 2. In the console tree, double-click the appropriate **domain node** and then choose **users** or select the **folder** that contains the desired user. 3. In the details pane, right-click the **user account** that you want to add, and then choose **Properties**. 4. Choose the **Member of** tab, and then select **add**. 5. In the **Choose Groups** dialog box, choose **Schema Admins**, and then select **add**.
Enable write access to the schema	Run Active Directory Schema and make sure that **The Schema may be modified on this server** check box is selected in the **Change Operations Master** dialog box.

Lesson 8 Activities

Complete the following activities to better prepare you for the certification exam.

1. Describe the Active Directory schema.

2. Describe the process of loading Active Directory schema.

3. Describe the process of preparing the schema for modification.

4. Discuss why modifying the schema requires great care.

5. Describe why you might want to delete objects from Active Directory and how you would do so.

6. Discuss the minimal guidelines your schema modification policy should include.

7. Describe how Active Directory avoids write conflicts during schema replication.

8. Describe the benefit of having a schema operations master.

9. Discuss the value of indexing attributes.

10. Each schema object must have a globally unique number, known as an Object Identifier. Describe an Object Identifier.

Answers to Lesson 8 Activities

1. The Active Directory schema is a list of definitions. These definitions describe both the kinds of objects that can be stored in Active Directory and the types of information about those objects that can be stored. The definitions are themselves objects that are stored. This allows Active Directory to manage the schema objects with the same object management operations used for managing the rest of the objects in Active Directory.

2. To load Active Directory schema you should perform the following steps:
    1. Log on as Administrator.
    2. Choose **Start** and then select **Run.**
    3. In the **Run** dialog box, type **regsvr32 schmmgmt.dll** and then choose **OK**.
    4. In the **regsrv32** dialog box, choose **OK**
    5. Open **My Console**.
    6. On the Console menu, choose **Add/Remove Snap-in**.
    7. In the **Add/Remove Snap-in** dialog box, choose **Add**.
    8. In the **Add Standalone Snap-in** dialog box, choose **Active Directory Schema** and then select **OK**.
    9. Choose **Close**, and then select **OK.**
    10. On the Console menu, choose **Save**.

3. Schema modification is disabled on all domain controllers. This includes the initial schema operations master. You must first enable write access to the schema before you can modify the schema. You do this by following these steps:
    1. Run **Active Directory Schema**.
    2. Make sure that **The Schema may be modified on this server** check box is selected in the **Change Operations Master** dialog box.

4. Schema modification impacts your entire network. Every domain controller in the forest stores a replica of the schema and each of those replicas is updated whenever you make modifications to the schema.

5. Existing objects of the deactivated class type are not deactivated. Objects from deactivated classes and deactivated class attributes will appear in searches. If you are certain that you no longer need objects of a given class, you can follow these steps:

    1. Deactivate the class.
    2. Search for all objects that are instances of that class.
    3. Delete those objects from Active Directory.

6. At a minimum, your schema modification policy should include guidelines for the following procedures:

    - Initiating schema modifications, which includes policies for submitting schema change requests to an approving committee, validating the need for requested schema changes and approving requested changes
    - Planning schema modifications, which includes policies for ensuring that the proposed schema modifications meet the specifications of the needed change and ensuring that an effective recovery plan is in place
    - Modifying the schema, which includes policies for supervising and testing changes and ensuring directory integrity

7. Windows 2000 Server maintains two copies of the schema: one stored in cache and one stored on disk in the Active Directory.

    The cached schema is used for read purposes and is used to maintain consistency with any running threads.

When an administrator writes to the schema, the schema writes are first recorded in the disk copy. After a schema write, Active Directory waits five minutes before it copies the schema from the disk to the cache. The old cache remains in memory, and existing threads under the old cache continue to use the old cache until their work is finished. In addition, during this five-minute interval, no objects that use a new or modified class or attribute can be added to the schema. When the new cache is built, all new threads refer to it. This behavior keeps the cache consistent.

Once this occurs the updated Active Directory schema is then replicated to all domain controllers throughout the forest.

8. Having a schema operations master prevents potential conflicts by designating a single domain controller in the forest to store the write-enabled copy of the schema.

   By default, the first domain controller installed in the forest is the schema operations master. However, you can change the domain controller that serves as the schema operations master at any time. In addition, by default, the first schema operations master is not enabled for schema modification. You must manually enable schema modification.

9. Indexing the attribute speeds search performance when a search is performed on that attribute. Additionally, this also gives you the ability to create reports that are sorted on the indexed attribute.

10. An Object Identifier is expressed as a string of numbers delimited by decimal points, for example, a.b.c.w.x.y.z. Object Identifiers are hierarchical, with the root controlled by the International Standards Organization (ISO). ISO allocates a branch of the Object Identifier tree to subordinate vendors or to name registration authorities. The name registration authority issues the leading digits a.b.c. The remaining digits, w, x, y and z, are reserved for your organization to extend as necessary.

Lesson 8 Quiz

These questions test your knowledge of features, vocabulary, procedures, and syntax.

1. Schema modifications are performed:

   A. Only on the root domain controller.
   B. On a single domain controller.
   C. By coordinating the activities on multiple domain controllers.
   D. Only with careful planning and consideration.

2. What types of schema objects cannot be deactivated or modified?

   A. Classes and attributes defined as system.
   B. Classes with objects that have been indexed in the Active Directory and replicated in the Global Catalog.
   C. Classes and attributes that are registered with the system.
   D. Classes that have no Object Identifier.

3. If a replication failure occurs:

   A. You must reverse the changes and then force replication.
   B. You must force replication of the schema so that objects can be recognized.
   C. Active Directory will automatically repair the failure.
   D. Active Directory will force the failed domain server off-line.

4. When you update the schema:

   A. A new cache is built from the schema database.
   B. The old cache remains in memory.
   C. Existing threads are terminated and restarted with the new schema.
   D. Existing objects are modified immediately.

5. Inheritance is:

   A. The ability of an object to copy attributes from another object.
   B. Another name for replication.
   C. The granting of the child's rights to a parent object
   D. The ability of a child class to take on attributes of the parent class.

6. Processes that are used to modify the schema include:

   A. Using Active Directory Schema in MMC.
   B. Using scripting with ADSI.
   C. Using Active Directory Computers and Users.
   D. Installing software applications.

7. Replication latency is encountered when:

   A. An object's mandatory attributes are created after the object is created.
   B. If instance of an object is replicated before its schema class.
   C. A delay is encountered between object instance replication.
   D. An object's attributes are replicated before the object instance.

8. When you create a new class you must provide:

   A. A common name and an LDAP display name.
   B. A unique X.500 Object Identifier.
   C. The parent class.
   D. The class type.

9. The 88 class type is:

   A. A unique class that supercedes structural classes.
   B. A special type of class based on the 1988 X.500 specification.
   C. Used to create structural, abstract and auxiliary classes.
   D. A special type of class defined prior to 1998

10. You cannot deactivate:

    A. Classes that have been added to the schema after installation.
    B. Objects and classes that have been deleted and re-created.
    C. Classes of the subclass-Of, auxiliary-Class, or poss-Superior lists.
    D. Attributes in the must-contain or may-contain lists of existing active classes.

Answers to Lesson 8 Quiz

1. Answer B is correct. Changes to a schema can only be implemented from a single domain controller

   Answer C is correct. Active Directory replicates the schema on other domain controllers thus controlling their activities.

   Answer D is correct. Without careful planning and consideration, changes to the schema may result in serious disruptions to the network.

   Answer A is incorrect. Schema modifications can occur on any domain controller.

2. Answer A is correct. You cannot modify or deactivate classes and attributes that are defined as system.

   Answer B is incorrect. You can modify or deactivate any class other than those defined as system. Bear in mind that you may pay a great price for doing so.

   Answer C is incorrect. In a sense, all classes and attributes are registered with the system.

   Answer D is incorrect. There are no classes that have no Object Identifier.

3. Answer C is correct. Active Directory will automatically replicate the schema from the schema operations master. This triggers an immediate schema cache update on the target domain controller. Once the target domain controller's schema has been updated, Active Directory then invokes a new replication cycle and replicates the object(s) that failed to the target domain controller.

   Answers A and B are both incorrect. You should never force replication without careful planning and consideration.

   Answer D is incorrect.

4. Answers A and B are correct. A new cache is built from the schema database and the old cache remains in memory.

   Answer C is incorrect. Existing threads continue to use the old schema in cache until they have terminated.

   Answer D is incorrect. Active Directory waits five minutes before it copies the schema from the disk to the cache.

5. Answer D is correct. The ability of a child class to take on attributes of the parent class is known as inheritance.

   Answer A is not correct. The ability of an object to copy attributes from another object may be a useful thing, but it is not inheritance.

   Answer B is incorrect. Replication refers to Active Directory's ability to reproduce itself on another domain controller.

   Answer C is incorrect. An object of a parent class does obtain rights from a child class.

6. Answers A and B are correct. You can modify the schema using Active Directory Schema in MMC or by using scripting with ADSI.

   Answer C is incorrect. You cannot modify the schema using Active Directory Computers and Users.

   Answer D is correct. Installing schema aware applications can modify the schema.

7. Answer B is correct. Active Directory will automatically repair any failed replication.

   Answer A is incorrect. All attributes must be created prior to the creation of a class that references them.

   Answer C is incorrect. There is a natural delay between the time an object is replicated on one domain controller and the time it is replicated on another.

   Answer D is incorrect. An object's attribute cannot be replicated before the object.

8. A is correct. You must provide a common name and an LDAP display name.

   B is correct. You must provide an X.500 Object Identifier that is issued by a name registration authority and that has probably been extended by your organization.

   C is correct. You must provide a parent class as the parent class defines what attributes the new class inherits and the location in which objects of the new class are created.

   Answer D is correct. You must provide a class type, either structural, abstract, auxiliary or 88.

9. Answer B is correct. An 88 class type is a special type of class based on the 1988 X.500 specification.

   Answer A is incorrect. An 88 class type does not supercede structural classes.

   Answer C is incorrect. You do not need an 88 class to create structural, abstract or auxiliary classes.

   Answer D is incorrect. The 88 class type is a special class for types of classes defined prior to 1993.

10. Answer C is correct. You cannot deactivate classes of the subclass-Of, auxiliary-Class, or poss-Superior lists.

    Answer D is correct. You cannot deactivate attributes in the must-contain or may-contain lists of existing active classes.

    Answer A is incorrect. Classes that have been added to the schema after installation are the only classes that can be deactivated.

    Answer B is incorrect. Classes cannot be deleted; they can only be deactivated.

Lesson 9

Active Directory Data Recovery and Maintenance

The way you plan to back up, restore, and maintain your Active Directory directory service should be carefully planned when you are defining your network architecture. Your processes for these tasks may affect early decisions on the installation options and hardware requirements for your Windows 2000 network.

Successful backup, recovery planning, and database maintenance involves a good understanding of how Active Directory handles data storage, data maintenance, and the changes to its database through transactions.

After completing this lesson, you should have a better understanding of the following topics:

- Active Directory Data Store Model
- Data Store Files
- Active Directory Maintenance
- Active Directory Recovery
- Active Directory Backup Process
- Database Planning

Active Directory Data Store Model

Active Directory functionality can be defined as a layered architecture where the layers represent the server processes providing directory services to client applications.

The Extensible Storage Engine (ESE) database uses a concept of distinct transaction and log files guaranteeing the reliability of Active Directory. Each request to the DSA (Directory System Agent) to add, modify, or delete an object or attribute is treated as an individual transaction. As these transactions occur on each domain controller, they are recorded in a series of log files that are associated with each NTDS.DIT file.

By default, the Active Directory database file is stored on <drive>\winnt\NTDS\Ntds.dit. Likewise by default, the log files are stored in the same directory.

The Data Store (Figure 9.1) is one of the four key service components of the Active Directory architecture. They are the Directory System Agent (DSA), the Database Layer, the Extensible Storage Engine, and the Data Store.

Figure 9.1 Active Directory Data Store Model

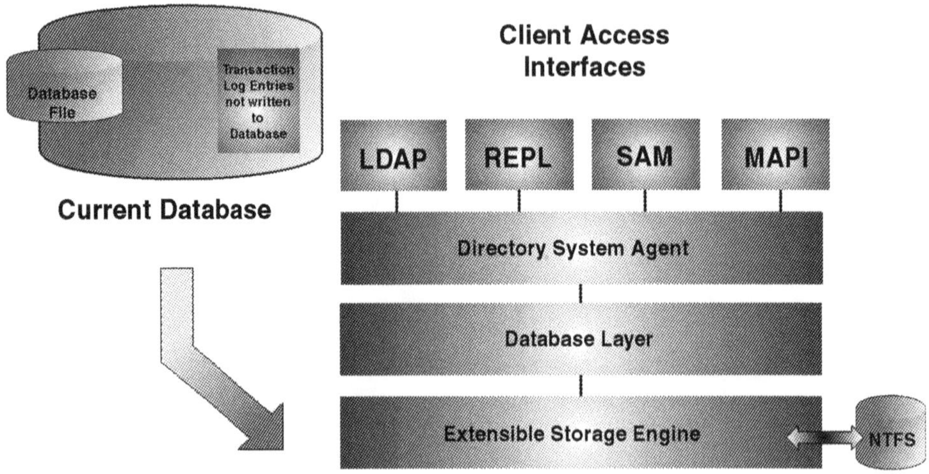

The Data Store (the database file NTDS.DIT) is manipulated only by the Extensible Storage Engine database engine, which is stored in the \winnt\NTDS folder on the domain controller. You can administer the file using the NTDSUTIL tool located in the\winnt\System32 folder on the domain controller.

Active Directory uses a fault-tolerant transaction-based database to accept, track, and maintain data. The Data Store model is based on the ESE database and includes:

- A database file that contains all objects in Active Directory
- Transaction log files that provide fault tolerance for the database
- The database that resides in the multi-layered architecture of Active Directory

Using the Data Store Process

Active Directory writes transactions to log files. It then applies the transactions to the database. If there is some kind of system failure, Active Directory uses these files to rebuild the data that was not written to the database. The most current version of the database includes all of the data in the previous version of the database file plus any transactions not written to the database file due to the system failure. Figure 9.2 shows the steps in the average transaction.

Figure 9.2 Data Store Process

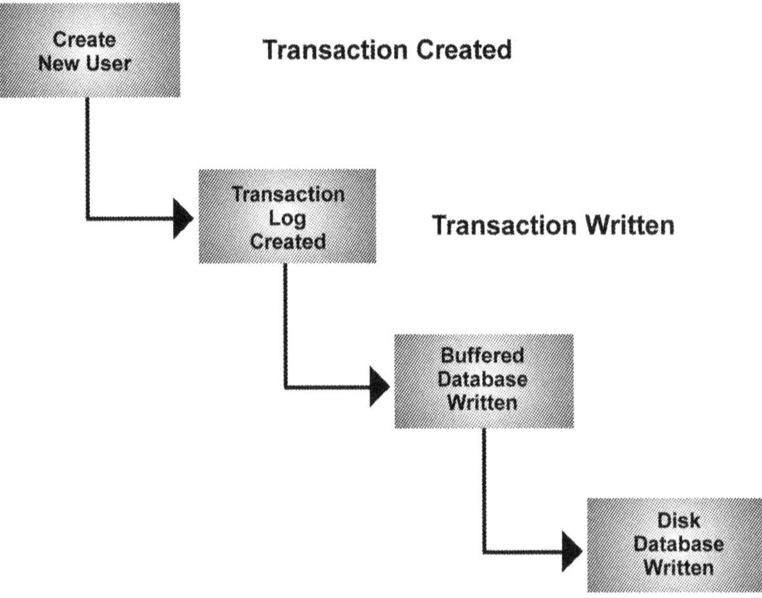

Following are the steps involved in an average transaction:

1. A transaction is created when there is a change to the Active Directory (**Create New User**).
2. The transaction is written to the log file.
3. When the transaction is written to database page in the memory buffer, it is committed.
4. The change is written to the database file on disk.
5. The pointer is advanced to the next uncommitted entry in the transaction file after the change has been written to the database.

Note: If the system is under heavy load, you can expect delays in logged transactions being written to the database file.

Data Store Files

When you restore or back up Active Directory, you restore or back up the following files (Figure 9.3):

Figure 9.3 Data Store Files

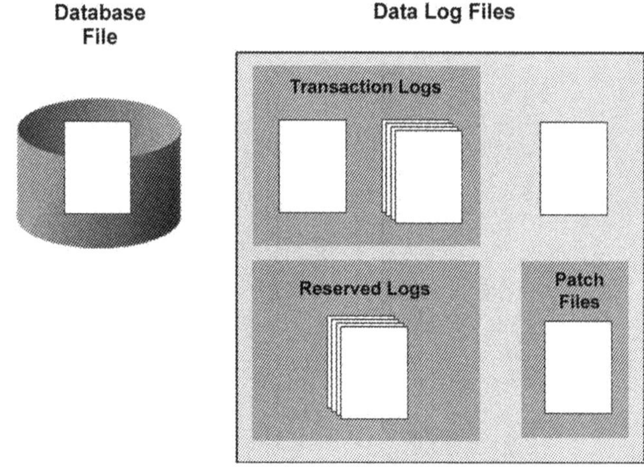

Database File—This file is made up of all the objects in the Active Directory.

Log Files—These files store, track, and manage transactions. Table 9.1 describes the different kinds of log files.

Table 9.1 Log Files

File Type	Description
Transaction logs	Before transactions are written to the database, these files track, maintain, and store the transactions. Transactions are stored in two different kinds of logs, current transaction logs, and previous transaction logs.
Checkpoint files	Transactions that have already been written to the database file have their pointers stored in the Checkpoint file.
Reserved log	Used as a store for low disk space conditions.
Patch files	Manages data during an online backup.

Working with Database Files

The Active Directory database file contains all objects and their associated information for each domain controller. It is stored by default in the system\NTDS directory.

You need to back up the database file regularly. To back up System State data, follow these steps:

1. From **Backup**, choose the **Backup** tab.
2. In **Click To Select the Check Box For Any Drive, Folder, or File That You Want To Back Up**, select **System State**.

3. This will back up the System State data plus any other data you have selected for the current backup operation.

The database uses the following three tables to store information:

- The object table
- The link table
- The schema table

Object Table

As stated in the name, the object table holds objects and their attributes. Each object is in a row and the attributes are in a column. Space is assigned by the database if the attribute actually contains data.

Link Table

The link table holds the relationships between objects in the object table.

Schema Table

The schema table holds the definition of all types of objects that you can create in Active Directory.

Tip: The database file size is reported when it is opened. The reported size will not change during normal server operations. If you shut down the server, the new size is reported when the server starts up again.

Understanding Log Files

If Active Directory is stopped unexpectedly, the database does not successfully copy to disk. The database performs a recovery on the next startup. The database reads the log files in order and reapplies changes until it is up-to-date.

Transaction Log Files

The transaction log is a collection of files that holds all transactions before they are written to the database file. The transaction logs are used to recover the database. Two types of transaction logs exist:

- Current Transaction Log Files
- Previous Transaction Log Files

Current Transaction Logs

The default log filename is EDB.LOG. The ESE can use the following logging types:

- Noncircular logging which creates a new log file when the current one fills up
- Circular logging that overwrites the oldest file when the log reaches a specified number of files

Warning: Noncircular logging consumes disk space, as it does not automatically delete the log file. This continues until the administrator removes the old log files after a backup or restart.

Circular logging is the default setting for Windows 2000.

The directory usually contains the following log files (Table 9.2) stored in the same directory as the database file:

Table 9.2 Log Files

Filename	Description
EDBxxxxx. LOG	EDB.LOG is the *current transaction* log file. The number of transactions contained in the log varies, based on the size of the transaction. When circular logging is turned off and the EDB.LOG file is full of transactions, it is renamed to EDB00001.LOG. This will continue to increment using hexadecimal notation as each log fills. Checking to see if there is an unbroken series of log filenames can answer questions about the state of the log files. The size of every .LOG file when it is created is exactly 10 megabytes (MB).
EDB.CHK	EDB.CHK stores the database checkpoint. If there is a failure, the file determines the point in the log file where the recovery of the information can start. Without the EDB.CHK file, the information store would have to recover from the beginning of the oldest log file and check every page in every log file to determine if it has been written to disk. This file improves the speed and efficiency of the process of making the database consistent.
RES1.LOG RES2.LOG	RES1.LOG and RES2.LOG are the reserved log files or placeholderstoset aside the last 20 MB of disk space on the current drive or directory. This gives the log files sufficient room for a smooth shutdown if all other disk space is full.

Note: If circular logging is set to on, running out of space for log files is not an issue.

To understand transaction log file flow, refer to Figure 9.4.

Figure 9.4 Transaction Log Files

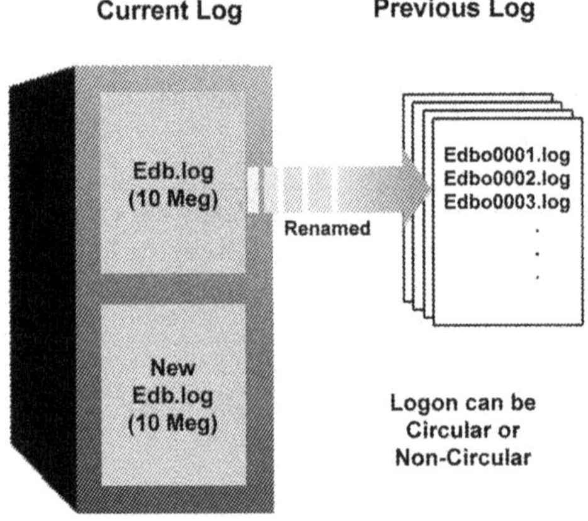

Previous Transaction Log Files

As shown in Table 9.2, as each log file fills, a new EDB.LOG file is created, and the previous file is renamed. When the transactions of the previous log file are committed to the database file, the information is no longer needed, and these log files can be cleaned up. The server will do garbage collection deleting of unneeded previous log files every 12 hours on each domain controller.

Circular logging, which is the default, causes the oldest file to be overwritten. This allows for the maximum recoverability. As noncircular logging consumes disk space, you can enable or disable circular logging with the following registry key:

HKEY_LOCAL_MACHINE\CurrentControlSet\Services\NTDS
Parameters\CircularLogging
Where 1 = circular logging
Where 0 = non-circular logging

Checkpoint Files

EDB.CHK is the Checkpoint file. By default, it is stored in the same directory as the database file. This file contains a pointer indicating the transactions in the transaction logs that have been applied to the database file. Each time a transaction is written to the database, the checkpoint advances to the next uncommitted entry (Figure 9.5).

Figure 9.5 Checkpoint Files

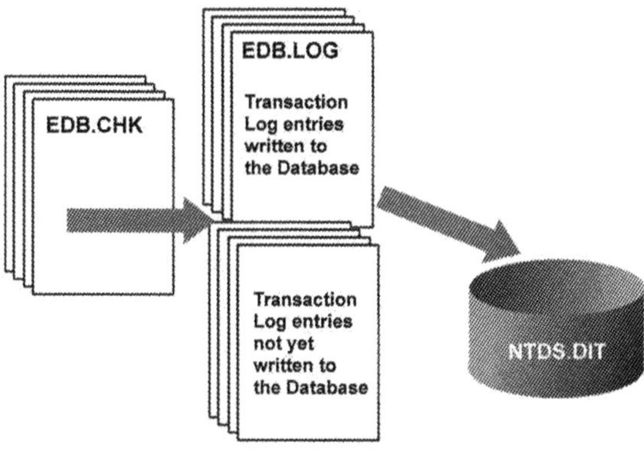

Each time the database is opened, there is a check to see if the database is up to date with the related checkpoint. For example, did the database fail before updating the checkpoint? If the database is not up to date, the log files are replayed from the point that the Checkpoint file indicates. A database can be recovered without a checkpoint, but the checkpoint allows faster recovery by directing recovery to begin closer to the logged operations that must be redone.

Note: Active Directory can decide which transactions have or have not been committed to the database file. However, the Checkpoint file leads to a faster recovery by decreasing the amount of data to be read.

Reserved Log Files

By default, there are two reserved log files stored in the same directory as the database file. These files are RES1.LOG and RES2.LOG (Figure 9.6), and each takes up 10 MB of space.

Figure 9.6 Reserved Logs

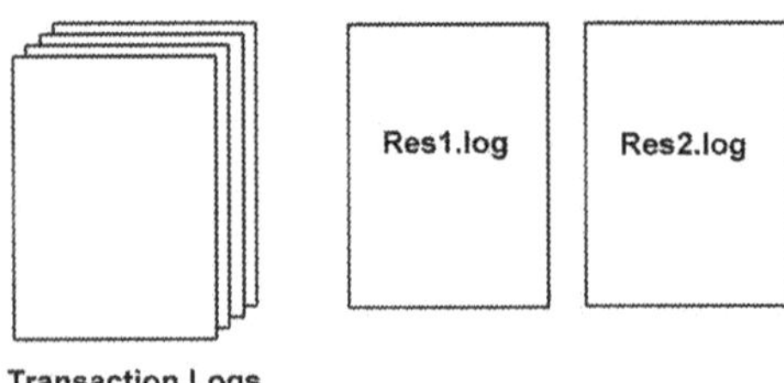

The reserved log files take over the transaction log when Active Directory tries to create a new EDB.LOG and there is not enough disk space. All of the unresolved transactions in memory are moved into the reserved logs.

Warning: When the reserved logs are used, Active Directory shuts down and records an out of disk space error message in the event log.

Patch Files

Patch files are the transactions written to the database during the backup (Figure 9.7). These files end with a .PAT suffix and are stored by default in the same directory as the database files.

Figure 9.7 Patch Files

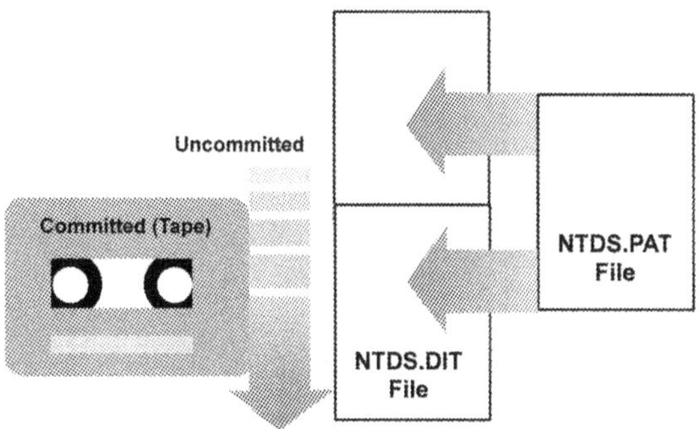

Once a transaction has been committed to the database, it is recorded on the database pages (buffered files) that are approximately 8KB in size. The backup process uses patch files when data is split across multiple pages. This split transaction is written to both the database file and the patch files. During a restore, only some pages of the split transaction may be written to the database file. The patch file is used to resolve split transaction issues.

The following steps occur during a backup:

1. A .PAT is created for the current database.
2. The backup for the current database begins.
3. Split transactions may be written for a portion of the database that has already been backed up and is recorded in both the NTDS.DIT and the .PAT file.
4. The .PAT file is written to the Backup.
5. The .PAT file is deleted from the directory.

Active Directory Maintenance

Databases become fragmented over time, and this happens to the Active Directory directory as well. Unneeded objects make the database larger than it needs to be and all this results in performance degradation. Active Directory automatically runs processes that perform the following tasks:

- Delete the unused files and objects, reducing space requirements
- Defragment disks to optimize disk storage

Windows 2000 also contains a number of manual processes you can perform to decrease database size and to identify lost objects.

Understanding Automatic Database Cleanup

Automated database cleanup removes unneeded data and defragments the database file. At 12-hour intervals a process called garbage collection, runs on every domain controller. This process consists of the following tasks:

- Deleting unneeded transaction log files
- Deleting obsolete objects from Active Directory
- Performing online database defragmentation

Deleting Transaction Log Files

These transaction files have already been written to the database and, once that occurs, they are no longer necessary. The garbage collection process removes them.

Deleting Obsolete Objects

When an object is deleted, it is tagged with a tombstone. Objects with a tombstone remain in the database for the life of the tombstone (the default is 60 days) and are invisible to client requests. This process allows enough time for the tombstone to replicate to all the domain controllers in the network. During garbage collection, objects that have exceeded the tombstone lifetime are physically removed from the database.

Defragmenting Online Databases

When files are updated, the computer saves these updates on the largest continuous space on the hard disk it can find. These are often on a different area of the disk than the other parts of the file. When files are fragmented, the computer searches the hard disk when the file is opened to find all of the parts of the file. This slows down response time.

Disk Defragmenter resolves this problem by rewriting the files on disk back into contiguous segments. In Active Directory, defragmentation rearranges the way data is written in the directory database file to compact it, increasing the speed of access and retrieval. Active Directory automatically performs online defragmentation of the database at certain intervals as part of the garbage collection process. Online defragmentation does not decrease the size of the database file (NTDS.DIT), but it optimizes data storage in the database and reclaims space in the directory for new objects. This can prevent data storage difficulties.

To start Disk Defragmenter, you can do one of two things: either from the **Start** menu, choose **Programs**, **Accessories**, **System Tools**, and then select **Disk Defragmenter**, or run **Computer Management**, and select **Storage** and **Disk Management** (Figure 9.8).

Figure 9.8 Disk Management Window

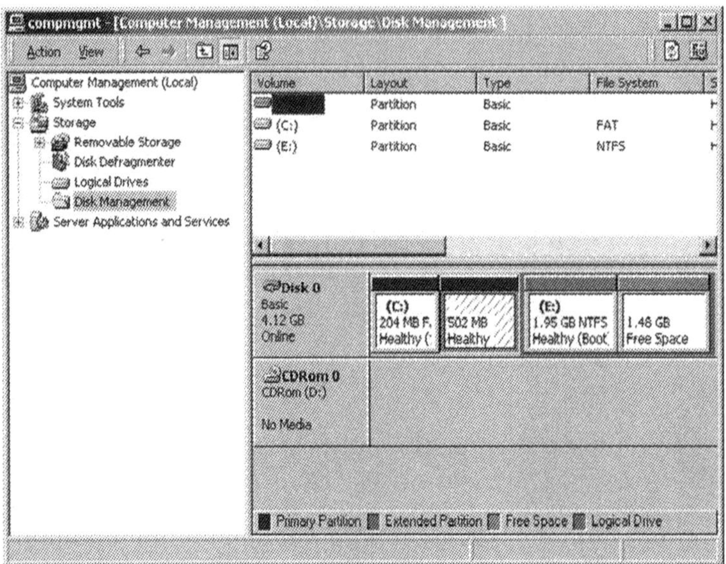

You can analyze the volume to see how many fragmented files and folders are present and then decide if you need to defragment the volume.

The amount of time that the defragmentation process takes depends on a number of factors—the size of the volume, the number of files on the volume, the amount of fragmentation, and available local system resources.

Disk Defragmenter

The window for disk defragmentation is divided into two main areas, as shown in Figure 9.9. The volumes on the local computer are displayed in the top portion. The lower portion shows how fragmented the volume is. The condition of the disk is displayed in color. The color key is explained in Table 9.3.

Figure 9.9 Disk Defragmenter

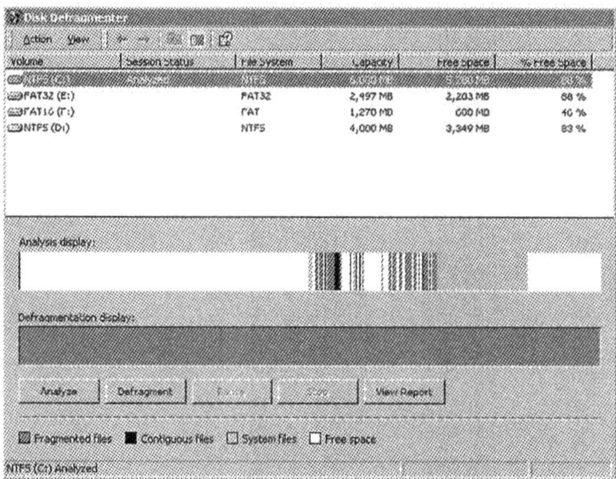

Table 9.3 File Color Key

Color	Description
Red	Fragmented files.
Blue	Contiguous (unfragmented) files
White	Free space on the disk.
Green	System files that Disk Defragmenter cannot move. These system files are not part of the Windows operating system but include files belonging to NTFS (New Technology File System) (when applicable) and the system-paging file.

Always analyze volumes before defragmenting them. By comparing the Analysis Display band to the Defragmentation Display band, you can see the improvement after you have defragmented your drive. After you have performed the analysis, a dialog box tells you if you need to defragment the volume.

You can only defragment local file system volumes, and you can only run one Disk Defragmenter console at a time.

Understanding Manual Database Cleanup

Manual database cleanup uses an offline defragmentation tool that can decrease the size of the Active Directory database as well as monitor the LostAndFound container for misplaced objects.

Offline Database Defragmentation Tool

The offline defragmentation tool initiates a new, compressed version of the database file. If the original database was fragmented, the new database file could be significantly smaller. You may want to run offline defragmentation in a test environment where you can view the file size difference after deleting a percentage of objects. For your production environment, offline defragmentation should not be necessary as online defragmentation is available.

To start the Offline Defragmentation Tool follow these steps:

1. Restart the server and choose **F8** to choose the **Directory Service Repair** module.
2. Use **NTDSUTIL.EXE** to create a defragmented copy of the database file.

Warning: There must be enough disk space to create the new defragmented database file.

LostAndFound Container

As part of your regular maintenance routine, you should examine the files in the LostAndFound.

Sometimes objects are created on one domain controller when its parent container is deleted from another domain controller; or an object is moved into another container when the opposite process is occurring at another domain controller. Active Directory replication does not know where to put these objects, so they end up in the LostAndFound container.

To view the LostAndFound container follow these steps: from **Active Directory Users and Computers**, choose the **View** menu for the domain, and select **Advanced Features**.

Active Directory Recovery

No computer is failure-proof, but strategic planning and preventative measures can make your network more failure-resistant. You should develop plans and procedures for recovering from failures even before they occur. This minimizes time lost and data damage. If you keep records about your hardware and software configurations and back up regularly, you can prevent failures from being catastrophic.

After a computer failure, when the domain controller is back up and running, it needs to be restored with Active Directory.

Replication—If there is more than one domain controller in a domain, Active Directory is restored through normal replication with the replication partners.

NTBACKUP Backup and Restore Wizards—You would use the NTBACKUP tool to restore the System State from a backup copy to recover the Active Directory files. You would use this option if there were no other domain controllers in the domain with which the domain controller can replicate.

In planning for Active Directory backup and recovery, you need to understand how the Active Directory database can be recovered. Three different ways of recovering Active Directory are available:

A non-authoritative restore—This is the restore of a domain controller where the objects in the restored directory are not treated as authoritative, that is, restored objects are updated with changes held in other replicas of the restored domain.

An authoritative restore—This is a restore operation on a domain controller where the objects in the restored directory are treated as authoritative, that is, all the existing copies of those objects are replaced through replication. You must use the NTDSUTIL.EXE utility to perform an authoritative restore.

Recovery without a restore—The restoration of lost data or the reconciliation of conflicting or erroneous data after a system failure. Recovery takes place through replication.

Backup and Recovery Tools

The Backup utility available in Active Directory helps you protect data from accidental loss, for example if your system encounters hardware or storage media failure. In this case, you can restore data through one of the following methods:

- Use Backup to create a duplicate copy of the data on your hard disk
- Use Backup to archive the data on another storage device such as a hard disk or a tape
- Restore the data from the archived copy

Backup can be used for the following procedures:

- To archive selected files and folders on your hard disk
- To restore the archived files and folders to your hard disk (or any other disk you choose)
- To create an Emergency Repair Disk (ERD) to help you repair system files if they become corrupted or are accidentally erased
- To make a copy of any remote storage data and any data stored in mounted drives
- To make a copy of your computer's System State, which includes the registry, the Active Directory database, and the Certificate Services database
- To schedule regular backups to keep your archived data up-to-date

To understand the available backup and recovery tools, refer to Figure 9.10.

Figure 9.10 Backup and Recovery Tools

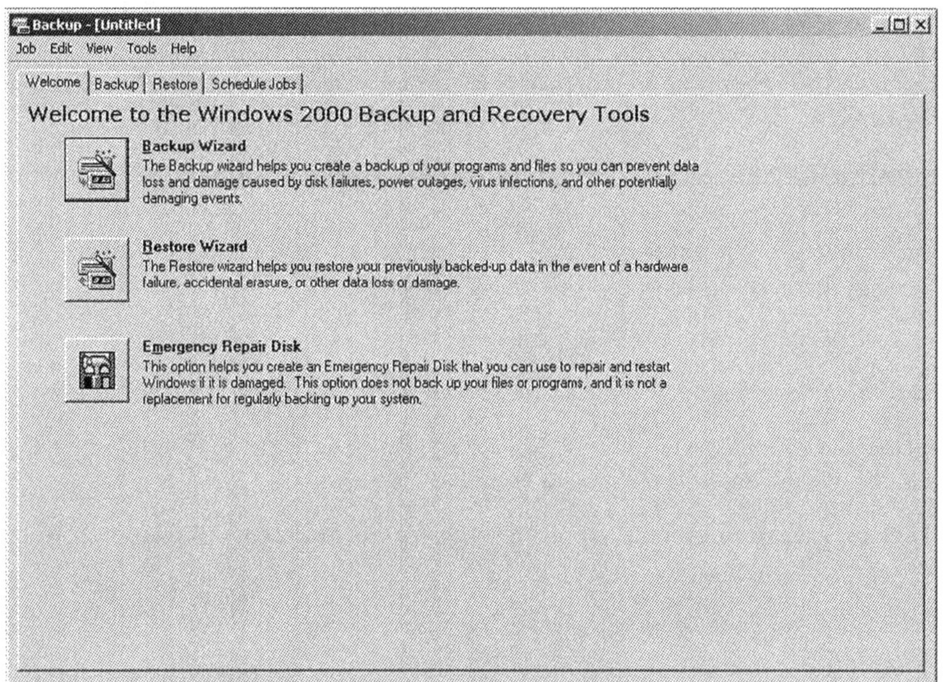

Activating a Non-Authoritative Restore

In cases where Active Directory needs to be recovered from hardware failure or replacement, but where data on other domain controllers is known to be stable, you only need to perform a non-authoritative restore from the most recent backup. After the non-authoritative restore, Active Directory replication automatically begins circulating changes that have happened since the last backup from other domain controllers.

Tip: To maintain the integrity of your data, it is important to have more than one controller per domain.

With a non-authoritative restore the entire replica of the database can be restored. The recovery of the back-up information depends on the transaction and replication logs.

To implement a non-authoritative restore, follow these steps:

1. Restart the server and choose **F8** to have the domain controller start in a directory Safe mode.
2. From the **Advanced Options** menu, choose **Directory Services Restore Mode** and select **Enter**. This ensures that the controller is not connected to the network.
3. At the **Please Select Operating System to Start** prompt, choose **Microsoft Windows 2000** and choose **Enter**.
4. Log on as administrator and on the desktop warning box that indicates that Windows is running in Safe mode, choose **OK**.
5. From the **Start** menu, choose **Programs**, **Accessories**, **System Tools**, and choose **Backup**.
6. From **Backup and Recovery Tools**, choose **Restore Wizard** (Figure 9.11), and then select **Next**.

Figure 9.11 Restore Wizard What to Restore Page

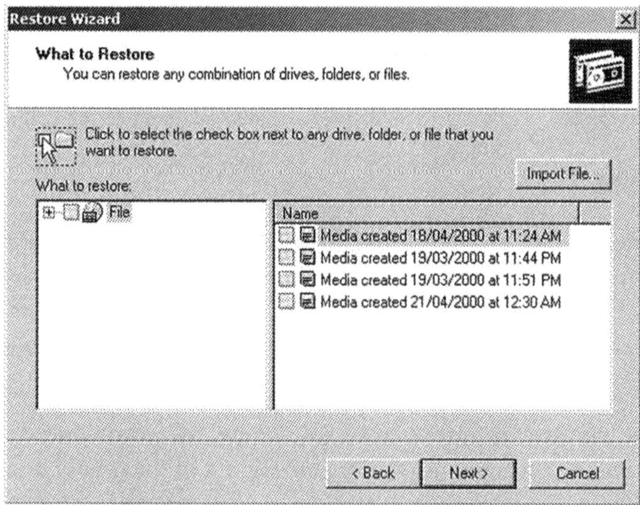

7. From **Restore Wizard What to Restore**, expand the media type that contains the data you want to restore.
8. Expand the appropriate media until the data you want is visible.
9. Choose the **data**, and select **Next**.
10. Either choose **Finish** to complete the restore process, or select **Advance** to specify advanced restore options.

Windows 2000 Backup ensures that all the necessary files are placed in the proper locations when they are restored.

A key is written to the registry and this signals to Active Directory that a restore is in progress. This forces a consistency check and a re-index the next time you start Active Directory. After these checks are complete, the key is removed.

The format of the key is:
HDKEY_LOCAL_MACHINE\SYSTEM\CurrentControlSet\Services\NTDS\
Restore In Progress

When the server is back online, directory replication brings the server up-to-date through replicating all of the changes that have taken place since the backup.

Activating an Authoritative Restore

If you have inadvertently deleted or modified objects stored in the Active Directory database, and those objects are replicated or distributed to other servers, you will need to authoritatively restore those objects so that they are replicated or distributed to the other servers. If you do not authoritatively restore the objects, they will never be replicated or distributed to your other servers because they will appear to be older than the objects currently on your other servers.

You can use the NTDSUTIL utility to mark objects for authoritative restore and so ensure that the data you want to restore is replicated or distributed throughout your organization. On the other hand, if your system disk has failed or the Active Directory database is corrupted, then you can use the normal non-authoritative restore to bring back the data without using the NTDSUTIL utility.

In some situations, you may want to do both. For example, you have unintentionally deleted the container that holds all your user data. The normal restore is non-authoritative, so that when you bring the controller back up, the replication of the deletion would spread throughout your forest. So that this does not happen, you would first do an authoritative restore on the container. The part of the database that you have tagged as authoritative would not be replicated throughout the forest.

Note: You can authoritatively restore an entire domain, an OU (Organizational Unit), or a single object.

With an authoritative restore, you can choose which data in the database should be the master copy. This prevents replication from overwriting the information that you have indicated as being the master copy.

To implement an authoritative restore, follow these steps:

1. Perform a non-authoritative restore.
2. Restart the computer, and choose the **F8** key to start the domain controller in repair mode.
3. From the **Advanced Startup Options** menu, choose **Directory Services Restore Mode**, and select **Enter**. This ensures that the domain controller is not connected to the network.
4. On the desktop warning box that indicates that Windows is running in Safe mode, choose **OK**.
5. From the **Start** menu, choose **Programs**, **Accessories**, and then select **Command Prompt**.
6. At the command prompt, type `NTDSUTIL.EXE`.
7. At the NTDSUTIL prompt, type `authoritative restore`. Choose **Enter**.
8. Type in the following, replacing the italics with the information for your own system: **`Restore subtree`** ***`OU=accounting,DC=MyCompany,DC=msft`***
9. After sucessful implementation, exit from **NTDSUTIL.EXE**, and restart your server.

Tip: The best time to do an authoritative restore is immediately after using the Restore Wizard to restore your Active Directory database.

Your Active Directory database will now be the same as it was when it was backed up. In the preceding example, it would be brought up-to-date with the rest of the system except for the Accounting OU. The restored domain controller would replicate the Accounting OU to all its replication partners, bringing them up-to-date with an authoritative restore.

Using a Transaction Logging Restore

For a recovery without a restore, you can use transaction logging to recover data without having to fully or partly restore Active Directory.

Note: You must not enable circular logging when you use transaction logging to recover data.

For example, you have had a power failure and your server fails. Those transactions in the transaction log not written to the database would be replicated when the server came back online.

Active Directory Backup Process

As soon as you start planning your network, you should start planning your backup strategy. In this stage, you need to accomplish the following tasks:

- Determine how to configure your disks for critical file storage
- Choose the appropriate hardware with capacity and speed
- Create a backup strategy

Configuring Hard Drives

When designing your network configuration, you should choose to store your log files on a physically separate hard disk. This enhances system performance and provides fault tolerance. As log files are written sequentially, disk access time will approach zero if the sequential writes are not interrupted by other requests.

Tip: A dedicated physical disk for your log files optimizes your network performance.

To optimize your system, consider having the following elements on separate hard disks:

- Windows 2000 operating system
- Active Directory database file
- Transaction logs

Determining Hardware Needs

Not only do you need to consider operating system needs when planning your network, but you also need to plan the hardware necessary for backup data storage.

Ideally, you should set up a test system so that you can predict the size of your Active Directory. By creating a sample population of objects and their attributes, you can determine the size of each object and thus predict the size of your Active Directory database.

Creating a Backup Strategy

When creating your backup strategy, you should consider the following points:

The method you choose for backup—Choose the method that meets your organization's needs for speed and matches how much tape space you have available.

Off-site storage of backup tapes—Plan to store the tape backups of your organization's most critical data at another location. Disasters such as fire can destroy both servers and backup tapes. Consider the tombstone lifetime to determine how long a backup is useful.

Capacity and speed of your hardware—Hardware capacity determines how fast backups or restores can be completed.

Test restores—It is important to test the integrity of your Backup. Periodically, you should choose a backup of a server at random and perform a test restore on a test server. Using a different tape device will also check the reliability of the tape machine.

Start the Backup program and then choose the folders and files you want to back up (Figure 9.12).

Figure 9.12 Backup Options

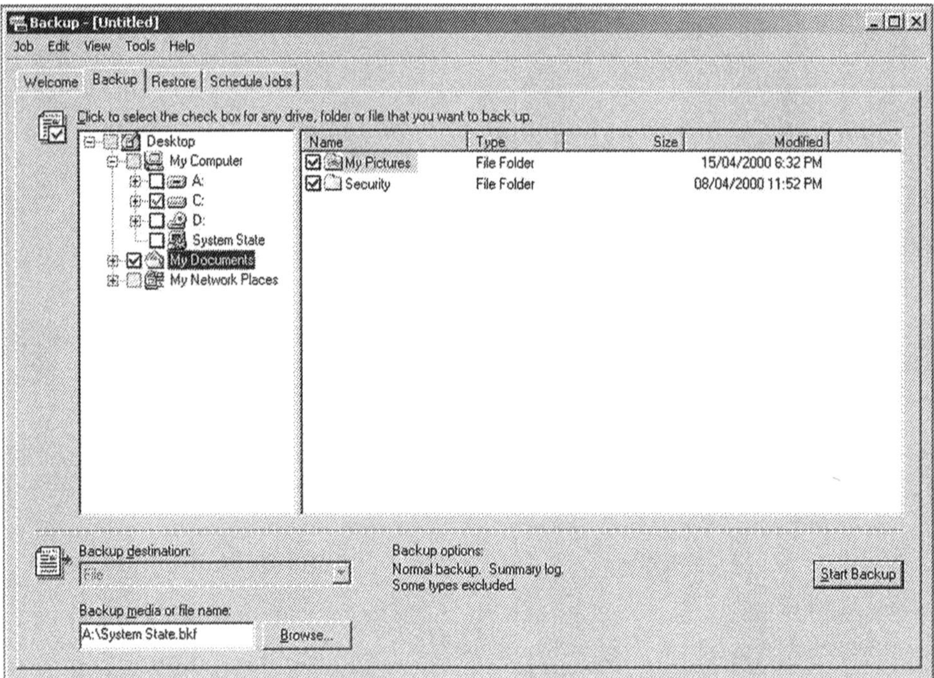

To create a backup on a server in a domain, follow these steps:

1. From the **Start** menu, choose **Programs**, **Accessories**, **System Tools**, and select **Backup** (Figure 9.12).
2. Choose the **Backup Wizard** .
3. Choose **Next**.
4. Choose **Only Back Up the System State Data**, and select **Next**.
5. In **Backup Media or Filename**, type **`c:\bkup.bkf`** (where **`c:\bkup.bkf`** represents the Backup filename).
6. After you verify that the Backup job description is correct, choose **Finish**.

7. When the backup is complete, choose **Close**.

To restore Active Directory from a backup, follow these steps:

1. Restart the server, and choose **F8** to have the domain controller start in a directory Safe mode.
2. From the **Start** menu, choose **Programs**, **Accessories**, **System Tools**, and select **Backup**.
3. In **Backup and Recovery Tools**, choose **Restore Wizard**. Select **Next**.
4. Choose **Import File**.
5. In **Catalog Backup File**, type ***c:\bkup.bkf*** (where ***c:\bkup.bkf*** represents the Backup filename), and choose **OK**.
6. In **What To Restore**, expand the path, choose **System State**, and then select **Next**.
7. In **Completing the Restore Wizard**, choose **Finish**.
8. In **Enter Backup Filename**, verify that the filename is correct, and choose **OK**. The restore will begin and display its progress.
9. When the restore is complete, choose **Close**, and select **Yes**.

Database Planning

For Active Directory database planning you will need to consider the following:

- Estimate the Active Directory database size
- Plan for Active Directory domain controller recovery

Estimating an Active Directory Database Size

By creating a sample population of objects, you can ascertain the size of each object. This will allow you to determine the size of your Active Directory database. This will help you to understand the effect of increasing the numbers of objects, as growth patterns are linear. Table 9.4 can help you estimate the size of your Active Directory:

Table 9.4 Estimating Guidelines

Task	Guidelines
Determining the number of objects in your organization	• Include users, printers, and groups • For security principles add 3,600 bytes per object • For non-security principles add 1,100 bytes per object • Double your estimated number of objects
Adding attributes to objects or applications that add objects to the Active Directory increase the size	• 100 bytes per string attribute, more if the string size is greater than 10 characters • For binary data, estimate the size of data and add 25% for buffering

When you test your predictions, use as many as possible of the attributes that you will use in production. A good source of test data for your objects could be the Microsoft Exchange Server Directory. It can be used to create the most valuable sample that you can produce.

Once you have determined the amount of disk storage you require, double it. This will allow for any errors and ensure that you can add scope for your needs in the future.

Vocabulary

Review the following terms in preparation for the certification exam.

Term	Description
authoritative restore	In Backup, a restore operation on a Windows 2000 domain controller where the objects in the restored directory are treated as authoritative, replacing through replication all existing copies of those objects. Authoritative restore is applicable only to replicated System State data such as Active Directory data and File Replication Service data. You use the NTDSUTIL.EXE utility for an authoritative restore.
backup	A duplicate copy of a program, a disk, or data, created for archiving purposes or to ensure that valuable files are not lost if the active copy is destroyed or damaged.
backup and recovery	A method available in most database management systems that allows a database to be restored to the latest transaction (complete unit of work) after a software or hardware error has made the database unusable. The process starts with the latest backup copy of the database. The change file, or transaction log, for the database is read. Each logged transaction is recovered through the last checkpoint on the log.
backup and restore	The process of maintaining backup files and putting them back onto the source medium if required.
Checkpoint file	A file containing information describing the state of the system at a particular time.
circular logging	In circular logging, the oldest files are written over and disabled. This allows for the maximum recoverability.

Term	Description
defragmentation	A process in Active Directory that rearranges how the data is written in the directory database file to compact it. The process of defragmentation rewrites parts of a file to contiguous sectors on a hard disk, increasing the speed of access and retrieval.
EFS	Encrypting File System is a Windows 2000 file system that allows users to encrypt files and folders on an NTFS volume disk to keep them safe from access by intruders.
ESE	Extensible Storage Engine stores all Active Directory objects, reserves storage only for space that is used, stores multiple-value attributes and properties, and communicates directly with individual records in the directory Data Store on the basis of the object's relative distinguished name attribute. When more attributes are added, more storage is dynamically allocated.
FAT	File Allocation Table is a list maintained by some operating systems to keep track of the status of various segments of disk space used for file storage.
log file	A file that stores messages generated by an application, service, or operating system. These messages track the operations performed. Log files are usually plain text (ASCII) files and often have a .LOG extension. In Backup, the log file contains a record of the date the tapes were created and the names of files and directories successfully backed up and restored. The Performance Logs and Alerts service also creates log files.
LostAndFound	A repository for orphaned objects. When Active Directory replication does not know where to put these objects, they end up in the LostAndFound container.
non-authoritative restore	A restore of a backup copy of a Windows 2000 domain controller in which the objects in the restored directory are not treated as authoritative. The restored objects are updated with changes held in other replicas of the restored domain.

Term	Description
NTDSUTIL utility	The NTDSUTIL utility lets you mark Active Directory objects for authoritative restore. When the object is marked, its Update Sequence Number is changed so that it is higher than any other Update Sequence Number. This ensures that any replicated data you restore is properly replicated or distributed throughout your organization.
NTFS	New Technology File System is an advanced file system designed for use specifically with the Windows NT operating system. It supports long filenames, full security access control, file system recovery, extremely large storage media, and various features for the Windows NT POSIX subsystem. It also supports object-oriented applications by treating all files as objects with user-defined and system-defined attributes.
on-media catalog	Information stored on backup storage media. The on-media catalog contains a list of files and folders that have been backed up in a backup set.
patch file	Manages data during an online backup.
permissions	Rules associated with an object to regulate which users can gain access to the object and in what manner.
registry	In Windows 2000, a database repository for information about a computer's configuration. The registry contains information that Windows 2000 continually references during operation, such as: • Profiles for each user. • The programs installed on the computer and the types of documents each can create. • Property settings for folders and program icons. • What hardware exists on the system. • Which ports are being used. The registry is organized hierarchically as a tree and is made up of keys and their sub- keys, hives, and value entries.

Term	Description
replication	The process of copying data from a Data Store or file system to multiple computers to synchronize the data.
reserved log	Used as a store for low disk space conditions.
System State	In Backup, a collection of system-specific data that can be backed up and restored. For all Windows 2000 operating systems, the System State data includes the registry, the system boot files, and the Certificate Services database (if the server is operating as a certificate server). If the server is a domain controller, the System State data also includes Active Directory directory services database and the SYSVOL directory.
SYSVOL	A shared directory that stores the server copy of the domain's public files, which are replicated among all domain controllers in the domain.
tombstone	Object marker that designates how long an object will remain in the database (the default is 60 days). This time period allows the tombstone to replicate to all domain controllers in the network. During garbage collection, objects that have gone past the tombstone lifetime are physically removed from the database.
transaction	The pairing of two or more actions performed together as a single action; the action succeeds or fails as a whole. Both transactions succeed or neither is executed.
transaction logs	File that record transactional changes that take place in a database. The transaction logs provide a basis for updating a master file and establishing an audit trail.

In Brief

If you want to...	Then do this...
Determine the increase in size of the Active Directory database caused by adding attributes to objects	• Allocate 100 bytes per string attribute, more if the string size is greater than 10 characters • For binary data, estimate the size of data and add 25% for buffering
Back up System State data	1. In **Backup**, choose the **Backup** tab. 2. In **Click To Select the Check Box For Any Drive, Folder, or File That You Want To Back Up**, select **System State**.
Create a backup on a server in a domain:	1. From the **Start** menu, choose **Programs**, **Accessories**, **System Tools**, and select **Backup**. 2. Choose the **Backup Wizard**. 3. Choose **Next**. 4. Choose **Only Back Up the System State Data**, and select **Next**. 5. In **Backup Media or Filename**, type ***c:\bkup.bkf*** (where ***c:\bkup.bkf*** represents the Backup filename). 6. After you verify that the Backup job description is correct, choose **Finish**. 7. When the backup is complete, choose **Close**.
Determine the number of objects in your organization and estimate required space	Include users, printers, and groups; for security principles add 3,600 bytes per object; for non-security principles add 1,100 bytes per object; and double your estimated number of objects. This should enable you to predict the required space.

If you want to...	Then do this...
Perform a non-authoritative restore	1. Restart the server, and choose **F8** to have the domain controller start in a directory Safe mode. 2. From the **Start** menu, choose **Programs**, **Accessories**, **System Tools**, and select **Backup**. 3. In **Backup and Recovery Tools**, choose **Restore Wizard**, and then select **Next**. 4. In **Restore Wizard What to Restore**, expand the media type that contains the data you want to restore. 5. Expand the appropriate media until the data you want is visible. 6. Choose the **data**, and choose **Next**. 7. Either choose **Finish** to complete the restore process, or select **Advanced** to specify advanced restore options.
Plan your backup strategy	**Select a method for backup**—Choose the method that meets your organization's need for speed and matches how much backup space you have available. **Off-site storage of backup tapes**—Plan to store the tape backups of your organization's most critical data at another location. Disasters such as fire can destroy both servers and backup tapes. Consider the tombstone lifetime to determine how long a backup is useful. **Determine the capacity and speed of your hardware**—Hardware capacity determines how fast backups or restores can be implemented. **Testing restores**—It is important to test the integrity of your backup. Periodically, you should choose a backup of a server at random and perform a test restore on a test server. Using a different tape device will also check the reliability of the tape machine.

If you want to...	Then do this...
Start Disk Defragmenter	From the **Start** menu, choose **Programs**, **Accessories**, **System Tools**, and then select **Disk Defragmenter** or run **Computer Management**, choose **Storage**, and then select **Disk Management**.
Start the offline defragmentation tool	1. To choose the **Directory Service Repair** module, restart the server, and select **F8**. 2. Use **NTDSUTIL.EXE** to create a defragmented copy of the database file.
Use the offline defragmentation tool	1. Back up **Active Directory** using the **Backup Wizard**. 2. Restart the domain controller, choose the correct installation from the **Start** menu, and select **F8** to display the **Advanced Options** menu. 3. Choose **Directory Services Restore Mode**, and select **Enter**. To have the system boot again, select **Enter**. 4. Log on using the Administrator account. 5. From the **Start** menu, choose **Programs**, **Accessories**, and then select **Command Prompt**. 6. At the command prompt, type **NTDSUTIL**, and choose **Enter**. 7. Type **files**, and then choose **Enter**. 8. Type **info**, and then choose **Enter**. Make note of the path and find enough disk space for the compacted database to be stored. 9. Type **compact to < *drive*> :\ < *directory*>** . 10. Type **quit**, and choose **Enter**. Type **quit** again. 11. Copy the new NTDS.DIT file over the old NTDS.DIT file in the current Active Directory database path. 12. Restart your computer.

If you want to...	Then do this...
Restore Active Directory from a backup	1. Restart the server, and choose **F8** to have the domain controller start in a directory Safe mode. 2. From the **Start** menu, choose **Programs**, **Accessories**, **System Tools**, and select **Backup**. 3. In **Backup and Recovery Tools**, choose **Restore Wizard**, and then select **Next**. 4. Choose **Import File**. 5. In **Catalog Backup File** type ***c:\bkup.bkf*** (where ***c:\bkup.bkf*** represents the Backup filename), and choose **OK**. 6. In **What To Restore**, expand the path, choose **System State**, and select **Next**. 7. In **Completing the Restore Wizard**, choose **Finish**. 8. In **Enter Backup Filename**, verify that the filename is correct, and choose **OK**. The restore will start and display its progress. 9. When the restore is complete choose **Close**, and select **Yes**.

Lesson 9 Activities

Complete the following activities to better prepare you for the certification exam.

1. Explain how you back up the Active Directory/System State.

2. You are viewing Active Directory Users and Computers and find some objects in the LostAndFound container. Describe where these objects could have come from, and what you should do with them.

3. You need to back up your domain controller. Describe the steps you take.

4. Now that you have backed up your Active Directory, you want to replicate between domain controllers from the computer that you used to back up your domain controller. Describe the steps.

5. You have backed up your domain controller, and you now want to restore that backup. Explain the steps.

6. While your domain controller is in the process of making a large number of changes to the Active Directory, the power failed. Describe what will happen when the domain controller is restarted.

7. You have installed Active Directory on a domain controller using all of the defaults. While monitoring the performance of the domain controller, you discover that there is a lot of activity on the disk that holds the system volume. Describe what you can do to alleviate the activity level.

8. Explain what the LostAndFound is, and what it does in the Active Directory.

9. Describe the best practices for maintaining Active Directory.

10. You need to estimate the size of your Active Directory database. Describe how you would accomplish that.

Answers to Lesson 9 Activities

1. The Active Directory is backed up using the built-in Windows 2000 Backup routine.

   Active Directory is part of the machine's System State, which includes the registry, class registration database, and the system boot files. A Windows 2000 Server that is a certificate server also contains the Certificate Services database. A Windows 2000 machine that is a domain controller includes the Active Directory and the SYSVOL directory.

   Follow these steps to back up the System State using the Backup Wizard:

   1. Start the **Backup Wizard**, and then choose **Next**.
   2. Choose **Only Back Up the Distributed Service Set**, and select **Next**.
   3. Choose **Backup Media or Filename**.

   If you do not want to use the wizard, you can manually back up your data by following these steps:

   1. Choose **Backup** from the **Backup** interface property page.
   2. Choose **System State**, and then select a **backup destination**.
   3. Choose **Start Backup**.
   4. Confirm **backup description**, and then choose **OK**.

   To back up only the System State from the command line, type the following command from the DOS prompt:
   C:\> ntbackup backup systemstate /f d:\active.bkf

2. They could be the result of replication of objects to containers that no longer exist. Check the objects to decide if they should be moved or deleted.

3. Create a backup on a server in a domain:
    1. From the **Start** menu, choose **Programs**, **Accessories**, **System Tools**, and select **Backup**.
    2. Choose the **Backup Wizard**.
    3. Choose **Next**.
    4. Choose **Only Back Up the System State Data**, and select **Next**.
    5. In **Backup Media or Filename**, type *c:\bkup.bkf* (where *c:\bkup.bkf* represents the Backup filename).
    6. After you verify that the Backup job description is correct, choose **Finish**.
    7. When the backup is complete, choose **Close**.

4. To replicate between domain controllers:
    1. Log on as Administrator.
    2. Verify that **Active Directory Sites and Servers** is connected to your local servers.
    3. Choose the **NTDS Settings** object for ***ServerName*** (where *ServerName* represents your server).
    4. Right-click the **connection object** for ***OtherServer*** (where *OtherServer* is the domain you wish to replicate to).
    5. Choose **Replicate Now**.
    6. Choose **OK**.

5. To restore Active Directory from a backup:
    1. Restart the server, and choose **F8** to have the domain controller start in a directory Safe mode.
    2. From the **Start** menu, choose **Programs**, **Accessories**, **System Tools**, and select **Backup**.
    3. In **Backup and Recovery Tools**, choose **Restore Wizard**, and then select **Next**.
    4. Choose **Import File**.

   5. In **Catalog Backup File,** type *c:\bkup.bkf* (where *c:\bkup.bkf* represents the Backup filename), and choose **OK**.
   6. In **What To Restore**, expand the path, choose **System State**, and select **Next**.
   7. In **Completing the Restore Wizard**, choose **Finish**.
   8. In **Enter Backup Filename**, verify that the filename is correct, and choose **OK**. The restore will begin and display its progress.
   9. When the restore is complete choose **Close**, and select **Yes**.

6. Any changes that had been committed in the transaction log will be applied to the directory.

7. You should relocate the Active Directory database file and log files to separate hard disks.

8. LostAndFound is a container. As part of your regular maintenance routine, you should examine the files in the LostAndFound. Sometimes objects are created on one domain controller when its parent container is deleted from another domain controller; or an object is moved into another container when the opposite process is occurring at another domain controller. Active Directory replication does not know where to put these objects so they end up in the LostAndFound container.

   To view the LostAndFound container, use the **Active Directory Users and Computers**. Choose the **View** menu for the domain, and select **Advanced Features**.

9. The following list provides best practices for maintaining Active Directory:
   - Plan for backup and recovery when you plan the layout of Active Directory
   - Keep the database and transaction logs on separate drives
   - By keeping the database files and transactions on physically separate hard disks, system performance is greatly improved
   - Estimate the size of your Active Directory, and then double it to decide on space requirements
   - Develop, document, and enforce a backup policy

10. To determine the number of objects in your organization, follow these steps:
    - Include users, printers, and groups
    - For security principles add 3,600 bytes per object
    - For non-security principles add 1,100 bytes per object
    - Double your estimated number of objects

    To determine how adding attributes to objects or applications that add objects to the Active Directory increase the size, follow these steps:
    - 100 bytes per string attribute, more if the string size is greater than 10 characters
    - For binary data, estimate the size of data, and add 25% for buffering

Lesson 9 Quiz

These questions test your knowledge of features, vocabulary, procedures, and syntax.

1. There are four different log files in the Data Store files. What are their names?

   A. Transaction logs, database file, reserved log, patch files.
   B. Transaction logs, Checkpoint files, reserved log, RES1.LOG.
   C. Database file, RES1.LOG, EDB.CHK, EDBxxxx.LOG.
   D. Transaction logs, Checkpoint files, reserved log, patch files.

2. What function does the Extensible Storage Engine (ESE) have in Active Directory?

   A. Stores all Active Directory objects.
   B. Enables you to create up to a 17-terabyte database that can theoretically hold up to ten million objects per domain.
   C. Reserves storage only for space that is used.
   D. Stores multiple-value attributes and properties.

3. What tables does the Active Directory database use to store information in?

   A. Object table
   B. Transaction table
   C. Schema table
   D. Link table

4. What are the features of Checkpoint files?

   A. A faster recovery by decreasing the amount of data to be read.
   B. The oldest file written over is disabled.
   C. They are the transactions written to the database during the backup.
   D. Deleting unneeded transaction log files.

5. What happens when files are fragmented?

    A. The computer searches the hard disk when the file is opened to find all of the parts of the file.
    B. Defragmentation rearranges how the data is written in the directory database file to compact it.
    C. Objects that have gone past the tombstone lifetime are physically removed.
    D. Slows down response time.

6. What is the difference between authoritative and non-authoritative restores?

    A. An authoritative restore restores an entire domain, an OU or a single object.
    A non-authoritative restore restores the entire replica of the database. The recovery of the back-up information depends on the transaction and replication logs.
    B. In an authoritative restore, objects in the restored directory are treated as authoritative, replacing through replication all existing copies of those objects.
    In a non-authoritative restore, the restored objects are updated with changes held in other replicas of the restored domain.
    C. In an authoritative restore, directory partition replicas are writable on each domain controller.
    In a non-authoritative restore a file replication service is used by the Distributed File System (DFS) to synchronize content between assigned replicas.
    D. In an authoritative restore, transactions in the transaction log not written to the database would be replicated when the server came back online.
    In a non-authoritative restore, if there is more than one domain controller in a domain, Active Directory is restored through normal replication with the replication partners.

7. How do you use the Backup tool?

    A. It is a shared directory that stores the server copy of the domain's public files.
    B. Delete the unused files and objects to reduce space requirements.
    C. Archive selected files and folders on your hard disk.
    D. Optimize disk storage.

8. Garbage collection is an automatic procedure. What does it do?

   A. It is a storage place for low disk conditions.
   B. Performs online database defragmentation.
   C. Writes transaction log files that provide fault tolerance.
   D. It runs in every domain controller.

9. You are developing a backup strategy. What do you need to consider and what tasks do you need to accomplish?

   A. The method you choose for backup.
   B. Capacity and speed of your hardware.
   C. Test restores.
   D. Estimate the Active Directory database size.

10. You need to optimize your system. What do you need to consider having on separate hard disks?

   A. Windows 2000 operating system; Extensible Storage database; Transaction logs
   B. Windows 2000 operating system; Active Directory database file; Microsoft Management Console (MMC)
   C. Windows 2000 operating system; Active Directory database file; FAT
   D. Windows 2000 operating system; Active Directory database file; Transaction logs

Answers to Lesson 9 Quiz

1. Answer D is correct. The four correct logs are the transaction log, the Checkpoint files, reserved log, and the patch files.

   Answer B is partly correct. RES1.LOG is the name of a patch file.

   Answer A is incorrect. A database file is one of the Data Store files but not one of the logs.

   Answer C is incorrect. A database file is one of the Data Store files, RES1.LOG is the name of the first patch file, EDB.CHK is the name of the Checkpoint file, and EDBxxxx.LOG is the name of a transaction log.

2. Answers A, B, C, and D are correct. ESE has the following functions in Active Directory:

   - Stores all Active Directory objects
   - Enables you to create up to a 17-terabyte database that can theoretically hold up to ten million objects per domain
   - Reserves storage only for space that is used; for example, if a user object has 50 attributes, and you create a user with values for only four of those attributes, space is consumed only for those four attributes and when more attributes are added, more storage is dynamically allocated
   - Stores multiple-value attributes and properties and this means that there can be multiple values for a single attribute or property; for example, the database can store multiple telephone numbers for a single user without requiring multiple telephone number attributes

3. Answer A is correct. The object table holds objects and their attributes.

   Answer C is correct. The schema table holds the definition of all types of objects that you can create in Active Directory.

   Answer D is correct. The link table holds the relationships between objects in the object table.

   Answer B is incorrect. There is no current transaction table.

4. Answer A is correct. Active Directory can decide which transactions have or have not been committed to the database file. However, the Checkpoint file leads to a faster recovery by decreasing the amount of data to be read.

   Answer B is incorrect. A feature of circular logging is that the oldest file written over is disabled.

   Answer C is incorrect. The transactions written to the database during the backup are patch files.

   Answer D is incorrect. Deleting unneeded transaction log files is part of automatic database cleanup.

5. Answers A and D are correct. When files are updated, the computer saves these updates on the largest contiguous space on the hard disk that it can find. These are often on a different sector than the other parts of the file. This slows down response time.

   Answer B is incorrect. It explains what happens when you defragment a disk.

   Answer C is incorrect. The reference is to deleting obsolete objects.

6. Answer A is correct. You can authoritatively restore an entire domain, an OU or a single object. With a non-authoritative restore the entire replica of the database can be restored. The recovery of the backup information depends on the transaction and replication logs.

   Answer B is correct. In an authoritative restore, objects in the restored directory are treated as authoritative, replacing through replication all existing copies of those objects. In a non-authoritative restore, the restored objects are updated with changes held in other replicas of the restored domain.

   Answer C is incorrect. In Active Director replication, directory partition replicas are writable on each domain controller. File replication service is a service used by the Distributed File System (DFS) to synchronize content between assigned replicas.

   Answer D is incorrect. In recovery without restore, transactions in the transaction log not written to the database would be replicated when the server came back online. In replication, if there is more than one domain controller in a domain, Active Directory is restored through normal replication with the replication partners.

7. Answer C is correct. With backup you can archive selected files and folders on your hard disk.

   Answer A is incorrect. The SYSVOL is a shared directory that stores the server copy of the domain's public files.

   Answer B is incorrect. Deleting the unused files and objects, so reducing space requirements is part of Active Directory maintenance.

   Answer D is incorrect. Defragmentation optimizes disk storage.

8. Answer B and D are correct. Garbage collection performs online database defragmentation, and it runs in every domain controller.

   Answer A is incorrect. A reserved log is a storage place for low disk conditions.

   Answer C is incorrect. Writing transaction logs is part of Active Directory maintenance.

9. Answers A, B, and C are correct. You need to consider the method you choose for backup, the capacity and speed of your hardware, and you need to test restores. You also need to consider off-site storage of backup.

   Answer D is incorrect. Estimating the Active Directory database size is part of database planning.

10. Answer D is correct. You should put each of these three items on their own server to improve performance.

    Answer A is incorrect. The ESE is part of the Data Store.

    Answer B is incorrect. The main MMC window provides commands and tools for authoring consoles and is an application in Windows 2000.

    Answer C is incorrect. FAT is the File Allocation Table. A list maintained by some operating systems to keep track of the status of various segments of disk space used for file storage.

Lesson 10

Windows 2000 Upgrade Strategies

Your network may consist of Microsoft Windows 2000 domain controllers as well as domain controllers running versions of Microsoft Windows NT. Before upgrading the NT domain controllers, you should first understands the implicationsimplications of having a mixed Windows network environment as versusopposed to having a fully completed upgrade, in whichwhere all your domain controllers are running Microsoft Windows 2000. Before attempting a network upgrade you should be able to accomplish the following tasks:

- Describe how a fully upgraded Windows 2000 environment differs from an environment with mixed Microsoft Windows 2000 and NT servers
- Describe the recommended paths to upgrade Microsoft Windows NT domain models.
- Explain the steps involved in an upgrade.
- Plan an upgrade.

Upgrading the network requires you to create and implement an upgrade strategy as well as testing and deploying.

After completing this lesson, you should have a better understanding of the following topics:

- The Mixed-Mode Domain
- Upgrading to Native Mode
- How to Upgrade to Windows 2000
- Planning a Windows 2000 Upgrade

The Mixed-Mode Domain

If you have a domain that contains both Microsoft Windows NT and Windows 2000 domain controllers, then you have what is known as a mixed-mode domain (Figure 10.1). In mixed-mode domains, means are provided to allow the disparate domain controllers to continue to provide the following elements:

- Domain services
- Domain controller communication
- Functionality

Figure 10.1 Mixed-Mode Domain

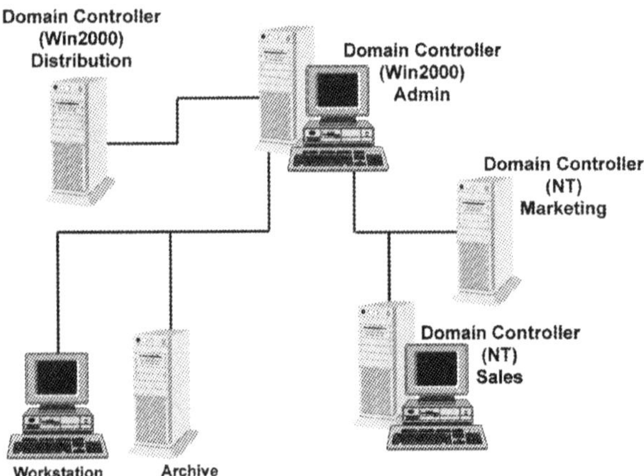

Differences exist between mixed-mode domains and native mode domains in the way the following features are handled:

- How requests to Primary Domain Controllers (PDC) are handled.
- Communication between domain controllers.

- Available services.
- Security.

Before you make a decision whether to remain in mixed mode or move to native mode, you should understand these differences.

Note: Earlier versions of Microsoft Windows NT are referred to as downlevel operating systems.

Workstations, member servers, and domain controllers running downlevel operating systems will look for a Primary Domain Controller (PDC) when they need to make changes to the Security Account Management (SAM) database. Each Windows 2000 domain designates a single-domain controller to act as a PDC emulator (Figure 10.2) to provide support for these downlevel clients.

Figure 10.2 PDC Emulator in a Windows 2000 Domain

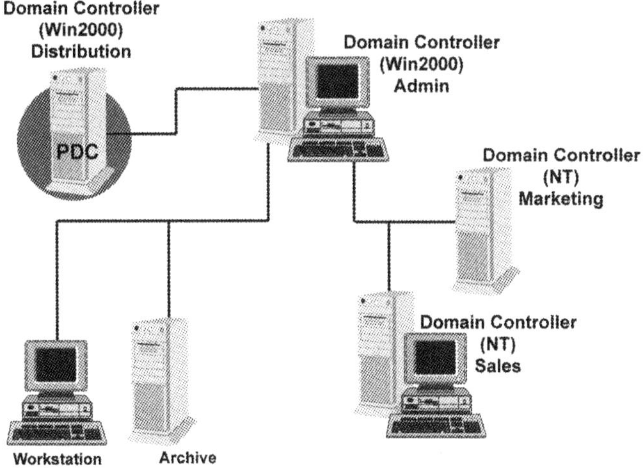

PDC Emulator Single Operations Master

The Primary domain controller (PDC) emulator acts as a Microsoft Windows NT primary domain controller in domains that have Microsoft Windows NT Backup Domain Controllers or computers without Windows 2000 client software. The PDC emulator is an operations master and must reside on one, and only one, domain controller in an Active Directory forest. The PDC emulator supports the Kerberos and NTLM protocols. ,This allowsing Microsoft Windows NT domain controllers to synchronize with a Windows 2000 environment running in mixed mode.

Every domain must have a domain controller that acts as a PDC emulator as long as the domain contains either clients without Windows 2000 client software or Microsoft Windows NT Backup domain controllers. This is illustrated in Figure 10.3.

Note: The first domain controller upgraded to Windows 2000 in an Active Directory domain assumes the role of the PDC emulator.

Figure 10.3 PDC Emulators in a Forest

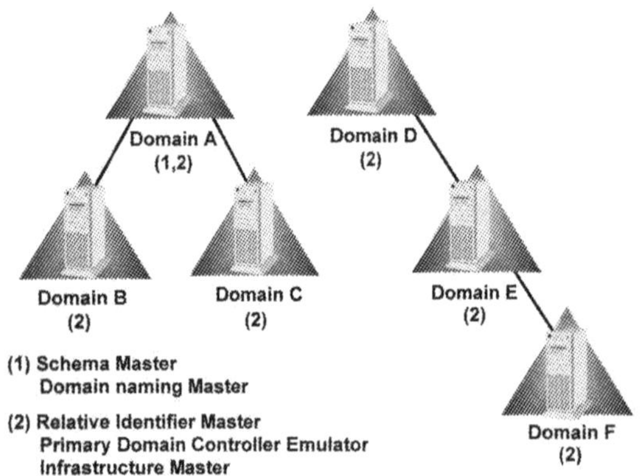

Downlevel clients may make the following requests from the Active Directory PDC emulator:

- Account changes.
- Account database replication to Microsoft Windows NT Backup Domain Controllers (BDCs).
- Supplying browsing information to downlevel clients running the Browser service.
- Authentication services for Microsoft Windows NT LAN Manager (NTLM) logon requests.

PDC Emulator and Replication

The PDC emulator exchanges updates to Active Directory in the following two ways:

- When contacting Windows 2000 domain controllers, it uses the Windows 2000 replication protocol and provides support for multimaster replication
- When the PDC emulator is contacting Backup Domain Controllers, it uses the NTLM replication protocol and acts as a single master

PDC Emulator and Downlevel Client Authentication

All objects are stored in Active Directory in a mixed-mode domain. Downlevel logon operations are not affected because Active Directory exposes the data to downlevel clients as a flat Microsoft Windows NT-style data store. A Windows 2000 domain controller uses the NTLM protocol to authenticate downlevel clients.

PDC Emulator Failure and Recovery

Downlevel clients that have not installed the Windows 2000 distributed services client package will not be able to change domain passwords or browse domain resources if the PDC emulator fails. A failure of the domain controller that is the PDC emulator, which is a single operations master, is visible to all users. This is why the PDC emulator role must be carefully planned. You mightmay want to keep the PDC emulator role on a domain controller that holds no other operations master role.

If the PDC emulator unexpectedly becomes unavailable, unexpectedly and it cannot be returned to service quickly, you will need to seize the role of the PDC emulator and force it to another domain controller.

The proceduresoperations used to seize the PDC emulator operations has used to seize the PDC emulator operations have been designed to facilitate the seizure with few, if any, severe side effects. The user- interface for a

seizure is just like the interface for a normal transfer of operations roles. However, because of the critical nature of the PDC controller, the seizure requires an extra confirmation from you. You should choose **OK** to the confirmation when you know the current PDC emulator will be offline for a significant period of time. period. You should transfer the PDC emulator role back to the original domain controller when it comes back online.

Warning: Remember that it is always preferable to transfer the operations master role rather than to seize the role.

Note: Remember that it is always preferable to transfer the operations master role rather than to seize the role.

To seize the PDC emulator, follow these steps:

1. From the **Start** menu, choose **Run**, or open a command window.
2. TypeType **`NTDSUTIL`**, and choose **Enter**.
3. At each of the following prompts, supply the indicated information, and then choose **Enter**.
4. At **NTDSUTIL**, type **`roles`**.
5. At **FSMO maintenance**, type **`connections`**.
6. At **server connections**, type **`connect to server,`** followed by the Fully Qualified Domain Name (FQDN) of the controller that is to be the new PDC emulator.

7. At **server connections**, type **`quit`**.
8. At **FSMO maintenance(Figure 10.4)**, type **`seize PDC`**.
9. At **NTDSUTIL**, type **`quit`**.

Figure 10.4 FSMO Maintenance Prompt

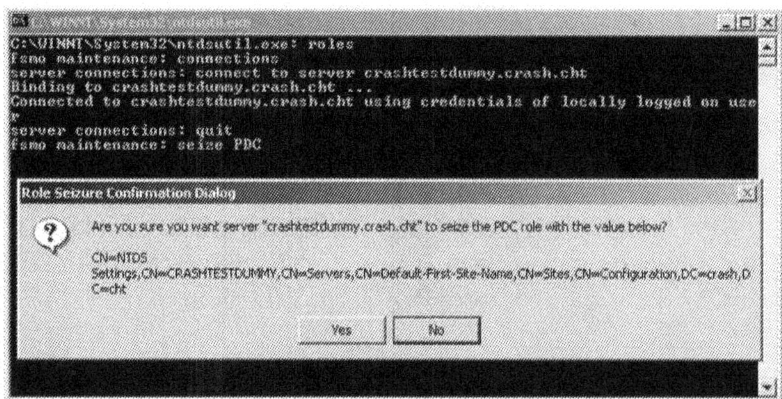

The PDC Emulator in a Fully-UpgradedFully Upgraded Domain

When all Microsoft Windows NT, Microsoft Windows 95, and Microsoft Windows 98 clients, servers, and domain controllers are all upgraded, downlevel support for client directory write operations, single-master replication, and browsing become unnecessary.

Once a domain is converted to native mode, the PDC emulator still plays a role. Password changes performed by other domain controllers in the domain are replicated preferentially to the PDC emulator. When an authentication request fails due to a bad password at one of the other domain controllers in the domain, the domain controller, where the failure occurred, will forward the authentication request to the PDC emulator before failing the request. This is done in case the password had been recently changed. Account lockouts are also processed on the PDC emulator.

Security Principles

In Active Directory, all objects are uniquely identified by:

- A Security Identifier (SID) that identifies the domain.
- A Relative Identifier (RID) that is supplied by the domain controller that creates the object.

The RID must be unique for each object. This is because all objects within a domain use the same domain identifier. I n Microsoft Windows NT, only the PDC was able to create security principles. All Backup Domain Controllers thus expected security principles to have consecutively incremented RIDs. Active Directory uses a multimaster replication protocol that allows each domain controller to create objects. This prevents the use of consecutively numbered RIDs.

In a mixed-mode environment, some means of centrally managing the RID allocation is needed,.. Each domain contains a domain controller acting as the RID operations master to provide this functionality. The old-style, master-slave replication protocol must be used for downlevel clients as long as downlevel domain controllers are part of the Active Directory domain. While domain controllers running Windows 2000 can supply RIDs from their allocated pool, only the RID Master can create security principles for downlevel clients. By default, the upgraded PDC is the RID Master.

Services in Mixed Mode

Not all Windows 2000 services are available in mixed mode; therefore, you need to consider the interoperability issues that arise with the following features:

- Logon Service
- File Replication Service
- Remote Access Service

Logon Services

A Windows 2000 client first uses Domain Name System (DNS) to locate a Windows 2000 domain controller. In a mixed-mode domain, if it cannot find one, it uses the NTLM protocol to log on to a Microsoft Windows NT domain controller. If this is the case, Windows 2000 Group Policy Objects

(GPOs) and logon scripts are not processed. You should install at least one Windows 2000 domain controller in all sites that have Windows 2000 network clients. This will eliminate inter-site logon and authentication traffic.

File Replication Service

Microsoft Windows NT uses the LAN Manager Replication (LMRepl) service to replicate policy and logon script files. LMRepl is not supported by Windows 2000. In Windows 2000, File Replication Service (FRS) replaces the LMRepl service. These replication architectures must be bridged in mixed mode.

Warning: Servers hosting import directories are migrated first. Plan on upgradingto upgrade the servers hosting the Microsoft Windows NT export directory to Windows 2000 last.

As best practices, you should incorporate the following tasks into your routine:

- Manually disable the Directory Replication Service before each domain controller or member server upgrade
- Create a batch file that copies the Microsoft Windows NT scripts directory to the system volume of a Windows 2000 domain controller
- Schedule the copy task to run at regular intervals to keep the scripts and policies up-to-date

---

Note: Every Windows 2000 domain controller has a replicated System Volume because of the File Replication Service. Any change made to a logon script is replicated to all domain controllers. Member servers cannot host the System Volume.

When you configure the export servers, consider the following recommendations:

- If the Microsoft Windows NT export server is the PDC, change the export server by removing the export directory
- Choose the server that you believe will be the last server upgraded to Windows 2000 and add the directory to the export list using Server Manager because if you do not do this, you will need to nominate yet another export server as you subsequently upgrade your servers

Note: It is important to remember that you will need to point each server configured as an import directory to the newly selected export server.

Remote Access Service

Microsoft Windows NT Remote Access Service (RAS) runs in the security context of a special service account, LocalSystem. When a service logs on as LocalSystem, it logs on with NULL credentials,credentials; no username or password is provided.

By default, Active Directory will not accept the querying of object attributes, such as Microsoft Windows NT RAS dial-in access permissions, by means of a NULL session. The object attribute query functionality can be provided when the following conditions are met:

- When the Microsoft Windows NT RAS server is a Backup Domain Controller (BDC) and the domain is in mixed mode; t his allows the server to have local access to the Security Accounts Manager (SAM)
- When the Microsoft Windows NT RAS contacts a Microsoft Windows NT BDC server by chance, and the domain is in mixed mode (t his event is not predictable)
- When Active Directory security has been loosened to grant read permissions to the Everyone group on any user object, whereby t he domain can be in either mixed or native mode; this option can be set during promotion of a domain controller by choosing the option to weaken the permission for RAS access

Security in Mixed Mode

If you run in mixed mode for both Microsoft Windows NT and Windows 2000 clientsclients, you will need to keep security information consistent between them. To do so, you will need to maintain the following aspects:

- Trust relationships
- System policy

You will also need to understand how objects in the Security Accounts Manager (SAM) map to Active Directory.

Trust Relationships

In a Windows 2000 forest, Windows 2000 uses transitive trust relationships between domains. However, transitive trusts are not recognized by downlevel domain controllersdownlevel domain controllers do not recognize transitive trusts. These domain controllers must use explicit one-way trusts between domains to authenticate users from a different domain. These two different trust relationships are compared in Figure 10.5.

Figure 10.5 Trust Relationship Comparison

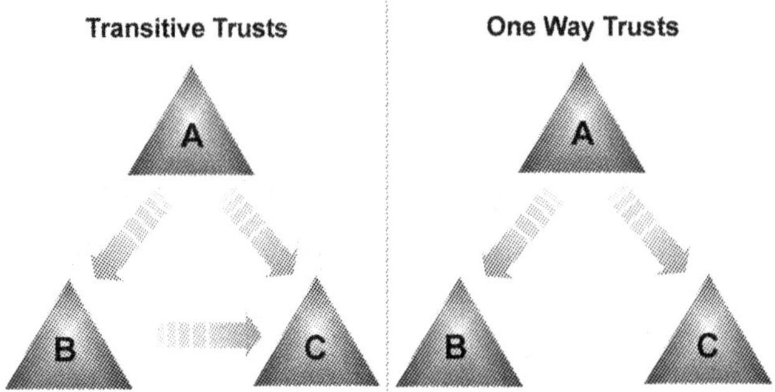

System Policy

Microsoft Windows NT 4.0-based clients and servers still process Windows NT 4.0-style Windows NT 4.0 style system policy in a Windows 2000 Active Directory environment. Therefore, you may need to maintain Windows NT 4.0-style Microsoft Windows NT 4.0 style system policy. If so, there is a Group Policy option that allows you to turn on Windows NT 4.0 style system policy. Once these clients and servers are upgraded to Windows 2000, then by default they will only process Windows 2000 Group Policy.

Warning: If you use the Group Policy option that allows you to turn on Microsoft Windows NT 4.0 style Group Policy, then the conflicting Windows 2000 Group Policy will be overridden by the Microsoft Windows NT 4.0 style policies.

Group Policy

Windows NT 4.0-style Microsoft Windows NT 4.0 style policies are defined in the System Policy Editor and processed at user logon. Since style policies can be complex and extremely detailed, such policies were created only by the most knowledgeable systems engineers. Windows NT 4.0-style

The successor to the System Policy Editor is Windows 2000 Group Policy (Figure 10.6). Using Windows 2000 Group Policy, you can create policies that can control all aspects of the environment, both large and small. Group policies are usually set at the site and domain level.

Figure 10.6 Windows 2000 Group Policy Snap-In

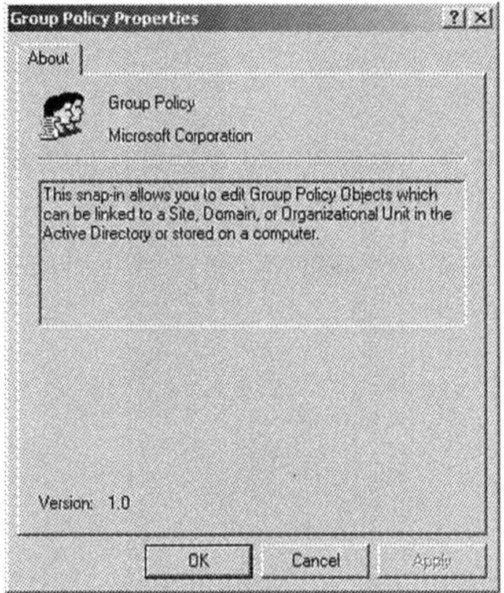

With the Group Policy snap-in, you can specify the following settings:

- registryRegistry-based policy settings
- securitySecurity settings
- softwareSoftware installation
- scriptsScripts
- folderFolder redirection

Enabling Windows NT 4.0-style Microsoft Windows NT 4.0 style Group Policy

Plan very carefully before you enable Windows NT 4.0-style Microsoft Windows NT 4.0 style policy in addition to Windows 2000 Group Policy. To ensure that consistent application of policy is maintained, you may want to consider mirroring your existing Windows NT 4.0-style Microsoft Windows

NT 4.0 style system policies in a Windows 2000 Group Policy. The system policies can be eliminated when all Microsoft Windows NT member servers and client computers have been upgraded to Windows 2000.

The SAM Database

When the PDC is upgraded in a domain, it includes the migration of administrative control, permissions, and security principles from the Microsoft Windows NT SAM to Active Directory.

From the SAM on a Microsoft Windows NT domain controller, security objects are migrated in the following ways:

- User accounts are placed in the Users container.
- Computer accounts are placed in the Computer container.
- Built-in local groups are placed in the Builtin container.
- Global groups are placed in the Builtin container.
- Non built-in groups are placed in the Users container.

The domain controllers' Organizational Unit (OU) receives the PDC's computer account. The permissions for NT File System (NTFS) files and folders, shared folders, printers, local groups, user rights, and registry keys are retained.

Note: All security principles created from downlevel clients are placed in the Users container after the upgrade.

While in mixed mode, the PDC emulator replicates directory objects to Microsoft Windows NT domain controllers. This limits the scalability of Active Directory to 40 megabytes (MB). This limitation is imposed on Active Directory by Microsoft Windows NT domain controllers.

Tip: If you wish to take full advantage of Active Directory scalability, you should upgrade all domain controllers as soon as possible to Windows 2000 and switch to native mode.

Even after all domain controllers are upgraded to Windows 2000, the network will still be running in mixed mode. You can promote your network to native mode, the final operational state. When your network is in native mode, the following parameters are in effect:

- Downlevel servers and clients can run in native mode
- All domain controllers must be running Windows 2000
- No additional Microsoft Windows NT domain controllers can be added to the network.

Choosing Native Mode

Native mode provides enhanced management features and many other advantages. Mixed and native mode management features are compared in the following tableTable 10.1.:

Table 10.1 Mixed and Native Mode Management Features

Feature	Mixed mode	Native mode
Multimaster replication	Yes	Yes
Group types	Global, Local	Universal, Global, Domain Local, Local
Nested security groups	No	Yes
Cross-domain administration	Limited	Full
Password filters	Installed on each domain controller individually	Installed on all domain controllers automatically
Transitive trusts	No	Yes
Queries using Desktop Change/Configuration Management	Only on Windows 2000 domain controllers	Yes

Choosing Mixed Mode

After the upgrade, you may want to remain in mixed mode for a period of time periodtime. This depends upon the upgrade strategy that you choose for your organization. If you remain in mixed mode, you can retain a BDC in your network. If you need to roll back your domain to a Microsoft Windows NT domain structure, you can consider the following steps:

- Force a resynchronization of the BDC's SAM.
- Promote the BDC to a PDC

If it becomes necessary, you can even replace existing Windows 2000 domain controllers with Microsoft Windows NT domain controllers until you have returned to the domain structure of Microsoft Windows 2000.

Upgrading to Native Mode

When you upgrade from a current Microsoft Windows NT domain model to a Windows 2000 Active Directory domain model, the planned path that you take depends on the current state of your present Microsoft Windows NT domain model and the operating systems of clients and other servers on the network (Figure 10.7). How you get the desired result depends upon the upgrade path you follow, based carefully on the version of your current operating system and the Microsoft Windows NT domain model currently employed.

Figure 10.7 Upgrade Paths for Different Operating Systems

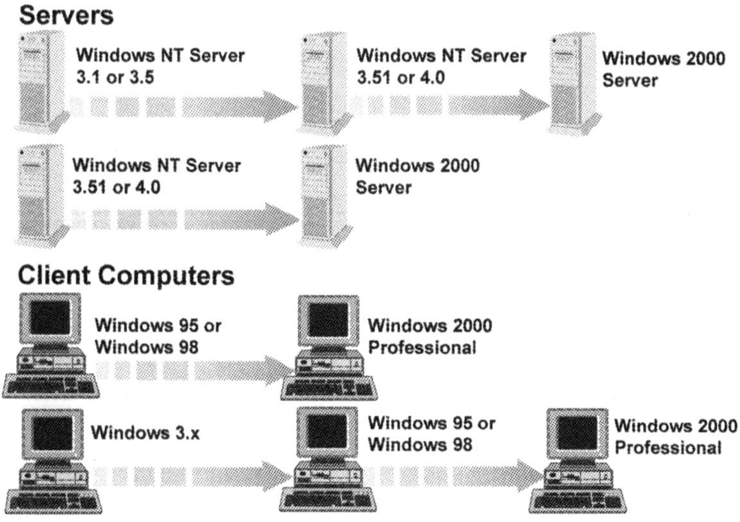

Microsoft Windows NT Operating Systems

To upgrade from Microsoft Windows NT Server versions 3.1 or 3.5 you must first upgrade to either Microsoft Windows NT Server v3.51 or 4.0 before you can upgrade to Windows 2000. If you are running Microsoft Windows NT Server 3.51 or 4.0, you can upgrade directly to Windows 2000.

The upgrade path to Windows 2000 for the different versions of Microsoft Windows NT Workstation is exactly thethe same as the upgrade path for the similar version of Microsoft Windows NT Server. Microsoft Windows NT Workstation versions 3.1 or 3.5 must upgrade to either Microsoft Windows NT Workstation v3.51 or 4.0 before upgrading to Windows 2000 Professional.

Microsoft Windows NT 3.51 Client Issues

Downlevel domain controllers do not recognize transitive trusts. Since it does not recognize transitive trusts, a computer running Microsoft Windows NT 3.51 cannot authenticate groups and users in domains other than the login domain. Also, Microsoft Windows NT 3.51 is unable to authenticate any user and group accounts that have been moved between Windows 2000 domains because it does not recognize the SID history attribute. You should avoid using Microsoft Windows NT 3.51 on computers in Windows 2000 domains.

Windows Client Operating Systems

If you are upgrading a Windows 95 or 98 system then you can upgrade directly to Windows 2000 Professional.

Note: Any version of Windows 95 can be upgraded directly to Windows 2000 Professional.

If you are upgrading a Windows 3.x system, you must first upgrade to either Windows 95 or Windows 98 before upgrading to Windows 2000 Professional.

Upgrading a Single-Domain Model

You upgrade a single-domain model Microsoft Windows NT domain into a single Active Directory domain (Figure 10.8). Using Organizational Units (OUs), you delegate authority to specific objects in the Active Directory domain. OUs are created in the Active Directory domain to logically reflect your administration model. An OU is a container that can contain other OUs and this allows you to create a hierarchical tree of OUs.

Once you create your OU hierarchy, you can organize objects into their respective OU container. When this is accomplished, you will have a more logical representation of the information to be managed. Another benefit of doing this is that you can take advantage of the ability to delegate the administration of OUs as well as apply Group Policy to them.

Figure 10.8 Upgrading from a Single Microsoft Windows NT Domain

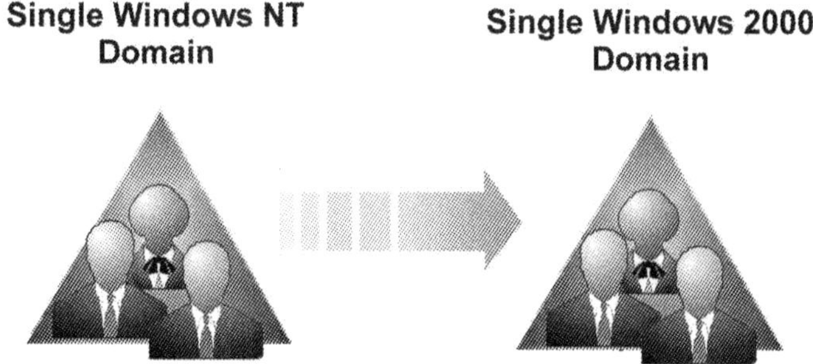

Upgrading a Master Domain Model

There are multiple domains in a Microsoft Windows NT master domain model. One of these domains has been designated as the master domain and it is where the accounts are usually stored. The remaining domains are referred to as resource domains.

When you upgrade this model (Figure 10.9), you retain your previous domain structure, and each Microsoft Windows NT domain is upgraded in place. You should upgrade your master domain model from the top down, where the master domain is the first domain to be upgraded.

Figure 10.9 Upgrading a Master Domain Model

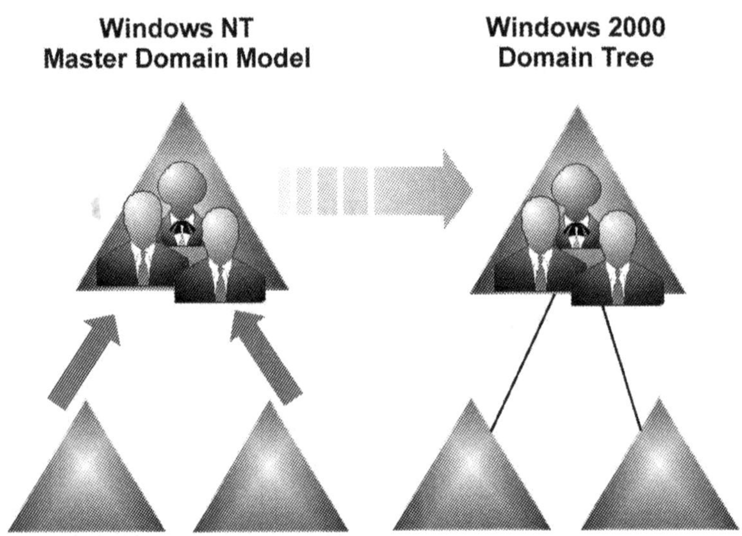

Note: This process requires the temporary use of explicit trusts until all domain controllers are upgraded.

Upgrading a Multiple Master Domain Model

There is more than one master domain in a Microsoft Windows NT multiple master domain model. Each master domain contains user accounts and global groups. This model is most often used when the following factors apply to an organization:

- Contains a large number of accounts
- Account management is decentralized
- Does not want domain synchronization traffic between geographically separate sites

Refer to Figure 10.10 to see the upgrade possibilities with a multiple master domain model.

Figure 10.10 Upgrading a Multiple Master Domain Model

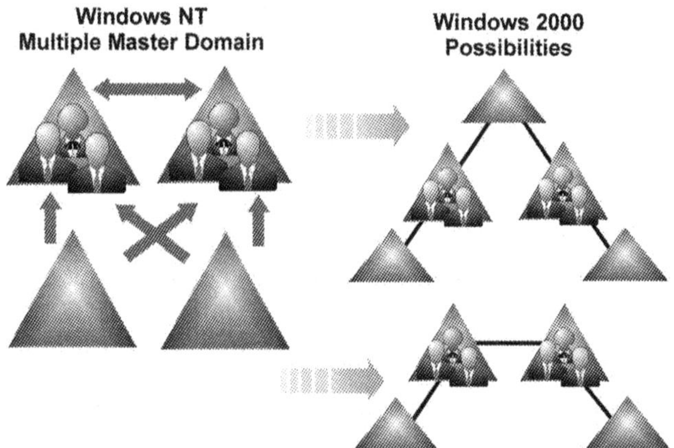

The following two upgrade approaches are possible with a multiple master domain model:

- Building a single-domain tree.
- Building a domain forest

Building a Single-Domain Tree

To build a single-domain tree that encompasses all master domains, you simply create an empty root domain. The existing master domains are incorporated as child domains of the new empty root domain. Existing Microsoft Windows NT resource domains can be implemented at the next level of the tree.

Building a Domain Forest

To build a domain forest, you build one domain tree for each member master domain and its subordinate resource domains. If you build a domain forest, each domain tree will be able to retain the following elements:

- A common schema
- A common Global Catalog
- Common configuration

Users will be able to access resources from anywhere in the forest by using transitive trusts. Business units will be able to implement their own tree in their own domain structure with their own security policies.

Upgrading a Complete Trust Model

When there are multiple Microsoft Windows NT domains that are all joined by two-way trusts, you have a complete trust domain model. This model is found when an organization is decentralized to the point that it cannot agree upon a common resource owner or common root.

Obviously, an organization does not usually intend to create a complete trust domain model. A complete trust domain is typically the result of the following factors:

- An explosion of grass roots domains
- Unplanned growth
- Mergers
- Acquisitions

Refer to Figure 10.11 to see how an upgrade to a complete trust domain model can be approached:

Figure 10.11 Upgrading a Complete Trust Domain Model

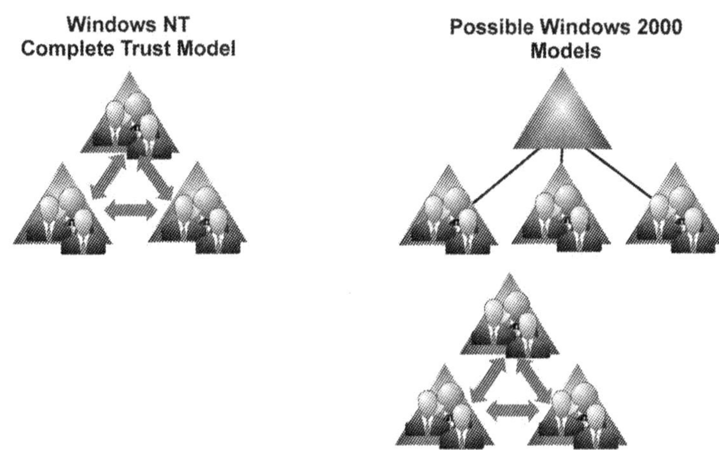

An upgrade to a complete trust domain model can be approached in two ways:

- Upgrading to a single forest with multiple domains.
- Upgrading to create separate forests

Upgrading to a Single Forest with Multiple Domains

Each division within the organization can maintain its own domain. Each of these domains areis made a child of a common, empty root domain. This allows your domains to share the following elements:

- A common schema
- A Global Catalog
- Configuration

All domains in the forest will be connected through transitive trusts (Figure 10.12). This is the reason why you will not need to create manual trust relationships.

Figure 10.12 A Single Forest with Multiple Domains

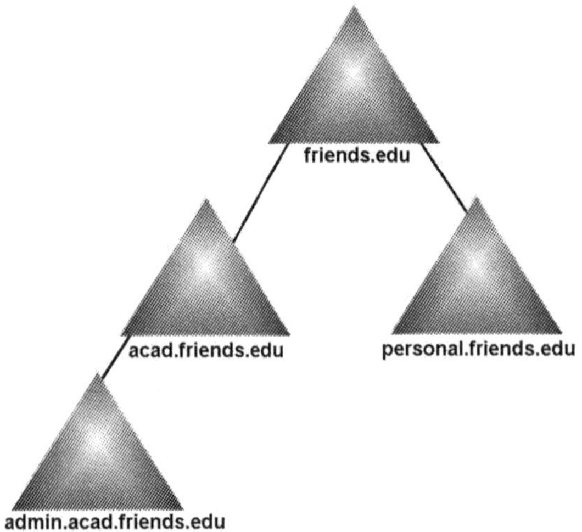

Upgrading to Create Separate Forests.

Between domains in separate forests, you can establish Windows 2000 explicit trust relationships. These trust relationships will have to be managed. Since each forest will have a separate Global Catalog, searches for resources will have to be performed against each distinct forest in the enterprise.

How to Upgrade to Windows 2000

Not all systems in your network have to be upgraded to take advantage of Windows 2000 features. When planning your upgrade to Windows 2000, you should review all the procedures involved. Windows 2000 Server is designed to support mixed networks containing downlevel clients and Windows 2000 servers and workstations with full interoperability.

You need to consider the following points:

- A plan to upgrade your PDCs
- The order in which you will upgrade BDCs

- When you will upgrade workstations
- When you will upgrade member servers
- A plan to test and verify the upgrade

Note: The first domain controller to be upgraded in a domain is always the PDC.

Upgrading the Primary Domain Controller

It is important to carefully choose the first domain to upgrade because the first PDC you upgrade creates the root of your Active Directory forest (Figure 10.13). The first domain controller in the forest will act as the schema operations master and the Global Catalog Server. There should be sufficient processor power and memory installed on this server to provide an adequate level of service. You must ensure that the first domain controller has sufficient hardware resources.

Figure 10.13 The First Upgraded Domain Controller

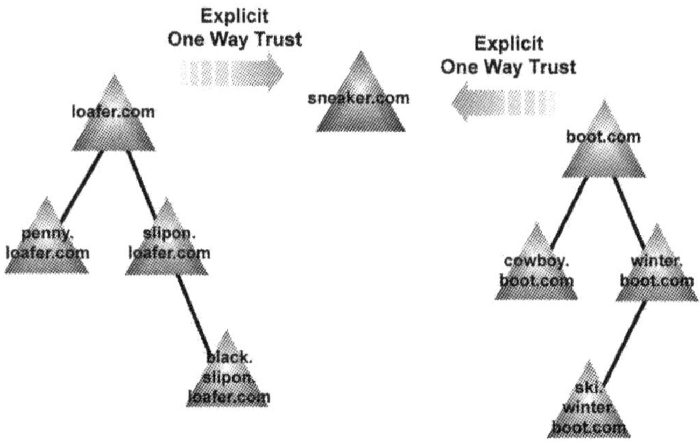

As you upgrade further domains, they should join the forest you created when you upgraded the first PDC. These upgraded domains create new trees in the same forest, or they may join an existing tree.

Active Directory Setup installs all necessary components on the domain controller including the following features:

- The Active Directory database
- Kerberos v5 authentication software

Existing SAM security principles are upgraded to Active Directory. These include the following elements:

- User accounts
- Local groups
- Global groups
- Computer accounts

Once you have upgraded the first PDC, and the first Windows 2000 domain controller is running in the first domain in the forest, you should upgrade the PDCs of any additional domains. When this has been accomplished, you should then upgrade the BDCs.

Upgrading the Backup Domain Controllers

You should migrate Backup Domain Controllers as quickly as possible to minimize the impact of running in mixed mode. The upgrade process will implement the following features:

- Recognize the server as a Backup Domain Controller
- Automatically start the promotion process to install the BDC as an Active Directory domain controller
- Add the BDC to the replication topology.

When determining when to upgrade each BDC, You will need to address the following questions:

1. Have you tested all required software applications for compatibility with Windows 2000?
2. Are there any resources or services that are not compatible with Windows 2000?
3. Does the BDC need to retain a domain controller role in the Windows 2000 domain?

Note: Remember that after upgrading you can demote any Windows 2000 domain controller to a member server.

Tip: Consider retaining one BDC in each Windows 2000 domain until you have decided to switch to native mode.

Upgrading Workstations and Member Servers

You can upgrade workstations and member servers in any order. You can also design and implement aan independent strategy from that used to upgrade associated domain controllers and account domains.

An OU structure is visible only for machines that have the Active Directory client software installed. Any other machine will not see OUs. The domain controller will expose all objects as a flat store if a downlevel client queries a domain controller for security principles. This allows these downlevel clients to find objects at the domain level, no matter in which OU the objects actually reside.

Note: Downlevel clients will continue to access Active Directory using NetBIOS.

You can upgrade workstations and member servers before upgrading domain controllers. However, you will not be able to access the features of Active Directory if you do so.

Testing Your Upgrade

It is very important to verify that network resources have been upgraded successfully after you upgrade a domain controller. You should test and verify the following elements:

- The domain upgrade
- User and group accounts
- System policies
- Active Directory install
- Hardware configuration

The Domain Upgrade

After the domain upgrade has been performed to, use the following tools and log files to verify the upgrade:

- DCPROMO.LOG
- LISTDCS.VBS
- LISTDOMAINS.VBS

You can verify the domain upgrade by checking the DCPROMO.LOG file. To list all the domain controllers within a domain, run the LISTDCS.VBS script that comes with the Windows 2000 Resource Kit, for example:

cscript listdcs.vbs LDAP://dc=username,dc=companyname,dc=msft

To list all domain-naming contexts within a given tree run the LISTDOMAINS.VBS script that comes with the Windows 2000 Resource Kit, for example:

cscript listdomains.vbs LDAP://dc= companyname,dc=msft

Tip: Lightweight Directory Access Protocol (LDAP) is case-sensitive in these commands.

User and Group Accounts

To verify user and group accounts, log on from a client computer. You should verify that the following features are available:

- Users who could log on to the domain before the upgrade can still log on after the upgrade
- User and group accounts that existed in the Microsoft Windows NT Server 4.0 domain still exist in the Windows 2000 domain
- All commands in the logon script batch file for a user or group run successfully

Use the administrator account to log on to the domain and then access the Active Directory Users and Computers (Figure 10.14).

Figure 10.14 Active Directory Users and Computers

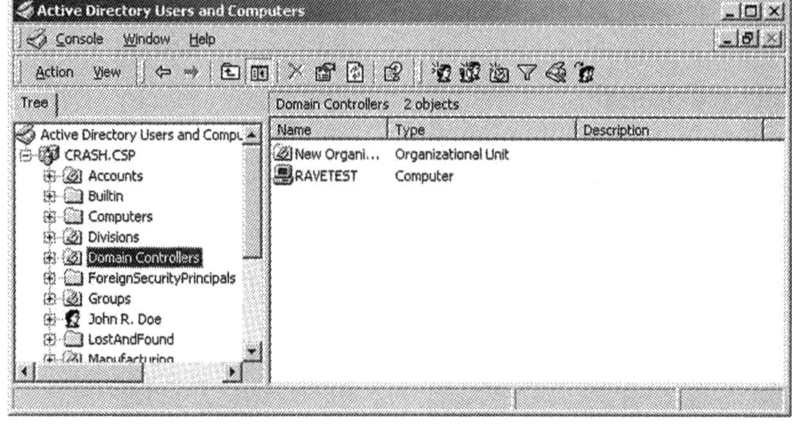

System Policies

To verify that domain members can still retrieve the correct system policy, complete the following tasks:

- Create Group Policy that mirrors your Microsoft Windows NT 4.0 system policies.
- Log on as different users who belong to different system policy groups.
- Confirm that the system policies assigned to groups are still being applied.

When you create Group Policy that mirrors your Microsoft Windows NT 4.0 system policies, you ensure that Group Policy is applied consistently across your network clients.

Active Directory Install

You can use Event Viewer to verify the installation of Active Directory. Event Viewer (Figure 10.15) will display which Active Directory components were installed in the directory service log. The components will be displayed as informational log entries.

Figure 10.15 Event Viewer Console

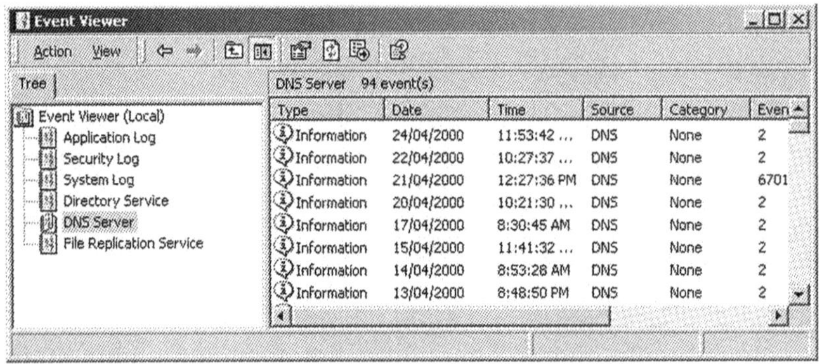

Hardware Configuration

Microsoft Windows NT uses Plug-and-Play to install hardware during the upgrade. Plug-and-Play is a standard set of protocols and procedures that regulate how the operating system, a hardware device, and the Basic Input Output System (BIOS) work together to install and configure hardware devices automatically.

Make sure that all hardware has been properly installed and configured and is still functioning correctly. Run the **Add New Hardware Wizard** in **Control Panel** to re-install the hardware device if setup fails to install a hardware device properly.

Planning a Windows 2000 Upgrade

An in-place upgrade is the simplest upgrade path to Windows 2000. An in-place upgrade retains your current domain model so that you retain your existing Microsoft Windows NT domain relationships within the Windows 2000 domain structure.

Note: You can restructure the Windows 2000 domain at a later time if necessary.

Existing Domain Structures

Consider the following elements when examining your current Microsoft Windows NT domain structure:

- Domain model
- Existing trust relationships
- Number and locations of domain controllers within each domain
- Your current DNS structure.

Domain Model

For each Microsoft Windows NT domain model, a different recommended Active Directory domain model exists. Your forest structure will be influenced by your current Microsoft Windows NT domain model.

Existing Trust Relationships

Any trusts existing before the upgrade will be preserved. It is important to know which trusts need to remain explicit because upgraded domains will have transitive trusts.

Number and Locations of Domain Controllers within Each Domain.

The Number number of domain controllers and their location within each domain indicatesindicate the effort and time that will be required to upgrade a given domain. The more domain controllers exist in a domain, the longer it will take to fully upgrade the domain to Windows 2000.

Your Current DNS Structure

Your current DNS structure influences the naming of Active Directory domains. You can use existing, registered DNS names for Active Directory.

Recovery Plan Strategies

Before performing an upgradeupgrade, it is important that you develop a recovery plan to ensure against accidental loss of data during the upgrade process. Before performing an upgrade complete the following tasks:

- Back up all services running on PDCs and BDCs
- Test the backup tapes.
- Fully synchronize all BDCs with the PDC.
- Take one BDC offline before upgrading the PDC and the other BDCs to Windows 2000 Server.

As a test before beginning the upgrade, perform the following steps:

- Promote the offline BDC to a PDC

Test the data backup.

- Demote this PDC to a BDC.
- Verify that the data did not become lost or corrupted.
- Keep this BDC available for a week or more after the domain upgrade is complete
- Back up all other BDCs regularly.

At each step in your upgrade process, you should be able to answer the following questions:

1. How would you roll back the system to a recovery state?
2. What administrative tools do you need to accomplish the upgrade?
3. What administrative tools do you need to roll back to the recovery state?

Designing the First Tree

The first domain created in the forest is the root domain (Figure 10.16). Since the root domain holds the configuration and schema information for the entire forest, Windows 2000 Server will not allow you to delete or rename the initial root domain without removing the entire forest. Planning the implementation of the first tree is crucial because it begins with the promotion of the first domain controller in the forest. To design the initial forest tree, you need to complete the following tasks:

- Examine the existing domain structure
- Examine existing explicit trust relationships
- Identify any domains you do not want to include in the forest
- Determine the number of domain controllers and their locations within each domain
- Identify where in the DNS naming hierarchy you will place your Active Directory root domain

Figure 10.16 Hierarchical Forest with Root Domain

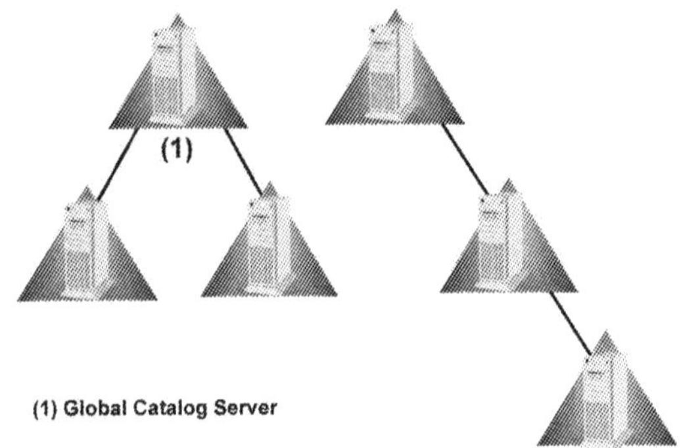

Examine the existing domain structure

Knowing the number of existing account and resource domains you have will help you create the Active Directory tree design. Your existing Microsoft Windows NT account and resource domains can be upgraded. If you only have one account domain, it can be the root domain. You can have the resource domains be children of the account domains. With more than one account domain, you can create a root domain and have the account domains be its children (Figure 10.17).

Figure 10.17 Account Domains

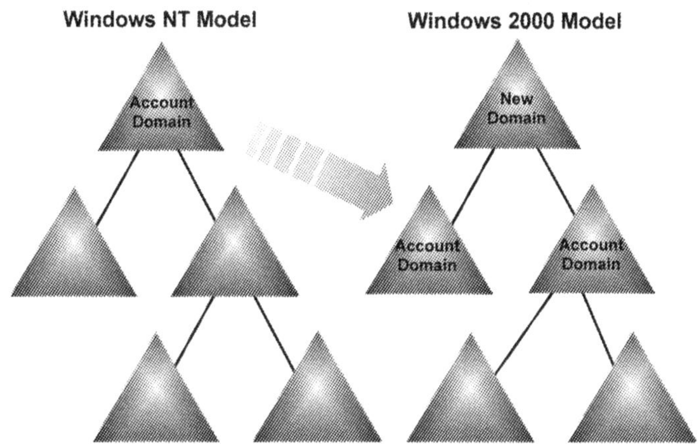

Examine Existing Explicit Trust Relationships

You will need to examine existing explicit trust relationships, both one-way and two-way. Domains upgraded to Windows 2000 that belong to the same forest will be connected with transitive trusts. It is important to know which trusts will need to remain explicit. Any trusts existing before the upgrade will be preserved.

Identify Domains You Do Not Want to Include in the Forest

These domains would use explicit one-way trusts to connect to the forest to retain resource access (Figure 10.18).

Figure 10.18 Retaining Access to Resources from a Separate Domain

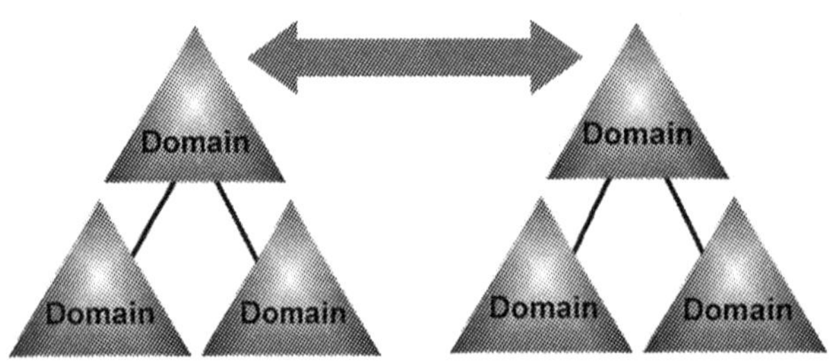

Determine the Number of Domain Controllers and Their Locations within Each Domain.

Knowing the number and location of member domain controllers will give you an indication of how much effort will be required to upgrade a given domain. You will also be able to plan the order in which member domain controllers are upgraded.

Identify Where in the DNS Naming Hierarchy You Will Place Your Active Directory Root Domain.

Choose where you will place your Active Directory root domain carefully. You cannot move your Active Directory root domain without re-installing the Active Directory forest.

Designing a Site Topology

Within a network, a site is a physical unit of replication and is not necessarily tied to the logical Active Directory structure. With domain controllers at different physical locations, a domain can span multiple sites. On the other hand, if needed, a site can span multiple domains. Sites guarantee that the domain controller that is physically closest to a particular group of users, computers, or both will be contacted first.

You should consider the following subjects when you design your site topology:

- The physical sites that will reside within the forest
- If any, the domains that will span physical sites
- The current and planned link speeds between sites
- The type of network that is installed or planned (a privately leased point-to-point Wide Area Network (WAN), a network that accesses the Internet, a dial-up network)

Considering these topics will help you to identify the physical locations for sites and subnets (Figure 10.19).

Figure 10.19 Physical Sites in a Forest

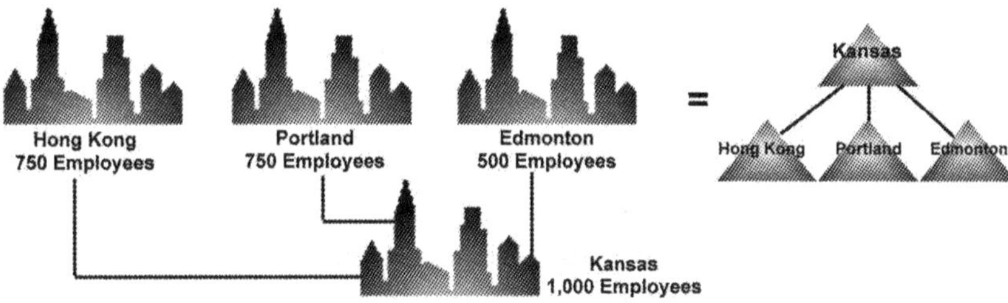

Ordering Domain Upgrades

To determine the order in which you upgrade your Microsoft Windows NT domains, you will need to consider the following points:

- The number of account and resource domains in the network
- Any existing trust relationships
- The final Active Directory domain structure that you want to implement.

The first thing you must do is to identify the Microsoft Windows NT domain that will become the Active Directory root domain. In most cases, this will be the Microsoft Windows NT account domain. Next, identify the Microsoft Windows NT resource domains that will become child domains of the root. You may need additional trees to accommodate multiple DNS root names in your forest.

In the case where multiple Microsoft Windows NT account domains are present, YOU you Mustmust decide whether to make the additional account domains child domains of an empty Active Directory root domain or to make each account domain the root of a separate tree.

Upgrading Domain Controllers

Within each domain, the PDC should always be upgraded first. In a multiple domain model, you need to determine the order in which PDCs are upgraded.

If you have resources that use local groups on Access Control Lists (ACLs), it will be easier if you upgrade initially to a single domain. It is better to use groups of users rather than users on ACLs because you have far fewer objects to manage.

Should you decide to remain in mixed modemode, you need to consider fault tolerance. You should upgrade at least one additional domain controller for each domain as quickly as possible.

If you decide to switch to native mode, once the first PDC has been installed, you should upgrade all of the BDCs in the domain as quickly as possible and then switch to native mode to minimize the impact of mixed-mode behavior. You can independently upgrade workstations and member servers in the domain in any order.

Tip: If needed, you can upgrade workstations and member servers before upgrading the domain controllers.

Once you decide to switch to native mode, another thing to consider is that you should upgrade the PDC and BDCs for a resource domain and add that domain to the tree. When you do so, the local groups and global groups in the resource domain become Windows 2000 domain local groups and global groups respectively.

Note: Recall that domain local groups are only available in native mode.

Vocabulary

Review the following terms in preparation for the certification exam.

Term	Description
downlevel operating systems	A term for earlier versions of Microsoft Windows NT.
in-place upgrade	The simplest upgrade path to Windows 2000, it retains your current domain model so that you retain your existing Microsoft Windows NT domain relationships within the Windows 2000 domain structure.
mixed-mode domain	A domain that contains both Microsoft Windows NT and Windows 2000 domain controllers.
native mode domain	In this domain, all domain controllers must be running Windows 2000.
Organizational Unit (OU)	A container that can, in addition to other types of objects, contain other OUs, thus allowing you to create a hierarchical tree of OUs.
Plug-and-Play	A standard set of protocols and procedures that regulate how the operating system, a hardware device, and the BIOS work together to install and configure hardware devices automatically.
seize a role	Forces a role, such as a PDC emulator, from one domain controller to another domain controller.
site	A physical unit of replication that guarantees that the domain controller that is physically closest to a particular group of users, computers, or both, will be contacted first.

In Brief

If you want to...	Then do this...
Seize the PDC emulator	1. From the **Start** menu, choose **Run**, or open a **command window**. 2. Type **NTDSUTIL**, and choose **Enter**. 3. At each prompt, supply the following information and then press **Enter**: 4. At **NTDSUTIL**, type **roles**. 5. At **FSMO maintenance**, type **connections**. 6. At server connections, type **connect to server**, followed by the Fully Qualified Domain Name of the controller that is to be the new PDC emulator. 7. At **server connections**, type **quit**. 8. At **FSMO maintenance**, type **seize PDC**. 9. At **NTDSUTIL**, type **quit**.
Upgrade from Microsoft Windows NT Server v3.1 or v3.5 to Windows 2000 Server	You must first upgrade to either Microsoft Windows NT Server v3.51 or NT Server v4.0 before you can upgrade to Windows 2000. Once you accomplish this upgrade, you can upgrade to Windows 2000 Server.
Upgrade to Windows 2000 Server from Microsoft Windows NT Server v3.51 or v4.0	You can upgrade directly to Windows 2000 Server.

If you want to...	Then do this...
Upgrade to Windows 2000 Server from Microsoft Windows NT Workstation v3.1 or 3.5	You must upgrade to either Microsoft Windows NT Workstation v3.51 or v4.0 before upgrading to Windows 2000 Professional.
Upgrade to Windows 2000 Professional from Microsoft Windows NT Workstation v3.51 or v4.0	You can upgrade directly to Windows 2000 Professional.
Upgrade a Windows 95 or 98 system to Windows 2000 Professional	You can upgrade directly to Windows 2000 Professional.
Upgrade a Windows 3.x system to Windows 2000 Professional	You must first upgrade to either Windows 95 or Windows 98 before upgrading to Windows 2000 Professional.
Build a single-domain tree that encompasses all master domains	First, create an empty root domain. Incorporate the existing master domains as child domains of the new empty root domain.
Verify a domain upgrade	Check the DCPROMO.LOG file.
List all the domain controllers within a domain	Run the LISTDCS.VBS script that comes with the Windows 2000 Resource Kit, for example, cscript listdcs.vbs LDAP://dc=user,dc=company,dc=msft
List all domain-naming contexts within a given tree	Run the LISTDOMAINS.VBS script that comes with the Windows 2000 Resource Kit, for example, cscript listdomains.vbs LDAP://dc= company,dc=msft

If you want to...	Then do this...
Verify the installation of Active Directory	Use the Event Viewer. It will display which Active Directory components were installed in the directory service log. The components will be displayed as informational log entries.
Test your recovery plan	• Take one BDC offline • Promote the offline BDC to a PDC • Test the data backup • Demote the PDC to a BDC • Verify that the data did not become lost or corrupted

Lesson 10 Activities

Complete the following activities to better prepare you for the certification exam.

1. Explain the differences found in mixed mode.

2. Discuss the role of the PDC emulator.

3. Explain what types of requests downlevel clients can make from the Active Directory PDC emulator.

4. Describe Remote Access Services (RAS) under Microsoft Windows NT and how it is handled in Windows 2000.

5. Discuss the importance of selecting which Primary Domain Controller (PDC) will be the first upgraded to Windows 2000.

6. Clarify why you should avoid continuing to use Microsoft Windows NT v3.51 on computers in Windows 2000 domains.

7. Explain the benefits of having an OU hierarchy.

8. Describe the importance of a recovery plan and how you would test it.

9. Discuss the factors you need to consider in determining the order in which you upgrade your Microsoft Windows NT domains.

10. Discuss Microsoft Windows NT 4.0 style policies and Windows 2000 Group Policy. Describe the benefits derived from Windows 2000 Group Policy.

Answers to Lesson 10 Activities

1. In a mixed-mode domain the following differences occur:
   - How requests to Primary Domain Controllers (PDCs) are handled
   - Communication between domain controllers
   - Available services
   - Security

2. The Primary Domain Controller (PDC) emulator acts as a Microsoft Windows NT Primary Domain Controller in domains that have Microsoft Windows NT Backup Domain Controllers (BDCs) or computers without Windows 2000 client software. The PDC emulator is an operations master and must reside on one and only one domain controller in an Active Directory forest. The PDC emulator supports the Kerberos and NTLM protocols, allowing Microsoft Windows NT domain controllers to synchronize with a Windows 2000 environment running in mixed mode.

   Every domain must have a domain controller that acts as a PDC emulator as long as the domain contains either clients without Windows 2000 client software or Microsoft Windows NT BDCs.

3. Downlevel clients may make the following requests from the Active Directory PDC emulator:
   - Account changes
   - Account database replication to Microsoft Windows NT BDCs
   - Supplying browsing information to downlevel clients running the Browser service
   - Authentication services for LAN Manager logon requests

4. Microsoft Windows NT Remote Access Service (RAS) runs in the security context of a special service account, LocalSystem. When a service logs on as LocalSystem, it logs on with NULL credentials; no username or password is provided.

   By default, Active Directory will not accept the querying of object attributes, such as Microsoft Windows NT RAS dial-in access permissions, by means of a NULL session. The object attribute query functionality can be provided when the following conditions are met:

   - The Microsoft Windows NT RAS server is a BDC and the domain is in mixed mode; this allows the server to have local access to the SAM
   - The Microsoft Windows NT RAS contacts a Microsoft Windows NT BDC server by chance and the domain is in mixed mode (this event is not predictable)
   - When Active Directory security has been loosened to grant read permissions to the Everyone group on any user object, whereby the domain can be in either mixed or native mode; this option can be set during promotion of a domain controller by choosing the option to weaken the permission for RAS access

5. It is important to choose the first domain to upgrade carefully because the first PDC you upgrade creates the root of your Active Directory forest. The first domain controller in the forest will act as the schema operations master and the Global Catalog server. Sufficient processor power and memory should be installed on this server to provide an adequate level of service. You must ensure that the first domain controller has sufficient hardware resources.

6. Since it does not recognize transitive trusts, a computer running Microsoft Windows NT 3.51 cannot authenticate groups and users in domains other than the login domain. Also, Microsoft Windows NT 3.51 is unable to authenticate any user and group accounts that have been moved between Windows 2000 domains because it does not recognize the SID history attribute.

7. Once you create your OU hierarchy, you can then organize objects into their respective OU container. When this is accomplished, you will have a more logical representation of the information to be managed. Another benefit of doing this is that you can take advantage of the ability to delegate the administration of OUs as well as apply group policy to them.

8. You develop a recovery plan to ensure against accidental loss of data during the upgrade process. Before performing an upgrade you should complete the following tasks:

   - Back up all services running on PDCs and BDCs
   - Test the backup tapes
   - Fully synchronize all BDCs with the PDC
   - Take one BDC offline before upgrading the PDC and the other BDCs to Windows 2000 Server
   - Keep this BDC available for at least a week after the domain upgrade is complete
   - Back up all other BDCs regularly

   At each step in your upgrade process, you should be able to answer the following questions:

   1. How would you roll back the system to a recovery state?
   2. What administrative tools do you need to accomplish the upgrade?
   3. What administrative tools do you need to roll back to the recovery state?

   To test your recovery plan perform the following steps:

   - Promote the offline BDC to a PDC
   - Test the data backup
   - Demote this PDC to a BDC
   - Verify that the data did not become lost or corrupted

9. To determine the order in which you upgrade your Microsoft Windows NT domains, you will need to consider the following elements:

   - The number of account and resource domains in the network
   - Any existing trust relationships
   - The final Active Directory domain structure that you want to implement

10. Microsoft Windows NT 4.0 style policies are defined in the System Policy Editor and processed at user logon. Since style policies can be complex and extremely detailed, such policies were created only by the most knowledgeable systems engineers.

    The successor to the System Policy Editor is Windows 2000 Group Policy. Using Windows 2000 Group Policy, you can create policies that can control all aspects of the environment, both large and small. Group policies are usually set at the site and domain level.

    With the Windows 2000 Group Policy snap-in, you can specify the following settings:

    - Registry-based policy settings
    - Security settings
    - Software installation
    - Scripts
    - Folder redirection

Lesson 10 Quiz

These questions test your knowledge of features, vocabulary, procedures, and syntax.

1. In upgrading an existing Microsoft Windows NT Workstation v3.5 to Windows 2000 which of the following can you do?

   A. You can upgrade straight to Windows 2000 server.
   B. You must upgrade to Microsoft Windows NT Workstation v3.51 before upgrading to Windows 2000 Workstation.
   C. You must upgrade to Microsoft Windows NT Workstation v4.0 before upgrading to Windows 2000 Workstation.
   D. You must upgrade to Windows 2000 Professional before upgrading to Windows 2000 Server.

2. When will you need to seize the role of the PDC emulator and force it to another domain controller?

   A. Before you upgrade the current PDC emulator to Windows 2000.
   B. When you need to add another domain to the forest.
   C. During backups of the PDC emulator.
   D. If the PDC emulator becomes unavailable unexpectedly and it cannot be returned to service quickly.

3. What role does the first domain controller in the forest perform?

   A. Acts as the schema operations master.
   B. Determines the order in which all other domain controllers are upgraded.
   C. Determines the order in which workstations and member servers are upgraded.
   D. Acts as the Global Catalog server.

4. What must you do to verify the installation of Active Directory?

   A. Run the LISTDCS.VBS script that comes with the Windows 2000 Resource Kit.
   B. Run the LISTDOMAINS.VBS script that comes with the Windows 2000 Resource Kit.
   C. Use the Event Viewer.
   D. Check the DCPROMO.LOG file.

5. If setup fails to install a hardware device properly, what will you need to do?

   A. Run the Add New Hardware Wizard in Control Panel.
   B. You must re-install the operating system.
   C. Check to verify that Windows 2000 supports the device.
   D. Replace the hardware.

6. What is the description of a mixed-mode domain?

   A. A domain that contains both Microsoft Windows NT and Windows 2000 domain controllers.
   B. A domain that contains Microsoft Windows NT Workstation clients.
   C. A domain that contains Windows 95 and 98 clients.
   D. A domain that incorporates multiple domains.

7. Why does Windows 2000 Server not allow you to delete or rename the initial root domain without removing the entire forest?

   A. Because the root domain holds the configuration information for the entire forest.
   B. Because the root domain determines the upgrade order for all subordinate domains.
   C. Because the root domain holds the schema information for the entire forest.
   D. Because the root domain maintains security for the entire forest.

8. What does the Primary Domain Controller (PDC) emulator do?

   A. Acts as a Microsoft Windows NT Primary Domain Controller in domains that have Microsoft Windows NT Backup Domain Controllers.
   B. It is an operations master.
   C. It supports the Kerberos and NTLM protocols.
   D. It must reside on one and only one domain controller in an Active Directory forest

9. Which of the following is applicable to a site?

   A. A site is tied to the logical Active Directory structure.
   B. A site cannot span multiple domains.
   C. A site must be unique within a domain.
   D. A site guarantees that the domain controller that is physically closest to a particular group of users, computers, or both will be contacted first.

10. How do you know when you have a complete trust domain model?

    A. All domain controllers are upgraded to Windows 2000.
    B. A common resource owner is agreed upon.
    C. A common root is agreed upon.
    D. There are multiple Microsoft Windows NT domains that are all joined by two-way trusts.

Answers to Lesson 10 Quiz

1. Answers B and C are both correct. You must upgrade to Microsoft Windows NT Workstation v3.51 or to Microsoft Windows NT Workstation v4.0 before upgrading to Windows 2000 Workstation.

   Answer A is incorrect. You cannot upgrade straight to Windows 2000 server from Microsoft Windows NT Workstation 3.5. Typically, your upgrade of a Microsoft Windows NT Workstation will be to Windows 2000 Professional.

   Answer D is incorrect. You cannot directly upgrade a Microsoft Windows NT Workstation v3.5 to Windows 2000.

2. Answer D is correct. If the PDC emulator becomes unavailable unexpectedly and it cannot be returned to service quickly, its role must be moved to maintain the services provided by the PDC emulator.

   Answer A is incorrect. The current PDC emulator is running Windows 2000 Server already.

   Answer B is incorrect. The PDC emulator does not need to be moved to add another domain to the forest

   Answer C is incorrect. You do not need to move the role of PDC emulator during backups.

3. Answer A is correct. The first domain controller in the forest will act as the schema operations master.

   Answer D is correct. The first domain controller will act as the Global Catalog server.

   Answer B is incorrect. The order in which all other domain controllers are upgraded is not set by selecting the first domain controller to be upgraded.

   Answer C is incorrect. You can upgrade workstations and member servers in any order.

4. Answer C is correct. You use the Event Viewer. It will display which Active Directory components were installed in the directory service log.

   Answer A is incorrect. You run the LISTDCS.VBS script to list all the domain controllers within a domain.

   Answer B is incorrect. You run the LISTDOMAINS.VBS script to list all the domain controllers within a domain.

   Answer D is incorrect. You check the DCPROMO.LOG file to verify a domain upgrade.

5. Answer A is correct. You should run the Add New Hardware Wizard in Control Panel to re-install the hardware device.

   Answer C is correct. You should check to verify that Windows 2000 supports the device.

   Answer B is incorrect. You do not need to re-install the operating system because of a hardware failure.

   Answer D is incorrect. You may need to replace the hardware, but only if Windows 2000 does not support the device and the manufacturer does not provide Windows 2000 drivers. This is the last resort.

6. Answer A is correct. A domain that contains both Microsoft Windows NT and Windows 2000 domain controllers is called a mixed-mode domain.

   Answers B and C are incorrect. If a domain contains Microsoft Windows NT Workstation clients or Windows 95 and 98 clients, that does not make it a mixed-mode domain. Mixed mode only occurs when domain controllers are both Microsoft Windows NT and Windows 2000.

   Answer D is incorrect. A domain that incorporates multiple domains can be a master domain model domain, a multiple master model domain or a complete trust model domain.

7. Answer A is correct. The root domain holds the configuration information for the entire forest.

   Answer C is correct. The root domain holds the schema information for the entire forest.

   Answer B is incorrect. The root domain does not determine the upgrade order for all subordinate domains.

   Answer D is incorrect. The root domain does not maintain security for the entire forest. Security functionality is distributed throughout the network.

8. Answer A is correct. The PDC emulator acts as a Microsoft Windows NT Primary Domain Controller in domains that have Microsoft Windows NT Backup Domain Controllers or computers without Windows 2000 client software.

   Answer B is correct. The PDC emulator is an operations master.

   Answer C is correct. The PDC emulator supports the Kerberos and NTLM protocols, allowing Microsoft Windows NT domain controllers to synchronize with a Windows 2000 environment running in mixed mode.

   Answer D is correct. The PDC emulator must reside on one and only one domain controller in an Active Directory forest.

9. Answer D is correct. Sites guarantee that the domain controller that is physically closest to a particular group of users, computers, or both will be contacted first.

   Answer A is incorrect. A site does not necessarily reflect the Active Directory structure.

   Answer B is incorrect. A site can span multiple domains. A site is merely a unit of replication within the network.

   Answer C is incorrect. If needed, a site can span multiple domains.

10. Answer D is correct. You have a complete trust model when there are multiple Microsoft Windows NT domains that are all joined by two-way trusts.

    Answer A is incorrect. When all domain controllers are upgraded to Windows 2000, you no longer require explicit trusts. Trusts under Windows 2000 are transitive.

    Answers B and C are incorrect. A complete trust model is required when an organization is decentralized and no common resource owner or common root can be agreed upon.

GLOSSARY

Term	Description
ADSI	Active Directory Service Interfaces provides several standard interfaces for open synchronization and application integration.
API	Application Programming Interface provides application developers with consistent rules for designing programs to interact with the TCP/IP stack.
ATM	Asynchronous Transfer Mode is a very fast packet-switching technology capable of quality real-time video transmission.
attribute	A single property of an object. An object is described by the values of its attributes. The term attribute is often used interchangeably with property. Attributes are also data items used to describe the objects that are represented by classes defined in the schema. Attributes are defined in the schema separately from the classes; this allows a single attribute definition to be applied to many classes.
authoritative restore	In Backup, a restore operation on a Windows 2000 domain controller where the objects in the restored directory are treated as authoritative, replacing through replication all existing copies of those objects. Authoritative restore is applicable only to replicated System State data such as Active Directory data and File Replication Service data. You use the NTDSUTIL.EXE utility for an authoritative restore.

Term	Description
Auxiliary Class type	A list of attributes, which can be derived from existing auxiliary or structural classes.
backup	A duplicate copy of a program, a disk, or data, created for archiving purposes or to ensure that valuable files are not lost if the active copy is destroyed or damaged.
backup and recovery	A method available in most database management systems that allows a database to be restored to the latest transaction (complete unit of work) after a software or hardware error has made the database unusable. The process starts with the latest backup copy of the database. The change file, or transaction log, for the database is read. Each logged transaction is recovered through the last checkpoint on the log.
backup and restore	The process of maintaining backup files and putting them back onto the source medium if required.
BDC	Backup Domain Controllers.
bridgehead server	Bridgehead servers are the contact point for exchange of directory information between sites. The Active Directory Connector service uses the directories on the bridgehead servers for synchronization between the directories.
Checkpoint file	A file containing information describing the state of the system at a particular time.
child object	An object that resides in another object. For example, a file is a child object that resides in a folder (the parent object).
circular logging	In circular logging, the oldest files are written over and disabled. This allows for the maximum recoverability.
class	Definition for groups of objects that share a common set of characteristics, called attributes.

Term	Description
Connection Agreement	A configuration that establishes and maintains synchronization between containers within Active Directory and Exchange site containers.
container object	An object that can contain other objects. For example, a folder is a container object.
DACL	Discretionary Access Control List defines security groups, user accounts and associated permissions. DACLs define object permissions for resource security enforcement and access levels for each list member.
DC	Domain Controller
defragmentation	A process in Active Directory that rearranges how the data is written in the directory database file to compact it. The process of defragmentation rewrites parts of a file to contiguous sectors on a hard disk, increasing the speed of access and retrieval.
delegation	Allows a higher administrative authority to grant specific administration rights for containers and subtrees to individuals and groups. This eliminates the need for domain administrators with sweeping authority over large segments of the user population. Access Control Entries (ACEs) can grant specific administrative rights on the objects in a container to a user or group. Rights are granted for specific operations on specific object classes through ACEs in the container's Access Control List (ACL).
directory	An online storage location that contains objects that may have various kinds of structures and be related to one another in some way. For example, an online building directory of a mall contains names of businesses, locations, and telephone numbers.
distributed directory	The distribution of data across the network on many different computers in a manner that is transparent to the users.

Term	Description
DNS	Domain Name System is a hierarchical distributed database. DNS is the namespace used on the Internet to translate computer and service names into TCP/IP addresses. Active Directory uses DNS as its location service.
domain	Used to accomplish network management goals, such as structuring the network, delimiting security, applying Group Policy, and replicating information.
domain boundary	As domains are a security boundary, by default, administrative permissions for a domain are limited to the domain. For example, an administrator with permissions to set security policies in one domain is not automatically granted authority to set security policies in any other domain in the directory.
downlevel operating systems	A term for earlier versions of Microsoft Windows NT.
DSA	Directory System Agent
DSACLS.EXE	DSACLS.EXE is a command line tool in the Windows 2000 Resource Kits. It assists in the management of ACLs for directory services. DSACLS.EXE enables you to query and manipulate security attributes on Active Directory Objects. It is the command line equivalent of the Security page on various Active Directory snap-in tools.
EFS	Encrypting File System is a Windows 2000 file system that allows users to encrypt files and folders on an NTFS volume disk to keep them safe from access by intruders.
ESE	Extensible Storage Engine

Term	Description
ESE	Extensible Storage Engine stores all Active Directory objects, reserves storage only for space that is used, stores multiple-value attributes and properties, and communicates directly with individual records in the directory Data Store on the basis of the object's relative distinguished name attribute. When more attributes are added, more storage is dynamically allocated.
FAT	File Allocation Table is a list maintained by some operating systems to keep track of the status of various segments of disk space used for file storage.
firewall	An electronic boundary that prevents unauthorized users from accessing certain files on a network; or, a computer used to maintain such a boundary.
forest	A collection of one or more Active Directory trees that trust each other. All of the trees in a forest share a common schema, configuration, and global catalog. When a forest contains multiple trees, the trees do not form a contiguous namespace. All trees in a given forest trust each other through transitive trust relationships. Unlike a tree, a forest does not need a distinct name.
FQDN	The full computer name is a Fully Qualified Domain Name for the computer. In addition to these, a computer might also be identified by the FQDN comprised of the computer (or host) name and a connection-specific domain name, where one is configured and applied for a specific network connection on the computer. The full computer name is a combination of both the computer name and the DNS domain name for the computer.
FRS	File Replication Service

Term	Description
Global Catalog (GC)	Built automatically by the Active Directory replication system, it contains a partial replica of every Windows 2000 domain in the directory. When given one or more attributes of the target object, the GC allows users and applications to find objects quickly, without knowing what domain they occupy. The attributes in the global catalog are those used most frequently in search operations, and those required to locate a full replica of the object.
Global Catalog server	A Global Catalog server is simply a domain controller server that is also configured to act as a Global Catalog. Global Catalog servers are identified as such in DNS and can be located by users using DNS. The Global Catalog contains a partial replica (i.e. a subset of attributes) of all objects in the Forest. This means that some attributes of every object in every domain database in the forest are maintained in the Global Catalog. The Global Catalog is used for fast forest-wide searches of enterprise objects. The Global Catalog is also used during logon to determine universal group membership, since universal groups do not reside within any particular domain.
Group SID	Group Security Identifier is an alphanumeric structure for security principles that integrates with non-Microsoft operating systems.
GUID	Globally Unique Identifier identifies the type of object or attribute in remote installations. It is part of the Access Control Entry (ACE).
HTTP	HyperText Transfer protocol is a computer language used for creating Web pages.
inheritance	The ability of a child class to take on attributes of the parent class.

Term	Description
in-place upgrade	The simplest upgrade path to Windows 2000, it retains your current domain model so that you retain your existing Microsoft Windows NT domain relationships within the Windows 2000 domain structure.
IPSec	Internet Protocol Security supports network-level authentication, data integrity, and encryption to secure intranet, extranet, and Internet Web communications.
KCC	The Knowledge Consistency Checker is a service that automatically generates a replication topology.
KDC	Kerberos Key Distribution Center.
Kerberos	The Kerberos protocol is the primary authentication procedure in Windows 2000. It is a security system that authenticates users. At logon, it establishes identity, which is used throughout the session. Kerberos does not provide authorization to services or databases.
kernel mode	Provides direct access to memory. Kernel mode consists of four components: Microsoft Windows 2000 Executive, Device Drivers, the Microkernel, and the Hardware Abstraction Layer (HAL).
LAN	Local Area Network
latency	The time lag between the beginning of a request for data and the moment it begins to be received. The time necessary for a packet of data to travel across a network.
LDAP	Lightweight Directory Access Protocol is used to access a directory service and is the primary access protocol for Active Directory.

Term	Description
log file	A file that stores messages generated by an application, service, or operating system. These messages track the operations performed. Log files are usually plain text (ASCII) files and often have a .LOG extension. In Backup, the log file contains a record of the date the tapes were created and the names of files and directories successfully backed up and restored. The Performance Logs and Alerts service also creates log files.
LostAndFound	A repository for orphaned objects. When Active Directory replication does not know where to put these objects, they end up in the LostAndFound container.
LSA	Local Security Authority
MAPI	Messaging Application Programming Interface
metadata	Another term for attributes and classes.
mixed-mode domain	A domain that contains both Microsoft Windows NT and Windows 2000 domain controllers.
MMC	Microsoft Management Console..
MSDSS	Microsoft Directory Synchronization Services is a component of Microsoft's Services for Netware v.5 product that makes it easy for administrators to synchronize changes between Active Directory and Novell's Directory Services.
multimaster replication	A replication model in which any domain controller accepts and replicates directory changes to any other domain controller. This differs from other replication models in which the computer stores the single modifiable copy of the directory and other computers store backup copies.

Term	Description
native mode domain	In this domain, all domain controllers must be running Windows 2000.
NDS	Network Directory Services is available to administrators for managing directory objects.
non-authoritative restore	A restore of a backup copy of a Windows 2000 domain controller in which the objects in the restored directory are not treated as authoritative. The restored objects are updated with changes held in other replicas of the restored domain.
non-homed	New Active Directory objects that are mail-enabled, but do not have mailboxes.
NTDSUTIL utility	The NTDSUTIL utility lets you mark Active Directory objects for authoritative restore. When the object is marked, its Update Sequence Number is changed so that it is higher than any other Update Sequence Number. This ensures that any replicated data you restore is properly replicated or distributed throughout your organization.
NTFS	New Technology File System is an advanced file system designed for use specifically with the Windows NT operating system. It supports long filenames, full security access control, file system recovery, extremely large storage media, and various features for the Windows NT POSIX subsystem. It also supports object-oriented applications by treating all files as objects with user-defined and system-defined attributes.
object classes	Another term for Classes within the schema.

Term	Description
objects	A distinct named set of attributes that represent something concrete, such as user data, printers, applications, or servers. The attributes hold data describing the thing that is identified by the directory object.
on-media catalog	Information stored on backup storage media. The on-media catalog contains a list of files and folders that have been backed up in a backup set.
operations master roles	A domain controller that has been assigned one or more special roles in an Active Directory domain. The domain controllers assigned these roles perform operations that are single-master, which means they are not permitted to occur at different places on the network at the same time. The domain controller that controls that particular operation owns the operations master role for that operation. The ownership of these operations master roles can be transferred to other domain controllers.
OUs	Organizational Unit is an entity or group of entities organized in a logical manner by the system administrator according to business or system functions or policies. They also enable the delegation of administration to distinct subtrees of the directory.
Owner SID	Security Identifier is an alphanumeric structure for security principles; an owner SID is the owner of an object, who is responsible for granting access permissions and granting rights for the object.
parent object	The object in which another object resides. A parent object can be the child of another object. For example, a subfolder that contains a file is both the parent of the file (child object) and a child object of the parent folder.

Term	Description
parent-child trust relationship	The two-way, transitive trust relationship established when you add a domain to an Active Directory tree. The Active Directory installation process automatically creates a trust relationship between the domain you are creating (the new child domain) and the parent domain.
partition	A unit of replication within the database.
patch file	Manages data during an online backup.
PDC	Primary Domain Controller
permissions	Rules associated with an object to regulate which users can gain access to the object and in what manner.
permissions inheritance	A mechanism that allows a given Access Control Entry (ACE) to be copied from the container where it was applied to all the children in the container. Inheritance can be combined with delegation to grant administrative rights to a subtree of the directory in a single update operation.
Plug-and-Play	A standard set of protocols and procedures that regulate how the operating system, a hardware device, and the BIOS work together to install and configure hardware devices automatically.
polling	Procedure that checks for changes in each directory defined in the Connection Agreement.
QOS	Quality of Service

Term	Description
recovery	If a replication failure occurs, Active Directory will automatically replicate the schema from the schema operations master. This triggers an immediate schema cache update on the target domain controller. Once the target domain controller's schema has been updated, Active Directory then invokes a new replication cycle and replicates the object(s) that failed to the target domain controller.
registry	In Windows 2000, a database repository for information about a computer's configuration. The registry contains information that Windows 2000 continually references during operation, such as: • Profiles for each user. • The programs installed on the computer and the types of documents each can create. • Property settings for folders and program icons. • What hardware exists on the system. • Which ports are being used. The registry is organized hierarchically as a tree and is made up of keys and their sub-keys, hives, and value entries.
REPL	Replication. Active Directory DSAs connect to each other by using a proprietary RPC interface when they are replicating directories.
replication	The process of copying data from a data store or file system to multiple computers to synchronize the data. Active Directory provides multimaster replication of the directory between domain controllers within a given domain. The replicas of the directory on each domain controller are writeable. This allows the update to be applied to any replica of a given domain. The replication service automatically copies the changes from a given replica to all other replicas.

Term	Description
replication latency	Replication takes time. At any moment, all the domain controllers in your forest may not have equal replicas. The delay between an action and replication throughout your network is referred to as replication latency. It is possible that an instance of an object of a newly created class may be replicated to a domain controller prior to the arrival of the new schema class. If this occurs, it is called replication latency.
reserved log	Used as a store for low disk space conditions.
resource	Any part of a computer system or a network, such as a disk drive, printer, or memory, that can be allotted to a program or process while it is running or shared over a local area network.
RFC	Request for Comments
RID	The Relative Identifier is the second part of a Security Identifier (SID). It identifies an account object within the issuing domain.
root domain	The domain at the top of the hierarchy.
RPC	Remote Procedure Call is a call by one program to a second program on a remote system.
SACL	System Access Control List contains a list of events that can be audited for an object. An administrator can audit all attempts to create a user object in a given Organizational Unit (OU) by creating an auditing entry for the OU. If the audit directory service access policy is enabled on a domain controller, then access to the audited objects appears in the security log of the domain controller.
SAM	Security Accounts Manager is an interface used by Windows clients that use Windows NT 4.0 or earlier to connect to the DSA. In addition, replication from backup domain controllers in a mixed-mode domain goes through the SAM interface.

Term	Description
schema	The definition of all objects that can be created in Active Directory. This includes their characteristics or attributes. For each object class, the schema defines what attributes an instance of the class must have, additional attributes it may have, and what object class can be a parent of the current object base.
schema object	Another term for attributes and classes.
schema operations master	Designates a single domain controller in the forest to store the write-enabled copy of the schema and thus prevents potential conflicts.
security descriptors	Access control information attached to every container and object on the network. This information controls the type of access allowed to users and groups. Windows 2000 automatically creates the security descriptor when a container or object is created, for example a file.
security principles	Users, groups and computers who are assigned or granted access control permissions. Group memberships, security policy profiles, and security identifiers define security principles.
seize a role	Forces a role, such as a PDC emulator, from one domain controller to another domain controller.
services	The useful actions that can be performed on the resources in the directory. For example, the contents of the directory can be queried, listed, and printed. Active Directory is the directory service included in Windows 2000
SIDs	Security Identifiers (SIDs) are unique, alphanumeric structures for security principles. Every user, group or computer has a SID, which identifies the domain where the SID was issued and has an account object within the issuing domain. SIDs are transparent to the user, never reused, and are only used by the system.

Term	Description
site	One or more well-connected TCP/IP subnets. A site allows administrators to configure Active Directory access and replication topology quickly and easily to take advantage of the physical network. When users log on, Active Directory clients locate Active Directory servers in the same site as the user. A site is separate in concept from domains, is delimited by a subnet and is typically geographically bounded. A site can span multiple domains, and a domain can span multiple sites. Sites are not part of the domain namespace. Sites control replication of your domain information and help to determine resource proximity.
site link	A link between two sites that allows replication to occur. Each site contains the schedule that determines when replication can occur between the sites that it connects.
site link bridge	The linking of more than two sites for replication using the same transport. When site links are bridges, they are transitive. All sites linked for a specific transport implicitly belong to a single site bridge for that transport.
SSL	Secure Sockets Layer is a protocol that creates a secure connection, or channel, over which all data between a Web client and a secure Web server are encrypted.
Structural Class type	Can be derived from another structural class or an abstract class. It can include auxiliary classes in its definition. It is the only type of class from which Active Directory objects can actually be created.
synchronization	Two directories are synchronized when their databases contain equivalent, though not necessarily identical, content.
syntax	Specifies the type of attribute value, such as a Distinguished Name, an Object Identifier, or a Case Sensitive String.

Term	Description
System State	In Backup, a collection of system-specific data that can be backed up and restored. For all Windows 2000 operating systems, the System State data includes the registry, the system boot files, and the Certificate Services database (if the server is operating as a certificate server). If the server is a domain controller, the System State data also includes Active Directory directory services database and the SYSVOL directory.
SYSVOL	A shared directory that stores the server copy of the domain's public files, which are replicated among all domain controllers in the domain.
TCP/IP	Transmission Control Protocol/Internet Protocol
tombstone	Object marker that designates how long an object will remain in the database (the default is 60 days). This time period allows the tombstone to replicate to all domain controllers in the network. During garbage collection, objects that have gone past the tombstone lifetime are physically removed from the database.
topology	The relationship among a set of network components. In the context of Active Directory replication, topology refers to the set of connections that domain controllers use to replicate information among themselves.
transaction	The pairing of two or more actions performed together as a single action; the action succeeds or fails as a whole. Both transactions succeed or neither is executed.
transaction logs	Files that record transactional changes that take place in a database. The transaction logs provide a basis for updating a master file and establishing an audit trail.

Term	Description
transitive trust	A trust relationship among domains, where if domain A trusts domain B and domain B trusts domain C, then domain A trusts domain C.
tree	A set of Microsoft Windows 2000 domains connected together via a transitive two-way trust, sharing a common schema, configuration, and global catalog.
UNC	Universal Naming Convention
URL	Uniform Resource Locator is a standardized addressing system for locating Internet resources.
USN	Update Sequence Number is assigned by the domain controller when an object is updated. USNs are stored in a table maintained by each domain controller and are incremented after each update. This occurs for both originating and replicating updates.
WAN	A Wide Area Network that spans a large geographical area and consists of multiple LANs and leased lines from telephone carrier service providers.

INDEX

88 Class type, 387

abstract Class type, 387

Access Control Entry, 111-112

Access Control List, 20, 110-112, 167, 212

access, 1, 3-5, 9-10, 20-24, 28-29, 45-47, 55, 61, 65, 67-68, 70, 74, 103, 105-108, 110-112, 114, 116-117, 120-121, 123, 131-132, 159, 166-171, 178, 181, 184, 208, 210-212, 216-217, 220, 222, 224, 253, 267, 305, 307, 313, 368, 386, 393, 401, 433, 444, 476, 478, 490, 495-497, 503-504, 506

account name, 261-262, 49

ACE, 111-112

ACL, 111-112

Active Directory Connector Management, 260-263, 277-278

Active Directory Connector Sites and Services, 260

Active Directory Connector, 253-257, 259-263, 265, 267, 269, 271, 273, 275, 277-281, 283, 285, 287-289, 291, 293, 295, 297, 299, 301, 303

Active Directory duties

Active Directory Installation Wizard, 173, 175, 180, 218, 225, 227, 369

Active Directory Knowledge Consistency Checker, 221, 308

Active Directory Object Manager, 314

Active Directory Replication Monitor, 318, 332

Active Directory Schema, 9, 191, 367-371, 373-377, 379-381, 383-385, 387-389, 391-395, 397, 399, 401, 403, 405, 407, 409, 411, 413, 415, 417

Active Directory Service Interfaces, 3, 28, 369, 374, 377

Active Directory Sites and Services, 123, 178, 217, 221, 223, 226, 308, 328, 336-337, 339, 342, 345-348

Active Directory User and Computers, 190

Active Directory Users and Computers, 117-119, 123, 125, 130, 132-133, 138, 158, 189, 228, 277, 399-400, 437, 497

Active Directory, 1-13, 15-25, 27-29, 31, 33, 35, 37, 39, 41, 43, 45-51, 53, 55-59, 61-71, 73-75, 77-79, 81-85, 87, 89, 91, 93, 95, 97, 99, 101, 103-107, 109, 112-114, 117-121, 123-125, 130-133, 138, 157-158, 161, 164, 169-173, 175-185, 189-191, 208, 210-211, 214-230, 253-257, 259-265, 267-273, 275-285, 287-293,

295, 297, 299, 301, 303, 305-315, 317-329, 331-339, 341-349, 351, 353, 355, 357, 359, 361, 363, 365, 367-381, 383-389, 391-395, 397, 399-403, 405, 407, 409, 411, 413, 415, 417, 419-425, 427, 429-433, 435-439, 441-445, 447, 449, 451, 453, 455, 457, 459, 461, 463, 465, 467, 472-473, 476, 478-480, 482-483, 485, 487, 493-498, 500-502, 504-506

Active-Directory-integrated

ADC Installation Wizard, 259

ADC service, 256, 264, 272

ADC, 253-262, 264, 270, 272, 276-281, 292

add site,

adding, 11, 47, 55, 62, 116, 122, 127, 166, 180, 183, 208, 210, 220, 267, 306, 317, 328, 346, 367, 387, 399

addresses, 12, 17, 45-46, 55, 57, 61, 66, 183, 275

administration model, 157, 162, 170-171, 487

administration, 1, 3, 9-10, 20, 63, 67-68, 70, 72-74, 103, 108, 114, 116-119, 121, 123-124, 157-159, 161-163, 166, 169-172, 210, 223, 262, 264, 287, 329, 487

administrative authority, 10, 103-105, 107, 109, 111, 113-115, 117, 119, 121, 123, 125, 127, 129, 131, 133, 135, 137, 139, 141, 143, 145, 147, 149, 151, 153, 155, 170, 219

administrative control, 4, 103-104, 113, 117-119, 121-123, 158, 162, 169, 171, 210, 482

administrative model, 10, 103, 116, 161-162, 164, 172

administrative, 1, 4, 10, 71-72, 78-80, 103-105, 107-109, 111, 113-119, 121-123, 125, 127, 129-131, 133, 135, 137, 139, 141, 143, 145, 147, 149, 151, 153, 155, 158-159, 161-164, 169-172, 175, 184, 191, 207, 210, 216, 219, 223-225, 227, 229, 253, 262-263, 278-279, 287, 336, 347, 381, 482, 501

administrator, 4, 10, 17, 21-22, 54, 78, 103, 109, 112-114, 116-117, 121, 133, 157, 161, 164, 175, 185, 219, 224, 226-230, 253, 256, 263, 265, 267, 277, 291, 318-319, 324, 326, 328, 332, 380, 399, 426, 440, 497

Administrators, 1, 3-5, 10, 21, 64, 76, 103, 113-114, 116-118, 121-122, 130, 133, 158, 163-164, 169-171, 179, 189, 209-211, 214, 217, 219, 223, 253, 277, 291, 306, 323, 332, 373

ADSI, 3, 28, 369, 374, 376-377

Advanced Features, 120, 132-133, 277, 437

advanced, 78, 120, 132-133, 138, 178, 186-188, 191, 274, 277, 323, 373, 422, 437, 440-441, 443

American Standard Code for Information Exchange, 46

API, 22, 28-29

Application Programming Interface

architecture, 2, 22, 24, 327, 419-421

ASCII, 46

assessment tools

assigning, 49, 73, 108, 118-119, 121-122, 222, 338

Asynchronous Transfer Mode, 24, 337

ATM, 24, 337

attribute indexing

attribute replication

attribute syntax, 370, 373

attribute, 9, 23, 29, 48, 74, 105-106, 112, 120, 164, 169-170, 187-188, 190, 307, 310, 317, 321-324, 370, 373, 375, 378, 380, 384-386, 388-394, 396-397, 420, 425, 478, 486

attributes, 4, 8-9, 15, 17, 20, 29, 70, 103, 108-109, 112, 118, 121, 170, 187-188, 190-191, 262, 277, 310-311, 323, 344, 367-368, 370-371, 373-375, 377-378, 382-385, 387-397, 399, 402, 404, 425, 445, 448, 478

authentication, 21-22, 24-25, 105, 184, 212-213, 220, 266, 314, 342, 473, 475, 477, 494

authoritative answer, 56

authoritative restore, 438, 442-443

authorization, 105

automatic generation

Auxiliary Class type, 387

availability control

backup and recovery, 437-440, 447

backup and restore, 437

Backup Domain Controller, 478, 494

Backup Operators

backup optimized

backup plan

backup strategy, 444-445

Backup utility, 438

backup, 16, 29, 55, 281, 314, 419, 424-426, 431-432, 437-442, 444-447, 472-473, 476, 478, 494, 500-501

bandwidth, 18, 75, 221, 281, 292, 307, 318, 334-335, 338, 342-343

BDC, 478, 484, 494-495, 500-501

benefits, 1, 10, 61, 163, 219-220

best practices, 171, 404, 477

bi-directional replication ring

bi-directional, 218, 231, 317, 326, 328

boundary, 10, 158, 224

bridgehead server, 265-266, 292, 316

bridgehead, 265-266, 281, 291-292, 316

bridges, 316, 339, 341, 345, 347-348

built-in local, 482, 74, 114

built-in, 74, 114, 171, 179, 482

business model, 71

cache, 379-381

Central Processing Unit, 317-318

centralized management, 276

centralized model

change control, 221, 308

Checkpoint file, 429-430

child class, 382-384, 388

child object, 133, 136

child, 11-12, 50, 53, 61-62, 66, 74, 108-110, 112, 117-118, 120, 133, 135-136, 138-139, 175-176, 208-209, 214, 217-218, 220, 224-226, 333, 382-384, 388, 490-491, 506

circular logging, 426, 428-429, 444

class attributes, 4, 8, 396

class types, 387

class, 4, 8-9, 21, 70, 112, 118, 169, 367, 370-373, 375, 379-380, 382-389, 392, 394-397, 402

classes and attributes, 9, 368, 370-371, 374, 377-378, 394, 397, 402

classes, 4, 8-9, 20, 368, 370-375, 377-379, 382-385, 387-388, 394-397, 399, 402, 404

CN, 48-49, 369

collision, 323-324

combined model

Comma-Separated Value, 273

Common Names, 48

complete trust model, 490

components, 2, 7, 18, 22, 26-27, 45, 48, 50, 69, 74, 78, 105-106, 254-255, 259-262, 277, 337, 370-371, 420, 494, 498

Computers, 6, 11-12, 17-19, 49, 51, 56, 78-79, 83, 106, 109, 117-119, 123, 125, 130, 132-133, 138, 158, 164, 179, 183, 187, 189-190, 220, 224, 226, 228-229, 262-263, 277, 311, 314, 343, 367, 399-400, 437, 472, 482, 486, 497, 504

configuration container, 254, 70, 75

configuration partition, 311

configuration replication, 218

configuration, 11, 14, 66, 70, 75, 79, 174, 210, 214, 218-219, 224, 226, 254, 262, 266-267, 281, 287, 305, 310-311, 319-320, 324, 326, 328, 345, 348, 369, 444, 490-491, 496, 499, 501

conflict resolution, 305, 323

conflict, 61, 280-281, 305, 323-324, 380

connecting, 77, 257, 324-325

connection agreement, 254, 256, 262-263, 265-267, 270-277, 280-281, 283-284, 286-291

connection object, 326, 329, 348

connection, 12, 67, 72, 180, 221, 254-256, 260, 262-263, 265-267, 270-277, 280-292, 308, 318, 324-329, 334-335, 338, 343, 348-349

connectivity and bandwidth, 343

connector, 253-257, 259-263, 265, 267, 269, 271, 273, 275, 277-281, 283, 285, 287-289, 291-293, 295, 297, 299, 301, 303

console, 77-80, 122-123, 181, 223, 228-230, 256, 262-263, 277-278, 330, 337, 339, 342, 346, 369, 375-376, 400, 436, 498

Contact object

container object, 6, 10, 21, 164

container, 6, 10, 21, 70, 74-75, 109, 111, 117-119, 158, 164, 179, 185, 189, 254, 256, 263, 267-268, 275-276, 283, 310, 436-437, 442, 482, 487

contiguous, 11, 14, 54, 208-209, 217-219, 433

control delegation

control features, 161

control, 4, 10, 17, 20, 70, 73-74, 103-114, 116-124, 130-132, 135, 157-158, 161-162, 167, 169, 171-172, 174, 210, 212, 214, 216, 221, 224, 255, 267, 305, 308, 325, 330, 334-335, 338, 343-344, 368, 374-375, 480, 482, 499, 506

controller, 13, 16, 19-20, 22, 30, 56-57, 64, 70, 75-77, 112, 124, 172-175, 177-184, 208, 211-212, 214, 217-218, 220-229, 262, 265, 281, 292, 305, 307-308, 311-324, 326-327, 332-336, 338, 342-346, 368-369, 379-380, 382, 392, 394, 420-421, 424, 429, 432, 437-438, 440, 442-443, 447, 470-478, 482, 493-496, 501, 504, 506

convergence, 311-312, 379

cost factoring

cost factors, 338

counters, 277, 279-280, 291, 330-331

CPU, 317-318, 328, 332

create and manage, 117, 345

create new, 103, 117-118, 169, 214, 218, 387, 392, 396-397, 402, 422, 494

create, 10-11, 22, 29, 60, 66, 69-70, 73-74, 76-79, 83, 103, 111-114, 116-118, 122-123, 125-126, 131, 135, 137-138, 157-158, 161-162, 164, 166-167, 169-170, 172, 175-178, 190, 208-210, 212-214, 217-218, 220, 222-223, 225, 227, 229, 256, 262-263, 275-276, 282, 318, 325-329, 336-338, 342-343, 345-347, 370, 372-373, 377, 379, 383-384, 386-388, 392, 396-397, 402, 422, 425, 430, 436, 438, 444, 446, 448, 469, 476-477, 480, 487, 490-492, 494, 498, 502

creating domain

creation, 22, 126, 130, 157, 172, 281, 305, 310, 345, 384-385, 389

credentials, 105, 175, 226-227, 478

cross-link, 212-213

CSV, 272-273

Custom Recipient object

custom, 77-78, 131, 263, 268, 276, 283

cycles, 267, 317-318, 328

DACL, 20, 23, 112, 116, 167, 212

DAP, 47

Data Store files, 419, 423

Data Store, 27, 29-30, 419-423, 473

database cleanup, 432, 436

database file, 30, 54-55, 63-64, 178, 181, 369, 420-426, 428-433, 436, 445

database migration

database planning, 419, 447

database, 10, 19, 25, 27, 29-30, 46, 50-51, 54-55, 58, 61, 63-64, 177-178, 180-181, 224, 226-227, 307, 312, 316, 318, 368-369, 381, 419-426, 428-433, 436-438, 440, 442-445, 447, 471, 473, 482, 494

DC, 48-49, 208, 214, 217-218, 220-222, 224-225, 227-228, 230, 333-334, 369, 443, 496

DCPromo.exe, 173, 335

default containers, 178-179

default domain controller

Default First Site Name, 178, 336, 348

default topology

defining, 58, 68, 114, 120, 159, 161-162, 216, 224, 256, 291, 325, 373, 388, 419

defragmentation, 432-434, 436

delay, 267, 311, 328

delegating, 10, 108, 113-114, 117, 122-123, 130, 171, 219

Delegation of Control Wizard, 117-120, 123, 130-131

delegation tools, 104, 119

delegation, 20-21, 74, 103-107, 109, 111, 113-125, 127, 129-131, 133, 135, 137, 139, 141, 143, 145, 147, 149, 151, 153, 155, 161, 169-172

deleting, 75, 113, 189, 267, 273, 429, 432-433, 436

deletion file

deletion methods

deletion nmethods

deletions, 220, 272-274, 277, 307

deployment, 45, 68-69, 76, 164, 280-281, 291-292

descriptor, 106, 110-111

design, 45, 58, 76, 80, 158, 160-162, 164, 170, 281, 290, 495, 501-502, 505

diagnostics, 278

direction, 103, 213, 230, 263, 268, 276, 281, 326, 350

Directory Access Protocol, 3, 46-47, 181, 211, 253, 386, 496

directory mappings

directory partition, 309-311, 369

directory service maintenance

Directory Service module, 23, 27, 30

directory service schema, 367

directory service, 1, 3, 5, 23-24, 27-28, 30, 45, 47, 50, 105, 112, 124, 219-220, 264, 313, 316, 332, 349, 367, 378, 419, 436, 498

directory structure, 1, 6, 18, 58, 68-69, 124, 291, 504

Directory System Agent, 27-28, 420

directory, 1-101, 103-110, 112-114, 116-126, 128, 130-134, 136, 138, 140, 142, 144, 146,

148, 150, 152, 154, 156-158, 160-162, 164, 166, 168-192, 194, 196, 198, 200, 202, 204, 206, 208, 210-212, 214-230, 232, 234, 236, 238, 240, 242, 244, 246, 248, 250, 252, 253-467, 470, 472-480, 482-488, 490, 492-498, 500-502, 504-506, 508, 510, 512, 514, 516, 518, 520, 522, 526, 528, 530, 532, 534, 536, 538

Discretionary Access Control List, 20, 167, 212

Disk Defragmenter, 433-436

distinguished name, 29, 48-49, 369, 389

Distributed File System, 334-335

distributed model

distributed, 1, 3-5, 46, 70, 103, 105, 170-171, 221, 308, 312, 327, 334-335, 442, 473

Distribution group, 165

Distribution List object

distribution, 164-166, 262-263, 276, 283

DNS data storage

DNS domain name, 66-67, 83, 175, 218

DNS name, 54, 57, 61, 64, 66-67, 73-74, 80, 82, 208, 215-218, 224, 226, 229

DNS Server, 13, 61, 63, 66-67, 80, 82, 174-175, 181-182, 214

DNS zone database

DNS, 2, 12-14, 45-47, 50-51, 54-58, 60-61, 63-68, 73-74, 78, 80, 82-83, 85, 164, 174-175, 180-183, 208, 214-219, 224, 226, 229, 476, 499-501, 504, 506

documentation, 167

domain boundary

Domain Components, 48

domain controller plan

domain controller, 13, 16, 19-20, 22, 30, 56-57, 64, 70, 75-77, 112, 124, 172-175, 177-184, 208, 211-212, 214, 217-218, 220-229, 262, 265, 281, 292, 305, 307-308, 311-324, 326-327, 332-336, 338, 342-346, 368-369, 379-380, 382, 392, 394, 420-421, 424, 429, 432, 437-438, 440, 443, 447, 470-478, 482, 493-496, 501, 504, 506

domain database, 19, 224, 307

Domain local group

Domain local groups, 166-169, 263, 506-507

Domain Name System, 2, 12, 45-47, 50, 164, 174, 208, 476

domain names, 12, 45, 47, 52, 65, 68, 73, 84, 215, 217, 223

domain namespace, 50-51, 54, 58, 218, 221

domain object, 175

domain operations master, 313

domain structure, 58, 70, 72, 76, 157-159, 161, 163, 165, 167, 169, 171-173, 175, 177, 179, 181, 183, 185, 187, 189, 191, 193, 195, 197, 199, 201, 203, 205, 335, 484-485, 487-488, 490, 499, 501-502, 505 domain trees, 13-14, 177, 212-213, 216-219, 222

domain, 2, 6, 10-22, 25, 29-30, 45-58, 60-62, 64-68, 70-78, 82-84, 103, 106, 110, 112-114, 116-119, 122-124, 133, 157-169, 171-187, 189, 191, 193, 195, 197, 199, 201, 203, 205, 207-231, 261-263, 265, 275-276, 280-282, 285, 288, 291-292, 305-308, 310-324, 326-329, 332-338, 342-348, 368-369, 374, 379-380, 382, 392, 394, 399-401, 420-421, 424, 429, 432-433, 437-440, 442-443, 446-447, 469-480, 482-491, 493-502, 504-507

domain-naming master role, 313

downlevel operating system

drag-and-drop, 253

DSA interfaces

DSA, 27-29, 420

DSACLS.EXE, 119, 121

duties, 103, 291

dynamic update*****, 63, 82, 175, 183

EDB.CHK, 429

EFS

e-mail, 3, 47, 79, 165, 253, 275, 332

emulator, 314, 471-475, 483

Encrypting File System

Enterprise Admins group, 214

Enterprise CA, 337

Enterprise Certification Authority, 337

environment, 3, 19, 63, 70-72, 76, 166, 212, 277, 281-282, 291-292, 338, 374, 404, 436, 469, 472, 476, 480

ESE, 27, 29, 420-421, 426

event log, 277-278, 332, 431

EX.CSV file

Exchange Administrator, 277, 291

Exchange Directory, 255, 262, 265, 270, 273, 275-277, 281-282

Exchange duties

Exchange Server, 253-257, 265, 272, 275, 280, 448

Exchange, 46, 253-257, 262-265, 267-270, 272-277, 280-285, 287-288, 290-292, 316, 342, 448

explicit domain, 229

explicit one-way, 479, 503

extensibility, 1, 4

Extensible Storage Engine, 27, 29-30, 420-421

extensible, 9, 27, 29-30, 368, 420-421

FAT

fault tolerance, 4, 19-20, 55, 64, 69, 77, 157, 182-184, 218, 220-221, 308, 322, 335, 421, 444, 506

features, 3, 20, 30, 40, 63, 82, 95, 120, 132-133, 150, 161-162, 188, 201, 244, 277, 280, 300,

360, 368, 375, 413, 437, 461, 470, 476, 483-484, 492, 494-495, 497, 517

File Allocation Table

File Replication Service, 30, 320, 476-477

files, 4, 54-55, 64, 79, 113, 166, 178, 180, 225, 257-259, 261, 273-274, 332, 419-421, 423-434, 437-438, 441, 444-445, 477, 482, 496

firewall, 67-68, 80, 255

first domain, 56, 73, 172, 174-175, 178-179, 214-215, 217, 223-225, 313, 336, 369, 374, 382, 472, 488, 493-494, 501

first, 5, 8, 52, 56, 73-74, 105-106, 126-127, 136, 162, 164, 172-175, 177-179, 182, 186, 190-191, 208, 210, 214-215, 217-218, 220-221, 223-225, 227, 264, 271, 283, 286-288, 311, 313, 328, 334, 336, 342, 347-348, 369, 371, 374, 380, 382, 394, 401, 442, 469, 472, 476-477, 486, 488, 493-494, 501, 504, 506

first-level, 51, 53, 66, 172

forest database, 224

forest, 10, 13-15, 17, 21-22, 62, 66-67, 69-70, 73, 75-76, 118, 159, 167-168, 175, 177-179, 183, 190, 207-209, 211-220, 222-224, 228-231, 305, 307, 310-314, 334, 368, 374, 379-380, 382, 393, 399, 404, 442, 472, 479, 489-494, 500-506

formulas, 265

forward lookup query, 57

FQDN, 474, 53, 84, 218

Frame Relay network, 337

from Windows NT Server

FRS, 30, 320, 477

Full Control, 109, 117, 131-132, 135

Fully Qualified Domain Name, 12, 53, 218, 474

GC, 15, 311, 319, 334, 392

generator, 327

Global Catalog server, 17, 28, 178, 186, 210, 217, 220, 222, 228, 292, 311, 396, 493

Global Catalog, 11, 14-15, 17, 28, 70, 159, 167-168, 178, 185-186, 190-191, 210, 214, 217, 220, 222, 228-229, 292, 311, 319-320, 334, 391-394, 396, 490-493

Global group, 168

Global groups, 166-168, 263, 482, 489, 494, 506

Globally Unique Identifier, 112

Group object

Group Policy, 10, 121-124, 161-162, 178-179, 219, 342, 476, 480-482, 487, 498

group scope, 167

Group Security Identifier

Group SID, 111

Group, 7, 10, 17-18, 24, 50, 81-83, 105-107, 109-114, 116-118, 121-124, 126, 129-131, 135, 138-140, 157, 161-168, 170-172, 178-179, 189, 210, 214, 219, 222, 262-263, 291, 314-315, 334-336, 342, 345, 347, 367, 377-

378, 384, 399-402, 476, 478, 480-482, 486-487, 496-498, 504

grouping, 7, 343, 384

groups, 3-4, 10-11, 20-21, 49, 51, 70, 74, 106, 108-115, 117-118, 121-126, 129, 131, 157-158, 164-169, 171, 179, 184, 186-187, 212, 217, 224, 228, 256, 262-263, 275, 283, 311, 315, 371, 384, 400, 482, 486, 489, 494, 498, 506-507

Guests, 138-140, 263

GUID, 112, 324

guide, 124

hierarchical structure, 12, 51, 62, 74, 103, 157, 208

hierarchy, 10-11, 28, 50-51, 60-62, 66, 72-73, 75, 110, 114, 116, 121, 138, 158, 161-162, 166, 181, 208, 215, 217-218, 253, 487, 501, 504

high watermark vector, 322-323

host name, 53, 67, 182

host, 12, 51, 53, 58, 67, 83, 182, 222, 224-225, 292, 477

how to, 18, 45, 114, 125, 157-158, 207, 224, 316, 402-403, 444, 469, 492

HTTP, 3

HyperText Transfer Protocol, 3

identifier, 105-106, 111-112, 314, 375, 386, 389, 397-399, 476

implementation, 3, 45, 59, 76, 104-105, 121, 157, 159, 161, 163, 165, 167, 169, 171-173, 175, 177, 179, 181, 183, 185, 187, 189, 191, 193, 195, 197, 199, 201, 203, 205, 280-281, 402, 443, 501

implementing, 58, 159, 161, 172, 184, 214, 216, 218, 291, 402

incremental transfers

index, 391-392

Information Technology, 83, 116, 159

infrastructure network, 224

infrastructure operations master, 315

infrastructure, 2, 4, 6, 8, 10, 12, 14, 16, 18, 20, 22, 24, 26, 28, 30, 32, 34, 36, 38, 40, 42, 44, 46, 48, 50, 52, 54, 56, 58, 60, 62, 64, 66, 68, 70, 72, 74, 76, 78, 80, 82, 84, 86, 88, 90, 92, 94, 96, 98, 100, 104, 106, 108, 110, 112, 114, 116, 118, 120, 122, 124, 126, 128, 130, 132, 134, 136, 138, 140, 142, 144, 146, 148, 150, 152, 154, 156, 158, 160, 162, 164, 166, 168, 170, 172, 174, 176, 178, 180, 182, 184, 186, 188, 190, 192, 194, 196, 198, 200, 202, 204, 206, 208, 210, 212, 214, 216, 218, 220, 222, 224, 226, 228, 230, 232, 234, 236, 238, 240, 242, 244, 246, 248, 250, 252, 254, 256, 258, 260, 262-264, 266, 268, 270, 272, 274, 276, 278, 280, 282, 284, 286, 288, 290, 292, 294, 296, 298, 300, 302, 304, 306, 308, 310, 312, 314-316, 318, 320, 322, 324, 326, 328, 330, 332, 334, 336, 338, 340, 342, 344, 346, 348, 350, 352, 354, 356, 358, 360, 362, 364, 366, 368, 370, 372, 374, 376, 378, 380, 382, 384, 386, 388, 390, 392, 394, 396, 398, 400, 402, 404, 406,

408, 410, 412, 414, 416, 418, 420, 422, 424, 426, 428, 430, 432, 434, 436, 438, 440, 442, 444, 446, 448, 450, 452, 454, 456, 458, 460, 462, 464, 466, 470, 472, 474, 476, 478, 480, 482, 484, 486, 488, 490, 492, 494, 496, 498, 500, 502, 504, 506, 508, 510, 512, 514, 516, 518, 520, 522, 526, 528, 530, 532, 534, 536, 538, 540

inheritance, 74, 108-110, 112, 117-118, 121, 133-134, 136, 138, 140, 379, 382

inheriting, 109

in-place upgrade, 499

installation, 47, 122, 157, 172-176, 180-181, 190, 214, 218, 225-227, 254-255, 257-259, 261, 369, 376, 378, 394, 419, 481, 498

instances, 8, 260, 384, 388, 392, 397

inter- replication

interaction, 69

inter-domain, 168, 211, 216

International Standards Organization, 3, 398

Internet Protocol Security

Internet Protocol, 18, 174, 182

Internet, 1, 3-4, 12, 18, 46-47, 51, 53, 58, 61-62, 65-68, 73-74, 80-83, 174, 182, 216, 505

InterNic, 60-61, 66

interoperability, 2-4, 47, 476, 492

inter-site advantages

inter-site replication, 316, 318-319, 326-327, 338, 344, 348

inter-site, 316, 318-319, 326-327, 337-340, 342, 344, 346-348, 477

interval, 189, 267, 316, 332, 380

intra- replication

intra-site replication, 316-319, 329

intra-site, 316-319, 327, 329

IP port configuration

IP, 12, 18, 46, 55, 57-58, 66-67, 72, 75-76, 174, 182-183, 319, 330, 333, 336, 338-341, 343, 345, 347

IPSec

ISO, 3, 398

issues, 6, 157, 159, 183, 398, 431, 476, 486

IT, 1, 3, 5, 9-11, 15-16, 19, 22, 27-28, 45, 47, 49, 52-53, 56-58, 61-63, 66-70, 72, 74, 79-80, 83, 105-106, 109-111, 113, 116, 118, 120-123, 125-126, 135, 140, 159, 161-162, 167, 171-175, 178-180, 183, 185, 190-191, 208-209, 212, 215, 217-218, 220-222, 226, 253, 256, 260, 262, 273-274, 281, 292, 306-307, 311-318, 320-323, 325-330, 332, 335-336, 338-339, 343-344, 349-350, 367-370, 373-374, 376, 379-381, 384, 387-388, 392, 396, 403, 421-422, 424-426, 429, 431-433, 437, 440, 443, 445, 448, 473-474, 476, 478, 482, 484-487, 490, 493, 496, 500-503, 506

KCC, 308, 317, 325-329, 348

KDC

Kerberos, 210, 212, 472, 494

kernel, 22-24

Key Distribution Center

key, 69, 75, 105, 107, 129, 161, 163, 181-182, 222, 266, 420, 429, 434-435, 441-443

Knowledge Consistency Checker, 221, 308, 317, 325-327, 332

LAN, 18, 75, 292, 333, 342, 473, 477

latency, 311-312, 318, 334, 338, 379

LDAP Distinguished Name, 48-49

LDAP port, 280

LDAP Relative Distinguished Name, 48-49

LDAP standard

LDAP, 3-4, 28, 46-49, 56-57, 181-182, 186, 190, 211, 217, 253-255, 275, 280, 292, 386, 389, 397, 402, 496

level, 22, 52, 66, 105-106, 113-114, 116-122, 161-162, 164, 167, 169-170, 172, 209-210, 228, 278, 323, 332, 480, 490, 493, 495

levels, 114, 117, 161-163, 167, 169, 171, 278-279, 332

Lightweight Directory Access Protocol, 3, 46-47, 181, 211, 253, 386, 496

link bridge, 77, 339-342, 347-348

link table, 425

link, 18, 21, 75, 77, 316, 318-319, 326, 334, 336-342, 345-348, 376, 425, 505

Local Area Network, 18, 76, 292

local authority

local name, 57

Local Security Authority, 23-25

locate, 3, 6, 13, 47, 55-57, 185, 187-188, 211, 217, 257-258, 334, 393-394, 476

locating, 20, 56-57, 185, 217

location service, 46

log file, 180, 273-274, 332, 422, 426, 428, 496

logical, 2, 5-8, 10-11, 16-18, 28, 70-72, 75, 262, 333-335, 384, 487, 504

logon, 17, 20-21, 49, 76, 121, 127, 136, 162, 180, 210, 220, 222, 257, 314, 334, 343, 370, 473, 476-477, 480, 497

lookup queries, 57-58

LostAndFound, 436-437

LSA, 24-27

Mailbox object

main purposes, 334

management tools, 280, 291

management, 1, 69, 77, 79, 116, 121, 123, 126, 129-130, 157, 161, 168, 181, 185, 219, 224, 256, 260-264, 276-278, 280, 291, 330, 367, 369, 376, 387, 433-434, 471, 483-484, 489

MAPI, 29

mapping, 116, 269, 309, 330

mappings, 54

master model upgrade

master, 19, 55, 64, 182-183, 312-315, 368, 375, 379, 382, 401-403, 442, 472-474, 476, 487-490, 493

MB, 184, 430, 483

Megabyte

membership, 165, 167-170, 222, 263, 334, 401-402

Messaging Application Programming Interface

metadata, 9, 323-324, 370

methods, 68, 104, 114, 117, 122, 253, 273, 309, 319, 376, 438

Microsoft Active Directory Connector, 253, 255, 257, 259, 261, 263, 265, 267, 269, 271, 273, 275, 277, 279, 281, 283, 285, 287, 289, 291, 293, 295, 297, 299, 301, 303

Microsoft ActiveX, 330

Microsoft Directory Synchronization Services, 253

Microsoft DNS Server, 181

Microsoft Exchange, 253, 257, 342, 448

Microsoft Management Console, 77, 123, 181, 256, 278, 330, 369

Microsoft Windows NT Backup Domain Controller

mixed mode, 184-185, 471-472, 476-479, 483-484, 494

mixed-mode domain, 29, 469-470, 473, 476

mixed-mode, 29, 469-470, 473, 476, 506

MMC console installation

MMC, 77-80, 130-131, 181, 185, 191, 256, 262, 329-330, 336, 347-348, 369, 374-377

mode, 22-24, 79-80, 157, 166, 168, 184-185, 226-227, 314, 337, 440, 443, 447, 469-472, 475-479, 483-485, 494-495, 506-507

model, 10-11, 45, 71, 75, 103, 116-117, 157, 159-162, 164, 169-172, 208, 210, 282-285, 287-288, 305, 309, 339, 341, 379, 382, 419-421, 485, 487-491, 499-500, 506

models, 24, 72, 170-171, 207, 210, 469

modes, 22, 24, 79, 166

modification, 329, 367, 372, 374-375, 379, 382, 401-403

modifications, 220, 307, 313, 367, 369, 371, 373-375, 377-379, 381-383, 385, 387, 389, 391, 393, 395, 397, 399, 401-405, 407, 409, 411, 413, 415, 417

MOVETREE.EXE, 314

moving between sites

moving, 75, 189, 346

MSADC, 253, 255-257, 259, 261, 263, 265, 267, 269, 271-275, 277, 279, 281, 283, 285, 287, 289, 291, 293, 295, 297, 299, 301, 303

MSDSS, 253

multimaster model

multimaster replication, 16, 19, 183, 220, 305-307, 312, 323, 379, 473, 476

multimaster, 16, 19, 183, 220, 305-307, 312, 323, 379, 473, 476

multiple master domain model, 489

multiple master model

multiple, 4, 9-10, 13, 16, 19, 29, 55-56, 72, 76, 118, 123, 159-160, 166-167, 170-171, 207-208, 210, 213-214, 216, 219, 221, 253, 256, 270, 281, 287, 291-292, 306, 308, 322, 326, 333, 337-338, 341, 343, 346, 370, 381, 389, 431, 487, 489-492, 504, 506

multiple-domain, 166, 180, 184, 207-211, 213, 215, 217, 219, 221, 223, 225, 227, 229, 231, 233, 235, 237, 239, 241, 243, 245, 247, 249, 251, 282, 284-290, 309

multiple-link, 338

multiple-site multiple-domain, 282, 287-290

multiple-tree, 207, 214-215

name resolution, 4, 7, 45, 55

name, 2-4, 6-8, 10-13, 17-18, 29, 45-50, 52-58, 60-68, 73-74, 80, 82-84, 111, 123-127, 129, 134, 136, 158, 164, 168, 174-175, 178, 181-182, 187, 189-191, 208-209, 214-218, 224, 226-227, 229, 257, 261-262, 266-267, 272-274, 315, 324, 336-337, 342, 348, 369-371, 386, 388-389, 392, 397-399, 402, 425, 474, 476

names, 6, 12, 14, 30, 45-55, 58, 61, 65-66, 68, 73-74, 83-84, 127, 129, 164, 208, 215-218, 223-224, 373, 386, 389, 402, 500, 506

namespace, 11-12, 18-19, 46-47, 50-51, 54-55, 58, 130, 209, 217-218, 221, 333, 335

naming conventions, 6, 14, 45-46

native mode, 157, 166, 168, 184-185, 314, 469-471, 475, 478, 483-485, 495, 506-507

native, 157, 166, 168, 184-185, 314, 469-471, 475, 478, 483-485, 495, 506-507

NDS, 3, 253, 308-309

nesting, 162-163, 166-167, 169

NetBIOS name, 48-49, 175, 218

NetBIOS, 48-49, 53, 175, 218, 226, 495

Network Basic Input/Output System

Network Directory Services

Network Monitor, 329-330

network, 1, 3-5, 7, 10, 17-18, 21, 25, 28, 45-46, 53, 55, 57, 61-63, 67-70, 72-73, 75-76, 78-79, 81, 83, 85, 103, 105-106, 111, 113-114, 159, 161, 164, 166, 172, 175-176, 178, 180, 219-222, 224-227, 266, 270, 280-281, 290-292, 305-308, 311-313, 315-318, 320, 322, 324, 327-330, 335-339, 341-344, 367, 369-370, 373, 375, 379, 396, 419, 433, 437, 440, 443-445, 469, 477, 483-485, 492, 496, 498, 504-505

new object, 4, 9, 127, 136, 138, 276, 370, 379

new objects, 275-276, 396, 433

non-authoritative restore, 437, 439-440, 442-443

non-homed, 275

nontransitive, 22

Novell Directory Services, 3, 253, 308-309

NSLOOKUP, 58, 181-182

NT Directory Services, 326

NT File System, 30, 111, 178, 482

NT.LDF file

NTBACKUP, 437

NTDS, 30, 178, 180, 326, 330, 349, 369, 420-421, 424, 429, 432-433, 442

NTDS.DIT, 30, 180, 369, 420-421, 432-433

NTDSUTIL, 30, 421, 436, 438, 442-443, 474-475

NTFS, 30, 111, 178, 225, 482

NTLM, 472-473, 476

object class, 8, 70, 112, 367, 370

object classes, 4, 8-9, 20, 370

object deactivation, 395, 395

object identifier, 375, 386, 389, 397-399

object mapping

object update, 321

object, 4, 6-10, 15, 17-18, 20-21, 23, 29, 48-50, 55-56, 64, 70, 74, 77, 103, 105-113, 116-120, 122-123, 127, 131, 133, 136, 138-140, 157, 164, 167, 169-170, 172, 175, 185-190, 210, 219, 222, 256, 264-265, 268, 272-273, 275-276, 279, 307, 310, 314, 321-324, 326, 329-330, 340, 344-345, 348, 367, 369-370, 372-373, 375, 379-380, 384, 386, 388-389, 392-395, 397-399, 420, 425, 433, 437, 442, 445, 447, 476, 478

one-way, 22, 222, 263, 266, 282, 479, 503

on-media catalog

operations master functions, 312

operations master roles, 183, 312-313

operations master, 183, 312-315, 368, 375, 379, 382, 401-403, 472-474, 476, 493

optimize, 213, 221, 274, 308, 432, 445

options, 79, 119-120, 219, 254-255, 259, 275-276, 419, 440-441, 443, 446

Organizational Unit, 10-11, 74, 109, 112, 114, 117, 125, 134, 158, 162-164, 169, 178-179, 190, 283, 442, 482

Organizational Units, 10-11, 48, 69, 74, 123, 157-158, 160, 162, 172, 219, 262-263, 311, 487

organizational, 10-11, 48, 58, 69, 71-72, 74, 109, 112, 114, 117, 122-123, 125, 134, 157-158, 160, 162-164, 169, 172, 178-179, 190, 219, 262-263, 283, 311, 442, 482, 487

OU model, 170

OU, 10-11, 48, 58, 74-75, 109-110, 112-114, 116-123, 125-126, 130-138, 140, 157-158, 160-164, 169-172, 179, 187, 189, 262-263, 283, 442-443, 482, 487, 495

Owner SID, 111

owner, 103, 111, 113, 116, 123, 138, 171, 490

ownership, 3, 106, 111, 113-114, 116, 122

paged, 275

parameters, 114, 218, 267, 330, 335, 429, 483

parent class, 382-383, 387

parent object, 109-110, 138, 140

parent, 10-12, 46, 48, 50, 61, 74, 109-110, 117, 136, 138, 140, 162, 189, 208-210, 214, 218, 224, 226, 345, 382-383, 387, 402, 437

parent-child trust relationship

parent-child, 28, 209

partial replica, 17, 220, 222, 311

partial, 15, 17, 220, 222, 311, 319

partition, 16, 54, 178, 219, 225, 309-311, 369

partner, 216, 227, 264, 267, 272, 307, 319, 323, 325-326, 328

patch file, 431

PDC emulator, 314, 471-475, 483

PDC upgrade

PDC, 281, 314, 470-476, 478, 482-484, 493-494, 500-501, 506

Performance Monitor, 277, 279-280, 329-331

permission inheritance, 110

permission set, 111

permission, 107, 109-111, 113, 117, 132, 135, 139, 167, 223, 478

permissions inheritance, 117

permissions tools

permissions, 22, 24, 79, 103, 106-113, 116-121, 123, 131-136, 138-140, 161, 164-172, 175, 183, 189, 210, 219, 224, 226, 257, 266, 378, 478, 482

physical structure, 2, 7, 17-18, 335

physical unit, 504

physical, 2, 7, 10, 17-18, 70-72, 75-77, 159, 292, 333, 335-336, 343, 444, 504-505

placement guidelines

plan, 6, 9, 18, 58, 60, 62, 68-70, 72, 74, 76, 114, 116-117, 158, 161, 163, 169, 207, 214, 226, 281, 292, 343-344, 373, 379, 402-404, 419, 445, 447, 469, 477, 481, 492-493, 500, 504

planning, 60, 62, 65, 68-69, 72, 76, 106, 109, 157, 160-161, 164, 166-172, 214, 270, 280-281, 308, 342, 403-404, 419, 437, 444-445, 447, 469, 492, 499, 501

Plug-and-Play Manager, 24

Plug-and-Play, 24, 499

policies, 10, 24, 122, 159, 162, 164, 180, 210, 219, 224, 404, 477, 480, 482, 490, 496, 498

policy object, 122-123, 219

polling, 266-267, 316

port mapping, 330

port, 255, 280, 330

Power Manager, 24

Power Users

preventing, 108, 110, 322

Primary Domain Controller, 281, 314, 471-472, 493

primary, 22-23, 47, 54-55, 64, 113, 181-182, 275-276, 281, 314, 470-472, 493

principals, 25, 106

principle, 111-112, 224, 308-309

private, 28, 53, 66-68, 80, 83

promotion, 172, 174, 177, 181, 218, 478, 494, 501

propagation dampening, 305, 322

propagation, 305, 312, 322, 328

properties, 29, 78, 107-108, 115, 117-120, 123, 129, 132-140, 162, 170, 175, 184, 223, 229-230, 263, 278, 283-284, 286, 288-290, 339, 346-347, 349, 379, 386, 390, 392, 394, 400

protocol, 3, 18, 46-47, 53, 63, 82, 174, 181-182, 211, 253, 255, 319, 329, 337, 346-348, 386, 473, 476, 496

public, 28, 67-68, 80, 83, 277, 291

publish, 122, 185, 190-191

publishing, 50, 56, 62, 122, 190, 219

QOS, 24

Quality of Service, 24

query, 4, 13, 17, 47, 55, 57-58, 75, 121, 161, 164, 182, 186, 211, 217, 228, 391, 394, 478

RAS, 478

Read, 107, 110, 116, 140, 170, 380, 393, 430, 478

recipient, 256, 262-263, 268, 275-277, 281, 283, 285, 291

recovery plan, 404, 500

recovery, 282, 379, 404, 419, 421, 423, 425, 427, 429-431, 433, 435, 437-441, 443, 445, 447, 449, 451, 453, 455, 457, 459, 461, 463, 465, 467, 473, 500-501

referral, 56

registered name, 83

registrar, 61

registry, 107, 266, 330, 429, 438, 441, 482

Relative Identifier, 106, 314, 476

Remote Access Service, 476, 478

Remote Procedure Call, 29, 329

REPADMIN.EXE, 329

REPL, 29

replica, 16-17, 19, 57, 220, 222, 227-228, 230

replicating update, 321

replication availability configuration

replication concepts, 305-306

replication control, 73

replication frequency control

replication latency, 312, 334, 338, 379

replication model, 305, 309, 379

Replication Monitor, 318, 329, 332

replication monitoring

replication partner, 227, 307, 319, 323, 325-326, 328

replication port

replication topology generator, 327

replication topology, 64, 182, 305, 307, 310, 315, 317-318, 322, 324-325, 327-329, 332, 342, 494

replication, 2, 10, 15-17, 19, 28-30, 64, 73, 75-77, 158, 162, 167-168, 182-184, 191, 207-208, 210, 218, 220-222, 226-227, 255-256, 270-271, 273-274, 277, 280, 282, 291-292, 305-339, 341-351, 353, 355, 357, 359, 361, 363, 365, 369, 379-380, 392-394, 437-440, 442-443, 473, 475-477, 494, 504

Replicator

Request for Comments, 3

reserved log, 430

reserved, 66, 114, 398, 430-431

resolving, 55-56, 222, 309, 324

resource, 3, 7, 13, 47, 55, 57, 63, 65-68, 82-83, 103, 112, 119, 121, 167, 172, 175, 180-181, 183, 208, 216, 219, 221-222, 291-292, 335, 369, 376, 378, 399, 487, 490, 496, 502-503, 505-506

resources, 1, 3, 5, 7, 11, 21-22, 28, 46, 61, 68, 70, 72, 74, 82, 103, 105, 116, 118, 122, 124-126, 158, 161, 166-167, 171, 190, 207, 210-212, 216-219, 221, 224, 277, 291-292, 308, 327, 345, 434, 473, 490, 492-494, 496, 504, 506

restoration, 438

reverse lookup query, 57-58

RFC, 3-4, 46, 48, 63, 65-66

RID, 106, 314-315, 476

rights, 4, 10, 20-22, 103, 106, 111-114, 116-117, 120, 123, 169-170, 211, 219, 482

root domain, 12-13, 51, 53-54, 61-62, 66, 73, 84, 178-179, 209, 214-215, 217-218, 222-224, 333, 399, 490-491, 501-502, 504, 506

root name, 11, 60-62, 178, 216

root, 11-13, 48, 51, 53-54, 60-62, 65-66, 73, 84, 130, 162, 174, 178-179, 209, 214-218, 222-224, 333, 369, 398-399, 490-491, 493, 501-502, 504, 506

root-level domain, 51

root-level, 51

router, 255

RPC, 29, 319, 329-330, 338

SACL, 112, 116, 167

SAM migration

SAM, 29, 49, 471, 478-479, 482, 484, 494

scalability, 1-2, 4, 45, 262, 483

schedule customization

schedule, 77, 267, 270-272, 292, 316, 318, 337-339, 344, 348-350, 438, 477

scheduling

Schema Admins Group, 377-378, 399-402

schema calls

schema master, 313

schema modification, 367, 372, 374-375, 379, 382, 401-403

schema object, 367, 395, 398

schema operations master, 313, 368, 375, 379, 382, 401-403, 493

schema policies, 404

schema table, 425

schema, 4, 9, 11, 13, 28, 70, 191, 210, 214, 217-218, 220, 224, 310-311, 313, 319, 324, 326, 367-385, 387-389, 391-395, 397-405, 407, 409, 411, 413, 415, 417, 425, 490-491, 493, 501

scope, 10, 58, 61, 70, 118, 123, 165-168, 170, 211, 219, 448

search, 29, 49, 61, 74, 116, 186-188, 190, 211, 217, 222, 228, 275, 334, 392, 394, 397

secondary, 54-55, 64, 181-182

second-level, 51-52

Secure Sockets Layer

secure, 65, 82, 167, 183

Security Account Management, 471

Security Accounts Manager, 29, 49, 478-479

Security group, 167

Security Identifier, 111, 314, 476

security subsystem, 22-24, 105

security, 1-4, 8, 10, 20, 22-25, 28-30, 49, 74, 103-106, 110-112, 114, 119-122, 125-126, 129, 132-135, 137-138, 140, 157-159, 164-168, 179-180, 184, 191, 210, 212, 216, 219, 223-224, 281, 308-309, 314, 317, 330, 384, 471, 476, 478-479, 482, 490, 494-495

seize a role

server object, 345

server pairs

server, 1, 4, 9, 13, 17, 19, 28, 48, 54-57, 61, 63-64, 66-67, 80, 82, 113, 124, 134, 161, 172-178, 181-183, 186, 208, 210, 214, 217-218, 220, 222, 224-225, 227-228, 253-258, 260-261, 265-266, 270, 272-273, 275, 280-281, 292, 306, 311, 316, 322-324, 329-330, 332, 335, 339, 345-346, 349, 369-370, 378, 380-381, 396, 401-402, 420, 425, 428-429, 436, 440, 442-448, 474-475, 477-478, 486, 492-495, 497, 500-501

servers, 17, 47, 54-55, 57, 63-64, 67-69, 75-76, 80, 82-83, 113, 124, 126, 167, 178, 182-184, 190, 208, 217, 225-227, 229, 255, 265-266, 281, 291-292, 306, 311, 330, 332, 336, 345, 347-348, 392, 394, 442, 445, 469, 471, 475, 477-478, 480, 482-483, 485, 492-493, 495, 506

service location, 263-264, 334

Service Resource Records, 55, 57

Service, 1, 3, 5, 12, 15, 23-24, 27-28, 30, 45-47, 50, 55, 57, 60, 62-64, 82, 105, 112, 124, 171, 175, 181, 219-220, 256-257, 263-265, 272, 278, 280, 312-313, 316, 320, 332, 334, 342, 349, 367, 378, 419-420, 436, 473, 476-478, 493, 498

services, 1-44, 46, 48, 50-52, 54-58, 60, 62, 64, 66, 68, 70, 72, 74, 76, 78, 80, 82, 84, 86, 88, 90, 92, 94, 96, 98, 100, 104-106, 108, 110, 112, 114, 116, 118, 120-124, 126, 128, 130, 132, 134, 136, 138, 140, 142, 144, 146, 148, 150, 152, 154, 156, 158, 160, 162, 164, 166, 168, 170, 172, 174, 176, 178, 180-182, 184, 186, 188, 190, 192, 194, 196, 198, 200, 202, 204, 206, 208, 210, 212, 214, 216-218, 220-226, 228, 230, 232, 234, 236, 238, 240, 242, 244, 246, 248, 250, 252, 253-254, 256, 258, 260, 262, 264, 266-268, 270, 272, 274, 276, 278-280, 282, 284, 286, 288, 290-292, 294, 296, 298, 300, 302, 304-312, 314, 316, 318, 320, 322, 324, 326, 328-330, 332, 334, 336-340, 342, 344-348, 350, 352, 354, 356, 358, 360, 362, 364, 366, 368-370, 372, 374, 376-378, 380, 382, 384, 386, 388, 390, 392, 394, 396, 398, 400, 402-404, 406, 408, 410, 412, 414, 416, 418, 420, 422, 424, 426, 428-430, 432, 434, 436, 438, 440, 442-444, 446, 448, 450, 452, 454, 456, 458, 460, 462, 464, 466, 470-474, 476, 478, 480, 482, 484, 486, 488, 490, 492, 494, 496, 498, 500, 502, 504, 506, 508, 510, 512, 514, 516, 518, 520, 522, 526, 528, 530, 532, 534, 536, 538, 540

settings, 10, 24, 79-80, 117, 123, 126, 131-132, 223-224, 259, 274, 278, 326, 349, 481

shared folder, 190, 223

shared system volume, 177-178, 226-227

shares, 190, 223

SID, 106, 111-112, 314, 476, 486

Simple Mail Transfer Protocol, 319, 329

single access point, 4-5

single domain, 10, 19, 72, 158, 166, 171, 184, 207-208, 210, 324, 335, 379, 382, 506

single master operations

single operations master, 472-473

single upgrade

single, 1, 4-5, 10-12, 19, 29, 67, 70, 72, 76, 80, 114, 122-123, 158, 166, 171, 181, 184, 207-210, 215-217, 223, 256, 260, 270, 275-276, 282-285, 288, 312, 321-322, 324, 326-327, 335, 337, 339, 343, 348, 370, 379, 382, 392, 442, 472-473, 487, 491-492, 506

single-site multiple-domain, 282, 284-286

single-site single-domain, 282-284

site control

site design, 290

site link bridge, 77, 339-342, 347-348

site link cost factors, 338

site link, 75, 77, 316, 318-319, 326, 334, 336-342, 345-348

site structure, 58, 76, 342

site topology, 17, 75-76, 333-334, 504-505

site uses

site, 17-19, 58, 61, 72, 75-77, 81, 118, 123, 178, 180, 221, 226, 256, 276, 282, 284-285, 287-288, 290, 292, 305, 307, 315-319, 325-329, 332-348, 480, 504-505

SMTP, 319-320, 329, 337-339, 347

snap-in, 9, 78, 121-122, 130-132, 256, 260, 262, 329-330, 336, 347-348, 369, 374, 377, 481

sniffer, 329

Software Installation, 122

special, 107, 110, 122, 312, 387, 478

SRV, 55, 57, 63, 66-67, 82-83, 175, 180-182

SSL

standard, 3, 12, 46, 64-65, 74, 107-108, 162, 181-182, 217, 499

standards, 3, 9, 12, 45-46, 48, 65, 218, 398

strategies, 45, 58, 67-68, 291, 469, 471, 473, 475, 477, 479, 481, 483, 485, 487, 489, 491, 493, 495, 497, 499-501, 503, 505, 507, 509, 511, 513, 515, 517, 519, 521, 523

strategy, 45, 47, 49, 51, 53, 55, 57, 59, 61, 63, 65, 67, 69, 71, 73, 75, 77, 79-81, 83, 85, 87, 89, 91, 93, 95, 97, 99, 101, 161, 292, 367, 402, 444-445, 469, 484, 495

Structural Class type, 387

structure plan

structure upgrade

structure, 1-2, 5-8, 10-12, 15-18, 45, 51, 53-54, 58, 61-62, 66, 68-72, 74, 76, 103, 114, 116, 122, 124-125, 157-165, 167, 169, 171-173, 175, 177, 179, 181, 183, 185, 187, 189-191, 193, 195, 197, 199, 201, 203, 205, 207-208, 214-215, 218, 254, 262, 291, 315, 327, 335, 342, 374, 379, 484-485, 487-488, 490, 495, 499-502, 504-505

sub-domain, 50, 66, 214

subnet grouping

subnets, 18, 72, 75-76, 317, 333, 336, 343, 345, 505

subsystem, 22-24, 105

synchronication

synchronization formula, 265

synchronization management

synchronization, 3, 253-256, 263-268, 271, 275-277, 280, 291-292, 308-309, 311, 321, 489

synchronized, 222, 255-256, 265, 268, 275-277, 281, 287, 290-291

synchronous, 319

syntax, 40, 95, 150, 201, 244, 300, 360, 370, 373, 389, 413, 461, 517

System Access Control List, 112, 167

System State, 312, 424-425, 437-438, 446-447

SYSVOL, 178

table, 18-19, 26, 51-52, 58-59, 80-81, 107-108, 114-115, 119-120, 128, 163, 165, 255, 269,

278-279, 283-284, 286, 288-290, 309-310, 320-321, 330-331, 424-428, 434-435, 447-448, 484

Take Ownership, 113, 122

Task Manager, 256

tasks, 69, 75, 108, 114, 131, 157, 161, 170-171, 207, 253, 270, 332, 345, 375, 419, 432, 444, 469, 477, 498, 500-501

TCP, 12, 46, 72, 76, 174, 181-182, 255, 280, 319, 330, 333, 336, 338, 343

TCP/IP

technical recommendations, 281

technical requirements, 71, 280

test environment, 281-282, 404, 436

test model scenarios

test, 40, 95, 150, 164, 201, 228, 230, 244, 280-282, 300, 360, 404, 413, 436, 445, 448, 461, 493, 496, 500-501, 517

to complete trust domain model

to native mode, 168, 184-185, 469, 471, 475, 483, 485, 495, 506

tombstone, 433, 445

tombstoning, 189

tool, 30, 119, 121, 180, 226, 253, 421, 436-437, 9, 18, 58, 78-80, 104, 114, 119, 121, 123, 125, 130, 184, 223-225, 227, 229, 262-263, 278-280, 291, 329, 336, 347, 376, 433, 438-440, 446-447, 496, 501

top-level, 51-52, 66

topology cost control

topology design

topology, 17, 64, 75-76, 182, 281, 290-291, 305, 307, 310, 315, 317-318, 322, 324-325, 327-329, 332-336, 338, 342-343, 494, 504-505

traffic, 17-18, 57, 68, 75, 159, 166-168, 191, 207, 210, 222, 265, 292, 305, 316, 319, 329-330, 335, 338-339, 342-345, 477, 489

transaction logs, 426, 429, 445

transaction, 320, 420-422, 426, 428-433, 440, 443-445

transitive trust, 13, 70, 208, 214, 219, 222, 479

transitive trusts, 22, 210, 212, 479, 486, 490-491, 500, 503

transitive, 13, 22, 70, 208, 210, 212-214, 218-219, 222, 230, 326, 339, 347-348, 479, 486, 490-491, 500, 503

Transmission Control Protocol, 174, 255

Transmission Control Protocol/Internet Protocol

transport site link, 338-339

transport, 320, 337-342, 344, 346-347

tree implementing

tree shares

tree, 10-12, 15, 17, 22, 49, 53, 62, 80, 103, 113-114, 117, 120, 122, 175-177, 207-219, 222-223, 225, 228-230, 263, 305, 318, 327, 337,

339, 342, 346, 374, 398, 400, 487, 489-490, 494, 496, 501-502, 506

troubleshooting, 58, 173, 254, 277, 282, 291

trust relationships, 11, 13, 20-21, 70, 207, 211-212, 214, 216, 219, 222, 229-230relationships, 479, 491-492, 499-501, 503, 505

trusting, 21-22, 211, 229

two-way, 22, 70, 208, 212, 214, 231, 263-264, 266, 490, 503

type, 15, 51, 55, 78, 80, 103, 107-108, 111-112, 114, 116-117, 123, 125-126, 131, 134, 136-137, 164, 167, 171, 174, 181-182, 187-188, 223, 226-227, 229, 256, 259, 261-262, 267, 326, 336-337, 342, 376, 379, 387, 389, 396, 441, 443, 446-447, 474-475, 505

types, 8-9, 22, 48, 68, 77, 107-109, 164, 168, 256, 278, 310, 320, 326, 369-370, 373, 387, 392, 425-426

UNC, 4

Unicode, 30, 46

Uniform Resource Locator, 3

Universal group, 168, 222, 334

Universal groups, 166-168, 184

Universal Naming Convention, 4

update request, 320

Update Sequence Number, 321

update, 16, 48, 63, 65, 82, 117-118, 164, 175, 183, 270, 307, 309, 311, 313, 320-324, 379, 381, 392

upgrade design

upgrade order

upgrade strategy, 469, 484

upgrade test

upgrade to, 276, 469, 486, 490-492

upgrade, 265, 276, 281, 469, 471, 473, 475, 477-479, 481-497, 499-501, 503-507, 509, 511, 513, 515, 517, 519, 521, 523

up-to-date vector, 322

URL, 3-4

usage, 4, 69, 170, 291-292

User object, 29, 49, 74, 112, 117, 276, 373, 388, 478

User Principal Name, 48-49

Users, 1, 3-6, 15, 17-18, 20-21, 24-25, 28, 45, 49, 55, 61-62, 65, 68-70, 76, 79, 81-82, 103, 105-106, 108-111, 113, 116-119, 121-123, 125, 129-133, 138, 158, 161, 164, 166, 168-169, 179, 186-187, 189-190, 210-212, 216, 220, 222, 224, 228-229, 256, 262-263, 270, 275, 277, 283, 285, 291, 305-307, 310-311, 314, 317-318, 323, 334, 336, 342-343, 345, 367, 371, 373, 384, 388, 399-400, 402, 437, 473, 479, 482, 486, 490, 497-498, 504, 506

uses, 7, 10, 16, 22, 25, 28, 46-47, 51, 62, 67, 83, 111, 124, 130, 158, 211, 221, 257, 265, 305-309, 319, 322, 330, 337, 342, 369, 379, 382,

420-421, 425, 431, 436, 473, 476-477, 479, 499

USN, 321, 323, 332

utility, 58, 181, 214, 332, 399, 438, 442

value, 8, 188, 273, 307, 321, 324, 327, 330, 332, 337-338, 373, 384, 388-389, 393, 397

vector, 322-323

verification, 132, 157, 180

WAN, 55, 221, 281, 307, 505

Web browser

Web page, 330

Wide Area Network, 55, 221, 281, 307, 505

Windows NT, 29, 49, 74, 184, 265, 276, 281, 314, 330, 335, 469-473, 475-490, 497-500, 502, 505-506

workstation logon traffic, 343

workstation logon, 76, 343

workstation, 76, 210, 221, 335, 343-344, 403, 486

write enable

X. OID

X., 3, 27, 47, 81., 386-387, 389, 398-399, 430., 471, 486

zone data, 55, 60, 64

zone database file, 54-55, 63-64

zone, 54-55, 57, 60, 63-66, 82, 85, 174-175, 182, 214

zones, 12, 54, 61, 67, 82, 181-183

www.ingramcontent.com/pod-product-compliance
Lightning Source LLC
Chambersburg PA
CBHW080130060326
40689CB00018B/3739

9780595148110